THE ROYAL
SOCIETY OF ARTS
1754 – 1954

By DEREK HUDSON and
KENNETH W. LUCKHURST

With a Foreword by
H.R.H. THE DUKE OF EDINBURGH, K.G.

and an Introduction by
THE EARL OF RADNOR, K.C.V.O.

LONDON
JOHN MURRAY, ALBEMARLE STREET

’Ἀρ’ οὖν οὐ περὶ πάντα οὕτω φήσομεν ἔχειν;
Πῶς; Περὶ ἕκαστον ταύτας τινὰς τρεῖς τέχνας
εἶναι, χρησομένην ποιήσουσαν μιμησομένην;
PLATO *Republic* X 601D

FIRST EDITION 1954

*Made and printed in Great Britain by William Clowes and Sons Ltd, London and Beccles
and published by John Murray (Publishers) Ltd.*

Contents

PART I

Merit Rewarded

PART II

Exposition and Education

CONTENTS

List of Illustrations in the Text

List of Half-tone Illustrations

Foreword

BY HIS ROYAL HIGHNESS THE DUKE OF EDINBURGH, K.G.
President of the Society

THE Royal Society of Arts is essentially a forward-looking body. By active origination, practical example and wise exposition it has led the way for two hundred years towards advancement in many familiar and practical aspects of life.

Now, at its Bicentenary, it is entitled to look back for a moment and review the way it has trodden and the paths it has opened up. As this new history of the Society shows, the retrospect is full of interest and surprises. By its persistent and unobtrusive activities the Society has been an agent behind many notable developments, the good effects of which are felt to-day, but it has always tended to do good by stealth, and its great achievements are far too little known.

I hope that the publication of this book will help to remedy this state of affairs and that in doing so it will serve not merely as a timely act of homage to the past, but also as an inspiration for the future, to the Society itself and to all who are engaged in voluntary service of any kind.

Introduction

By the Right Hon. the Earl of Radnor, K.C.V.O.
Chairman of the Council

When the Council of the Royal Society of Arts first began to consider its plans for celebrating the Society's bicentenary there was one project which at once suggested itself and was adopted. *The History of the Royal Society of Arts* by Sir Henry Trueman Wood, in which the story of the Society's foundation and work was first extensively recorded, had covered only the first 130 years of its existence, for Wood modestly preferred to carry his record only up to the commencement of his Secretaryship, while *The Story of the Royal Society of Arts*, which was compiled by his successor, Mr. G. K. Menzies, although it continued the narrative almost up to the recent war, was intended only as a brief introduction to the subject. The Council therefore felt that the time was ripe for the preparation of an entirely new book, in which the whole story of the Society's work during its first 200 years might be re-told as fully as the capacity of a single volume could make convenient. This task was entrusted jointly to Mr. Derek Hudson and the present Secretary, Mr. K. W. Luckhurst, and it is my privilege, as Chairman of Council during the bicentenary year and also as the lineal descendant of the Society's first President, Viscount Folkestone, to contribute a few words of introduction.

I suppose that the outstanding impression which must be made on any reader of this record will be of the remarkable diversity of the interests and activities of the Royal Society of Arts. Its versatility not merely as between one period and another of its 200 years of existence but also at any one period during that 200 years is quite bewildering. What a world of human enterprise is comprised in those three words "Arts, Manufactures and Commerce" as they have been interpreted in practice by this one institution during the past 200 years! It is, of course, to this essential and outstanding characteristic of the Society that all who are privileged to be associated with it would especially attribute its peculiar fascination, and herein lies the great interest of the present book for the reader. It treats, quite literally,

> Of shoes—and ships—and sealing wax—
> Of cabbages and kings

and of countless other things besides. From the authors' point of view, however, this very quality has presented their greatest difficulty, for although they have been given a very rich mine to work, and have dug from it "things new and old", the task of constructing their diversified material into a unified story has not been inconsiderable.

Yet with all this multiplicity and variety of activity there is one cord which binds the whole together. The first official announcement published by the Society describes its proposals as a "design for the publick Good", and the reader of this record cannot fail to be impressed by the frequency with which similar phrases recur as the primary touchstone by which all the proposals brought before the Society have been ultimately tested. Besides this desire to serve the community there has, at bottom, been only one other motive controlling the activity of the Society and that has been its determination to perform that service on an entirely independent basis. In a day when the ramifications of State action emphasise by contrast the peculiar value of voluntary activity this element in the Society's story is of the greatest importance.

Authors' Note

THIS history has been written at the request of the Council of the Royal Society of Arts, with the idea that its publication should form part of the Society's celebration of its bicentenary year. The task of planning such a book within pre-defined limits has not been easy. The Society's aims have been so many and so various that we have been continually conscious of our shortcomings as chroniclers. But one factor has remained constant—our admiration for the Society's courage, for its public spirit and for all that it has achieved in its avowed object of "the Encouragement of Arts, Manufactures and Commerce".

The material in the Society's archives is rich and copious. We have been fortunate in having been allowed to use it freely, and we have therefore been able to publish many interesting details for the first time and to throw new light on matters hitherto only imperfectly known or understood. While necessarily viewing the Society's past through two individual pairs of eyes—one focused from within the Society, the other from outside—we have tried to assess its activities fairly and to see them proportionately as a whole. According to our own ideas of what has seemed interesting or important or entertaining, we have attempted to present a fresh picture for readers in 1954 of a venerable Society which began its unselfish labours in 1754, has kept at them persistently ever since and is still as flourishing to-day as it has ever been.

The history of the Society has already been recorded in two volumes, both written by Secretaries of the Society. The first was the detailed and comprehensive *History of the Royal Society of Arts* by Sir Henry Trueman Wood (John Murray, 1913). The second —an abridgment of the first—was *The Story of the Royal Society of Arts* by G. K. Menzies (John Murray, 1935). We should like to express our indebtedness to both these books and also to The

Studio Ltd. for permission to draw upon material published in *The Story of Exhibitions* by one of the present authors.

We have each written ten chapters, D. H. concerning himself principally with the general history of the Society and its work for the Fine Arts, and K. W. L. dealing primarily with the scientific and technical aspects of its achievement. But we have both shot the arrow of criticism into each other's territory and accept a joint responsibility for the whole.

Our grateful thanks are due to Sir Harry Lindsay, chairman of the Society's History Committee, for helpful criticism; to Mr. John Grey Murray, who has interested himself in the book at every stage; to Miss Margaret Clark, the Society's librarian, for greatly assisting our researches; and to Mr. W. T. Tuck, who has not only deciphered and typed our manuscript but has made some useful comments in the process. We are also grateful to Sir William Ogg, Dr. Douglas McKie, Sir Frank Brown, Mr. Percy Harris and Mr. G. K. Menzies for advice on various points.

D. H.
K. W. L.

PART I

MERIT REWARDED

CHAPTER 1

A Meeting at Rawthmell's

1

To attempt to define the spirit of an age is exceedingly rash. To halt the march of history at specific decades or centuries, in order to seal them off for convenient analysis, is a dangerous temptation for the historian. Accepting these risks, we may say that the nineteenth century in Britain was, broadly speaking, an age of confident progress touched by self-righteousness. The men who then led their country into an era of commercial prosperity and international prestige that it is unlikely to know again were indeed continually uplifted as individuals by a strong, simple idealism and a faith in human destiny that seem to their descendants of the twentieth century highly enviable qualities. Yet the Victorians did not press forward so resolutely that they could not spare the time—fairly frequently—to pat themselves on the back. With so many plums in their pie, there was perhaps a suggestion of Jack-Horner-ism about the way they gloated over them. We in the twentieth century have far fewer plums, and some of those we might have been most proud of seem to be poisoned; we contemplate our pie with distrust and diffidence, but perhaps with the saving grace of humility. Though the romantic vision is clouded, the battle for progress still goes on.

If there is a gap in feeling between the nineteen-fifties and the eighteen-fifties, the contrast between the eighteen-fifties and the seventeen-fifties is equally great. It is true that both periods have characteristics in common. In the middle of the eighteenth century, as in the middle of the nineteenth, there was uncertainty and experiment—but how different was the spirit of that age from our own! It was an age of insatiable curiosity and creative power, the

3

time, as Dr. Trevelyan has said, "when our fathers conquered Canada and half India, rediscovered and began to settle Australia, and traded on an ever-increasing scale all over the inhabited globe; reorganised British agriculture on modern methods; began the Industrial Revolution in our island, thence in later times to spread over the whole world. . . ." And yet the impression persists that the eighteenth century was primarily an age of decadent dilettantism, of elegant but ineffectual drawing-room small talk. In England at least, this was not so. The century's own traditions of reason and good manners have served to obscure the energy with which private individuals—often in contrast to the lethargy of established institutions—made striking advances for the public good.

Beginning with just such a group of private individuals, meeting in a London coffee-house in 1754, we can follow in the history of the Society which they founded "for the Encouragement of Arts, Manufactures and Commerce"—now known as the Royal Society of Arts—one of the most remarkable examples of continuous, disinterested public service which the British nation has provided. Throughout two hundred years, in three centuries, under ten sovereigns, we can trace the fortunes of a determined band of pioneers and see in their advance an illustration of the spirit of their country, now thwarted, now triumphant, but never failing to meet the challenge of the hour.

2

"There was never from the earliest ages", says the preface to Rolt's *New Dictionary of Trade and Commerce*, published in 1756, "a time in which trade so much engaged the attention of mankind or commercial gain was sought with such general emulation." England was on the threshold of her second industrial revolution. Her mechanical inventors—men like Hargreaves, Arkwright, Crompton and Watt—would soon be achieving advances in every branch of production. On all sides local crafts were beginning to give way to the mechanised factories. Josiah Tucker said that in Birmingham in 1757 "almost every Master-Manufacturer hath a new Invention of his own, and is daily improving on those of others".

In England the Royal Society, which covered all departments of science, was founded in the reign of Charles II and for fifty years received no challenge to its supremacy as a learned institution. But the middle of the eighteenth century saw the founding of various technical societies which had as their object the study of the remarkable progress that was being made in trade, commerce and the industrial arts. The Royal Society of Arts was one of the first associations of this kind to be established in Great Britain. It is, however, twenty-three years younger than the Royal Society of Dublin, which was founded under the title of the "Dublin Society for Improving Husbandry, Manufactures, and other Useful Arts" in 1731, and the Welsh Society of Cymmrodorion, founded in 1751.

The story of the Society has its formal beginning at Rawthmell's Coffee House, Henrietta Street, Covent Garden, on March 22, 1754. We may think of Henrietta Street in those days—even more than to-day—as a relatively quiet refuge from the roar of the Strand, from the clatter of horses' hooves and iron wheels, the shrill cries of ballad singers and street vendors, the hand-bells of postmen and scavengers.

Coffee-houses played a highly important part in eighteenth-century London. They were embryo clubs, where customers for the price of their coffee could read the newspapers and talk by the hour. Each house acquired its own distinctive clientele. The coffee-houses of Covent Garden and Temple Bar were favourite resorts for authors and wits, but Rawthmell's was also favoured by doctors like Dr. George Mead, George II's physician, and by several men of science who were Fellows of the Royal Society. The actual site of Rawthmell's has been identified as 25 Henrietta Street—which is now covered by the red brick of Saint Peter's Hospital.

Anyone who studies the first volume of "The Minutes of the Society for the Encouragement of Arts, Manufactures and Commerce" must pause to admire the elaborate penmanship of the title page with its ornamental scrolls. He may well doubt whether this was written at Rawthmell's (and he will be right, for it was copied from a series of rough notes—the scribe inserting his name at the foot of the first page, I. Champion). In the final paragraph of the Minutes of that first meeting on March 22, 1754, are set down the names of the founding fathers of the Society. "At this Meeting were present the Right Honble. Lord Viscount Folkstone [sic], the Right Honble Lord Romney, the Revd. Dr. Steven Hales, Jn°. Goodchild Esq., Messrs. Lawrence, Baker, Crisp, Brander, Short, Messiter, & Shipley." We may imagine them, these "Noblemen, Clergy, Gentlemen, & Merchants", as the minute-book puts it, grouped purposefully round a secluded table, with their wigs and hats bent over the coffee and a pile of public prints pushed determinedly aside. Or perhaps they had a private room.

3

Dr. Hales, Henry Baker, Gustavus Brander and James Short were all distinguished men who had been elected Fellows of the Royal Society. But the last name on the list of the eleven attending the Society's first meeting gives the clue to the driving-force behind its inception and the rapid progress made in its early years. William Shipley (1714–1803), brother of Jonathan Shipley, Bishop of St. Asaph and friend of Franklin, was an obscure drawing-master at Northampton when he conceived the scheme on which he based the Society of Arts. If Northampton had not supported a successful horse-fair, and if the poor people of Northampton had not had to pay exorbitant prices for winter fuel, perhaps the Society would never have come into existence.

Shipley's plan for the Society, suggested to him by local experience, was simply this—that industry should be stimulated by means of prizes drawn from a fund contributed by public-spirited people. The idea of the prizes came to him from the Northampton horse-fair. He learned that its success was largely due to the institution of horse-racing meetings and that many of these meetings had been promoted by the King and others who had presented plates or prizes. When he turned his attention to the fuel situation at Northampton, he found that the poor were suffering because merchants bought up fuel at low prices in the summer and sold it at high prices in the winter. And so he set to work to raise a fund which would be used to buy fuel at summer prices and sell it to the poor in the winter without profit. Shipley was clearly inspired by something of the charitable spirit of Good King Wenceslas. The plan succeeded: thanks to Shipley and his friends, the workers of Northampton bought their fuel cheaply in 1751 and 1752. We can be sure their fires burned the brighter for his generosity.

After pondering the lessons of these two experiences, Shipley approached a distinguished scientist in London to whom he had been given an introduction; this was the physiologist and inventor, the Rev. Dr. Stephen Hales, F.R.S. Dr. Hales welcomed Shipley's proposals and promised to mention them to various influential friends. Having thus made a start, Shipley returned to Northampton, where he published a leaflet entitled "Proposals for raising by subscription a fund to be distributed in Premiums for the promoting of improvements in the liberal arts and sciences, manufactures, etc." He followed this up by "A scheme for putting the Proposals in execution", which was published in London. The second leaflet propounded a definite scheme for a society and drafted rules for the conduct of the proposed competitions, which were worked out in considerable practical detail.

Shipley soon realised that the leaflets by themselves, though useful for attracting attention, would not carry the embryo society very far. He therefore decided to go back to London and to live there permanently. The outcome of three months' hard canvassing in the capital was not encouraging, and at the end of it he found that he had only fifteen promises of support. Luckily for him, two of these were from Lord Folkestone and Lord Romney, both influential and public-spirited men who became respectively the first and second Presidents of the Society of Arts.

4

We come back to that first assembly at Rawthmell's. The Society's minute-book makes it quite clear that the Society immediately set to work on the basis established by Shipley—the double plan being to use premiums as a means of encouragement and to raise a public fund to provide the premiums. The Society's first concern was with two raw materials, cobalt and madder, which until then had had to be imported at great expense, but the home-supply of which in quite small quantities would have far-reaching effects. In the words of the Minutes: "It was proposed to consider whether a reward should not be given for the finding of Cobalt in this Kingdom; as there is reason to believe it may be discovered here, if diligently sought after.... It was also proposed to consider whether a Reward should not be given for the Cultivation of Madder in this Kingdom."

Cobalt and madder! The names recur as a persistent theme in the early Minutes and Letter Books. A society must start somewhere—and for a society that was to know few frontiers in its two hundred years' campaigning for the betterment of mankind, cobalt and madder was as good a starting-point as any other. But then, as now perhaps, not everyone understood the significance of these terms. At an early meeting "Mr. Shipley made a Motion to have the Word Cobalt explained in our future Advertisements, that ye Common People might have a Chance for our promis'd Premium for that Oar ...". What the Society had in mind was to make available cheap dyestuffs, so as to enable the British textile industry to stop sending textiles abroad to be dyed. Cobalt is, in fact, a hard white metal remarkable for the brilliant colours of some of its compounds; and the plant madder was, until the introduction of the coal-tar colours in the nineteenth century, the principal source of all red dyes.

But Shipley was not a drawing-master for nothing and the artistic aims of the Society were not forgotten at the first meeting. The Minutes continued:

It was likewise proposed, to consider of giving Rewards for the Encouragement of Boys and Girls in the Art of Drawing; And it being the Opinion of all present that ye Art of Drawing is absolutely Necessary in many Employments Trades, & Manufactures, and that the Encouragem^t thereof may prove of great Utility to the public, it was resolved to bestow Premiums on a certain Number of Boys or Girls under the Age of Sixteen, who shall produce the best pieces of Drawing, & shew themselves most capable, when properly examined. ...

The Society's endeavours for the encouragement of the Arts were thus early linked with the advancement of industrial design, and, though by no means restricted to any particular approach, the Society has never lost sight of this practical aspect throughout its long history.

At the second meeting, again at Rawthmell's Coffee House, on March 29, 1754, the following offers were decided upon:

1. For the best quantity of cobalt (not less than 20 lb.) produced in this country—£30.
2. For raising and curing not less than 20 lb. of madder—£30.
3. For the best drawing by a child under fourteen years of age—£15.
4. For the best drawing by a child between fourteen and seventeen—£15.

The offers were duly announced in the *Daily Advertiser*, one of those narrow, closely printed newspapers that lay among the coffee-cups on the tables at Rawthmell's. But the advertisements were a bold act of faith. The Society well knew that so far it lacked the resources to pay the premiums. The concluding sentences of the Minutes of the second meeting show how this obstacle was faced:

... And whereas the Number of Subscribers to this Society at present are too few to raise the Sums proposed to be given according to yᵉ above Advertisement. — The Right Honble Lord Viscount Folkestone & the Rᵗ Honᵇˡᵉ Lord Romney have generously promised to make up whatever Deficiencies may happen on that Account. The Society desired they would be pleased to accept of their thanks for this generous offer.

5

After April 24, 1754, several meetings of the Society were held in a circulating library at Crane Court, Fleet Street. Not all of them were well attended. We are reminded of the precarious state of the Society in its first year by the entry in the Minutes for May 22, 1754: "Present, Messrs. Baker & Messiter. The Evening being very wet and no more Company was expected; after waiting about half an Hour, they broke up without proceeding to Business." And again on September 11: "As the Subscribers were most of them in the Country, the Secretary,[1] after waiting about two Hours, went away without proceeding to Business." Other gatherings were fortunately more fruitful. The response to the invitations regarding cobalt and madder was discussed, but they seem to have led to little immediate result (an early letter from a learned Doctor states that he has examined a specimen sent in from Truro "and after many trials of it, made with various sorts of glasses, finds, that it will not *stain glass blue in fusion*; and that it is not the *Cobalt which will make Zaffer*").

The results of the drawing competitions were, however, much more encouraging. Thirty-six boys and nine girls entered as candidates, and the Society enlisted the services of "Five of the most Eminent Masters of Drawing . . . to assist in determining ye Merit of the Drawings". Their decisions were made known at a meeting at Peel's Coffee House in Fleet Street, at the east corner of Fetter Lane, on January 15, 1755. It had been agreed at the previous meeting that Shipley should "treat with the Master of Peel's Coffee House, about getting his Dining Room . . .". Peel's was a good house which acquired a reputation for the files of newspapers it maintained.

Of the prize-winners only two are now remembered as artists, Richard Cosway (later a Royal Academician and an eminent miniaturist) and John Smart (also a successful miniaturist). They were respectively first and second in the class open to children under fourteen, the prize of £15 being divided between them and three others. Shipley had a special interest in Cosway, whose work was so impressive that he was brought up to London at the instance of the Society, and who later appears to have become a pupil in the art school which Shipley established in the Strand. The drawing with which Smart won his prize is reproduced in plate 9, and a portrait of his master by Cosway, done a few years later, in plate 1.

---

[1] William Shipley acted as Secretary without pay for the first year of the Society's existence.

At the same meeting at Peel's, it was decided to organise the Society on a more regular basis with a President and officers. On February 5, 1755, Lord Folkestone was elected the first President, and the following as Vice-Presidents: Lord Romney (who succeeded to the presidency in 1761), Charles Whitworth, James Theobald and Stephen Hales. John Goodchild was appointed Treasurer and William Shipley Secretary; and Shipley and Henry Baker were elected "perpetual members".

Henceforth meetings were held more systematically. To begin with, there were "ordinary meetings" on alternate Wednesdays, and subsequently on every Wednesday from November to May, with less frequent meetings during the other months. The day-to-day business of the Society was conducted at these "ordinary meetings", but they were not empowered to alter the "rules and orders" of the Society—this could only be done at "general meetings", which were held as and when required. Smollett refers to the democratic constitution of the Society, and the dangers arising from it, in *Humphrey Clinker* (1771), where one of his characters is made to write to a friend: "We are become members of the Society for the Encouragement of the Arts, and have assisted at some of their deliberations, which were conducted with equal spirit and sagacity. My uncle is extremely fond of the Institution, which will certainly be productive of great advantages to the public, if from its democratical form, it does not degenerate into cabal and corruption."

Though the Society's sole object, in its opening phase, was to encourage arts and industries by the offer of prizes, Smollett did not exaggerate its initial success or the remarkable potentialities for good which it soon manifested. From 1755 onwards the membership expanded rapidly, and within a few years it reached 2,500. The subscription was fixed at "not less than" 2 guineas, but those who could afford it—in those early days—paid 3 guineas and peers were expected to pay 5 guineas. The charge for life membership was 20 guineas. The Society's income rose steadily from £360 in 1755 to £632 in 1756, £1,203 in 1757 and £4,614 in 1763. Considering that it has never received any official aid, the way in which this philanthropic Society has stood on its own feet from the start is surely a great tribute to, and vindication of, the public spirit of the British people.

6

The progress of the Society from 1755 onwards was not a fluke but was the direct result of careful and economic management. The total receipts for the years 1755–63 were £22,295; the total expenditure £18,756. Of this, £8,496 went in money prizes and medals, £3,507 on a special grant for a system of land carriage for fish, £291 on the Society's annual art exhibition, and the balance on general administration, including salaries, advertising, printing and rent.

After the experiment of the first premium list, a definite technique was evolved for the conduct of the prize competitions. Each individual offer was subjected to the following considerations: (1) whether the object for which the prize was proposed was an important one with more than temporary or local significance; (2) the precise requirements to be stipulated as the basis of competition; (3) whether the prize should consist of money or a medal; (4) how many prizes should be offered, and what should be their value; (5) how long the time-limit should be; (6) the best means of certification; (7) whether competitors needed to be given any preliminary information on the subject of the offer; (8) whether any permanent record in the form of a written account, drawings or, in the case of machines, a model should be required.

As the Society developed, these detailed investigations were referred to committees. The six principal committees dealt respectively with Agriculture, Chemistry, Polite Arts (as they were called), Manufactures, Mechanics, and Colonies and Trade. Members gave freely of their time: it was not unusual for a meeting of the Society, or of a committee, to be held on each night of the week.

A glance at the Guard Books containing the Society's early correspondence affords a vivid impression of the variety of matters that immediately engaged its attention. On April 18, 1755, for example, Dr. Hales wrote a letter "containing a proposal for

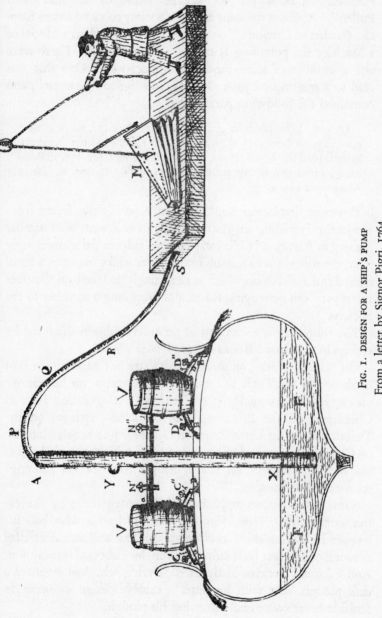

FIG. 1. DESIGN FOR A SHIP'S PUMP
From a letter by Signor Pigri, 1764

Publishing a Book on Silk Worms wrote by the Rev^d Mr. Pullen". At about the same time the Society received letters from Dr. Garden of Carolina, "on cultivating Vines and on a Model of a Machine for pounding Rice and other matters". There were also a number of anonymous communications. One that was read to a meeting on June 18, 1755, was signed "Centaur", and contained the following paragraph:

> Quaere, Whether it might not be of publick use, to propose a pecuniary or honorary Reward to such regularly-bred Surgeon, as shall read the best Lecture, or publish the best Treatise, in Anatomy, upon any of the principal parts of that Noble & Useful Animal—a Horse.

In this same first Letter Book there are copies of two letters from Benjamin Franklin, suggesting the establishment of a similar Society in America. (The early correspondence darts engagingly from the ridiculous to the sublime. There is, for instance, a letter from Lord Folkestone which is charmingly indexed on October 11, 1755: "On destroying Ratts, and proposing a member to the Society.")

The following is a selection of the many subjects discussed by writers in the Guard Books for 1757–66:

On making Rosin; on making Salt Petre in Patna; on the Rot in Sheep; on the Trade to the Baltic; on Carpets; on Education; on Grey or Norway Rats; on Tea; on Extinguishing Fires in Chimneys; on the Procuring Fish by Land-Carriage; on the Turbot fishing; on Linen Rags; on Cattle feeding in Salt Marshes; on Cyder; on a method of emptying Ships which spring a Leak at sea; on a drill plough; on Silk Worms in America; on Tanning; on American potash . . .

Some of the writers supplemented their suggestions by illustrative documents. Thus, Signor Pigri, the Italian who was interested in leaking ships, enclosed a song, as well as a delightful drawing of an eager little sailor working his elaborate contraption. And Edmund Greaves of Bradwell, Derby, who had invented a drill plough, sent with his letter a capable design showing an amiable horse contentedly drawing his plough.

Your most obedient Servant,
William Shipley.

I. WILLIAM SHIPLEY
Founder and first Secretary of the Society of Arts
From the portrait by Cosway, awarded a prize in 1759 and included in the first art
exhibition, 1760

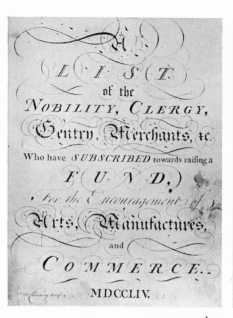

A
LIST
of the
NOBILITY, CLERGY,
Gentry, Merchants, &c.
Who have *SUBSCRIBED* towards raising a
FUND,
for the Encouragement of
Arts, Manufactures,
and
COMMERCE.
MDCCLIV.

Tho.ᵉ South	2. 2
Tho.ᵉ Allyne	2 2
John Thornton	21 00
James Chauvel	2 2
Francis Knollys	5. 5
Richard Halde	2 2
Ind. Scott	2 2
A. Addington	2 2
Sam: Johnson	2 2
Jno Phillps	2 2
Wm Southwaite	2 2
W Perrocc	3 3
W Horsley	3 3
Tho.ᵉ Salmon	2 2
George Echersall	2 2

2. THE SOCIETY'S FIRST SIGNATURE BOOK

(*a*) Title page   (*b*) A typical page of entries

3. JAMES BARRY, R.A.

From a pen-and-ink self-portrait

4. ROBERT ADAM

From a cameo by James Tassie

7

Of the proposals received, many were useless, others fruitful; all were carefully considered and usually referred to the appropriate committee. But, to understand the importance of the initiative of the Society in these early days, we must consider the development of its prize competitions, of which its miscellaneous correspondence was often the by-product. These competitions were remarkably elaborate, and they were most skilfully and thoroughly organised.

The premium list for 1764 provides an excellent example. It occupied ninety-one pages of text, and as many as 380 classes were open to competitors. In the Agriculture section there were ninety-two classes, covering the planting of several species of trees, the growing of experimental feeding stuffs for cattle and sheep, the collection of quantities of pure grass seed of named varieties, the best methods of cultivating certain crops, the production of madder and hemp, the manufacture of compost, keeping of bees, and invention of new implements for agriculture. The Chemistry section contained offers of twenty-three premiums covering the production of various minerals, varnishes, enamels, pigments and dyes. Under the heading of Manufactures, there were thirty classes, most of them for textiles; in Mechanics there were only five classes; but to encourage the development of the American and West Indian colonies, prizes were offered in 123 classes for the production of such things as raisins, wines, iron and potash, as well as various drugs and spices. There was also a special list of prizes to encourage fishing for turbot and cod in British waters.

In addition to all this, there were, under the heading "Polite Arts", some fifty separate awards for different kinds of drawing, divided according to the subject and the age and sex of the competitor. One notices, as anticipating a later speciality of the Society, the classes for "the best compositions of drawings or ornaments, being original designs fit for embroiderers, calico printers, paper stainers or any other art or manufacture". There were another fifty classes for medals and medallions, clay and wax models, etchings and engravings, cameos, paintings in enamel, and statuary in bronze and marble. Architecture was also represented, and a sum was offered for making an accurate survey of any county to the scale of one inch to a mile.

It will be recognised that prize competitions such as this—for which the entries were most carefully judged and, where necessary, tested—afforded a tremendous stimulus to scientific and artistic advance. In the first twenty-two years of the Society's existence, £16,625 was expended in premiums. But what was their actual influence in other than monetary terms? Four claims can be asserted with confidence. First, they resulted in the reafforestation of very considerable areas of land. Secondly, they played a predominant part in the earlier stages of the "agricultural revolution", being the means of introducing several new crops to this country and to the colonies and of the invention of new agricultural implements. Thirdly, they fostered the skill of draughtsmanship. And, fourthly, by stimulating the invention of many mechanical devices, they contributed largely to the progress of the Industrial Revolution.

8

It was clear to members of the Society from the earliest days that its objects would by no means be fulfilled unless thorough accounts of all the inventions and advances stimulated by the Society's initiative, and all the valuable information contributed by competitors for awards, were available for public appraisal. Thus there was an early proposal for the publication of an *Historical Register*, and, acting on instructions, Peter Templeman, the Secretary from 1760 to 1769, prepared two manuscript volumes, still in existence, which were bound up at a later date and entitled *Dr. Templeman's Transactions*. These volumes consist primarily of extracts and compilations from the minutes, lists of members, etc., but include one or two manuscripts which are of interest regarding the Society's early history.

Many of the early communications made to the Society were published as pamphlets, or in the book *De Re Rustica* (1771), or in the *Gentleman's Magazine* and other periodicals. A little later, descriptions (with engravings) of some of the machines rewarded by the Society were published by William Bailey, the Registrar, in 1772.[1] But the first publication which offered a regular selection from the Society's proceedings was the monthly *Museum Rusticum et Commerciale* (1764–6), though this had no official connection with the Society and did not confine itself to the Society's activities.

The failure of the *Museum Rusticum* provoked Robert Dossie, the friend of Dr. Johnson, and an active member of the Society whose name will figure frequently in subsequent pages, to commence his *Memoirs of Agriculture and other Œconomical Arts* which were issued in three volumes in 1768, 1771 and 1782. The first volume contains a resolution passed by the Society in June, 1767, to the effect that they "will occasionally publish in this Work such Pieces as they shall think proper to lay before the Public". This volume is entirely devoted to the Society's proceedings and, besides a list of awards and of receipts and expenditure, presents the whole early history of the Society in an admirable account prepared, presumably, by Dossie himself. The subsequent volumes contain a few papers not contributed to the Society; these volumes are largely given over to agricultural matters, though Volume III includes a complete list of the premiums for "Polite Arts" down to 1776. It is probable that Dossie's plan for continuing a general history of the Society was thwarted only by his death, the date of which cannot be exactly determined, though it certainly occurred not later than 1783.

The discontinuance of the *Memoirs of Agriculture* led directly to the commencement of the invaluable series of *Transactions*. Arthur Young, who was then very active at meetings of the Society, claimed to have originated the idea: "When I became chairman of the Committee of Agriculture," he wrote in his *Autobiography*, "I was the first to propose that annual publication, which afterwards took place." Some of the credit for carrying through the proposal, however, must probably be allowed to Valentine Green, the mezzotint-engraver. The first volume was published in 1783, and the series, which improved in interest and arrangement as it advanced, continued until 1851.

[1] See p. 174.

A number of single publications recording the Society's activities with varying degrees of authority also appeared during its early years. These will be found listed in Appendix C.

Throughout its existence the Society has always been officially known as "The Society for the Encouragement of Arts, Manufactures and Commerce" (with the addition of the prefix Royal in 1908). This long and cumbrous title was soon found, however, to be too much of a mouthful for regular use. As early as July, 1755, the *Gentleman's Magazine* was referring to the Society by the familiar name of the "Society of Arts", which has been usually employed ever since, and was first officially adopted in the Minutes in 1811. But in its early days the Society was known by several different names. In its own books of accounts, for example, it was sometimes called "The Premium Society", and Boswell and others refer to it as "The Society of Arts and Sciences". Another variant was "The Society for Useful Arts", and one of its early correspondents, impressed with its patriotic activities during the Seven Years' War, solemnly addressed it as "the laudable association of Anti-Gallicans". There is no doubt that the title "Royal Society of Arts and Sciences" would better describe its purpose and activities in modern times than the shorter "Royal Society of Arts", which, though hallowed by tradition, has become positively misleading.

CHAPTER 2

Setting up House

1

ON February 19, 1755, at one of the meetings in Peel's Coffee House, the Society made arrangements to acquire its first permanent offices. William Shipley, who had been staying since the foundation of the Society with his friend Messiter, a surgeon, in Great Pulteney Street, now decided to take a house in Craig's Court, Charing Cross, and he agreed to sub-let part of this house to the Society for £20 a year, including coals and candles. But the rooms proved too small. After a year the Society moved again—this time to a house in Castle Court, a narrow alley leading from the Strand to Chandos Street.

Castle Court was the Society's headquarters for the next two years, until its rising membership and increasing influence necessitated yet another change. The Society now came to terms with a firm of upholsterers and carpenters, Messrs. Williams and Woodin, whose premises in the Strand (opposite Beaufort Buildings) included the house afterwards known as 380 and 381 Strand, and a warehouse and yard behind it. Williams and Woodin agreed to build a Great Room for the Society on the site of this warehouse, and William Chambers, the distinguished architect of Somerset House, was put in charge of the work. He designed a fine upstairs apartment 80 feet long by 40 feet wide (almost exactly the dimensions of the large gallery of the Royal Academy at Burlington House). There was also a smaller room on the ground floor, the "Repository", in which the Society's first exhibition of models and machines was held in 1761. The rent for these rooms and a part of the house in the Strand was fixed—after an initial payment of £200—at £120 a year for three years, and

£100 a year afterwards, for a term of fifteen years from Midsummer 1759.

The site of the Strand premises occupied by the Society is now almost exactly covered by the width of Exeter Street. The Society spent busy and useful years there, but as the lease neared expiry the old complaint of lack of space was heard once more. In 1770 an announcement appeared in some of the daily papers inviting anyone who had proposals to make for the accommodation of the Society to communicate with the Secretary. In reply there came from the Brothers Adam, who were then engaged on their scheme for the Adelphi, an offer to include in their plan a suitable building to serve as headquarters for the Society, and it was finally agreed that they should build a house for a premium of £1,170 and a rent of £200 a year.

As every lover of London knows, and as many deplore, the great terrace built by the Brothers Adam, from the inspiration of the arched gallery in the Palace of Diocletian at Split, is now a thing of the past. Demolished in the nineteen-thirties, it has been replaced by a huge modern office-block entirely alien in character. Of the surviving examples of Adam building in the neighbourhood, the Society's house is by far the most important, and, as we shall see in a later chapter, generous contributions from members of the Council and an anonymous gift of £30,000 enabled the Society to purchase the freehold in 1922. The house fortunately escaped serious damage in the Second World War and stands to-day the same, at least externally, as when the Society took possession in 1774.

The design of the house seems to have been partly influenced by an appreciation of the premises enjoyed by the Society opposite Beaufort Buildings, in so far as the main features consist of the imposing Great Room on the first floor, and a large, though less pretentious, room on the ground floor (formerly the "Repository" and now the library). The building is really two houses in one, the part containing the public rooms communicating with what was originally a small self-contained residence intended, and for many years used, as the home of the Secretary. The main entrance gives on to a charming pillared hall and a graceful staircase leading to the first floor, where, besides the Great Room, there is a room used for council meetings and smaller rooms employed as offices. The external façade—bearing the legend "Arts and Commerce Promoted", as on the original design—is in Robert Adam's best manner.

The house is larger than might appear from the outside. There is a second floor which provides accommodation for several offices, and even a third floor, under the roof, approached by a turret staircase leading to a little room with a round port-hole window, still in use, and to other rooms given over to storage. Below the house is a labyrinth of cellars; there are even remains of an old roadway which used to dive down underneath the house and give access from the Strand to the Adelphi Arches.

Inside, not everything remains exactly as it was. The spacious entrance hall, for instance, comprises what were originally three separate compartments, and the main staircase, designed by Adam, used to run up to the second floor; it now ends at the first floor, giving airiness to the landing and providing space for an additional room above. For many years, also, the library, originally the "Repository", was furnished with show-cases, and the Adam pillars were taken away in the eighteen-sixties; but it has now been restored to its original appearance.

The following is an account of the ceremony of laying the foundation-stone by Lord Romney, as recorded in the form of Minutes of a meeting held on the day of the ceremony, March 28, 1772, at the Adelphi Tavern:

> Present Lord Romney
> > Duke of Northumberland
> > Honble. Charles Marsham
> > Sir Charles Whitworth
> > Edwd. Hooper Esq.
> > Owen Salusbury Brereton Esq.
> > Keene Fitzgerald Esq.

A Printed List of the Members of the Society, a Printed Book of the Rules and Orders of the Society, Lists of the president and Vice presidents according to the Minutes of Febry. 3d, an elevation of the Front of the Building, together with the Medal and two pallets of the Society in Copper, a Two Guinea Piece, a Guinea, a half Guinea, a Quarter Guinea, four Shillings, a half penny, and farthing coin'd during the Reign of his present Majesty wrapt in Tin Foil were inclosed in a Glass Vessell prepared acording to the Direction of the Meeting held February 25 and the Glass Stopper of the Vessell covered with Glaziers Putty. This Vessell with its Contents was deposited under the first Stone laid at the West End of the Front of the New Building, the Top of the Glass having a Sheet of Tin foil laid over it and the Space between the Glass and the Stone case in which it was placed filled up with Charcoal Dust.

Under a Stone at the East End of the Front of the Building were placed two Copper plates one pierced according to the direction of the Meeting, Feb^{ry} 25, and the other deeply engraved, with the Names of the president and Vice presidents. These plates were covered with Tin foil and the Space between them and the Stone filled with Charcoal Dust. After depositing the Glass Vessell and Copper Plates Ten Guineas were given by the Right Honorable Lord Romney to be distributed among the Workmen. The President Vice presidents and numerous Members of the Society who had attended the Ceremony then proceeded to dine at the Adelphi Tavern where the Remainder of the Day was spent with that Harmony and Good Humour which a Consciousness of promoting the Good of Mankind and of Society will never fail to inspire.

At this Meeting the Sum of one Thousand pounds was paid to Messrs Adam pursuant to the Resolution of the Society Decem^r 11. 1771. . . .

2

Before the Society moved into its new home, much consideration was given to the decoration of the Great Room with "proper historical or allegorical pictures" to be painted by eminent artists. The Society decided that there should be eight historical pictures, on subjects taken from English history, and two allegorical pictures, which were to be "emblematick designs relative to the Institution and views of the Society". Angelica Kauffman, Sir Joshua Reynolds, West, Cipriani, Dance, Mortimer, Barry and Wright were invited to paint the former, and Romney and Penny to execute the latter. This proposal was, however, refused and the Society had to content itself, for the time being, by placing portraits of its first two Presidents, Lord Folkestone and Lord Romney—by Gainsborough and Reynolds respectively—over the two fireplaces (subsequently moved downstairs to the library) which in those early days provided the only heating for the Great Room.

In 1777 James Barry, R.A. (1741–1806), who had been one of the artists originally approached, and who was then still a young man in his thirties, revived the proposal for decorating the Great Room by offering to undertake the task single-handed and to provide "a series of pictures analogous to the views of the Institution". This proposal was accepted, and the task occupied Barry for nearly seven years. He offered to do the work without payment, but in fact he received the proceeds of two exhibitions of the paintings held in 1783 and 1784 (amounting to about £500), was awarded a sum of £250 and a gold medal, and finally was granted a pension by the Society. Unfortunately this last gesture was made only a month before Barry's death, which took place in miserable circumstances. His quarrelsome nature had led to expulsion from the Royal Academy, where he was Professor of Painting for seventeen years, and latterly he seems to have eked out an existence mainly by the sale of his etchings from his own works. His body lay in state in the Society's Great Room for a day, before it was buried in St. Paul's beside the tomb of Reynolds.

Barry, like Haydon, was a painter who fixed all his hopes on a series of great canvases which he hoped would revolutionise English art; like Haydon, he was disappointed; yet his shortcomings must not blind us to the merit of his high ambition, his genuine talent and the considerable measure of success he attained. William Blake considered one of the pictures "equal to Raphael or Michael Angelo or any of the Italians". Samuel and Richard Redgrave, in their famous book on the British painters, published in 1866, describe the "painted epic" which Barry undertook for the Society as "a monument to be spoken of with great respect . . . no other work of the English school, even down to our own day, aspires to so high a rank in a region of art, in which even to be short of perfection is not to be disgraced". It is also well to remember that Dr. Johnson himself declared that he beheld in it "a grasp of mind which he could find nowhere else". A later critic, Professor Thomas Bodkin, has provided an excellent account of Barry in a lecture before the Society (published in the Society's

Journal, No. 4576, December 13, 1940) in which he speaks of "the tragedy of a great spirit, ruined by an uncompromising temper and by that kind of high ambition which, only when it fails, is called gross vanity".

In composing the Society's pictures, which are six in number, Barry aimed to trace the development of civilisation from primitive to modern times and to show its ultimate results in "Elyzium". His object was "to illustrate one great maxim or moral truth, viz., that the obtaining of happiness, as well individual as public, depends upon cultivating the human faculties". The first painting represents a primitive people living in a wild country, while Orpheus, playing on his lyre, speaks to them of the gods. In the second painting, perhaps the most graceful of the series, Barry turns to ancient Greece, in order to show the development of the first or agricultural stage of human progress by representing Ceres and Bacchus looking down on a "harvest home". The third picture suggests the climax of ancient civilisation in the ceremony of "Crowning the Victors at Olympia"; many of the principal figures of the great age of Greece are introduced, and Barry has given Pericles the features of the Earl of Chatham and painted his own portrait as the artist Timanthus. The fourth picture, "Commerce, or The Triumph of the Thames", presents the development of commerce in a whimsical mixture of mythology and history; the drawing is weak in places, and the whole can hardly be called a success; alongside Raleigh, Drake and Captain Cook appears Dr. Burney as the representative of music. ("It irks me", said a contemporary lady of fashion, "to see my good friend Dr. Burney paddling in a horse-pond with a bevy of naked wenches.") In the fifth picture, a fanciful account of a distribution of premiums by the Society of Arts, a large number of figures are skilfully related within a small space; while the sixth picture, which, like the third, is extremely large, has as its object "to bring together in Elyzium those great and good men of all ages and nations who were cultivators and benefactors of mankind".

The Society has always been proud to possess Barry's great paintings, which have remained on the walls for which they were intended for 170 years (apart from a short war-time interval) and have looked down on so many of its most important gatherings. Though slightly darkened by age and dirt, the canvases are well preserved. They have been several times inspected by experts and have been periodically cleaned. In 1846 Mulready reported that they were in excellent condition, and in the eighteen-sixties they were re-lined and stretched on new frames. During the Second World War the pictures were removed into the country for safety; they were in grave danger when Buxted Park, the home of Basil Ionides (a Vice-President of the Society) was burnt down, but were rescued undamaged.

3

We cannot find a better starting-point from which to consider some of the outstanding figures associated with the Society's early years than Barry's fifth picture,[1] a highly idealised conception of a distribution of the Society's premiums, which Barry has imagined as taking place, for this special occasion, in front of Somerset House, with St. Paul's in the background. From its position in the series, Barry apparently intended to suggest in this picture that the establishment of the Society of Arts was the final stage of human progress!

The picture shows (near the right side) the first President of the Society, Lord Folkestone, and Dr. Stephen Hales; while, over to the left, the second President, Lord Romney, stands near the Prince of Wales (later George IV). William Shipley, the founder, sits at the left-hand corner with a manuscript in his hand; Arthur Young, the agriculturist, is shown just above him with another farmer. Near the centre of the picture appears Mrs. Elizabeth Montagu, the earliest "blue stocking", who was the best known of the pioneer women members, and who is commending a young girl and her work to the consideration of the judges. Further to the right, again, Dr. Samuel Johnson is seen between the Duchesses of Rutland and Devonshire, whom he is trying to persuade to follow Mrs. Montagu's example.

The presence of the Prince of Wales reflects the feeling, held by

[1] Reproduced in plate 6.

many members at the time, that the Society would benefit by royal patronage. An interesting letter from Caleb Whitefoord, preserved in the Society's archives, shows that he took it upon himself in 1785 to discover the Prince's views of this proposal. Whitefoord says that he

> applied to a Gentleman, who sometimes has the Honour of being admitted to the Prince's presence; and I requested him that he would seize the earliest Opportunity of setting in a just & fair Light, the Society's Merits; and of soliciting his Royal Highness's Patronage.
>
> The Gentleman most readily & cheerfully undertook the Commission; and I am happy to be able to inform the Society, that he has succeeded in the main Object of it. I was last night favoured with a Letter from him, in which he tells me, that after a proper Introduction of the Subject, he had asked, if his Royal Highness should be applied to, whether he would chuse to confer on the Society, the Honour of becoming its Patron? The Prince was graciously pleased to answer in the *affirmative*; and added, "that it would allways give him Pleasure, to patronize whatever appeared so much calculated to promote the Public Good . . .".

The meeting of the Society which considered Whitefoord's letter disclosed differences of opinion, however, as to the desirability of having the Prince as Patron. The question was "postponed", never to be revived. In fact, King Edward VII was the first of the Society's royal patrons, although since 1816 the Society has enjoyed the association of a member of the Royal House in the more intimate capacity of President.

On the death in 1793 of Lord Romney—to whose careful interest and regular attendance the Society had owed much in its early years—the eleventh Duke of Norfolk was elected the Society's third President. He was an able man who gave liberal encouragement to literature and the arts, but he was decidedly eccentric, being rather too fond of drink and lacking in self-control. Perhaps one may read between the lines of a newspaper account of the Society's annual dinner in 1814 which stated that "the day was spent with that high conviviality which the Duke of Norfolk never fails to inspire". Nevertheless, from 1794 until his death in 1815, he fulfilled the duties of President conscientiously

26

and well. If at times he found himself out of his depth in the Society's affairs, he is not to be blamed—least of all in the following instance, recorded in a plaintive letter to John Samuel, one of the Assistant Secretaries:

> Sir,
>
> I herewith return the letter you sent me address'd to the president of the Arts and Sciences. It is from a person who says he has discovered the perpetual motion & conceives the Society will give a large premium.
>
> It is written in German, as I neither understand the language nor the subject I can only refer to the committee of foreign correspondence in case they think it deserving attention.
>
> I am Sir your obed^t serv^t
>
> Norfolk
>
> Aug: 25th 1799.

4

A treasured possession of the Society is the small note-book (of which two pages are reproduced in plate 2) in which the first members signed their names and recorded the amount of their subscriptions. Indeed this book, which was in use for about ten years, must be one of the most remarkable collections of eighteenth-century autographs in existence. The title-page, beautifully inscribed, records that it is "A List of the Nobility, Clergy, Gentry, Merchants, &c. Who have Subscribed towards raising a Fund, For the Encouragement of Arts, Manufactures, and Commerce. MDCCLIV", and the second page is headed: "We whose Names are underwritten, Promise to pay Annually during Pleasure, the several Sums to which our Names are respectively prefixed." Though not all the signatures which follow are written with the exquisite clarity of these preliminaries, many of them are, and many are adorned with highly elaborate flourishes—so that the student who reads them two hundred years later cannot fail to be struck by the manifest decline in our national calligraphy (checked, as one hopes it may be, by contemporary efforts towards a revival of the art).

It is a diverse list, made up of names distinguished in all walks of life. Among many others, this book contains the signatures of Samuel Richardson, John Wilkes, Samuel Johnson, George Colman, Joshua Reynolds, Robert and James Dodsley, Edward Gibbon, William Hogarth, Allan Ramsay, Thomas Chippendale, John Baskerville, Robert Adam, John Howard and Horace Walpole. Hogarth's name is boldly crossed out, perhaps by the painter's own hand; no one knows why, for he was duly elected in December, 1755, and subscribed for two years.

But this brief selection from the signature-book represents only a very small proportion of the eminent men who supported the Society in its early days. Great numbers of the peerage, for example, were generous with their contributions and patronage; among them, Lord North, the statesman, Lord Rodney, the admiral, and that illustrious Earl who gave his name to the sandwich. By no means all the members signed the signature-book. The following are only a few of the additional distinguished names that can be added after an examination of the printed lists of members covering the first ten years of the Society's existence: Thomas Arne, Sir Joseph Banks, Dr. Charles Burney, William Caslon, Sir William Chambers, Benjamin Franklin, David Garrick, Oliver Goldsmith, William Pitt, Francis Louis Roubiliac, Paul Sandby, Thomas Sheridan, Laurence Sterne, George Stubbs, Henry Thrale, Jacob Tonson, Benjamin West, Caleb Whitefoord, Henry Samson Woodfall...

In fact, the record of famous names is so extensive that it might almost seem easier to compile a list of the eminent men of the mid-eighteenth century who were *not* members of the Society. There could be no greater proof of the Society's popularity and of the esteem in which it was held. H. B. Wheatley has well summarised its distinctive appeal:

As the condition of England in the middle of the seventeenth century brought about the foundation of the Royal Society and the popular and widely-spread interest in the investigation of science, so the condition of the country in the middle of the eighteenth century brought about the formation of the Society of Arts for the encouragement of the applications of science for the general good. As Dryden, Weller, Evelyn, and the literary coterie of the Restoration period largely supported the Royal Society, so the circle that surrounded Dr. Johnson took a lively interest in the success of the Society of Arts.

The Society naturally treasures its association with the great man of the age, whose neat "Sam: Johnson" stands in the signature-book beside the promise to pay £2 2s. a year.[1] Boswell gives us several glimpses of him at the Society's meetings, in which he took a keen interest. There is some evidence that he was diffident about addressing his fellow-members. Sir William Scott said to Boswell "that Johnson had told him, that he had several times tried to speak in the Society of Arts and Sciences, but 'had found he could not get on'". William Gerrard Hamilton similarly reported that Johnson "rose in that society to deliver a speech which he had prepared; 'but (said he,) all my flowers of oratory forsook me' . . .". On the other hand, the learned Dr. Kippis testifies: "I once heard Dr. Johnson speak in the Society of Arts and Manufactures, upon a subject relative to mechanics, with a propriety, perspicuity, and energy, which excited general admiration."

Dr. Johnson's presence at the Society's meetings did not pass unnoticed. He said of Thomas Hollis, the republican and author, whom he did not much care for: "I remember once at the Society of Arts, when an advertisement was to be drawn up, he pointed me out as the man who could do it best. This, you will observe, was kindness to me. I however slipt away, and escaped it."

A friend whom Dr. Johnson greatly admired, and whose election to the Society he assisted, was Robert Dossie, who has already been mentioned as editor of *Memoirs of Agriculture* in which the Society's early proceedings are recorded. Boswell states:

> Johnson was well acquainted with Mr. Dossie, author of a treatise on Agriculture; and said of him, "Sir, of the objects which the Society of Arts have chiefly in view, the chymical effects of bodies operating upon other bodies, he knows more than almost any man." Johnson, in order to give Mr. Dossie his vote to be a member of this Society, paid up an arrear which had run on for two years. . . .

[1] See plate 2b.

The Society's records confirm that Dr. Johnson paid two years' subscriptions on March 25, 1760, and that Dossie was elected on April 2, 1760.

The name of James Boswell is also found in the list of members in 1760—the year he first visited London, before he knew Dr. Johnson—but Boswell never paid his subscription and so his membership lapsed. He was characteristically pleased with his own shrewdness when he related how he avoided payment of the arrears in his *London Journal* (1950, p. 60) under the date December 1, 1762:

> Soon after I came to London, I met with Mr. Mayne from Scotland, who reminded me that he had got me admitted a member of the Society for the Encouragement of Arts and Sciences in the year 1760; that the subscription was two guineas a year, and that three years were now unpaid, so that I owed six guineas. This was a most alarming piece of news to a man who was trying to calculate a livelihood out of moderate finances. However, I put the best face on it: told Mayne that I imagined the neglect of payment for one year made a man lose his place, so that I had but two guineas to pay. However, if I found it otherwise, I should pay the whole. This was really my idea.
>
> I went and called on Mr. Box, the collector (admirably named); found him a very civil man; told him that I had been in Scotland almost ever since my admission to the Society, and that I was now uncertain how long I might stay in London. If, therefore, it was possible to have my name struck off the list so that I should never be considered as having been a member, and might afterwards when sure of settling in London be admitted a member of that elegant, useful, and noble Society, it would make me very happy. I treated him with so much complaisance and put the argument so home to him that he agreed to my proposal, and I left him with a cheerful heart at the thoughts of having six guineas to spend which I had given up for lost. . . .

5

George Box, whom Boswell thought so "admirably named", was brought in as Assistant Secretary under William Shipley in 1756. In the following year, when Shipley was appointed Registrar, Box became Secretary. Little is known of Box, save that he was efficient and competent and (as Boswell tells us) "a very civil

5. THE SOCIETY'S "GREAT ROOM" IN 1809

6. PANEL ENTITLED "THE SOCIETY"
From the series executed for the Great Room by James Barry

7. THE SOCIETY'S HOUSE (1790)
From an aquatint by T. Malton

man". But three years later a committee decided that the Society required for its Secretary someone of "general and technical knowledge . . . a man of character and a man of learning". Apparently it was felt that Box did not possess exactly these qualities, yet the committee took "the liberty from the long experience of the diligence and integrity of your present secretary to recommend him to the office of assistant secretary and receiver". It was in the latter capacity, no doubt, that he was disappointed in his hope of receiving Boswell's subscription.

Box was therefore reinstated in his former post of Assistant Secretary, which he now held until 1779. An advertisement produced four candidates for the secretaryship, of whom Dr. Peter Templeman was elected by a large majority. He had been Keeper of the Reading-Room at the newly established British Museum since 1758, had written numerous medical books and was a fine scholar and linguist. He made an excellent Secretary from 1760 until his death in 1769, though during the long illness at the close of his life he was greatly assisted by Samuel More, who succeeded him as Secretary and held the post for the next thirty years.

When the advertisement for a Secretary was published in 1760, Oliver Goldsmith seriously considered sending in an application and went so far as to ask David Garrick for his support. But Garrick was unsympathetic. John Forster, in his life of Goldsmith, records that

> When . . . Goldsmith sought to obtain what a struggling man of letters was thought to have some claim to, the vacant secretaryship of the Society of Arts, Garrick made answer to a personal application for his vote, that Mr. Goldsmith having "taken pains to deprive himself of his assistance by an unprovoked attack upon his management of the theatre in his *Present State of Learning*, it was impossible he could lay claim to any recommendation from him".

In the end Goldsmith decided not to submit himself as a candidate. Perhaps his failure to secure the secretaryship may be viewed as a blessing to English literature and as no great loss to the Society's affairs. He was, however, elected a member of the Society in 1763, when his address was given at the Chapter Coffee House.

The solid, dependable qualities and the handsome presence of Samuel More, Secretary from 1769 to 1799, have been convincingly recorded in the portrait painted for the Society by Benjamin West. The esteem in which More was held is also suggested by the presentation to him in 1794 of a gold medal "for eminent services" and by his inclusion in Barry's picture of the Society. More's main interest, as West's portrait indicated, was in gem-engraving and die-sinking. It was during his secretaryship that publication of the Society's *Transactions* was commenced.

6

A few words may fittingly be inserted here to round off what has already been said about the Society's founder, William Shipley, who served as its Secretary from 1754 to 1757 and as Registrar from 1757 to 1760. There is some reason for thinking that the latter post was instituted as a means of providing an easy job for one whom the Society naturally held in honour, but whose abilities had been seen, as the Society expanded, to be those of an originator rather than an administrator. His official connection with the Society was not, in fact, long maintained. He took leave of it in the modest and self-effacing letter reproduced below:

October ye 1st, 1760.

Gentlemen,

Having lately engaged in Business of such Importance as to render me incapable of discharging my Duty to this Society as their Register, without very much injuring my own Affairs; I take this Method to inform you of my Intentions to resign my Office as Register; but though it will not suit me to serve you any longer in that Station, I shall on every Occasion use my uttmost Endeavours to promote the Interest of this Society as a Member thereof, and I acknowledge most gratefully the many Favours you have for several Years conferred uppon me, who remain with the greatest Respect,

Gentlemen,

Your most obedient, and very humble Servant,

WILLIAM SHIPLEY

Much of Shipley's time was now taken up by his art school,

which from 1760 onwards was carried on at 96 Strand. In 1768 he left London for Maidstone, where he was married and lived until his death in 1803. According to a Maidstone tradition, he was so absent-minded that while on his way to church to be married he caught sight of a rare butterfly, ran after it and consequently arrived late for the ceremony. Little more is known of his life at Maidstone, except that he established a local society on the lines of the Society of Arts and busied himself in philanthropic work. He still occasionally attended meetings of the Society and its committees. In 1776 he was awarded a silver medal for inventing a lighted buoy for saving life at sea. As it was not a particularly original invention, the award suggests that the Society retained a pleasing loyalty and affection for its founder.

William Shipley may be accounted one of the best of Englishmen: not in himself a man of extraordinary talents or ability, but made outstanding by the depth of his patriotism and by his steady determination to help his countrymen without thought of personal reward. His achievement in founding the Royal Society of Arts has given him a place in his country's history; but he is best recalled, perhaps, as typifying the lives of many like him, less often remembered, who have devoted their energies to disinterested public service. When his fellow-members paid their tribute to him by awarding him one of the first of the Society's gold medals in 1756, the inscription they chose was "To William Shipley, whose public spirit gave rise to this Society", and appropriately a similar description still appears beneath his portrait, by his pupil Cosway, in the entrance hall of the Society's House.[1]

[1] Maidstone honoured Shipley on March 22, 1952, when a memorial tablet to distinguish Knightrider House, his old home, was unveiled by Sir Edward Crowe, a Vice-President and Past-President of the Society. The tablet was the first of a series to be put up by the Friends of Old Maidstone, and had been designed and made by students of the Maidstone College of Art. It bears the inscription: "William Shipley, Founder of the Royal Society of Arts, lived here."

Cosway's portrait of Shipley is reproduced in plate 1.

CHAPTER 3

The Fine Arts: 1754–1854

1

THE Society was constituted "for the Encouragement of Arts, Manufactures and Commerce", and even in the early years interested itself freely in all three objects. But the Society's endeavours on behalf of the Fine Arts were from the outset so considerable and so far-reaching in their effects that, in displaying the varied work of the Society, there is every reason to follow its aims in the order in which they were first formally set out. In this chapter, therefore, we shall consider the steps taken by the Society to encourage the Fine Arts during the first century of its existence. It is a proud and inspiring record.

We have already described how the Society began its activity by offering premiums for cobalt and madder and for the best drawings by children under fourteen and between fourteen and seventeen. The premium system was a great success; the scope of the competitions was rapidly increased; and the annual prize competitions led to annual exhibitions of the work of the winners. The drawings chosen for exhibition were framed and mounted at the Society's expense and hung on the walls of the meeting-room for the inspection of members of the Society and their friends.

These small, informal exhibitions ministered to an enthusiasm for art which had been growing for a decade but which was something quite fresh in London life. It had been aroused by the collection of pictures formed at the newly established Foundling Hospital in Bloomsbury about 1746. Hogarth, Gainsborough, Wilson and others had presented portraits and landscapes to decorate the building, and the administrators of the hospital, inspired by gratitude to the artists and pride in their acquisitions, had opened the doors to the public. The response had been immediate. The Foundling Hospital soon became one of the show places of London.

Practising artists now began to draw their own conclusions from the simultaneous success of the Foundling Hospital display and of the annual small collections at the Society of Arts. It appeared to them that regular art exhibitions might provide not only a valuable advertisement for their works but also, perhaps, a source of revenue. In March, 1759, Robert Pine, an historical and portrait painter (who later emigrated to America and died in Philadelphia), proposed to the Society of Arts—of which he was a member—that they should hire a room for an exhibition of the works of "the present painters and sculptors". At that time the Society's meeting-room was hardly suitable for such an undertaking, and the proposal was not adopted. But the matter was raised again, on November 5, 1759, at the annual meeting of the contributing artists to the Foundling Hospital collection, who had all been elected governors of the hospital as a mark of appreciation.

On this occasion the incentive came from Francis Hayman, another member of the Society of Arts, a friend of Hogarth and Garrick who is best known for his ornamental paintings at Vauxhall. Hayman's proposal for "a public receptacle to contain the work of artists for the general advantage and glory of the nation and satisfaction of foreigners" was received with much applause. At a special meeting of artists at the Turk's Head, in Gerrard Street, Soho, a week later, it was agreed that an exhibition should be held annually, in April, and should include the various fine arts. The object was to be two-fold—to "raise to distinction" artists "who otherwise might languish in obscurity", and to form a provident fund for the support of infirm and aged artists: to this end an entrance fee of a shilling was to be charged. A committee consisting of sixteen artists, representing the various branches of art, was appointed to carry the plan into execution.

Where was the exhibition to be held? What more natural than an approach to the Society of Arts, which had already begun to take the part of a pioneer, and which numbered so many artists among its members? Another good reason for seeking the

Society's protection was that it had recently moved to its premises in the Strand opposite Beaufort Buildings, where the Great Room offered ample accommodation for an exhibition of pictures.

With the help of Dr. Johnson, the artists composed a letter[1] to the Society, which, with a short memorandum of their proposals, was dispatched on February 26, 1760. It read as follows:

> Sir,
>
> The Artists of this City having resolved to raise a sum for purposes of Charity by the Annual Exhibition of their Works entreat the Society to allow them the Use of their Room from the 7th of April to the 19th. This favour they consider as very important. The Publick concurrence of the Society will give to a new Practice that Countenance which Novelty must always need, and the Arts will gain Dignity from the Protection of those whom the World has already learned to respect.
>
> I am, Sir,
>
> Your most Humble Servant,
>
> F. HAYMAN, Chairman.

The accompanying note set out in unmistakably Johnsonian language ("Elegance and Ingenuity are most valuable when they contribute to the Purposes of Virtue . . .") the decisions reached at the Turk's Head the preceding November.

The letter was considered at the Society's weekly meeting on the day after it was received and was referred to a large special committee consisting of more than thirty members, including not only David Garrick but also several artists, among them Hayman himself, Reynolds and Allan Ramsay. When this committee reported to the weekly meeting, one thing immediately became evident—that the Society intended to exercise full control over the exhibition and to regard it as its own affair. The artists' proposals were accepted in principle but substantially altered in detail. In particular, the Society decided that they could not allow any charge for admission and that a committee appointed by the Society should settle any question of the hanging of the pictures in the event of disagreement among the artists. They also advanced the date of the exhibition by a fortnight.

[1] Published in Walpole Society, vol. vi (1917–18), p. 118.

The artists had no alternative but to accede to the Society's conditions, though they never ceased to think of the exhibition as theirs. They managed to get round the Society's ban on an admission fee by deciding, rather ingenuously, to charge sixpence each for catalogues.

2

And so the time drew nearer for the opening in the Great Room of the Society of the first specially organised art exhibition ever to be held in this country. Not that any particular credit can be claimed by Britain in this respect, for art exhibitions had been popular in Paris since 1667 (it is, indeed, a rather striking example of insular backwardness). Nevertheless, the occasion was so important for British artists that historians of the Society may be excused for dwelling on it at some length.

The exhibition committee was preoccupied with the question of preserving order. Officers of the Society were given discretionary power "to exclude all persons whom they shall think improper to be admitted, such as livery servants, foot soldiers, porters, women with children, etc., and to prevent all disorders in the Room, such as smoking, drinking, etc., by turning the disorderly persons out". These precautions proved necessary, for the rule that everybody should be admitted who came "with an order from any member of this society or from any known artist" seems to have attracted a number of undesirables. There was a bill of 13s. 6d. for "windows broke", and the artists complained of "the intrusion of persons whose stations and educations disqualified them for judging of statuary and painting, and who were made idle and tumultuous by the opportunity of attending a show".

All this is best viewed as a measure of the success of the exhibition as a whole and as an indication of natural public curiosity at such a unique display. Even someone reasonably well qualified by birth and breeding "for judging of statuary and painting" might have broken a window for sheer excitement at discovering the works of Reynolds, Richard Wilson, Cosway, Morland, Roubiliac, Paul Sandby and sixty-three others. The general public had never before enjoyed an opportunity of seeing Reynolds' paintings, and the four portraits he showed at once established his pre-eminence. Richard Wilson's four canvases, Roubiliac's model for his statue of Shakespeare, Hayman's picture of Garrick as Richard the Third and Cosway's portrait of Shipley must likewise have stood out by their excellence.

But here we touch on one of the undoubted shortcomings of this first art exhibition—that the visitor was offered no help in discriminating between the good and the less good. Indeed, he was positively confused, for the artists' pictures were scattered here and there on walls already hung with prize-winning entries for the Society's competitions. Some of the latter were distinguished by marks of approbation; whereas the canvases of painters like Reynolds and Wilson were not singled out in any way. It must certainly have been exceedingly puzzling—another excuse, perhaps, for a visitor to break a window as a protest against the apparent injustice of it all!

Although the Society had been obstinate in refusing to allow an entrance fee, the catalogues sold so well that the artists were left with a balance of £100 which they invested and applied "towards the advancement of art". The number of catalogues sold (6,582 in all) gives a clue as to the number of visitors; 300 catalogues were required each day in the first week, and during the second week the demand varied between 600 and 800: a reasonable estimate of the total attendance is over 20,000.

The great success of this first exhibition would alone ensure for the Society an honourable place in the history of British art. Not only was art appreciation given a powerful impetus and the custom of annual exhibitions inaugurated, but artists were offered enormous encouragement by the demonstration—achieved, it must be admitted, in spite of the Society's opposition—that large numbers of people were willing to pay to see a collection of pictures. The artists were quick to send a generous acknowledgment to the Secretary, again drafted by Johnson:

Sir,

You are requested by the Artists whose Works appeared in the late Exhibition to return their sincerest Thanks to the Society for the Use of their Room and the Honour of their Patronage. Whatever improvement the Arts of Elegance shall receive from the honest Emulation which publick Notice may excite will be justly ascribed to those by whose Example the Public has been influenced.

I am, &c.,

F. HAYMAN, Chairman of

the Committee.[1]

3

In due course the artists, having decided to hold another exhibition in the following year, once more approached the Society for the use of its room. They now felt themselves in a strong enough position to insist on their own terms—namely, that the exhibition should be postponed until June (to avoid the intermingling of their own works with those of the Society's prizewinners) and that the purchase of a catalogue, the price of which was to be increased to a shilling, should be a condition of admission. But the Society maintained its resolve not to have dictated to it the terms on which an exhibition should be held in its own hall. The proposal for an entrance fee was particularly distasteful, and the Society informed the artists that any exhibition in the Great Room must be "free and open to the Public". The artists' committee refused to accept the Society's conditions; they decided to look elsewhere for a suitable gallery.

This secession did not mean that the Society held no art exhibition in 1761, for a number of artists signified their willingness to accept its conditions and to continue to show their work under its auspices, but it did mean that the second exhibition was much less important than the first. In 1761 the great names—Reynolds, Hogarth, Gainsborough, Stubbs, Wilson, Roubiliac—were to be found in the exhibition of the independent group of artists at Spring Gardens, Charing Cross; while the Society of Arts' second exhibition, though larger and better organised than the first, offered few distinguished contributors apart from Cosway and Nollekens. As if to emphasise the split, the group that exhibited at Spring Gardens became known first as the Society of Artists of Great Britain and later (having received a royal charter) as the

[1] Walpole Society, vol. vi, p. 120.

Incorporated Society of Artists. Those who remained under the patronage of the Society of Arts formally assumed the title of the Free Society of Artists.

The Society of Arts decided to end its exhibitions after 1764, but those of the Incorporated Society and the Free Society continued in other premises. In October, 1768, a clash of personalities developed within the Incorporated Society, as a result of which William Chambers, the architect, approached King George with a plan for a Royal Academy. The King gave his consent; the Academy was formally established; and Chambers was appointed its first Treasurer. The long succession of Royal Academy exhibitions began in April, 1769, and, though the Incorporated Society and the Free Society continued to hold exhibitions of their own for some years afterwards, it was not long before they were compelled to concede that their main purpose was being fulfilled by the Academy and brought their activities to an end. Appropriately enough, the records of the Incorporated Society were finally deposited with the Royal Academy and those of the Free Society with the Society of Arts.

Looking back on the complicated art-history that was packed into this short space of ten years, between 1759 and 1769, we see that the part played by the Society of Arts in forwarding the interests and raising the status of the artist was considerable. The foundation of the Royal Academy can, indeed, be traced perfectly clearly, though indirectly, from its decision to sponsor the first art exhibition in 1760. That the Society itself might have initiated a Royal Academy of Arts as early as 1755 is shown by the draft of a scheme (preserved in Dr. Templeman's MS. volume of *Transactions*) submitted to it in that year by Sir Henry Cheere, advocating that the Society should apply for a charter for an Academy of Painting, Sculpture, etc. The objects of Sir Henry Cheere's scheme, and the methods proposed for attaining them, are identical with those defined in the "Instrument" granted to the Royal Academy by King George III. But, in retrospect, there seems little reason to regret that Cheere's scheme did not find favour. Had it done so, the Society of Arts would probably have been merged in the Royal Academy; Art, in the long run, would not have benefited, while agriculture, invention, industry and commerce would all have been losers; and the history of the Society might well have been narrower in its scope and, in view of the many points at which it has touched the life of the nation, less fruitful for good.

4

Although the sponsoring of the pioneer art exhibition in England was a most important achievement, the Society's main claim to the gratitude of artists and art-lovers—so far as the first century of its existence is concerned—rests on the system of competitions and prizes which it established, and which became for a period perhaps the most popular part of the Society's work. We have already seen how the first offers of prizes for drawings by children came to be made at the second meeting of the Society, on March 29, 1754; and we have noted the names of Cosway and Smart among the winners. The announcement of that first competition left no doubt that the Society's primary intention was to encourage industrial art, i.e. art applied to manufactures. The printed list of premiums for 1758 showed the same dominant purpose. A statement declared that "Fancy, Design, and Taste" were "greatly assisted by the *Art of Drawing*, and absolutely necessary to all persons concerned in Building, Furniture, Dress, Toys [the word was used in its old sense, to cover many kinds of trinkets from brooches to watch-chains] or any other Matters where Elegance and Ornament are required", and prizes were offered to young people, according to a careful schedule, for figure drawings, landscapes, casts and so forth.

The same list of 1758 offered prizes for designs for weavers, calico-printers, cabinetmakers and coachmakers, as well as for manufacturers of iron, brass, china, earthenware or "any other Mechanic Trade that requires Taste". These were all for the young; a prize for a copper medal was open to candidates a little older (but still under twenty-five). In the following years there were added to the list: engraving, mezzotint, etching, gemengraving, cameo-cutting, architectural and furniture design, bronze-casting and other specialities of that kind. However, though many prizes were awarded, the response in these classes seems to have been disappointing; there were many more entries in the purely artistic sections; with the result that, by 1778, nearly all the technical subjects had dropped out, and the list was confined to the artistic classes alone, including the methods of reproduction (engraving, modelling, carving, etc.) but omitting the industrial applications. It was not really that the Society failed to appreciate the importance of encouraging the industrial artists—in the observations attached to the list of Fine Art awards in 1778 we find the Society claiming, apropos of the weavers and calico-printers, that "the elegance of pattern adopted by them may with justice be attributed in a great degree to the rewards and attention bestowed upon them by the Society" (nor was this an idle boast); yet perhaps it is true to say that the majority of the Society's "Committee of Polite Arts" at this time were more interested in Art pure and simple than in industrial art, and that they were not prepared to exert themselves to attract entries in the industrial sections. It was not until the eighteen-forties that the Society, on the suggestion of its President, Prince Albert, resumed as a serious task the encouragement of "the application of the Fine Arts to our Manufactures".

Meanwhile, how did the foundation of the Royal Academy in 1768 affect the Society's work in the sphere of Fine Arts? It might have been expected that there would be nothing more for the Society to do; but this was by no means the case. For the Academy confined itself to the instruction of those art students who showed the highest promise, while the Society continued to offer prizes to all who cared to enter its competitions—provided only that they were young people who "are intended hereafter to become artists", or young people of the upper class who were studying art as amateurs. The Society therefore played a most valuable part in stimulating talent at that stage of an artist's development when he is still uncertain whether or not to commit himself to an artistic career, and when a gesture of encouragement from an official body can mean so much.

In general, the Society wisely confined its competitions to young people, though there were some exceptions in favour of older candidates (notably in the case of such arts as die-sinking, gem-engraving and casting in metals). The classes, age-limits and conditions were varied from time to time. At first the rewards were always pecuniary, but from 1758 onwards gold and silver medals were also provided, in two sizes, and in 1766 the "Honorary Palette" was devised—a minature copy of an artist's palette, bearing on the obverse the Society's title and on the reverse a scroll with the recipient's name; this was generally in silver, though sometimes in gold or silver-gilt. In 1782, on the strength of a legacy of £100 from John Stock, "Painter to His Majesty's Dockyards", the Stock Medallion was instituted: it was nearly always given for architecture, but occasionally for sculpture. The money prizes ranged from a few pounds up to, on rare occasions, £100 or even £150. Prizes of 15 or 20 guineas were common. Sometimes both a medal and a money prize were given.

5

During the period of ninety-five years from 1755 to 1849, the Society's Fine Art awards totalled more than three thousand. This is a record that implies a great deal of voluntary committee-work conscientiously performed. But the three thousand awards represent only a fraction of the hopes and fears, the ambitions and disappointments that the Society's challenge called forth year by year. How greatly British art benefited by the Society's encouragement can be seen from the many famous names that are included in the selected list of 450 successful candidates published in Sir Henry Trueman Wood's history of the Society.

The first in date, though not in importance, was Richard Cosway (1740-1821). Shipley's outstanding pupil, who was elected R.A. in 1771, became a successful portrait-painter and a favourite of the Prince Regent. He won a first prize in the Society's first competition, and later received four other prizes from the Society. The Society now possesses two of his works: his portraits of Shipley (plate 1) and Dr. Templeman.

With Cosway must be mentioned his friend John Smart (1741-1811), the miniature-painter, who was second to Cosway in that first competition with the drawing reproduced in plate 9. He received three other prizes from the Society, one of them in respect of a portrait in chalks of the founder.

G. M. Moser (1704–1803), the German-born chaser and enameller, and his daughter Mary Moser (d. 1819), the flower-painter, were both remarkable artists whose merit was recognised by the Society in its early years. The father received a premium in 1758 for designing a medal for the Society (which was, how-ever, rejected in favour of a design by "Athenian" Stuart), and his daughter was awarded a premium in the same year for an ornamental design. In 1759, at the age of fifteen, Mary Moser received another premium for a flower picture (reproduced in plate 8), and with it a special silver medal "as a further Reward for her extraordinary merit". This delightful painting of Miss Moser's, which normally hangs in the Society's Council room, was shown in the 1760 exhibition and for that reason was included in the Society's "Exhibition of Exhibitions" in 1951.

Both G. M. Moser and Mary Moser were elected R.A.s, the father being one of the founders of the Royal Academy and its first Keeper; he engraved George III's first great seal. Mary Moser was likewise a foundation member of the Academy and one of the two original women Academicians.

It is worth noting that Francis Towne (1740–1816), the land-scape-painter, was awarded a premium in 1759 for a design. His alpine water-colours did not receive the appreciation they deserved until more than a hundred years after his death.

The first sculptor of distinction to receive one of the Society's prizes was Joseph Nollekens (1737–1823), who won a premium for a drawing in 1759 and premiums for bas-reliefs in that year and the three following years. A considerable controversy arose over his premium for modelling in 1759, a rival candidate stating that "both Nollekens and himself had been assisted by Mr. Wilton [presumably Joseph Wilton, later Keeper of the Royal Academy], by touching both their Models in several Places; and that Mr. Wilton worked some time at Nollekens' Model". At first the Committee of Polite Arts were of opinion that Nollekens must forfeit his title to a premium, but at the next meeting of the committee (March 29, 1759) Nollekens' master Peter Scheemakers "said he believed Nollekens is capable of doing the Model himself, and that he don't believe Nollekens had any assistant", and Wilton said "that he might take the tool and make a stroke or two, but gave him no assistance in the finishing part in which lies the Judgment". The committee were then satisfied that Nollekens deserved his premium for the bas-relief, but a doubt had apparently now been implanted in their minds as to whether his entry for the drawing-prize was really as good as it looked, and he was therefore required to undergo a test in this respect. The following is a quotation from the Minutes of the Committee for Polite Arts for April 17, 1759:

> The Committee before whom Nollekens was to give Proof of his abilities having directed that the said Nollekens should be locked up in a Room by himself in order to give such Proof; and to make a rough sketch from the following subject viz. Lot his Wife and two Daughters leaving Sodom: Mr. Shipley acquainted the Committee that Nollekens had accordingly been lock'd up alone about 3 hours one Day and between three and four another Day during which time he had made a rough Sketch of the Subject directed by the Committee which being produced to and examined by them, They are of opinion that the said Nollekens has therein given Satisfactory Proof of his abilities and therefore recommend it to the Society to give him the whole Premium offered for this class (No. 72) being fifteen Guineas.

In 1760 Nollekens went to Rome, and from there submitted a bas-relief in marble for which he received 50 guineas. While in Rome, he met David Garrick who cried: "'What! let me look at you! Are you the little fellow to whom we gave the prizes at the Society of Arts?' 'Yes, Sir,' being the answer, Mr. Garrick invited him to breakfast the next morning, and kindly sat to him for his bust, for which he paid him 12L. 12s."[1]

It was in 1759 also that John Bacon the Elder (1740-99) received a premium, at the age of eighteen, for a figure of Peace. This sculptor, highly esteemed in his day—he was responsible, among numerous other works, for the monuments to Pitt in Westminster Abbey and to Dr. Johnson in St. Paul's—received many

---

[1] *Nollekens and his Times*, by J. T. Smith, 1949 edn., p. 3.

substantial prizes from the Society, and in 1778 was awarded a gold medal in recognition of his gift to the Society of his statues of Mars and Venus.

John Flaxman (1755–1826) came to the Society's notice at an earlier age than Nollekens or Bacon, for he won a premium for modelling in clay when he was only eleven. Two more premiums went to Flaxman in 1769—again for modelling in clay—and in 1770 he received the Palette in gold for modelling a statue of Garrick. The Society was also indebted to him for the design of its large medal in 1807, a beautiful piece of work which he presented to the Society and for which he, in return, was rewarded with the Society's gold medal. Other notable sculptors who won medals from the Society were William Behnes (d. 1864) and his pupil Thomas Woolner (1825–92), the only sculptor member of the Pre-Raphaelite Brotherhood.

Several interesting artists, apart from Nollekens and Flaxman, were winning the Society's prizes in the seventeen-sixties. Francis Wheatley (1747–1801), the landscape- and portrait-painter who became R.A., was one of these; he was yet another of Shipley's successful pupils. In 1763 Antony Devis (1729–1816) received a premium for a landscape. James Tassie (1735–99), the gem-engraver, and Philip Reinagle, R.A. (1749–1833), the animal- and landscape-painter, both won premiums in 1767. But more important, in the eyes of posterity, was the award of £20 in 1763 to George Romney (1734–1802).

The picture for which Romney received his award—it was really a sort of "consolation prize"—was his first important work, "The Death of General Wolfe". The Committee of Polite Arts originally allowed Romney a second prize of 50 guineas in this competition for historical paintings, but the committee's judgment required the confirmation of the members at large. At an extraordinary meeting, held soon afterwards, this confirmation was not forthcoming, and the second prize was taken away from Romney and given to J. H. Mortimer. The committee now recommended that a "bounty" of 25 guineas be given to Romney. The "members at large" seem to have accepted this in principle, but apparently thought the sum too generous; at least, the printed

8. FLORAL DESIGN BY MARY MOSER AT THE AGE OF FIFTEEN

Awarded a prize in 1759 and included in the first art exhibition, 1760

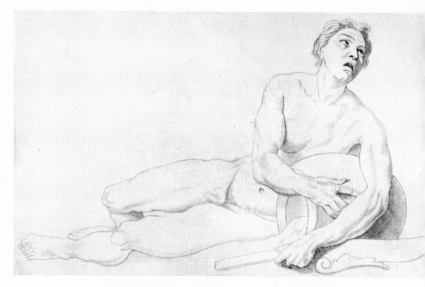

9. FENCIL DRAWING BY JOHN SMART AT THE AGE OF ELEVEN
Awarded a prize in the Society's first competition, 1754

10. PENCIL DRAWING BY EDWIN LANDSEER AT THE AGE OF TEN
A proficiency test to substantiate his claim to a prize, 1813

list of premiums and bounties (1754–76) records that Romney received only £20.

The reversal of a committee's award was by no means an unusual or suspicious event in the Society at this time, yet in Romney's case it gave rise to a remarkable amount of gossip and innuendo. Richard Cumberland wrote that "Romney, friendless, unknown, was set aside in favour of a rival better supported", and Romney's son John elaborated this statement by declaring that the original judgment was reversed through the influence of Joshua Reynolds who was jealous of Romney. Hayley says that Romney himself believed this to be true, though (according to Hayley) Romney felt that Mortimer deserved the prize. Numerous biographers of Romney have traced his life-long antipathy to Reynolds to this incident. There is nothing in the Society's records to support that interpretation. Reynolds was then a member of the Society, it is true, but he was not a member of the Committee of Polite Arts, and there is no mention in the Society's Minutes of his intervention in the discussion at any point. Nor need it be assumed that his opinion would have carried great weight, for he was not on particularly good terms with the Society in 1763, having been one of the artists who seceded from the Society's art exhibition in 1761.

The known facts of the Romney incident are well set out by W. T. Whitley in his *Artists and Their Friends in England*.[1] It should be added that, two years later, the Society gave Romney a premium of 50 guineas for his oil-painting of "The Death of Edward I".

From this curious episode we may turn, with unmixed satisfaction, to the Society's award in 1775 of a premium of 7 guineas to Thomas Bewick (1753–1828). The great wood-engraver can then only just have left his apprenticeship, so that this premium must have meant much to him. The prize was given for a charming little engraving on wood of a hunting scene, called "The Old Hound": it is well reproduced from the original cut in the prefatory memoir to the 1820 edition of the *Select Fables*, from which the reproduction on the next page was made.

[1] 1928, vol. I, pp. 191–2.

Young Thomas Lawrence (1769–1830)—later to become Sir Thomas Lawrence, P.R.A.—was a little unfortunate when, at the age of fourteen, he submitted a copy of Raphael's "Transfiguration" for a competition in 1784. The committee found that the drawing had not been executed within the specified time-limit; they therefore announced that it was disqualified and that Lawrence could not be awarded the gold medal. However, as in Romney's case, second thoughts caused the committee to relent. Lawrence was eventually awarded the Palette in silver-gilt and 5

FIG. 2. "THE OLD HOUND"
Wood-engraving by Thomas Bewick. Awarded a prize 1775

guineas, "as a token of the Society's approbation of his abilities": a trifle stingy, one might think, but it was quite impossible to run a series of competitions if the candidates did not keep to the rules. The award to Lawrence does not appear in the printed list but is recorded in the Society's Minutes, and Lawrence's receipt is still preserved by the Society.

The early years of the nineteenth century saw several distinguished artists honoured, at the outset of their careers, by the Society. J. S. Cotman (1782–1842), the Norwich painter, received the silver Palette in 1800 for a drawing of a mill (his rapid development was in striking contrast to the slow progress of his fellow-townsman John Crome). In 1801 William Mulready

(1786–1863), the genre-painter, also received the silver Palette for a drawing: we shall see that nearly fifty years later a collection of his work was to be exhibited in the Society's House. Another very successful competitor at this period was William Ross (1794–1860)—later Sir William Ross, R.A.—the miniature-painter, who carried off a tremendous array of Palettes and medals in the years between 1807 and 1817, and who, like Mulready, was later to be honoured by an exhibition in the Society's House (in his case, in the year of his death). Sir Charles Eastlake, P.R.A. (1793–1865), the historical-painter who was also for a time Director of the National Gallery, received a silver medal in 1810; and Samuel Cousins, R.A. (1801–87), the mezzotint-engraver, was awarded the silver Palette in 1813 and a silver medal in 1814, both for drawings, the first done when he was eleven years old.

As the nineteenth century advanced the Society recognised the early merit of many artists who became highly esteemed in Victorian England but whose work has since been drastically re-valued. For example, Sir Edwin Landseer, R.A. (1802–73), the animal-painter, received the silver Palette for a drawing of animals from life when he was only eleven[1] and won silver medals in the three following years. C. W. Cope, R.A. (1811–90), the historical-painter, received silver medals in 1828 and 1829, and J. C. Horsley, R.A. (1817–1903) was awarded silver medals at the ages of thirteen and fourteen. Portraits of Prince Albert by Cope and of "Queen Victoria and her Children" by Horsley are now to be seen on the Society's staircase. An artist whose repu-tation has weathered the years rather more successfully than theirs is W. P. Frith (1819–1909), the painter of "Derby Day", whose first silver medal was given to him by the Society when he was about seventeen. Hablot K. Browne (1815–82), better known as "Phiz", the illustrator of Dickens, was also seventeen when he won a silver medal for a group of figures in pencil. And an un-expected name on the list is that of Coventry Patmore, the poet, who received the silver Palette in 1838, when he was fifteen, for a

[1] A drawing of a dog, done at the Society's House to substantiate Landseer's claim to this prize, is reproduced in plate 10.

pencil drawing, but who did not continue to develop his talent as an artist.

No more striking example could, however, be chosen to illustrate the Society's encouragement of young artists in the first century of its existence than the record of its lavish recognition of the boyish genius of Sir John Millais, P.R.A. (1829–96). At a very early age Millais showed an extraordinary gift for sketching portraits from the life. His son J. G. Millais has described how, in 1838, he was brought to London from St. Helier by his parents, who were armed with an introduction to Sir Martin Archer Shee, the President of the Royal Academy. In the coach from Southampton they met Joseph Paxton, and during the journey, to quote the words of Millais' brother William, "Mr. Paxton fell asleep, and Jack at once went for him and got him into his book. Just as he had finished the sketch Paxton awoke, and, seeing what had been done, was so astonished that he entered into conversation with my mother, which resulted in a letter of introduction to the President of the Society of Arts, Adelphi, where my brother afterwards went."

The President of the Royal Academy was highly enthusiastic when he was shown the boy's drawings, but it was from the Society of Arts that Millais received the more practical encouragement, in the shape of his first medal. This silver medal was awarded him in 1839; he won two others in the years immediately following and later received a gold medal and a gold medallion. William Millais' first-hand description of one of the Society's prize-givings well suggests the importance of the work that the Society was doing, and emphasises the significance, to a young artist, of being publicly honoured by his elders on such great occasions. The passage is quoted from J. G. Millais' *Life and Letters of Sir John Everett Millais* [1]:

> I shall never forget the Prize-day at the Society of Arts when my brother had won the silver medal for a large drawing of "The Battle of Bannockburn." He was then between nine and ten years of age, and the dress the little fellow wore is vividly before me as I write. He had on a white plaid tunic, with black belt and

[1] 1900, vol. I, p. 14.

buckle; short white frilled trousers, showing bare legs, with white socks and patent leather shoes; a large white frilled collar, a bright necktie, and his hair in golden curls.

When the Secretary . . . called out "*Mr.* John Everett Millais," the little lad walked up unseen by His Royal Highness the Duke of Sussex, who was giving the prizes, and stood at his raised desk. After a time the Duke observed that "the gentleman was a long time coming up," to which the Secretary replied, "He is here, your Royal Highness." The Duke then stood up and saw the boy, and, giving him his stool to stand upon, the pretty little golden head appeared above the desk.

Unfortunately the Duke, being weak as to his eyesight, could make nothing of the drawing when it was held up to him, in spite of trying various glasses; but he was assured that it was a marvellous performance. He patted my brother's head and wished him every success in his profession, at the same time kindly begging him to remember that if at any time he could be of service to him he must not hesitate to write and say so. It so happened that Jack did avail himself of this kind offer. We had been in the habit of fishing every year in the Serpentine and Round Pond by means of tickets given to us by Sir Frederick Pollock, then Chief Baron; but a day came when this permission was withheld from everyone, and then my brother wrote to the Duke's private secretary, and we were again allowed to fish there. . . .

6

It is appropriate to refer here to the Society's attempt, unsuccessful though it proved, to provide for the establishment of a National Gallery of British Art, one of the first objects to which Henry Cole directed himself when he joined the Society in 1846. The admirable idea was that an exhibition of the work of a contemporary artist should be held each year, the profits from which were to be expended on purchasing one or more of that artist's works, and that these should be lent to the National Gallery until enough had been collected to fill a special gallery. Landseer was the first artist to be approached. He showed considerable hesitation, and Henry Cole eventually wrote to ask whether his silence might be taken for consent. Landseer's reply did credit to his modesty:

26th Fe^{by} 1847.

ST. JOHN'S WOOD.

Dear Sir,

Can you forgive my silence as I have not courage "to give consent"? I am very highly flattered by the proposal received from the Society of Arts, and I sincerely hope their project may be successful. To secure this desirable object I venture to recommend the Committee to select from amongst those you mentioned to me a more worthy and attractive exhibitor. With this feeling I beg very respectfully to decline the honor, and to thank you for the kind interest you have taken in my behalf.

My dear Sir, Sincerely yours,
E. LANDSEER

It comes as no surprise from the writer of this letter that, when elected President of the Royal Academy, in 1866, he should have declined the office in favour of Francis Grant.

William Mulready was the next to be asked. He gave his consent, and an important collection of more than two hundred of his works was exhibited at the Society's House in the summer of 1848, the *Morning Post* remarking: "We cannot remember that we ever witnessed a collection of pictures with one half the satisfaction with which we beheld these. They constitute the exhibition of the season." The profits were not large but sufficed for the purchase of three drawings by Mulready, which were presented to the National Gallery.

Soon afterwards Turner was approached, with a view to his works providing the second exhibition, but he declined from "peculiar inconvenience this year". William Etty, R.A., was then sounded by David Roberts as to whether he would take Turner's place and replied in the affirmative, saying that he felt "flattered they should have thought of my works. . . . If the Edinburgh Pictures could be got it would make a grand foundation and if the thing is done it ought to be done well". Five large and important pictures were duly lent by the Royal Scottish Academy and formed the nucleus of the exhibition of more than one hundred and thirty works by Etty which was shown in the Society's House in June, 1849. The exhibition came as a timely tribute to Etty's achievement, for his health had begun to fail, and he now retired from London to his native York. He was able, however, to supervise the hanging of his pictures and (in the words of Richard and Samuel Redgrave, the art-historians, both of whom were members of the Society's National Gallery Committee) he "was much moved by the congratulations of his friends". Etty died in November of the same year.

Unfortunately the Etty exhibition resulted in a loss, from which the Society was only able to extricate itself by diverting, with the donor's consent, a gift of £500 from the widow of a member, Mrs. Acton, which had been intended for the general purposes of the Society. The scheme for a National Gallery of British Art was now abandoned. It will be best remembered, perhaps, for having inspired the Mulready and Etty exhibitions, which have their place in British art-history.[1] In 1850 the Society turned to an exhibition "of works of Ancient and Medieval Art" which proved highly successful, largely owing to the exertions of Mr. (afterwards Sir) Augustus Wollaston Franks, the eminent archaeologist; but this had no connection with Cole's scheme.

7

The Society's system of Fine Art premiums continued in operation throughout the eighteen-forties. Even when it was being revised in the years before the 1851 Exhibition, with the avowed object—urged by the Prince Consort—of substituting the application of art to industry for the cultivation of pictorial art, the prizes for painting and drawing were not discontinued. But the Great Exhibition, a national turning-point in many different ways,

---

[1] It appears probable, nevertheless, that the Society did have an influence on the establishment of the Tate Gallery, Millbank, forty years later. For on March 11, 1890, the matter was once more brought to public notice by a paper read to the Society by James Orrock on "The Claims of the British School of Painting to thorough representation in the National Gallery." This paper was illustrated by a collection of works by English masters either not represented or inadequately represented in the National Gallery, a collection which remained on view in the Society's House for a few days after the meeting. In the *Journal* of June 27, 1890, the Society was pleased to note Henry Tate's generous offer of pictures from his collection and to reprint from *The Times* his letter to the Chancellor of the Exchequer which led to the foundation of the Tate Gallery.

affected the Society which sponsored it no less than it affected other British institutions. There was no prize distribution by the Society of any sort in 1851, and at the last distribution in 1853 only one solitary medal was given in the class of Fine Arts.

The Society, not for the last time in its history, had shifted the direction of its advance and turned its energies to different fields. This is not the place to anticipate a later chapter, which will record the work of the Society that led up to the Great Exhibition, but it is sufficient to mention the graceful tea service designed for one of the Society's competitions, in 1846, by "Felix Summerly" (the pseudonym of Henry Cole), and the enormously popular shilling colour-box which derived from a competition in 1851, to show that, though the emphasis of the Society's initiative was altered, art in general continued to benefit. In less than twenty years, eleven millions of these colour-boxes were sold.

Ever since its inception, the Society had, from time to time, encouraged and rewarded inventions and improvements connected with the arts. To take only a few examples: in 1764 a premium of 30 guineas went to Thomas Keyse for a method of fixing crayon drawings, and in 1781 a silver Palette was given to Thomas and William Reeves for improved water-colours. It is surprising that the Society has not done more for printing, but in 1819 it did, rather belatedly, present a gold medal to Aloys Senefelder for his invention of lithography.

The award of two prizes in 1822 and 1823 marked an important, if temporary, development in the technique of engraving. Although steel had been used by so early an artist as Dürer, copper was almost universally employed for engraving until the middle of the nineteenth century, and the introduction of soft steel by T. G. Lupton for mezzotint was rewarded, as an innovation, by the Society with a gold medal in 1822, and in the following year Charles Warren also received a gold medal for "improvements in the art of engraving on steel".

These awards followed an important investigation which was carried out by a committee of the Society in 1819 into possible means of preventing as far as possible the forgery of bank notes. While this committee were able to suggest several possible improvements, including machine engraving and, very tentatively, the use of soft steel, a much more promising line of development had already been pursued by Jacob Perkins, whose company, Messrs. Perkins, Fairman & Heath, had for many years before this been practising their "siderographic" method in America. This method consisted in the use of a steel roller to transfer the impression of an engraving from one piece of steel to another, and it thus made possible the production of an unlimited number of accurate impressions of a highly complicated design. This important aid to the defeat of the forger was described in a paper published in 1820 in the *Transactions*, but no prize was awarded for it, presumably because the process which it described was not new. Perkins did, however, receive from the Society several medals for other inventions.

The Society did a great deal in its early years to stimulate the arts of die-sinking and gem-engraving. As a result, the character of British medals was substantially improved. The five children of Thomas Pingo (1692–1776), the engraver to the Mint who cut the dies for the Society's first medal, were notably successful in these competitions, especially John and Lewis Pingo. The offer of prizes for medals was dropped in 1765 but reappeared in 1807. A number of medals for medal dies were subsequently taken by William Wyon, R.A. (1795–1851), and by several other members of the distinguished Wyon family. The Society's lists provide interesting evidence of the richness of hereditary talent in the artistic crafts.

The revival of gem-engraving in England in the latter part of the eighteenth century may be largely, and perhaps entirely, attributed to the Society of Arts. Edward Burch, R.A., and his pupil Nathaniel Marchant, R.A., were conspicuously successful in the Society's competitions for gem-engraving in the seventeen-sixties. The younger man was probably the greater artist; but collectively there is no doubt that they were the finest gem-engravers of their day. Burch pays handsome tribute in his *Catalogue of One Hundred Proofs from Gems Engraved in England* (1795) to "that truly laudable and patriotic Society for the Promotion and Encouragement of Arts, Manufactures and Commerce". He praises "the above honourable society who gave (with a liberal hand) premiums for history paintings, large and small medals for sculpture likewise, and engravings on gems; and it is with thankfulness that I acknowledge the share I had in these honors and emoluments. . . . What was most for the fame and opulence of their native country was generously undertaken by them, and carried on with a spirit which must do honor to any institution."

In the same year (1759) as the prize for gem-engraving was first offered, a prize was also announced for "casts or impressions in glass, commonly called pastes". As we have seen, 10 guineas were awarded in 1767 to that excellent modeller James Tassie, whose reproductions of gems were catalogued by that unusual rascal R. E. Raspe, the creator of *Munchausen*. The last award of any note in this section was a gold medal given to Thomas Moring in 1845.

Anyone who looks back on the work for the Fine Arts accomplished by the Society during the first century of its existence cannot fail to be struck by the vast extent to which the country's taste and talent benefited. Indeed the range and ramifications of its activities make its influence beyond computation.

CHAPTER 4

Pioneering in Agriculture

1

SURPRISE is not infrequently—and not unnaturally—expressed that a Society of Arts should interest itself in agriculture, and indeed the founder of the Society himself considered that, except when directly linked with manufacture by the production of raw materials, the subject was outside the scope of "arts, manufactures and commerce". Yet if agriculture is not a manufacture, it is certainly one of the greatest industries and one of the oldest "arts", and Robert Dossie points out that in his days it was closely linked with commerce. "Agriculture", he said, "is peculiarly important to us, as a commercial nation: the support of our trade depending on our manufactures; those manufactures on the rate of labour; and the rate of labour, in a great degree, on the price of the necessaries of life."

At any rate the Society, shaking off any scruples, soon took up this vital subject wholeheartedly, and for a considerable time it assumed the lead in the great movement commonly known as the agricultural revolution, which was then in its initial stages. The part played by the Society in this movement is commonly over-looked by historians, who, so far as the eighteenth century is concerned, focus attention upon a few individual "improvers". But essential though the work of the pioneers was, it was largely wasted until the rank and file of the farming community had begun to follow in their steps. Hence the need for a national centre of agricultural knowledge and stimulus, and this need was supplied solely by the Society of Arts until more specialised bodies of an equally national status were established.

For some time after its foundation the Royal Society had concerned itself with agriculture as with other applications of science, but by the middle of the eighteenth century it was strongly tending to become purely academic in its interests, and when the Society of Arts entered upon the task of developing agriculture the field was clear. Indeed, there is reason to believe, although the original documents are now unfortunately lost, that about the year 1775 a number of leading members of the new body who were also influential Fellows of the older society held a private meeting specially to discuss a division of labour between the two organisations, and that here it was unofficially agreed that the Royal Society should occupy itself with pure science and leave the study of its applications to the Society of Arts.[1]

The method which the Society chose for this great task, as for its encouragement of art, was the prize competition, but the offering of prizes for agricultural objects was by no means as simple a matter as it was for art. The settling of the terms of an offer required, first of all, a clear idea about the ultimate purpose to be served by it. If, for example, its subject was the growing of lucerne, was the intention to get more farmers to grow lucerne? or to get those who grew it to grow more? or to improve the quality of what was being produced? or to encourage better methods of cultivation? or to popularise new varieties? These and similar questions (many of which have already been listed[2]) had to be faced and settled before the terms of the offer could be drafted effectively.

And then there was the question of safeguards to ensure as far as possible that the claims submitted were genuine. Typical of the kind of certificates which the Society decided to demand are the following, which were submitted by John Crow of Faversham, a successful candidate for a prize for madder-growing in 1773:

[1] Attention was drawn to this circumstance by Dr. F. W. Gibbs, to whose three monographs, on "Robert Dossie and the Society of Arts" (*Annals of Science*, Feb. 7, 1951), "Peter Shaw and the Society of Arts" (*Ibid.*, Mar. 7, 1951) and "William Lewis, M.B., F.R.S." (*Ibid.*, Feb. 8, 1952) the authors are also indebted.

[2] See p. 12.

Feversham, October 31st, 1772.

These are to certify, that I, John Crow, of the parish of Feversham, in the county of Kent, have dug up, from one acre, and one perch of ground, fifty-one hundred, one quarter, and twenty-six pounds of dry and clean madder-roots: of which, I have sent a sample of seven pounds weight, of the same quality as the whole parcel. Witness my hand,

JOHN CROW

N.B. The above madder was three years growth, and no more; and grew in a field known by the name of Cutthorn, in the parish aforesaid.

Sworn before me, the day and year above written.

EDW. JACOB, Deputy Mayor of Feversh.

Sworn before me,

RICHARD LUSHINGTON, Mayor.

The above madder was weighed in our presence, viz.

RICHARD MARSH, Vicar of Feversham.

JAMES TAPPENDEN, Attorney at Fev.

JOHN CRESWELL,
THO. MORRIS, } Church-wardens.

HENRY ANDERSON.

JOHN BALDWIN.

This careful system of certification was, of course, essential, for substantial sums of money were at stake, and even in spite of it the Society was seriously defrauded in at least one case. The culprit was one of its own members, a certain Dr. John Stephens, of Lincoln's Inn Fields, who fraudently obtained from the Society a total of £195 over a period of some eight years. Stephens' idea was to send in under a fictitious name a forged certificate for the growing of some crop for which the Society had offered a premium, and then to appear at the Society's offices with a letter purporting to be written to him by the fictitious candidate and asking him, as a member of the Society, to collect the premium on his behalf.

The Society still possesses the receipts given by Dr. Stephens, and several of his forged certificates, the varied handwritings and signatures upon which are so cleverly executed that it is no wonder that they completely hoodwinked the Society's officials and the committee. Ultimately the fraud was detected through a foolish mistake made by Stephens on the first occasion only, when he submitted the claim in the name of an actual living person. Presumably Stephens thought that this would add to its verisimilitude, but the result was that years later the man concerned heard of the premium which he had so unknowingly been awarded, and inquiries began to be made. Stephens got wind of these and disappeared, and not even the following graphic description of him, appended to a notice issued by the Bow Street magistrate, could lead to his arrest:

> N.B. Dr. John Stephens is a comely person near six feet high, clear complexion, Dark Brown Brows, formerly with a full Bob Wig but of late wore either a Bag or a Queue and is about 40 years of Age.

Another point requiring very careful consideration was the form and amount of the award to be offered for any specific object. Arthur Young, the famous agriculturist, criticised[1] some of the awards offered by the Society in 1766 as not being financially attractive in proportion to the work required of those who competed for them. Indeed, it was inherent in the competitive method adopted by the Society that only the best candidates should get any recompense at all for the time, trouble and in many cases out-of-pocket expenditure incurred by them, whereas Arthur Young's view was that "in every object some certain offer for every acre is the way to advance the measure". In some cases, of course, it could be assumed that the competitors would be of such a type as to find these financial considerations immaterial, and then the Society made no attempt to reimburse even the winning competitors, but offered the "honorary premium" of a medal.

2

There was therefore much to learn on the administrative side when the Society embarked upon the encouragement of agriculture by the offer of premiums. But few of its earliest members

---

[1] *Farmer's Letters* (1767), p. 215.

knew much about agriculture either! At first, therefore, they
wisely turned their thoughts along the comparatively straightforward lines advised by the founder, such as the planting of
madder, for which, as we saw, a prize was first offered in 1754,
and the sowing of acorns and planting of other trees, which first
became the subject of a prize in 1757.

For the purposes of this history it will be more convenient to
consider these semi-agricultural objects in a separate chapter, and
merely to observe here that they soon led on to more strictly agricultural objectives, for in the same year in which the first forestry
prizes were offered, the Society also offered two gold medals, one
"For the best set of experiments with a dissertation on soils and
their different natures"; and the other "For the best set of experiments with a dissertation on the nature and operation of Manures",
both of them only to be awarded "if really deserving".

As it turned out, none of the entries was found to be "really
deserving", which is, perhaps, hardly surprising. In offering a
prize for the study of soils the Society was half a century ahead of
its time, for it was not until the famous lectures of Sir Humphry
Davy before the Board of Agriculture in 1803 that the science
of agricultural chemistry was really founded. A renewal of the
offer, therefore, some thirty years later, although on more specific
and practical lines, was equally unsuccessful. The subject of
manures, also, although at first sight a simpler and more experimental basis for a prize, requires a very precise and critical examination if permanent principles are to be disentangled from varying
circumstances, and it was not until 1798 that the Society felt able
to make an award in connection with this subject, when John
Middleton of Merton received a silver medal for a series of comparative tests on top-dressings.[1]

But the importance of these first two offers for agriculture lies
not in the sparse results which they achieved directly, but in the
significant stress which is laid in both of them upon *experiments*,

[1] Middleton's tests came out strongly in favour of organic manures, particularly night soil, as against chemicals such as soot and potash, and he consequently deplored the waste of much valuable material through the sewage
system.

for experiment was the keynote of every kind of agricultural activity which the Society sought to stimulate in future years. Nothing was taken for granted. If a prize was offered to encourage a new method of husbandry, the candidates were required to test it against more familiar methods and satisfy themselves and others that it was a genuine improvement. If the subject of the prize was the design of a new machine, the entries had to be thoroughly tried out against older types of implement. And even if a prize was offered to promote the wider growing of some new crop, the entrants had to maintain a careful and detailed record of their method of cultivation and glean as much information as possible about the special characteristics and potential uses of the plant.

But however firmly based on experience any single report might appear to be, the Society never hurried to build any final conclusion upon it. In agriculture there are so many factors, seen and unseen, known and unknown, that the utmost caution is necessary, and of this the Society was well aware. Indeed, the chief importance of the Society's work in agriculture during this period is that by its system of premiums it called into being a nation-wide team of researchers, experimenting and observing in widely differing conditions and sometimes over long periods. Men like Weston, Tull and Townshend had already blazed a trail, but the Society of Arts led a great body of practising farmers along it, and in farming breadth of experience is at least as important as depth.

Eighteenth-century farmers, even of the more enlightened type whose numbers were beginning to increase with the growth of enclosures, needed a very definite lead, and this was where these first two agricultural offers of the Society were defective: few farmers would know how to set about obtaining the information for which they called. After a few years, however, a change is to be observed in the way in which the Society framed its offers, and the kinds of trials which it required are precisely stipulated and detailed directions are given for carrying them out. This new technique is apparent from 1761 onwards and marks a fresh start—in fact, the real, serious start—of the Society's agricultural work.

11. DESIGN FOR SILK DAMASK BY LEWIS PINGO
Awarded a prize in 1758

(Country Life)

12. CARPET MADE AT EXETER, 1758
Very possibly the one for which Passavant was awarded a prize in that year.
It may now be seen at Petworth House, Sussex.

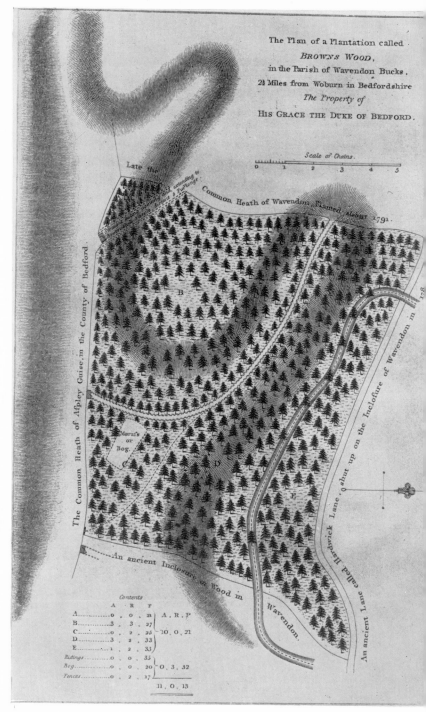

The Plan of a Plantation called
BROWNS WOOD,
in the Parish of Wavendon Bucks,
2½ Miles from Woburn in Bedfordshire
The Property of
HIS GRACE THE DUKE OF BEDFORD.

Scale of Chains.
0 1 2 3 4 5

Common Heath of Wavendon, Planted about 1791.

The Common Heath of Apsley Guise, in the County of Bedford.

Morals or Bog.

An ancient Inclosure or Wood in

An ancient Lane called Hardwick Lane, shut up on the Inclosure of Wavendon in 178

Wavendon.

Contents

	A	R	P	A . R . P
A	0	0	22	
B	3	3	27	
C	0	2	25	10 . 0 . 21
D	3	2	33	
E	1	2	35	
Ridings	0	0	35	
Bog	0	0	20	0 . 3 . 32
Fences	0	2	17	
				11 . 0 . 13

13. PLAN OF A WOOD AT WAVENDON, BUCKS
In respect of which John Farey was awarded a prize in 1805

The introduction of this new note of thoroughness and method is probably to be connected with the Society's removal to more commodious premises in the Strand at the end of 1759. Here there were proper facilities for committee meetings and investigations of all kinds, and in the autumn of 1760 standing committees were established to deal with the various branches of the Society's work.

The formation of an agriculture committee came about a little earlier than that, in the following way. In the spring of 1760 Peter Wyche, who had taken a prominent part in the Society's work for the development of the North American colonies, wrote a letter proposing that the Society should now pay attention to its own country's needs. "We are now", he wrote, "the greatest assembly of men that in any country ever sat in a disinterested manner for the good of its people, and what greater lustre can be added to the title we have assumed than really to consider and advance the landed property of these our islands." And he then went on to point out the Society's duty to give a lead because the ordinary husbandman, through an ignorance which was no fault of his own, would continue to cultivate "*more maiorum*, however stupid that might be".

As a result of Wyche's move a committee was appointed, and its members, who on the whole attended the weekly meetings very well, included such men of standing as Henry Baker, Benjamin Franklin, Sir Thomas Robinson, the re-builder and re-planter of Rokeby, Sir George Savile, the Whig politician, Thomas Hollis, F.R.S., Thomas Grignion, the clockmaker, divines such as Dr. Chandler, F.R.S., and Dr. James Fordyce, Alexander Small, the inventor of the chain plough, and last but not least Robert Dossie, who was a few years later to publish the first-fruits of the committee's labours in the three volumes of his *Memoirs of Agriculture*.

3

Besides stirring up the Society's interest in agriculture generally, Peter Wyche brought to the fore a particular problem in his letter

of March 1760. This was the dearth of winter feed, which necessitated the slaughter of countless animals each year. According to
Wyche, the survival of the animals through the winter depended
on six crops,[1] all of which had been introduced from abroad, viz.
rye grass, clover, trefoil, sainfoin, lucerne and the turnip. Turnips, of course, had long been cultivated in this country for animal
feeding, yet Lord Ernle says[2] that in 1768 they were still unknown
in many parts, and Dossie writing in that year[3] points out that in
any case it was highly unsatisfactory to depend on a single root
crop, which might fail in any season owing to the prevalent
turnip fly, or be ruined after harvesting by wet, or hard frost.
"We have lately suffered greatly on this account," he says, "not-
withstanding the use of turnips." The Society therefore began
to campaign very vigorously to extend the range of fresh feeds in
general cultivation, and paid equal attention to all three classes of
these crops, roots, green-stuffs and grasses.

Of the roots, carrots were the first to be sponsored, by the offer
in 1761 of a prize for the greatest area sown with carrots "for the
feeding of cattle only . . . on ground which has not been used for
carrots for at least 7 years". In 1762 parsnips, turnips and kohl-
rabi (if this latter may be grouped for convenience with the roots)
came into the list, swedes in 1769 and potatoes in 1772. No prize
was ever offered for growing the mangel-wurzel, although the
Society substantially assisted its first introduction into this country
by distributing seeds to the members and by publishing accounts
of it in the *Transactions*, and it awarded a "bounty" for its cultivation in 1814.

The two roots in connection with which the Society made the
most notable contributions were the potato and the swede.

Until the latter part of the eighteenth century the potato, although well established in Ireland, was only grown as a field crop
in a few parts of Britain, and then almost exclusively as a feeding-
stuff for animals. Among the pioneers of potato-growing in this

[1] Called at that time rather confusingly "foreign *grasses*" because they answered the same purpose as grass.
[2] *English Farming, Past and Present*, 5th ed., p. 202.
[3] *Memoirs of Agriculture*, vol. I, pp. 59–60.

country was Gilbert White, who found it most difficult to persuade the villagers of Selborne to take it up. Another great promoter of the potato was Arthur Young, who received a gold medal from the Society in 1779 for his work on the "clustered potato". It was largely through Young's influence that the Society began to push the crop by the offer of premiums.[1] Except for the single year 1783, when a gold medal was offered and awarded for growing potatoes specifically for the table, the Society's object at first was purely to encourage them as a feeding-stuff. In 1795, however, there was a sudden scarcity of wheat, not only in this country but also on the Continent, and in that year the Society made three separate offers for the growing of potatoes, one, as before, for growing them for sheep and cattle, one, a new one, for experiments with the seed, and a third (which was specifically announced as being introduced because of the scarcity of "bread-corn") for the growing of potatoes "fit for the table".

These efforts of the Society played an important part in the spread of potato cultivation in this country, but a greater achievement was in connection with the introduction of the swede, which came about in the following way.

John Reynolds, an enterprising tenant farmer of Adisham in East Kent, was attracted in 1767 by the Society's offer of a prize for cultivating kohl-rabi, and decided to enter for it. Kohl-rabi was still quite a novel crop, and as none of the English seedsmen whom he knew could supply him with seed he procured some from Holland, although even there he could only obtain a pound.

However, Reynolds determined to make the most of what he had, and to discover and report to the Society all he could about kohl-rabi by testing its reaction to as many different circumstances as possible. He therefore chose a field which had a variety of soils and had borne three different crops the previous season. Then, just to make the experiment a little more complicated, he only manured half the field, and ploughed it in strips at four different depths. Finally, the plants of kohl-rabi were set out in

[1] Gazely, "Arthur Young and the Society of Arts", *Jl. of Economic History*, I, 2, p. 149.

this patchwork at varying intervals, and one acre was left to be planted with cabbage, kale and broccoli as controls.

By this complex arrangement Reynolds certainly hoped to find out a great deal from a single experiment, but as things turned out he discovered a great deal more than he ever anticipated. For it happened that the seeds which the Dutchman sent to him were not of kohl-rabi at all but of swede, a plant which was well enough known on the Continent but had never before been grown in England. Needless to say, Reynolds was quick to perceive that a strange crop had come up, and he soon began to test the quality of its foliage and roots on his cattle and sheep—with the most excellent results. "Behold! what a noble production this is!" he wrote ecstatically to the Society. "Too much cannot well be said of its excellencies, so far as I am able to judge." And to prove the point, a small parcel accompanied the letter, with a personal note for George Box the Registrar:

> Mr. Reynolds' compliments to Mr. Box, desires his acceptance of a bit of butter (churned yesterday) made only from the herbage of my turnip-rooted cabbage, which I flatter myself will be acceptable, as a curiosity: being, as I dare say, the first ever made in England from this plant.

The Society quickly recognised the importance of Reynolds's discovery and made him a grant of £50. Reynolds also supplied the Society with seed from his plant and this was distributed to members of the Society, with the result that the virtues of the new plant soon became widely known and accepted.

4

In its anxiety to solve the problem of animal feeding-stuffs the Society, as we have seen, also turned its attention to leguminous crops. The 1761 list of offers included two of these, lucerne and white clover, to which sainfoin, beans, peas, tares and vetches were added the next year. Burnet also was taken up with some enthusiasm in 1762, and in 1766 the brassicas began to be encouraged, "borecole" (kale) and "cole seed" (colza rape) being included in that year and several kinds of cabbage a few years later.

The Society's offers were very effective in encouraging these crops, most of which were still quite unfamiliar to the average farmer.

But it was in connection with grasses that, next to roots, its most important work was done, for here it opened up what Arthur Young described as "an untrodden field".

The Society rightly attributed the generally poor quality of English pastures very largely to the method—or rather, lack of method—adopted in sowing them. The seed used was almost invariably the sweepings of the hay loft, and not only were these full of weeds, but no one knew whether even the grasses which they contained were the most suitable for the soil on which they were to be sown or for the purpose for which the sowing was to be made. Moreover, even those farmers who were enlightened enough to want to sow pure seed had nowhere where they could buy it, except the seed of rye-grass, an imported variety.

The Society's first task, therefore, was to remedy this deficiency, and to this end it made two separate sets of offers in 1762. The first was for growing and threshing the greatest quantity of "clean grass seed". With this offer there was no requirement regarding the varieties of grasses which might be submitted: the only point was the absence of weeds, and this had to be substantiated by certificates to the effect that the ground from which the seed was produced had not been contaminated with weeds by dunging within the past year, and that it had been weeded in the spring. The other offer went further and required the collection, by hand, of the greatest quantity of the seed of separate varieties of grass, the selection of the varieties being left to the competitors, provided that they chose species which were "really useful and valuable".

No successful claims were made for either of these awards, but there was a better response when, in 1764, the Society amended their second offer and laid down nine specific varieties of which illustrations could be found in current publications, viz. vernal, fine bent, meadow foxtail, sheep's fescue, crested dogstail, common poa, meadow fescue, yellow oat and annual poa. It was also suggested that as an alternative to submitting immediately seed gathered from the fields, it might be multiplied before submission by sowing in drills the next year.

A number of claims were submitted under these revised terms, for which awards were made in 1765 and 1766, and as the Society had now succeeded by these offers in obtaining the collection of considerable quantities of specific varieties of grass, it took its task a step further by offering larger prizes for sowing the greatest areas (over one acre) with each of these nine varieties. With seed-growing brought in this way to the mass production stage, sufficient quantities became available to meet the requirements of all who were willing to follow the Society's lead and lay down pastures with pure seed of deliberately selected varieties.

The foundation to improvement of pastures being thus securely laid, the way lay open for serious experimental work, and from 1769 onwards a number of offers were made for reports on the comparative merits of individual grasses and mixtures. Unfortunately, no satisfactory candidate was keen enough to rise to these offers, but a simpler test, for which an offer was made, did attract a successful entry. This was for comparative experiments conducted over a period of four years in rolling as against scarifying grass. The final stage in the series was reached in 1775 when offers were made for the best sets of experiments, continued over three years, to find "the most advantageous mixture of different seeds for laying down arable land to grass on wet or strong soils", and on "dry or light soils", respectively. This offer was continued until 1783, but without an award being made.

In all its work on winter feeding-stuffs the Society's primary search was for what it called a "vegetating pabulum"—a crop which would be green, alive and nutritious in the latter half of the winter; and besides offering premiums to farmers at home it entered into a wide correspondence overseas. It wrote to the sister societies in Edinburgh and Dublin, the newly founded agricultural societies in Switzerland, the academy of sciences at Paris and even to the Oeconomical Society at St. Petersburgh.[1] Among the more distinguished personal correspondents on the subject were John Wynne Baker of Dublin, who was awarded a gold

[1] See p. 150.

medal for his helpful communications, Valltravers of Switzerland, who was also awarded a gold medal, and, through Valltravers, Linnaeus.[1] All of these were made corresponding members of the Society. Benjamin Franklin, also, being actually present at some of the committee meetings, was able to give helpful information about grasses (particularly timothy grass) in North America.

5

Besides encouraging the production of more and better and more varied feeding stuffs for animals the Society fostered experiments in the manner of feeding them to the stock. In 1768 it began to offer prizes for accounts of the feeding of pigs, poultry and calves, and in 1789 it took up the more specialised problem of "soiling" or stall-feeding, first of horses and some years later of cattle. The most notable response to this offer came from J. C. Curwen, M.P., of Workington Hall, who was awarded two gold medals for stall-feeding. The second award, made in 1816, was for exploring the potentialities of stall-feeding for bringing beef-cattle to maturity more quickly than by pasturing, and Curwen mentions in his report that "the sanction of the Society's patronage in the system of soiling has had an extensive influence in spreading the practice through every part of this country".

Another problem in which it took a great interest was the way in which animals choked themselves by trying to gulp down roots too big for their gullets. A good many farmers tried to obviate this by slicing the roots by hand, but it was a laborious and somewhat dangerous process, and the Society decided in 1766 to offer a prize for a machine to serve the purpose instead. Dossie said[2] that this offer showed how useful the Society was as an initiator of inventions, for until it was published no one had ever thought of designing such a thing. But once the idea was propounded, a simple and efficient machine was very soon designed by James

[1] Linnaeus sent a list of grasses which are ready for grazing in the far north in May or June, and which, therefore, he thought, might be fit for grazing farther south in the early months of the year. (Guard Book, II, 50.)

[2] *Memoirs of Agriculture*, vol. I, p. 85.

Edgill of Frome, who was awarded a gold medal at the end of the year. Edgill's slicer consisted of a wooden tub, inside which the roots were pushed round by four wooden vanes and pressed by them against a set of adjustable knives fixed on the bottom. This implement, which anticipated the first patented slicer by almost forty years, appears to have been used in a good many parts of the country, and in a test in the presence of the Society's agriculture committee two men were able to slice twelve bushels of turnips with it in the space of an hour.[1]

The Society also took a keen interest in animal diseases. One of the very earliest prizes which it offered was for a cure for the dreadful scourge of sheep-rot or liver-rot. We now know that this is caused by the liver fluke, with its extraordinary life cycle, but the people of the mid-eighteenth century knew little more about it than Hartlib, one of whose prescriptions in his *Legacie* a century before was: "The colicke or pain in the belly is put away in the beholding of geese in the water, especially duckes."[2] The nostra submitted to the Society sounded rather less absurd than this, but they were little more effective. It is evident, however, from the papers sent in that some farmers clearly appreciated the very local character of the infection, and that certain meadows might hold it owing, as we now know, to the presence of infected water-snails. Among the less lethal diseases taken up by the Society were foot-rot, a remedy for which was rewarded in 1807, the scab, for which Sir Joseph Banks submitted a prescription in 1787, and that troublesome pest, the sheep fly, to which, unfortunately, no answer was found.

Another pest which at one time threatened the lives of the beasts seriously, if indirectly, was the turnip fly, for, as we have already seen, when turnips were the only known root for winter feed, the ravages of this fly meant slaughter or starvation for thousands of animals every year. This was therefore chosen as one of the first subjects for a prize, and the offer was repeated at intervals for a century. Unfortunately, the Society found, like the hero in the song, that it was "all my eye for we to try to keep fly

---

[1] Bailey's *Machines*. An engraving of the slicer is reproduced in plate 14.
[2] The *Legacie* does contain a more scientific remedy as well.

off the turmot". The only effective answer was to introduce other crops which were not attacked by this pest, and that of course the Society successfully did.

The Society also did much to encourage research into "potato-curl" or leaf-roll, the disease which started to afflict the potato as soon as it began to be developed as a farm crop. Premiums were offered annually from 1788, not merely to obtain a preventative but also to accumulate information as to "the nature and cause" of this new phenomenon. According to one of the reports, for which a medal was awarded in 1790, the disease first appeared in this country in Lancashire about 1764, and the immunity of certain varieties was an important point noted by several of the candidates.

Perhaps the most effective results in connection with plant diseases which the Society achieved by its offers were over the troubles of fruit trees known collectively as "blight". Two contributors to the *Transactions* went straight to the point. William Hampson, who was awarded a silver medal in 1795, observed that the larvae of various destructive creatures harboured in the moss and lichen growing on the trunks and branches of these trees, and that therefore the best preventative was to remove these lurking places; and four years later this suggestion was followed up by T. S. D. Bucknall who advocated washing the trees with soap-suds and painting them with a mixture of oil and sulphur or tobacco. Even to-day Bucknall would not be considered very far behind the times.

6

Another of the main elements in the Society's work for agriculture at this time was the investigation of the comparative merits of drill and broadcast husbandry.

The sowing of corn and other seed in straight rows by means of a drill (or "drill-plough" as it was at first termed), and concomitantly the horse-hoeing of the soil between these rows, which were spaced far enough apart to permit of this process, was the great innovation of Jethro Tull, an innovation so great, indeed, that his system soon became generally known as "the new husbandry". Not only did the use of the drill result in a great saving of seed, but as it permitted the soil to be worked after the seed had been sown (which was impossible with broadcasting) the system also benefited the crops as they grew up. Furthermore, it eliminated the wasteful use of fallows for soil recovery by enabling the soil to be kept clean and in good heart. Tull even alleged that the constant tillage made possible by his system rendered the use of manure unnecessary.

As soon, therefore, as the Society seriously entered upon its work for agriculture it was compelled to turn its attention to this great question. Its first efforts were quite simple. In 1761, it took the opportunity, when offering an award for growing lucerne, to add the significant footnote: "'Tis recommended that the culture of lucerne be by drilling and keeping it clean by hoeing." And the same year it offered a gold medal for designing the necessary implement, the "drill plough". The drill designed by Tull, though practical, was simple and imperfect, and left room for many improvements and modifications, and a friend of Peter Wyche drew the Society's attention to a description of the Spanish "sembrador" published in *Philosophical Transactions*, which showed the kind of improvement which was possible.

The offer for an improved drill soon attracted some entries, but for several years there were no new ideas among them. It was a principle with the Society in its judging of inventions that weak entries could be eliminated in committee by merely examining a model or reading the author's written account. But the more deserving entries had to be fully tried out before any award could be made, and when in 1765 some entries were at last received which could be taken seriously, it was decided to put them to the test. Trials were accordingly arranged to be held at "Mr. Seymour's Ground at Brumpton" at 10 a.m. on April 10, 1766.

It was quite an event for the agriculture committee, and in spite of the early hour thirty members turned up at the rendezvous, the Green Park Coffee House in Piccadilly, and proceeded together to the field. Here they found four drills, sent down the day before by the Registrar, and an ample supply of wheat, horse beans and turnip seed for the trials.

Two of the drills were soon ruled out, one of them being obviously very similar to Tull's, and a second "capitally deficient in some part, for that the committee could not by any means cause the same to work to any effect". But a third, designed by James Willey, was found to have an important improvement, and the fourth, designed by the Rev. Humphrey Gainsborough, a brother of the artist, was declared to be "an improvement upon such drill ploughs as are already known or in use, and the principles on which the same is constructed are entirely new". It was agreed, therefore, that the prize of £50 should be divided between Gainsborough and Willey.[1]

After these successes the Society still went on to encourage new designs, emphasising particularly the need for an implement which would be "strong and cheap". Probably the most interesting award after Gainsborough's was the one which was made in 1770 to the Rev. Benjamin Gale, D.D., of Killingworth in Connecticut, for a drill which delivered fertiliser with the seed. The enterprising Dr. Gale had sent over the complete implement from America; in fact, he had despatched two, but one was lost at sea, and he seems to have well deserved the gold medal which the Society gave him.

The Society did not confine its interest to entries for its competitions. It kept its eyes open for new developments at home and abroad. In 1765 it went to a good deal of trouble and expense to purchase from Switzerland a specimen of the plough designed by Châteauvieux,[2] and two decades later, although it was debarred by its own rules from giving a reward to a patented invention, it did all it could to publicise[3] the drill which was patented in 1783 by the Rev. James Cooke, the prototype of the modern machine.

But meanwhile the Society had been trying to get to the root

[1] Willey's plough is illustrated in plate 14.
[2] This machine is very fully illustrated and described in *The Complete Farmer* (1777).
[3] *Transactions*, V, 71 ff. Cooke also designed the first modern-type chaff-cutter.

of the matter, and to find out for certain whether drilling was really a better method than broadcasting. To this end it began in 1762 to offer gold medals for comparative tests of the two methods with all the principal crops.

When these offers were first made, thirty years had already passed since Tull had published his book *Horse-hoeing Husbandry*, and it was sixty years since he had invented his drill. One might have thought that by this time the soundness (in general) of his ideas was well established, and that all that the Society needed to do was to encourage more farmers to adopt them. Yet even the more progressively minded farmers were by no means sure as yet about so radical a change. For example, Sir Digby Legard, who won one of the Society's first awards in this connection, said, when submitting his entry for the prize in 1763: "I would reject the most plausible theory if unconfirmed by experiments. And even experiments themselves, if they are not executed with care, often varied in different soils, situation and circumstances, and repeated several years, are too apt to mislead."[1] Five years later, however, he was thoroughly converted, and wrote:

> After ten years' constant and very extensive practice; after the experience of a great variety of soils and seasons, I can recommend the drill and horse-hoeing culture as founded on reason and on truth. I have constantly attended, with all the impartiality I am master of, to the peculiar advantages, inconveniences, expences and benefits both of the old and new husbandry; and I cannot avoid giving my verdict in favour of the latter.[2]

Such a verdict was worth a great deal, yet the Society did not make up its own mind for many years to come, owing in part, no doubt, to the influence of Arthur Young, a most active member during the 'seventies and chairman of the agriculture committee for some years, who was strangely prejudiced against the new husbandry and held out for long against it. As late as 1792, the Society stated that the question "still continues to divide the opinion of some of the most ingenious and skilful agriculturists",[3]

[1] *Memoirs of Agriculture*, vol. I, pp. 323–4.
[2] *Ibid.*, pp. 373–4.
[3] Preface to *Transactions*, X.

after which Young wrote to Samuel More the Secretary, "I hope . . . that you are endued with a good stock of philosophic patience to see the triumphs of drill ploughs and horse-hoes. I perceive however that you so far agree with me that the point *is not yet ascertained*." (The italics are Young's.) Ten years later, however, the Society could at last announce that the long struggle between drill and broadcast husbandry was coming to a definite conclusion: "The Drill Husbandry", it stated, "continues to gain advocates, and repeated experiments confirm its advantages."[1]

But the Society had a second and equally important purpose in maintaining for so long its offer of prizes for these tests. This was to interest more farmers in the new husbandry, and to wear down their conservative resistance with proofs that the new method would repay them. The importance of its work in this connection was emphasised by Dossie in 1768:[2] "It is an unquestionable truth that Mr. Tull . . . was the first to introduce the use of this kind of husbandry into our country. He, nevertheless, only started the notion. The practice was very little pursued till the Society awakened the public attention to it by their premiums."

How much they needed "awakening" may be seen from the letters of John Boote, a Warwickshire farmer, who was awarded two gold medals for communications on this subject in 1787 and 1788. By that time, of course, most farmers had heard about the new husbandry, but the majority were still more than sceptical, and all Boote's neighbours thought that he was madly imprudent when in 1786 he applied the system, on a hitherto unprecedented[3] scale, to an area of 348 acres. "I suppose", he said, "no one person was ever held more cheap and more vehemently exclaimed against by all his neighbours than I was."

When Boote's drilled crops did remarkably well, their success was attributed to chance or to "something which they did not understand"; "and truly," he comments, "in this something which they did not understand was comprized the whole mystery: viz. a regular distribution of considerably less than half

[1] Preface to *Transactions*, XIX.
[2] *Memoirs of Agriculture*, vol. I, p. 73.
[3] It anticipated Coke of Holkham's far greater experiments by several years.

the quantity of seed usually sown broadcast, and that at proper depths and distances in the land".

In spite of all the scepticism Boote planned to continue his experiment on an even vaster scale, for, he says—waxing metaphorical with warmth of feeling—"I had one support unknown to them in which I placed my whole trust, viz, facts derived from experimental demonstration: this was my strong fort, which after weathering out many storms and tempests, at almost every fair and market, covered my entrance into a safe harbour, at the end of the year 1786, with a clear profit of £500 more than I should have gained if I had sown my land broadcast. . . . Indeed, if all the world had been unanimous, as all my neighbours were, in their opinion against me, and I had been left alone in the field, as in fact I was, supported only by Mr. Cooke's Drill, and a firm belief that similar causes produce similar effects, I should certainly have acted just as I have done."

Next year, when Boote drilled 450 acres, all the countryside flocked to watch the progress of his crops, "many from afar", and the evidence was plain to see. "Corn grown in the open field, carried in the open day, tythed in kind by the common tything man, exposed to view in barns and stackyards, threshed, dressed and measured by common servants and sold to common purchasers." This was the kind of propaganda the Society was after, and it cannot have failed to have its due effect.

Besides its great work on the new husbandry, the Society gave encouragement to the investigation of other practical problems of tillage, especially the subject of rotations. But as the discovery and testing of a new rotation involves a series of parallel and carefully recorded experiments lasting over periods of anything up to eight years or even longer, it was a task out of all proportion to the small rewards offered by the Society. The only new rotation for which an award was made was a four-year course evolved by John Middleton of Merton and consisting of winter tares, roots, clover and wheat, and probably the most important contribution of the Society in this direction was to emphasise by its offers and awards the potentialities of certain crops as preparatory to others.

The early varieties of bean appear frequently as a crop to be grown in the same year as autumn sown wheat or in connection with green crops; and potatoes are brought forward as being suitable to grow before wheat. Particular attention was also paid to spring wheat.

7

But we must now turn to the two other matters of agriculture in regard to which the Society made an outstanding contribution. These are land reclamation and mechanisation.

Under the first-named subject three separate problems came up for consideration—the improvement of land already under cultivation but in poor condition, the bringing into cultivation of waste land, and the gaining of entirely new land from the sea.

At the time when the Society began its labours, the amount of totally uncultivated land in this country was still a considerable proportion of the whole. "You may draw a line", wrote Arthur Young in 1773, "from the north point of Derbyshire to the extremity of Northumberland, of 150 miles as the crow flies, which shall be entirely across waste lands: the exception of small cultivation spots very trifling."[1] Nor was this true only of the north. Two years later Nathaniel Kent wrote:[2] "Within 30 miles of the *capital* there is not less than 200,000 acres of waste land."

In spite of this, food supplies at that time were reasonably adequate, and the obvious agricultural objective was to get better returns for the labour already being expended and from the land already in use for agriculture. But soon internal and external causes created an urgent need for more food, which meant that more land must come under the plough, while rising food prices at the same time provided the necessary economic incentive for heavy capital expenditure. It is to the credit of the Society, however, that it was active in encouraging land reclamation on a wide scale before these changed circumstances became really effective.

In most cases the principal reason for the poor condition or total neglect of land in this country was lack of drainage, and therefore,

[1] *Observations on the Present State of Waste Lands of Great Britain.*
[2] *Hints to Gentlemen of Landed Property.*

just as, in its development of drill husbandry, the Society's first step was to offer a prize for an improved drill, so when it turned to the problem of drainage it began by offering a prize for an improved implement for cutting drains. The offer, which was first made in 1764, was quickly responded to, and a series of awards were made for drain-ploughs between 1766 and 1770 to Cuthbert Clarke, Ducket and others.

The next step was to offer, in 1770, a premium for improving at least ten acres of land "lying waste or uncultivated", and an award was made in 1777 for work of this kind at Bedale in Yorkshire. Then, in 1780, a definite piece of enclosure was envisaged (to be effected, however, not by act of Parliament but by local arrangement). In this case the premium was for improving "waste moors", at least a hundred acres in extent and "absolutely uncultivated", and the enclosure had to be divided into fields, with buildings for a tenant and let on lease to "one who occupies no other land". In the same year a premium was offered for gaining at least twenty acres from the sea, a hint being given that this might be effected in the Dutch manner "by fixing whisps of straw upright in the sand".

After a few years awards began to be made under these various heads, and the Society was able to report in 1789: "Every traveller knows that the quantity of waste-lands in this kingdom is a disgrace to the country. The improvement, therefore, of wastelands has long been an object of the Society's attention . . . and at length such improvements are advancing to the great benefit of the nation, and the rewards offered by the Society will in time have the desired effect."[1]

Experiments in drainage lead inevitably into geological investigations. The drainage system devised by James Elkington, which became so famous at this time, was based on the simple geological fact that some strata are porous and pervious to water and others are not. These facts also appear, and are very clearly stated, in some of the accounts received by the Society at this time, as, for example, those of J. Wedge in 1792 and J. C. Curwen in 1804. Curwen, in particular, was at pains to explain the cir-

[1] *Transactions*, VII, v.

cumstances in which Elkington's system of draining off spring waters by the boring of deep holes could be effective.

The Society approached the same problem of sub-surface water by more orthodox methods, and it began in 1791 to offer a prize for the construction of hollow drains, "of brick, stone, or such-like durable materials", for draining "water arising from internal springs". The most notable result of this offer, although it achieved the same ends by different means and therefore received a "bounty" and not the advertised prize, was Adam Scott's mole-plough, rewarded in 1797.

The mole-plough, cutting an underground pipe by means of a pointed metal "mole", is very effective in clay land, as the channel which it cuts can last for a considerable period owing to the natural properties of the clay. Shallow "mole" drains had long been in use: they are described, for example, in Stephen Switzer's *The Practical Fruit Farmer* (1724). But the idea of a special implement for cutting them was new. Thanks to the publicity accorded it by the Society's award, however, it came rapidly into fashion, so that Young, in his *Agriculture of Essex*, published in 1807, speaks of it as being by that time not uncommon in that county, where it is particularly suitable.

But Scott's award also had certain unpleasant consequences. In return for his bounty Scott was required to present one of his ploughs to the Society, and according to the Society's invariable rule he had to agree not to patent his invention. In spite of this, a similar plough appeared a few months later in the London shops, patented, and selling at 10 guineas, four times the price at which Scott had said that his plough could be sold. What was worse, it was discovered that Scott himself had an agency for the sale of this "pirate". All that the Society could do was to publish a protest in its *Transactions*, republish a woodcut of Scott's plough, and encourage people to make copies of it despite the patent—and of course to debar Scott himself from receiving any further award.

During the first quarter of the nineteenth century the conditions caused by the Napoleonic Wars created a boom in land reclamation, and altogether the various works submitted successfully or unsuccessfully to the Society for reward during this period represented many thousands of acres added to the cultivated area of the country. Probably the most spectacular of these awards were those for "gaining land from the sea", usually areas well over a hundred acres in extent; and among these some of the outstanding achievements were on the banks of the Humber, where "warping", i.e. the depositing of silt on tidal flats by impounding the outflowing river waters, not only raised the level of the land but covered it with a rich surface of alluvial soil. A large gold medal was awarded in 1825 to Ralph Creyke for reclaiming 429 acres in this way.

8

We turn finally to the contribution made by the Society to the promotion of mechanisation. At the time when it began its work, mechanisation, even in the most primitive sense, was still a dream, in spite of the work of men like Tull. The oldest types of implement, such as the plough, were still cumbrous and inefficient, and such new implements as had been invented had hardly reached the practical stage and were certainly not yet in common use. A wonderful opportunity therefore lay before the Society, and it did not fail to seize it. "It may be safely asserted", claimed Sir Henry Trueman Wood, "that of all the implements used by the farmer during the fifty or sixty years from 1760 onwards . . . there was not one which was not either introduced or improved in consequence of the Society's exertions and influence."

We have already noted the origination of the drain-plough and the root-cutter, and the development of the seed-drill, which took place under the encouragement of the awards offered by the Society. But it was of little use to stimulate the design of these and other implements unless the improvements were made use of by many others besides the designer, and here the Society's Repository, or Industrial Museum, was of service. All the prize-winning implements, and others, like Châteauvieux's drill, which were specially purchased or presented, were added to the collection, and their display had a two-fold effect: not only were they copied (for none of them—with the notable exception of Cooke's drill—was patented) and put into operation in many parts of the country, as Dossie testifies,[1] but in some cases the exhibits themselves were improved as the result of suggestions made by visitors.

The first agricultural machine officially tested and rewarded by the Society was a "threshing mill", a model of which was presented to the Society by its designer in 1761. The threshing was done by a gate, weighing about half a hundredweight and rising and falling perpendicularly like a sash window, under which the corn was fed down a sloping hopper. The Society was sufficiently impressed by the model to have a full-size machine made for trial, but in spite of numerous improvements suggested by the committee it could not be made to give satisfactory results. The designer, however, a man called Lloyd of Hereford, was recompensed for his trouble by a bounty of £15.

Four years later another bounty of £15 was awarded to a Mr. Harvey of Connecticut who appears to have threshed with ribs projecting externally on a large revolving cone, and in 1769 50 guineas were awarded to John Evers for a machine with a revolving floor and a series of oscillating flails. The last of the very varied threshing devices for which the Society made an award was a machine with a set of revolving beaters, somewhat similar to the early patent of Michael Menzies, which was awarded a gold medal in 1801.

Meanwhile the Society had made an important contribution to the improvement of reaping. The ancient sickle was still universally employed in this country, and although the scythe was known, there was a strong prejudice against it. But in 1763, one of the members, William Hanbury, presented the Society with two Hainault scythes which he had purchased on the Continent, and these were sent to a Northamptonshire farmer for a thorough testing against the sickle. The outcome of the trial was, naturally, wholly in favour of the scythe, and the Society, which at that time had no regular arrangements for publicity, made known the results of the trial by inserting a full report, with the certificates of the witnesses, as advertisements in the newspapers.

When it came to mechanised reaping, the Society's efforts were not so creditable. It began in 1774 to offer an award for "a

[1] *Memoirs of Agriculture*, vol. I, p. 87.

machine to answer the purpose of reaping or mowing corn", and it continued the offer for forty-five years without ever making an award, in spite of the fact that a number of machines were brought out during this period and several of them were actually entered for the Society's premiums. What is more, two of the entries were subsequently proved to be of outstanding merit, and the Society therefore missed a great chance.

The first of these was a machine invented by John Common and sent in for the prize in 1812 by Earl Percy. This machine, the first successful adaptation of reciprocating blades to reaping, was turned down by the committee as being incomplete, so that they "could not fairly judge of it". To be fair, it must be added that the only trial of which the committee received a report was carried out at night and on a small patch of corn, apparently because the inventor was afraid of his design being stolen from him. But truth will out. For want of the Society's encouragement Common himself made no further progress, but some years later his design reached the hands of McCormick in America and brought to him and to his country all the glory of the invention of this vital implement.[1]

The other important machine which failed to impress the Society, the Rev. Patrick Bell's, used the alternative principle of a scissor action. This reaper was exhibited in Scotland in 1828 and 1829 and on the latter occasion was awarded a prize of £50 by the Highland and Agricultural Society, but when it was submitted in the following year to the Society of Arts, it was turned down as being already so well known as not to need the encouragement of a prize. Had this application been successful, the invention might well have interested manufacturers, but, as it was, very few of the machines were made, and the reaper went into cold storage until the enthusiastic reception accorded to McCormick's reaper at the Great Exhibition enabled Bell to put his machine very successfully into production.

Besides concerning itself with the invention of new types of implement the Society did not omit to foster the improvement of

[1] See Trueman Wood, *A History of the Royal Society of Arts*, pp. 128–9; and *Journal*, XXVI, 369, 419, 479.

the older ones, especially the plough. The Rotherham plough, particularly as improved by James Small and John Arbuthnot (the latter being a member of the Society and a close friend of Arthur Young), had shown that if only the design of the implement were modified, the vast teams of horses or oxen (in some cases numbering as many as twelve) which were required to tug the old-fashioned ploughs through the soil and forcibly rip it open would no longer be necessary. The Society seized on this great advantage of the newer ploughs and decided, in 1770, to offer a gold medal for an essay on "the principles of constructing a plough so as more effectually to diminish the friction". The medal was awarded in the next year to Cuthbert Clarke, who afterwards made a plough in accordance with his principles and sent it to the Society for exhibition in the Repository.

Through the influence of Arthur Young the Society held an interesting trial of ploughs at Morden, Surrey, in 1773, for the purpose of testing another innovation, an all-iron plough invented by a blacksmith friend of Young's, named Brand. Brand's implement was tried against an impressive "field", the other "runners" being a Rotherham plough, two of Arbuthnot's ploughs, Ducket's famous trenching plough, which had been awarded a bounty by the Society in 1769 and placed in the Repository, and a Surrey plough.

In order that the results might be as precise as possible, in accordance with the Society's invariable policy, the Committee made use of a spring dynamometer recently invented by the Secretary, Samuel More, and of a type still in use for approximate measurements, by which the force of the draught could be measured in hundredweight tensions. Brand's plough did well in this distinguished company, and although Arbuthnot's ploughs proved themselves to be the most efficient on the field, it was decided that the all-metal newcomer, for which the test had been organised, had its points, particularly the facility with which it could be taken to pieces for repair, and Brand was awarded a bounty of £20.[1]

Among other types of field implement in which the Society

1 Full details of the trial are given in *Annals of Agriculture*, I, 113–19.

interested itself were the horse-hoe, the cultivator and the harrow. It also did a good deal for the more static machinery of the farmyard. Besides its origination of the turnip-slicer the Society deserves credit for its work in connection with the chaff-cutter. The first suggestion that a machine should be designed to cut up straw for the feeding of animals seems to have been made in *Museum Rusticum* in 1764, and four years later we find the Society awarding James Edgill a bounty of 20 guineas for a machine which worked on precisely the same principles as the modern cutter. It consisted of curved knives mounted on a rotating flywheel and a trough along which the straw was pushed into contact with them.[1] Several improvements were produced in succeeding years through the encouragement of the Society's offers, and in 1794 the Rev. James Cooke, whose fame in connection with the drill has already been referred to, took out the first patent for a chaff-cutter. But Edgill's basic conception remained unchanged throughout, and he unquestionably deserves the prior recognition.

Special mention must also be made of another piece of farm apparatus which made its debut with an award from the Society. This is the movable iron hurdle, on wheels, which is still a familiar sight in sheep-farming country. This simple device was invented by Thomas Plowan, of Broome in Norfolk, who received a gold medal in 1804 for an idea for a "portable sheepfold" which would be more workmanlike than the ordinary wattle hurdle.

9

During the greater part of the period we have been considering, agriculture was invariably put at the top of the list of the Society's activities, and it is still safe to say that the work recorded in this chapter was the greatest and most fruitful task it has ever carried through. One must remember, too, that as a national agricultural centre the Society anticipated the first Board of Agriculture by forty and the Royal Agricultural Society by eighty years, and that what Coke of Holkham did intensively, and therefore conspicuously, the Society did extensively and over a period twice as long.

[1] See plate 14.

Even now one important aspect of its agricultural work has not been recounted. So far, we have been concerned solely with agriculture for food production: we have still to consider the production from the soil of raw materials for industry.

Before we do so, however, brief mention must be made of an important contribution made by the Society to the winning of food, not from the land but from the sea, for the Society of Arts was largely responsible for establishing the salted fish industry in this country.

When it began, in 1805, to offer a reward for "curing herrings by the Dutch method", the British herring fisheries were limited to the supply of fresh fish for home consumption, while the Dutch were known to do a large export trade, mainly to central Europe through Hamburg, with inferior herrings "cured" by a special method of their own. With the known wealth of first-class herrings in British waters, therefore, the Society saw so certain a possibility of an important new export trade that it continued this offer for many years, making several awards for gradual improvements in curing, until a reward of 50 guineas was won three times, in 1819, 1820 and 1823, by J. F. Denovan, of Leith, for a product fully up to the Dutch standard. Denovan had made many unsuccessful attempts in Holland itself to discover the nature of the Dutch process (which consisted simply in gutting and cleaning the fish and packing them in barrels with salt or brine) until finally he brought over six Dutch fish-curers to the west coast of Scotland and started a packing station there. In view of the superior quality of the Scotch herrings Denovan was quickly able to establish his products in the Hamburg market, and thus the foundations of the present export herring trade (four times as large as the home trade in fresh herrings) were laid.

CHAPTER 5

The Production of Timber and other Raw Materials

1

WE saw at the beginning of our last chapter that when the Society was first founded there was considerable doubt as to whether agriculture, in the sense of food production, came within its terms of reference. There was, however, no such doubt regarding the production, from the soil, of the raw materials of industry, especially as the Society felt that far too much money was going out of the country to purchase materials which could be produced at home. Above all there was one vital material, timber, of which the nation's reserves were fast running out, and the Society's success in encouraging the replenishment of this essential asset was a highly important achievement.

Originally this country had been richly endowed by Nature with great forests of timber trees, but by the eighteenth century this heritage had largely been squandered, partly by the extravagant use of wood as domestic fuel and for certain industries such as iron-smelting, but more because it hardly occurred to anyone that steps should be taken to let Nature replace at least part of what had been expended. Even those who felt a certain responsibility were also conscious of the fact that they themselves could expect little or no return for the labour and expense involved in replanting.

By the eighteenth century the position had become extremely serious, particularly as the possession of naval power was becoming increasingly vital to the country, for naval power meant "wooden walls" and "wooden walls" meant timber—timber of good quality. Now, although the Society of Arts is essentially peaceful in its aims, it has never failed to realise that national prosperity is indissolubly linked with national defence, and as early as 1757 we find it taking steps to encourage the production of timber, primarily for this reason. The move originated in March, 1755, with the presentation to the Society by Henry Baker, the naturalist, on behalf of the author, Edward Wade, of a pamphlet "to promote the planting of timber trees in the commons and waste ground all over the kingdom, for the supply of the Navy, the employment and advantage of the poor, as well as the ornamenting of the nation". In view of the navy's need, the first kind of timber proposed for encouragement was, naturally, oak, but other varieties of wood were also suggested, and finally in 1757 it was decided to offer prizes for the planting of three—oak, chestnut and elm. Further trees were added to the list from time to time, the most important being fir in 1758 and larch in 1773, and the offers continued to be published for nearly a century, the last actual award for tree-planting being made in 1835.

Throughout this period the form of the awards offered and made for tree planting was always the same. The Society realised that those who would be in a position to respond to its stimulus must inevitably be landowners, with sufficient means to invest capital, not for their own benefit but for that of their posterity, and for the national good. For such people the appropriate award was the "honorary premium" of the gold or silver medal, and this was offered on the competitive principle, the gold medal for the greatest number of a particular tree, or greatest area of ground, planted during a particular year, and the silver medal for the second greatest.

The first awards were made in 1758, and consisted of a gold medal to the Duke of Beaufort for sowing 23 acres at Hawksbury, Gloucestershire, with acorns, and of silver medals to two other landowners for sowing smaller areas. Scotch firs received their first award in 1760, and two years later there were the first awards for Spanish chestnuts and elms. The highest numbers of awards were for oaks, firs and larches, and it is probable that the

Society deserves the credit, not indeed for inaugurating the serious planting of larches in this country, for that was begun a little earlier in the century, but for popularising it. With this end in view it not only offered, and awarded in great numbers, premiums for planting larches, but further stressed the importance of this then unfamiliar tree by offering prizes for an essay on its "utility".

The adoption of a competitive medal system for tree-planting meant, of course, that the value of what was achieved as the result of the Society's offers was out of all proportion to their cost to the Society, for besides the trees planted by the successful candidates, account must be taken of those planted by the unsuccessful candidates. Some indication of the proportion of the latter may be found in the statement in Volume XII of the *Transactions* that in the preceding year (1793) the number of trees in respect of which actual awards had been made was 491,000 whereas the total number of trees certified by all the candidates for these awards was 808,000. And to these must be added the efforts of the many landowners whose practical interest in tree-planting was aroused by the Society's efforts although they did not actually submit claims for the premiums. Even the total planted by those who were awarded medals is unknown, for in some cases their claims were submitted in terms of acreage and not trees. It is quite impossible, therefore, to assess the total number of trees planted as a result, direct or indirect, of the Society's campaign. Trueman Wood says that "at the very lowest estimate this number must have considerably exceeded fifty millions, of which some twenty millions were firs and larches and some fifteen million oaks". The highest total in a single year was probably reached in 1806 when the number of trees planted by the successful candidates alone was 1,269,000.

But the Society's contribution to reafforestation cannot be assessed simply by the number of trees which it caused to be planted. Besides the offers for planting, awards were also offered from time to time for essays, based on experience and in some cases on deliberate experiments, on such questions as the best kind of trees to plant on boggy land, the best varieties to produce useful timber in exposed positions, and the best methods of protecting new plantations against rabbits and other pests. Much was also added to the knowledge of forestry methods through the fact that every candidate for one of the Society's awards for planting had to submit full details of how he had carried the planting out. Many of these statements were published in the *Transactions* with the announcement of the award, and besides their immediate usefulness these records acquired a unique value after the lapse of years. Attention was drawn to this in Volume 49, Part 2, of the *Transactions* (1833), where a list of the awards made between 1758 and 1779 was republished, with full details of the plantings, in order that they might be compared with the woods then standing and supply evidence as to the ultimate results to be expected from different planting methods.

2

The importance of a raw material does not depend solely on the quantity of it which is consumed, and there were several materials of great usefulness but, unlike timber, required in only small amounts, to which the Society also paid very particular attention. One of these was madder, an ancient and important dyestuff, which was one of the four objects for a prize proposed by Shipley and advertised in the year of the Society's foundation. For a considerable period the English had come to depend for this material upon the Dutch, who did not fail to take advantage of the monopoly, yet at one time it had been grown quite successfully in England, and indeed one variety is an indigenous plant. Altogether, therefore, it was a well-chosen object for "encouragement", and the Society was so convinced of this that it persisted for over twenty years in trying to establish the crop as a permanent feature of British agriculture. So anxious was it to gain this end that in 1761, to encourage a greater number of farmers to try the crop, it departed from the usual competitive principle and offered a flat rate subsidy of £5 for every acre planted with madder. This wide and generous offer attracted a good deal of attention, and over a period of five years some seventy-eight separate claims (representing a total of nearly three hundred acres) were made for the subsidy, among which it is interesting to note those made by Arthur Young in 1765 and 1767, for planting one acre on each occasion.

The campaign for madder lasted until 1779, the last actual award being made in 1775, and the total amount of cash awarded in connection with it was over £1,500, more than half the total of all the cash awards for agriculture during the same years. For a time, too, it achieved considerable success. The *Dictionary of Arts and Sciences* (Croker, Williams & Clark) stated, in 1765, that the culture of madder "is now again set on foot in this kingdom, under the laudable encouragement of a public society", while the Society itself claimed that it had stimulated the production of enough madder to threaten the Dutch monopoly, and that by the establishment of this threat it had caused the price of Dutch madder to be reduced permanently and its quality to be improved. But the best evidence of the effect of the Society's awards is provided by the Customs records for madder imports, which show that they dropped from nearly 20,000 cwt. in 1760 to only 13,000 cwt. in 1765, and although they soon went up again, madder continued to be grown in this country, but in a quantity sufficient to meet only a small proportion of increasing industrial requirements.

That the Society was justified in making this great effort is also shown by the fact that the French made a similar effort at just the same time. They, however, had the advantage of government support,[1] and also of a more favourable climate in the areas where planting took place, with the result that from being one of the heaviest importers of madder France became, by the end of the century, the leading European producer.

3

Besides its efforts to establish the production of madder and, as we shall see later, other dye-stuffs, the Society did what it could

[1] The Society of Arts gained parliamentary assistance in one particular, a modification of the tithing law (31 Geo. II, 1755, c. 12), which was made at the Society's request to assist madder-growers.

to encourage the production of several fibres. The first of these was hemp. The Royal Society had unsuccessfully tried to foster the growing of hemp for export, but the Society of Arts was primarily concerned about its importance for defence, as the raw material for naval sails and cordage, and it realised that its import from abroad was not only a drain on our foreign currency, but also likely to be cut off just when it was most needed, in time of war. With the Seven Years' War in progress and British ships and military forces engaged in many parts of the world, there was never a time when naval supplies were of greater importance. The Society therefore devised an ambitious scheme. Setting aside a total of £700 per annum for use as premiums, it divided the whole country into seven regions, and offered four prizes, totalling £100, for the four greatest areas planted with hemp in each of these. It need never have devised anything so elaborate. Offers were made on these lines for three years (1762–4), and during this period only seven different candidates put in claims, covering in each year, on an average, a total of only 120 acres out of the whole country.

After that, efforts were made from time to time, but with little effect, to encourage the production of other vegetable fibres, and at the time of the Napoleonic Wars a renewed attempt to encourage the production of hemp in the Scottish Highlands was equally unsuccessful, although, as we shall see, the Society did at that time cause the permanent establishment of hemp-growing in Canada. But at home the Society's ambition to promote the crop on a wide scale was never likely to be fulfilled, for, although hemp of a very good quality can be produced in this country, it is not a popular crop here because the high cost of the labour required for the treatment of the stalks renders it unprofitable as compared with the higher quality textile, flax, and still more with food crops.

A similar handicap has beset the successful home production of silk, although in that case the need for great skill in the rearing of the worms and the preparation of the raw silk before it is sent to the manufacturers has been a further complication. The Society, however, made several determined efforts in the eighteenth, and to a lesser extent in the nineteenth, century to establish the production of raw silk in this country.

The first of these originated with Edward Vernon,[1] who in 1766 sent the Society some specimens of English raw silk produced by himself. The quantity was not large, for Vernon complains in his covering letter that he "lost upwards of two thousand worms through the obstinacy of the proprietors of the mulberry trees denying me the liberty of plucking ye leaves under the idle pretence that it would kill the tree". Nevertheless the Society accepted this proof that good silk could be produced in England, and rewarded Vernon by presenting him with an Italian machine for winding silk from the cocoons. Moreover, in investigating his claims they found that he was by no means the only producer of silk in the country, and this encouraged them to begin in 1767 to offer substantial rewards for the planting of mulberry trees and the rearing of silkworms.

These premiums were continued for a great many years, and articles were published from time to time in the *Transactions*, but the only result was the occasional production to the Society of small quantities of cocoons, for which the appropriate awards were made. Owing to many difficulties, not the least of which has been disease, no attempt to produce raw silk in this country has succeeded permanently until the recent efforts of Lady Hart Dyke at Lullingstone Castle, Kent, described by her in a paper read to the Society in 1935.

When we turn to the most important of all home-produced textiles, wool, we find, strangely enough, that the Society did nothing in the eighteenth century, directly, at any rate, for its promotion, in spite of the important developments which were taking place at the time through the work of Bakewell and his followers. Indirectly, of course, the wool industry was benefiting from the Society's work for the production of winter feeding-stuffs, but it was not until 1812 that the Society made an award specifically for wool. Then it was for producing a foreign variety, merino, which was coming into great demand because of the in-

[1] *Not* John Delamare as Trueman Wood states (p. 265) (see Minutes, November 19, 1766).

creasing taste for finer quality cloths. But in spite of the example of George III ("farmer George"), who introduced this breed into England, and of several awards made by the Society, the merino did not permanently take on here, partly, no doubt, because of the poor quality of its mutton. In other parts of the Empire, however, and particularly in Australia, the introduction of the merino sheep had the most important results, but the Society's connection with these developments belongs to another chapter.

Another effort to promote high quality wool production involved the introduction of a far more exotic animal, the Kashmir shawl-goat. Kashmir shawls, although a very ancient type of product, first became fashionable in Europe in the early nineteenth century, and this led the Society in 1822 to begin to offer rewards for the establishment in England of flocks of the animal from whose wool they were produced. The offers were temporarily successful and several awards were made, but the flocks did not thrive and ultimately the effort was a failure.

4

Another group of raw materials of which the Society endeavoured to foster the production by British agriculture was of those required for the manufacture of chemicals and drugs, some of which closely affected the daily life of the people.

Personal cleanliness was not a characteristic of the eighteenth century, but our ancestors had a good excuse for their condition in the scarcity and high cost of soap, which was due to the shortage of alkali. The alkali then most commonly used in the making of hard soap was "barilla", which was prepared from the ash of various plants growing in or near the sea, the richest in "soda-ash" being the Spanish *kali* (hence the word *alkali*) or glasswort, of which large quantities were imported. The Society therefore endeavoured to establish this plant in England, and also to encourage the making of soda-ash of a stronger alkaline content than had so far been achieved from native kelp or seaweed. But although offers to stimulate either or both of these means of producing alkali were repeated annually from 1768 to 1800, little success attended the effort (at any rate, the Society was unable to make any awards), and Leblanc's discovery in 1790 of the chemical manufacture of soda finally made it unnecessary to continue it.[1]

A more successful, if less important, effort of the Society was its encouragement of the production of medicinal rhubarb, which it was persuaded to undertake by Robert Dossie in 1760. The difficulty here was that the Chinese, who had a monopoly of rhubarb growing, had long seen to it that the seeds of the "true rhubarb" were safely kept behind the stone curtain of the Great Wall. But it so happened that, a few years before, Sir Alexander Dick, the President of the Royal College of Physicians of Edinburgh, had got into touch, through his brother-in-law, the British Resident at the Court of the Tsar of Russia, with a Dr. Mouncey, the Tsar's chief physician (and, incidentally, one of the earliest Corresponding Members of the Society), and persuaded him, with the Tsar's connivance, to get a box of the seeds smuggled out of China through the help of the Russian medical service in Asia. The seeds thus obtained were successfully sown in the Royal Botanic Gardens at St. Petersburg, and when, in 1762, Dr. Mouncey retired from his Russian post and came and settled in Edinburgh, he brought a box of seeds with him (the produce of the first) and distributed them for experiment to members of the Royal College of Physicians in Edinburgh and to influential landowners and friends both in Scotland and in England. Among those who obtained seeds in this way was a Mr. English of Hampstead, and in 1769, when some of the plants which he raised from seeds were more or less mature, he sent the Society particulars of his plants and specimens of the root, and also a supply of seeds for distribution among the members. These were all submitted to careful investigation, with such satisfactory results that a gold medal was awarded to English for his culture of the true rhubarb and for his offer to "present a quantity of seed for the use of the public". Shortly afterwards, a medal was also awarded to Dr. Mouncey.

[1] For the parallel efforts to encourage the importation from British colonies of mineral potash (by which soft soap is prepared), see pp. 161–2.

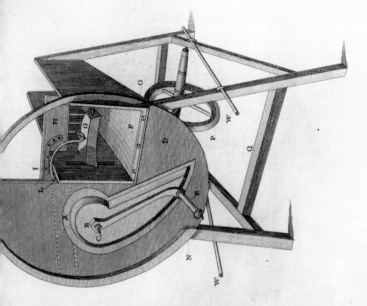

Chaff-cutter, invented by J. Edgill
Awarded a prize, 1769

"Drill-plough", invented by James Willey
Awarded a prize, 1766

Root-slicer, invented by J. Edgill
Awarded a prize, 1767

14. THREE AGRICULTURAL AWARDS OF THE SOCIETY

Loom designed by John Almond
Awarded a prize, 1771

Pinchbeck's crane, with safety device on
the walking wheel
Awarded a prize, 1767

Wm. Westgarth's hydraulic pump
Awarded a prize, 1769

*The downward flow of water in the left-hand cylinder
pumped another column upwards on the right*

15   THREE MECHANICAL AWARDS OF THE SOCIETY

Having found an attested source of "true rhubarb" seeds, the Society now went straight ahead. In 1770 it began to offer annually a gold medal for raising the greatest number of plants of *Rheum palmatum*, "not less than one hundred", and it is very satisfactory that the first candidate to be awarded one of these medals was Sir Alexander Dick himself. During the next quarter of a century nearly twenty awards were made, mostly of gold medals, a greater number than for any other agricultural object except the production of madder, and in several cases the crops introduced as the result of the Society's offers became permanently established. Such was the case, for example, at Bodicote, near Banbury, which continued until the recent war to be a centre for the production of medicinal rhubarb.[1] Here it was first grown in 1777 by William Hayward, an apothecary, who cultivated it for use in his own practice and was awarded the Society's silver medal in 1789 and the gold medal in 1794.

It is typical of the deeply humanitarian feeling of the Society that the other drug which it made strenuous efforts to promote in this country was opium, in which it began to take an interest in 1797 as the result of an approach by John Ball of Williton in Somerset. Ball, who had already won three awards for the growing of rhubarb, forwarded to the Society a small pot of opium produced from poppies grown in his garden, and mentioned in his covering letter that he "expected a pecuniary reward, particularly from such a respectable and opulent society". No doubt there was considerable emphasis on the "pecuniary" as he had already received three gold medals and would have little use for a fourth! At any rate, the Society, being seriously interested, was willing to come to terms, and offered him 50 guineas in return for a detailed account of how he had obtained the drug. To this he agreed, and the Society, armed with these particulars, began to offer a similar award, or a gold medal, for the production of opium on a substantial scale, at least 20 lb. of the drug being required. The award was successfully claimed in 1800 by a Londoner, Thomas Jones, who like Ball had already been induced by

---

[1] The Banbury variety is *Rh. rhaponticum*, the type commonly grown for consumption as food.

the Society to go in for rhubarb-growing, and further awards were made some twenty years later.

But opium-growing never became firmly established in this country as a sound commercial proposition. There were a good many pitfalls, and the vagaries of the weather always seriously threatened the quality as well as the quantity of the product. There was also the problem of the amount of labour required for the collection of the poppy-juice, although the experimenters met this difficulty by employing children, whose wages were certainly cheap enough. Thomas Jones, for example, paid them threepence per day at eight years old and "if tractable and well-disposed an additional penny for every additional year".

5

Besides the raw materials which are obtained out of the ground by the process of vegetation there are those which have to be won from it by mining, and in these also the Society took a considerable interest.

One of the first two objects (other than drawing) for which it offered a prize was the discovery of a cobalt mine in Great Britain; the other, as we have just seen, being for the planting of madder. Thus both of the practical subjects in which the Society first interested itself concerned the home production of colouring materials, and both of them were pursued with a thoroughness and determination which, particularly in the case of cobalt, cannot but surprise the modern student of its history.

Cobalt ore was required for the production of its silicates zaffre and smalt, which impart a beautiful blue to glass, and were also used at that time for the making of "powder blue" for washing linen. As Shipley reported to the Society at its second meeting, a total of over 200,000 lb. of smalt was imported in 1753, so that to open up a source of this material in this country was certainly a worth-while object. The difficulty was that, although cobalt had been found in Cornwall and was likely to be found elsewhere in Great Britain, the deposits would probably be too small or of too uncertain a quality to make the opening up of mines, for cobalt only, an economic proposition. The Society received samples from several localities and made an award in 1755 to Mr. Beauchamp of Truro (who generously suggested that £20 out of his premium of £30 should be left with the Society as a life composition fee), but no mine was ever put into operation.

Nevertheless, this apparently abortive effort of the Society had indirect consequences of considerable interest. The specimens which were received by it were first sent for assaying to the Assay Master at the Mint, and as that gentleman was unable to undertake the task, because his equipment and experience were limited to the assaying of gold and silver, Doctors Lewis and Morris and other chemists within the Society coped with the problem in their private laboratories. This experience showed very clearly the need for a central laboratory to which members of the public who found promising-looking minerals might send them for analysis, and to meet this need furnaces were installed early in 1757 in the kitchens of the Society's offices. When the Society moved to new quarters in 1759 similar arrangements were made there. The use of these laboratories, however, was restricted (apart from the Society's own experimental purposes) to the assaying of specimens of British ores.

Owing to the general ignorance in this country on the subject the Society's promotion of cobalt also led to its first deliberate venture into the international sphere. In 1756 it was decided to offer a gold medal for an essay on cobalt, describing where it might be expected to occur geologically, how it might be identified and assayed, and how zaffre and smalt should be made from it, and entries were invited from abroad, the advertisement being published both in English and German. Only five entries were received, but two of these were in German, two in Latin and only one in English. The winner was Dr. Lehmann of Berlin, and two other competitors were thought worthy of a silver medal.

Among other ores of which the Society encouraged the search or rewarded the discovery were manganese, which was discovered in 1804 by Dr. Dyce near Aberdeen, and chrome-ironstone (until then largely imported from America for the manufacture of pigments), discovered by Dr. Hibbert in Shetland in 1820.

But the Society's chief successes in connection with minerals were with non-metalliferous rocks. One need with which it particularly concerned itself was for the discovery of a British rock which would make as good a millstone as the French burrs. Periods of war with France, when these burrs could not be imported direct, emphasised the need, and we find the Society offering a prize in 1758, during the Seven Years' War, for British millstones nearest in quality to the French, and again during the Napoleonic period, when prizes were awarded in 1801–3 for pairs of stones from various Welsh and Scottish quarries, some of which were declared to be fully up to the French standard.

A few years later the Society attempted to popularise the use of British marbles, and with this in view it began to form what must have been an impressive collection which was exhibited in the repository for a good many years. Numerous contributions to this display were received from the Dublin Society, the Cork Institute and various individuals.

Over and above the Society's spasmodic efforts to promote the exploitation of particular British minerals it made its greatest contribution in this field by encouraging the survey of the whole of British mineralogical resources. In 1802 it began to offer three gold medals for mineralogical maps, on a scale of not less than ten miles to the inch, of England and Wales, Scotland, and Ireland, respectively, and there was a most notable result in 1815 when William Smith, who subsequently came to be known as the "father of British geology", was awarded a 50-guinea prize for his mineralogical map of England and Wales on a scale of five miles to the inch. This prize enabled Smith, who was a poor man, to publish his map which, incidentally, was the first of its kind and was on twice the minimum scale laid down by the Society. After this success the Society modified its offer and put up prizes for inch-to-the-mile mineralogical maps of counties, but these were never claimed.

Besides promoting the discovery of minerals the Society did a good deal to assist in the winning of them. It interested itself in this subject, as we shall see in the next chapter, mainly from the humanitarian point of view, and in the hope of reducing the hazards and mitigating the hardship of the miner. Prizes were also offered for many years, and a few were awarded, for improved devices for bringing minerals to the surface. Perhaps the most interesting of those rewarded was the endless chain device invented by Thomas Arkwright of Kendal, who received a prize of 25 guineas in 1801.

6

One further source of raw materials which the Society did not overlook was the sea. Until the exploitation last century of mineral oils, the most promising source of oil then known—and one which could be exploited from this country as the base—was the whale. The Society's efforts in this connection were directed to two main ends. In the first place it quickly seized upon the importance of the gun harpoon as a means of increasing production and, having rewarded its inventor, continued for a good many years to reward those who used it, in order to encourage its general adoption. Also, as we shall see in the next chapter, it was the means of introducing a method of "edulceration" or purification of the oil in order to make it fit and pleasant to use.

The rewarding in 1771 of Abraham Staghold, the inventor of the gun harpoon, is worth describing in some detail as it is an excellent example of the meticulous and painstaking manner in which the Society investigated the claims which were made upon it for rewards. There were four stages in the examination of this invention. First of all, a model of Staghold's apparatus was brought before the committee[1] at their headquarters, and Staghold himself, and an experienced harpooner summoned by the committee, were interviewed. Then, as the invention appeared to be a practical device, a range was fixed up on an open space in Deptford and shooting with an actual harpoon took place, in the presence of the committee, at targets placed at varying distances from the gun. Next, the results of these trials warranting still further investigation, a test was arranged actually on the water and

[1] It is interesting to note that John Hyacinthe Magalhaens (Magellan), a descendant of the great navigator, participated in these whaling tests.

with a moving ship. Two experts, sea captains engaged in the whaling industry, were called in to witness the trial, and the shooting was aimed at an "artificial whale", which, in the opinion of the experts, called for at least the same penetrating power in the missile as the skin and flesh of a whale. Even after this test, when the experts had given their view that in certain circumstances the weapon would be of great value to whalers, the committee were not satisfied. They awarded Staghold 20 guineas on the strength of "the satisfactory experiments already made", but decided that the invention must still be tried out in actual service. Six swivel guns and twenty-four harpoons were therefore ordered to be made for each of the two sea captains, at a cost of up to 60 guineas to the Society, and the captains undertook to put them to the test throughout a whole season's whaling. It was only on receipt next autumn of their favourable and detailed reports, based on actual practical experience, that the committee finally decided to recommend a further award of £30 to the inventor.[1]

The particular point about Staghold's gun harpoon which differentiated it from earlier weapons of this type and made it the first practical instrument was his method of dealing with the line and ring by which it was attached to the boat. Staghold was the first to arrange this in such a way as not to deflect the harpoon from its aim, and it was for this reason that the Society tested its accuracy with such care. After that, a number of further improvements were rewarded by the Society, but it was many years before the gun harpoon came into anything approaching general use. Nevertheless, the Society had with much deliberation pointed the way, and the great whaling industry of the present day owes much to it.

---

[1] Staghold's harpoon is illustrated in plate 17.

CHAPTER 6

The Society and the Industrial Revolution

1

WHEN we leave this great story of pioneering in the development of natural resources and turn to those manufacturing industries with which the Society's founder thought that it should rather have concerned itself, we find, somewhat paradoxically, that its record of achievement is a good deal more modest. This was entirely due to the enormous changes which occurred soon after the Society was founded and which it would have required a much more far-sighted man than Shipley to anticipate. In 1754, when Shipley established the Society, there were so few industries that the whole of them could be continuously reviewed by its small but representative body of members, and if such circumstances had continued, the Society would doubtless have established an over-all leadership in the industrial field comparable with that which it exercised for many years over agricultural development. But the scene soon changed, and British industry became a colossus, producing by the end of a hundred years the vast assortment of manufactured goods which crowded the aisles and nave of the Crystal Palace in 1851. Amid this complexity a small voluntary society had to find a less ambitious rôle, particularly when the premium system through which it mainly acted was operated by means of precisely defined and strictly limited prize offers. The proportion of the rapidly expanding industrial field which could be covered by the annual premiums list continually contracted, and the aim had to be to choose those subjects for prizes in which the greatest effect might be anticipated from the comparatively small incentive offered.

As far as industry was concerned, it was mainly in the field of mechanical invention (to which the French Academy of Science had applied it as early as the eighteenth century) that the premium method was really appropriate, and thus we find that by the early nineteenth century the committee of mechanics had become probably the busiest of the six standing committees.

Yet there was one direction—and a direction of which Shipley would have strongly approved—in which, in spite of all these limitations, the Society may be said to have exercised a degree of over-all leadership: in the whole of this wide field it consistently stood for humanitarian principles and the welfare of the workers, at a time when even the most enlightened people were quite insensitive to such considerations. This aspect of the Society's work is outstanding and calls for more detailed discussion at the outset.

2

It will be remembered that William Shipley's scheme for providing cheap fuel for the poor people of Northampton played its part in the formulation of his scheme for the Society, and it is not surprising, therefore, that as early as the Society's second year one of its public acts was primarily humanitarian in intent. This was the offer of prizes for "tinning copper and brass vessels of a large size in a perfect manner", of which Dossie says:[1] "In a commercial light this was not of great consequence. But as the health and lives of numbers of persons depend on the avoiding of untinned (and therefore potentially poisonous) vessels of copper or brass, or such as are imperfectly tinned, it may be well considered as very momentous." The immediate result of this offer was small. A single very modest award was made for what were apparently the first large vessels to be tinned in England. According to Dossie, however, a good deal more was ultimately achieved than that. "Many persons", he says, "are induced to be cautious; and some artizans do tin in a better manner than before." At any rate, it was an early demonstration of the Society's spirit.

Generally speaking, of course, the Society was more concerned with harm received during the processes of industry than with the

---

[1] *Memoirs of Agriculture*, vol. I, p. 170.

injurious effects of faulty manufacture, and it was not long before
we find it taking up the subject of dangerous and unhealthy trades.

Occupational hazards are many and various, but probably the
most dangerous trades are not those in which there are obvious
risks of physical accident but those in which the health of a large
proportion of the workers is insidiously undermined over a period
of years. The first of these trades to which the Society turned its
attention was water-gilding, a process in which gold is deposited
by applying it as an amalgam with mercury and then volatilising
the mercury by heat. The consequent mercurial vapours are extremely poisonous, and in 1771 the Society began to offer a prize
for some form of protection against them. This was awarded in
1771 to J. Hills, who invented an apparatus which drew off the
vapours on the same principle as the familiar fume chamber of a
chemical laboratory, but with a treadle-operated bellows instead
of a fan to increase the draught. Unfortunately the employers do
not appear to have been as concerned about the matter as the
Society, and Hills' apparatus never came into general use. In
1811, therefore, a further award was made, to Richard Bridgen,
for a different solution to the problem, a mask covering the
operator's nose and mouth and enabling him by means of a tube
to breathe air from behind his back.

Several other respirators and similar devices figured in the lists
of awards. One award, a prize of 5 guineas, granted in 1827 to
J. Callaghan of Lambeth for a simple metal-gauze face-guard for
the protection of foundrymen, is interesting for the human
understanding which lay behind it. "J. Callaghan is himself a
workman," announced the Society,[1] "and the Society have rewarded him in hopes that his fellow-labourers may be induced to
avail themselves of the invention of one of their own comrades,
though they would probably neglect the very same contrivance,
if offered to them from any other quarter."

A much more important award, consisting of the large silver
medal and 50 guineas, was made two years before to John Roberts,
a miner, for a device which embodied all the principles of the
modern gas mask. It was invented by Roberts to protect himself

[1] *Transactions*, XLV, 152.

against the hot and acrid fumes of the great fires which in those days burned at the foot of the pit shafts to induce ventilation of the mine, and it consisted of a goggled leather hood, completely covering the head and face, with an air inlet which contained flannel to catch the solid matter in the smoke, and a wet sponge (corresponding to the modern activated charcoal) to dissolve the poisonous gases. Like so many of the objects of the Society's awards, Roberts's mask was subjected to severe tests before the prize could be adjudged to him. A special chamber was erected inside the shell of a partly erected house in Southampton Row, and here Roberts was made to endure an inferno of heat and smoke but, according to the records, emerged, after a considerable time, without the slightest ill effects.[1]

Another form of poisoning contracted in various industries was that due to arsenic, the peculiar danger of which lies in the extreme difficulty of detecting its presence (as intending murderers long ago realised). In 1821, therefore, the Society began to offer a premium for an effective test for arsenic and continued the offer until 1827. During this period no submission was made to it, but in 1836 James Marsh produced to the Society the famous test now associated with his name and was awarded a gold medal. The account of this test which is recorded in the Transactions[2] seems to be the first ever published.

Perhaps the most important industrial poison, and certainly the one which the Society tried its hardest to combat, is lead, which occurs industrially in the best earthenware glazes and the best types of paint. The Society first concerned itself with this poison in 1783 when it began to offer a prize for a harmless method of preparing lead paint or, alternatively, for a base which would be equally durable and not substantially dearer than white lead. Ten years later, when this offer had produced nothing of value, the Society turned its attention to the use of lead as a glaze and began to offer a prize for a satisfactory substitute. This second problem seemed as intractable as the first, and it was only after the Society

---

[1] For a full description see Transactions, XLIII, 25, and Journal, LXXXVII, 1239. One of the engravings illustrating the article in the Transactions is reproduced in plate 16 of this book.   [2] Transactions, LI, 66.

had persisted for nearly thirty years in offering a prize for a solution that it found it possible to award medals to John Rose of Coalport, in 1820, and J. Meigh, in 1822, both for felspathic glazes. Unfortunately, experience has proved that felspar and other substitutes make a less effective and more expensive glaze than lead, and nowadays the problem is solved by greater care in the use of the lead.

A further group of dangerous trades which the Society endeavoured to ameliorate were those causing injury to the lungs by dust, which can, of course, by inducing silicosis and other grave conditions, be just as harmful as actual poisons. The first step was to offer from 1805 onwards a gold medal for "obviating the prejudicial effects of the operation of grinding needles", and later the offer was extended to other trades involving the process of dry grinding. Numerous awards were made, the most notable apparatus submitted being one invented by J. H. Abraham in 1821. This combined a device for carrying away as much of the dust as possible with a respirator fitted with magnets to attract the particles of steel still left in the air. Abraham's apparatus, with its double safeguard, proved highly efficient, but it never came into general use, not because of the apathy of the employers, but because of the attitude of the workers, who in this case objected to the protection because they feared that on account of its very efficiency their wages would be lowered through the reduction in the danger of their occupation. Abraham's drawing of his invention is reproduced in plate 6.

Besides the trades which are rendered dangerous or unhealthy by the materials with which they deal, others are prejudicial to the health of those engaged in them because of the conditions in which they have to work, and early in the nineteenth century the Society did what it could for two important trades—cobbling and tailoring—which were unhealthy by reason of the hunched-up attitude in which the workers traditionally sat. A number of awards were made in the first three decades of the century for stitching and other machines, which had the effect, of course, not merely of making the work of these trades more healthy but also of vastly increasing their output.

Miners' conditions also, as we have already seen, were a pre-occupation of the Society, and it helped to foster various developments in pumping and ventilation. For example, a gold medal was awarded in 1769 for William Westgarth's hydraulic pump,[1] which was already in use for the pumping of mines, and a gold medal and 100 guineas were awarded in 1816 to James Ryan for his ventilating system, which drained off the gas by "passages or gas drifts so arranged as to collect and draw off the gas at the highest level"—a system which was used very effectively in Staffordshire. Several improvements of the Davy lamp also resulted from the Society's offers.

The Society also made some attempt to improve the general working conditions of the ordinary factory. Heating and proper ventilation were the primary needs, and prizes for effective devices to provide these elementary requirements in the vast "Satanic mills" which were springing up were offered for many years, their most important result being the steam central heating system for which Neil Snodgrass was awarded 40 guineas in 1806.

But the most famous example of the Society's efforts to do away with unhealthy working conditions is its long-continued and ultimately successful campaign to obtain an apparatus for cleaning chimneys without the use of climbing boys. No one seems to have realised that this work involved the boys in any undue hardship until the philanthropist, Jonas Hanway, who had long been a zealous member of the Society, secured an Act of Parliament in 1788 which imposed certain restrictions upon the practice. Mere restrictions were not much good, however, and what was wanted was a method of doing the job without using boys at all. This was what the Society set out to find, by offering a prize for an efficient invention, and after some years, during which several types of apparatus were submitted to the Society but not approved, a gold medal was awarded in 1806 to G. M. Smart for the greatest number (over three hundred) of chimneys cleaned without the use of boys, and another gold medal two years later for the apparatus which he employed, which came to be known as the "scandi-

[1] Discussed on p. 113 from the mechanical point of view.

scope" and consisted, like the present-day apparatus, of inter-
locking rods with a brush on the end.

3

The Society's efforts to reduce the number of industrial accidents were perhaps a little less thorough-going than its work for
industrial hygiene. In most cases, no doubt, the solution of the
problem seemed to lie with the workers themselves, and the
Society concentrated on a few instances where accidents could
only be prevented by the invention of safety devices. One prevalent cause of frightful injuries was the running back of walking-
wheels attached to cranes, and the Society not only awarded
several prizes (one of them in 1767 to Christopher Pinchbeck) for
automatic brakes to prevent this disaster, but it actually had a
crane on one of the wharves below London Bridge fitted with
Pinchbeck's device, to serve as a permanent demonstration.[1] But
again we have the complaint about the workers' indifference to
their own safety, for "although", say the *Transactions* in 1786,
"it answered well the purpose it was designed for, yet, from that
unaccountable inattention to their safety which is daily seen among
labouring people, it has been suffered totally to fall into ruin".
As steam power came more and more into use and the explosion
of boilers became an increasing problem, several prizes were
awarded by the Society for safety valves and similar devices, and
during the Napoleonic Wars prizes were also offered and awarded
for means of preventing explosions in gunpowder mills. But
perhaps the Society's most interesting effort of this kind was its
offer of a prize for a means of preventing the premature collapse
of arches during the demolition of buildings. The solution of
this problem for which A. Ainger received a gold medal in 1825—
the use of a strengthening iron crossbar—was quickly adopted not
merely as a temporary precaution in demolition but also as a
normal constructional device in private houses and small buildings, for which purpose it is, of course, still commonly used.
The Society also found plenty to do in connection with the

[1] Pinchbeck's crane is illustrated in plate 15.

broader aspects of public safety. Its many efforts for lifesaving at sea and greater safety on the roads will be discussed in a later chapter, but we may here consider what it did for the fighting of fires and the rescuing of persons involved in them.

Probably the most sensational of all the Society's early trials took place on May 21, 1761, when a three-storey building which had been specially erected at the Society's expense near the end of Tichfield Street, Marylebone, was set on fire in order to test an extinguisher invented by Ambrose Godfrey,[1] the well-known chemist, of Southampton Street, Covent Garden. This device, called a "Fire Watch", consisted of explosive balls, fired by a match and fuse, which were thrown into the blaze and, as they burst, scattered a fire-quenching or "suffocating" liquid over the flames. There was no question of making an award to Godfrey, for his invention was patented, and the purpose of the test was, by means of a public demonstration, to popularise the use of what the Society had reason to believe had proved its value in actual fires.

The Society's first objective, of publicising the invention, was overwhelmingly achieved, for the crowd which flocked to see the trial was so immense (in spite of efforts to keep the exact time a secret in order to avoid the presence of a "mobb") that two hundred military guards were needed to control them, and the distinguished spectators included the Duke of York, Prince William and the Duke of Gloucester. The demonstrations, too, could not have been more convincing. The first test was confined to the ground- and first-floor rooms, which had been previously filled with combustible materials, and although the flames were allowed to get such a hold that Godfrey, in his report to the Society, says that in shutting the door upon them his "eyebrows and wigs were somewhat more than sing'd", the fire was so quickly put out by three of the bombs or "machines" that only the people in the front rows saw anything. The top-storey rooms were then set on fire and this time, to satisfy the crowd, the blaze was allowed to continue until the flames burst out of the windows and up the chimney; but when a single ball was thrown in, it completely extinguished them. Nevertheless, in spite of the resound-

[1] Details of earlier tests are given in *Notes and Queries*, ser. 7, vol. VIII, p. 257.

ing success of the demonstration, the effort failed to extend the use of Mr. Godfrey's extinguisher to any appreciable extent. The trouble was, of course, that then, as now, hardly one householder in a thousand troubled about buying a fire extinguisher until a fire had started—and then it was too late.

Later the same year we find the Society testing claims made for various fire engines, but without finding anything much better than the one of which its committee of mechanics recorded, on October 7, 1761, that "it appears to be complex, likely to be top-heavy at the same time that it would scarce reach to the second storey [what we should call the first storey]; and upon the whole liable to so many inconveniences in the practice as to render it not so useful as the common engines".

The Society had rather greater success with fire-escapes. Its first efforts, beginning in 1773 with the offer of a prize for a machine for preserving lives in case of fire, did not produce any very useful results, but a considerable number of awards were made for fire-escapes from 1810 onwards, and the first of these, of 50 guineas to John Davies, was for an apparatus very similar to the modern escape, with telescopic ladder and carriage, which was tried out with a "rescue" from the top storey of the Society's house.[1]

Besides its many efforts to prevent accidents, the Society attempted from time to time to ameliorate the lot of the victims of those which did occur as well as of sickness and infirmity generally. As early as 1760 it seriously considered offering a prize for artificial arms and legs, and in the early nineteenth century it made several such awards, as well as awards for a great variety of surgical and dental apparatus and instruments. Some thirty prizes were given at that time for forceps, saws, lancets, surgical trusses and obstetrical instruments, and collectively they make an important but forgotten contribution by the Society to human welfare. The Society also showed a constant concern for the blind and made a considerable number of awards, extending over the course of a century, for some of the very earliest devices to enable them to write and to calculate.

[1] See plate 16.

4

To round off this review of the Society's many-sided humanitarian activities we must consider finally what it did to help the poor, industrial and otherwise. Such questions as the workers' rates of pay were, of course, outside its scope, particularly in an age of *laisser-faire*, although in other respects its efforts on their behalf were often prompted by economic as well as humanitarian considerations. Nevertheless, it is significant that when the original aims of the Society came to be formulated in the Charter of Incorporation granted to it in 1847, they were stated to be "the employment of the poor, the increase of trade and the riches and honour of the kingdom"—in that order. Certainly, enough has been said already to prove that the gentler motives were never lacking even from its more utilitarian actions.

For example, in its early years the Society took a considerable interest in workhouses, many of the inmates of which (especially the women) did no useful work. As the Society pointed out, this state of affairs was not only economically wasteful but also morally harmful. Its first action was to award to William Bailey in 1758 a prize of £50 for a new plan for running workhouses on productive lines, and then, in order to stimulate the establishment of workhouses according to this proposal, it offered a whole series of awards to the masters of institutions whose inmates produced work of certain kinds, such as grinding corn, spinning thread and knitting various types of fabric. A number of these premiums were awarded for several years until the offers were discontinued. Another effort was made towards the end of the century to evoke a fresh "plan for the maintenance of the poor in parish workhouses" as a result of which a prize of 25 guineas was awarded to S. M. Good.

The Society also did not forget the poor who managed to keep outside the workhouses, and for them the dominant note in its policy was independence. As we shall particularly see in several cases quoted in the next chapter, it was constantly on the look-out for opportunities of providing remunerative employment, at home, for women and children; it also made persistent attempts

John Davies's fire-escape
Awarded a prize, 1810

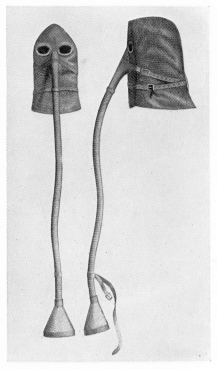

Respirator invented by John Roberts
Awarded a prize, 1825

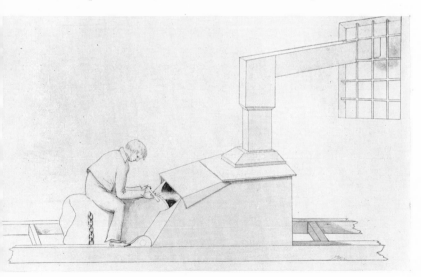

Dust-extracting device for needle-grinders, invented by J. H. Abraham
Awarded a prize, 1822

16. THREE HUMANITARIAN AWARDS OF THE SOCIETY

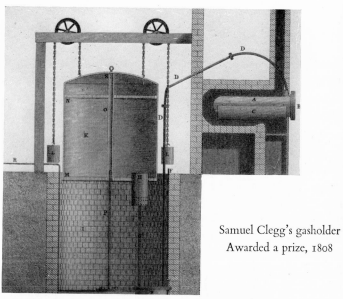

Samuel Clegg's gasholder
Awarded a prize, 1808

Sturgeon's electro-magnet
Awarded a prize, 1825

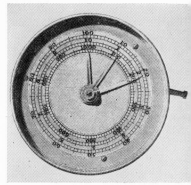

Brian Donkin's comptometer
Awarded a prize, 1819

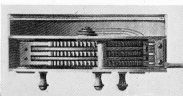

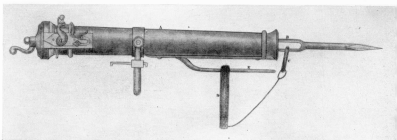

Staghold's gun-harpoon.   Awarded a prize, 1772

17. FOUR KEY INVENTIONS REWARDED BY THE SOCIETY

to promote the design of an efficient handmill, which would have enabled poor families to grind their own corn and so become independent of the miller. Unfortunately, there are technical difficulties in producing a good flour with stones small enough to be worked by hand, and these were only partially overcome as a result of the Society's offer, although a number of awards were made for handmills between 1757 and 1761 and again at the end of the century. As the purpose of these mills was primarily to help poor people, their price was as important a criterion as their efficiency, and the Society went so far as to require one of the winners, Samuel Parsons, before they would give him his prize, to undertake publicly, in the advertisement columns of several newspapers, that he would provide for sale at £5 mills similar to the one for which he had been awarded it and to state that the prize-winning mill was open to public inspection in the Society's repository.

5

Such, then, are some of the ways in which the Society endeavoured to keep alive an element of genuine humanitarianism in the hard-headed, materialistic world of the Industrial Revolution. We have considered them in detail because, collectively, they form its most distinctive, and most needed, contribution to the movement. We must now consider its more scientific contributions, many of which were, individually, of considerable importance.

It may be convenient to discuss them in relation to some of the great bases on which the fabric of the Industrial Revolution was reared. Several of these bases are dealt with in this history in other connections. The important work done by the Society to promote the production of raw materials was the subject of the previous chapter, and its work for the improvement of transport will be dealt with later, while its care for the interests of the workers has just been discussed. Let us now consider its work in connection with three other basic matters: industrial power, industrial equipment and industrial chemistry.

When the Society was founded, steam-power, except for a few

crude engines used for pumping mines, was a thing of the future, and all machinery depended on water, wind, animals or human beings for its motive power. In the words of George Cockings, one of the Society's servants, who aspired to write an epic on the Society's work, machines had to be "work'd by windy power or wat'ry force, Or by a circumambulating horse", and to develop these sources of power soon became an important object for the Society. Little was done about animal and human power (except for those measures to ensure human safety in the walking-wheel which have already been referred to), but in 1759 (the year, as it happened, when Smeaton presented to the Royal Society his "Experimental Enquiry concerning the Natural Powers of Water and Wind to turn Mills and other Machines depending on a Circular Motion") the Society began to offer prizes for models, of improved design, of "windmills" and "tidemills". By these terms were meant, of course, any machines operated by wind or tide, and not merely those for grinding corn (one use, for example, which the Society particularly had in mind was land drainage), and of all the sources of power then open to development these two offered by far the greatest potentialities. Unfortunately, however, they both presented the same awkward problem of converting into a steady uni-directional motion forces which constantly vary in intensity and direction.

Awards of the prizes for windmills were made in three successive years, 1760, 1761 and 1762, and whatever the mechanical merits of the successful models they certainly enhanced the general appearance of the Society's repository in which they were placed. Four awards were also made for ideas for harnessing the tides, including one of £60 to the Rev. Humphrey Gainsborough.[1] It is no wonder that none of these prize-winners hit on a really effective solution of this fascinating and still unsolved problem, but several made creditable efforts, to the testing of which the Society's committee devoted a great deal of time. A plaintive note in one of the Minutes records that "the committee have sat to June 25th [1761] inclusive 24 times on tide mills", and still their task was not complete. A considerable amount of money also was spent on the

[1] Gainsborough's agricultural drill has already been mentioned (p. 73).

making of special apparatus for the tests, such as a model mill-race with "artificial race" and waste trough, and a mechanical system for measuring as accurately as possible the power created.

In 1769 a somewhat different method of utilising water-power was rewarded with a bounty of 50 guineas. This was the hydraulic pumping engine of William Westgarth in which a downward flowing column of water pressing the piston of one cylinder was made to operate a pump which forced another column upwards. The bounty was given by the Society on the strong recommendation of Smeaton, who had persuaded Westgarth to offer his invention to the Society instead of taking out a patent. The Society unfortunately let Smeaton down rather badly, for Westgarth died just after the award had been made, and apart from depositing his model and drawings in the repository the Society did nothing to make the invention known until Smeaton in 1786, disturbed at the neglect of what according to William Bailey[1] he regarded as "the greatest stroke of art in the hydraulic way . . . since the invention of the steam engine", submitted a detailed description (without which the model was unintelligible), and this was published in the Transactions,[2] Smeaton being awarded a silver medal for his trouble.

Towards the end of the century the Society at length turned its attention to the ordinary water-wheel, which it had deliberately neglected earlier because it considered that it had already been brought to a reasonable degree of efficiency. In the meanwhile, however, the water-wheel had become the mainstay of many branches of industry; indeed, it retained its importance until well into the nineteenth century; and several awards were made by the Society for minor improvements in its mechanism and in the control of the water which was fed to it.

In the newcomer, steam, on the other hand, the Society was extremely slow to take an interest. One of the Vice-Presidents, Keane Fitzgerald, F.R.S., presented to the repository in 1768 his model for converting the alternate motion of the Newcomen engine into rotary motion, but singularly little notice appears to

[1] Catalogue of Machines (1782), vol. I, p. 192.
[2] V, 179. An illustration of the machine will be found in plate 15.

have been taken of it by the Society. In May of the same year the committee of mechanics actually decided to recommend the award of a silver medal for a "model fire engine" which produced rotary motion by different means from those used by Fitzgerald,[1] but they failed for some reason to bring forward their recommendation to the Society. Similarly, early in 1769 they examined a steam-engine (of which no description survives), designed by Richard Lovell Edgeworth, the friend of Erasmus Darwin, and resolved that it "appeared to be a very ingenious application of the expansive force of steam and merits the farther attention of the committee in order to determine its power", but the Minutes give no indication that the matter was ever taken further.

The first positive action by the Society for the development of the steam-engine was the introduction in 1783, just after Watt's second and third patents, of an offer for "increasing the quality or force in steam engines with less fuel". Unfortunately, although this excellent offer, with its enlightened objective of developing the efficiency of steam-engines in relation to their fuel consumption, was repeated year after year for half a century, it was never claimed. As time went on, however, a good many awards were made, first for improvements in the design of the steam-boiler, such as the Chevalier Edelcrantz's safety valve (1804) and several improved methods of feeding high-pressure boilers, and later for developments in the steam-engine culminating in the award of a gold medal to William Siemens in 1850 for the regenerative condenser.

Not long after steam-power had established itself as an industrial factor of real practical importance, discoveries began to be made which opened the door to the development of the second great source of modern industrial energy, electricity, and this time the Society of Arts did not fail to be "in on the ground floor". In 1825, five years after Oersted had made the primary discovery of the phenomenon of electro-magnetism with the voltaic pile, the English scientist Sturgeon submitted to the Society his invention of the soft-iron electro-magnet, the basis of the modern

[1] For fuller details see *The Story of Exhibitions* (Studio), p. 69.

generator, and it was in the pages of the *Transactions*[1] that this great discovery was first described, while Sturgeon's apparatus was put on view in the repository. The invention, which consisted of a horseshoe-shaped bar of soft iron, coated with varnish, on which was wrapped a spiral coil of bare copper wire, was modestly rewarded with a silver medal and 30 guineas.

Another early piece of electrical apparatus of some importance which was rewarded by the Society was Alfred Smee's galvanic battery, for which a gold medal was awarded in 1840. The special feature of this battery was the use of platinum-coated silver instead of copper for the negative plate as a means of reducing the accumulation of hydrogen on its surface.

6

Besides power, the industrial worker needs good tools and equipment, and here the Society was very much alive. As early as 1757 it began, on the advice of the distinguished chemist, Peter Shaw, to offer awards for the manufacture in England and from English materials of crucibles and retorts "for the distillation of acid spirits and for other chymical purposes". At that time these articles were all imported, mostly from Germany, but although the apparatus submitted in response to the offers was very carefully tested by Shaw and others and found of excellent quality, so that several awards were made, the Society's intention to establish a permanent manufacture in this country was not immediately fulfilled. Still, the object lesson had its effect before many years.

Between 1760 and 1770 there was quite a spate of awards for tools of various kinds, such as the 50 guineas awarded to William Bailey in 1761 for an auger, and the gold medal awarded in 1770 to Staghold, the inventor of the gun-harpoon, for a screw-jack, similar to that with which the modern motorist used to be equipped.

The same decade and the next saw a series of awards for measuring instruments, including gauges, balances and various

[1] XLIII, 37. One of the engravings illustrating that article is reproduced in plate 17.

instruments for land measurement, such as the "perambulator" for which R. L. Edgeworth received a silver medal in 1767, and Mr. Green's range-finder, or "instrument for taking distances at one station", rewarded in 1778. During the 'seventies the Society also made particular endeavours to establish a reliable universal measure of length and enlisted the assistance of a group of Fellows of the Royal Society in judging the entries. Two awards were made, both of them for proposals based on the pendulum but not attaining to any high degreee of accuracy. Some time later the Secretary, Samuel More, wrote a paper[1] advocating as the standard of weight the use of a piece of agate adjusted by grinding to equal the standard metal pound weight at the Exchequer, and as the standard of length, a brass cube of such a size as exactly to contain 1,000 oz. avoirdupois of soft water at 60° Fahrenheit.

Among numerous other measuring instruments for which awards were made may be mentioned two inventions of the famous mechanician Brian Donkin—a "tachometer" for measuring the velocity of machines by the centrifugal action of a revolving cup of mercury (this was awarded a gold medal in 1810) and a revolution-counting machine, awarded a gold medal in 1819, in which, as in the modern car milometer, the completion of a revolution by the mechanism controlling the first digit moved the mechanism controlling the second digit one notch forward. This positive step-by-step movement was a great advance on the creeping clocklike motion of earlier counters.[2]

But the measuring instruments in which the Society took the greatest interest were those for measuring time. Horology is the mechanician's playground, and it was a never-failing source of interest to the Society's committee of mechanics, particularly as the years advanced and the committee became more and more concerned with detailed mechanical refinements rather than basic discoveries. In the first half of the nineteenth century hardly a year passed without some award being made for horology, and the Society's encouragement of the science must have been a factor of great importance at a time of much development.

The Society also took a considerable interest in the develop-

[1] *Transactions*, XII, 292.　　　　[2] See plate 17.

ment of optical instruments. Following upon Dollond's invention of the achromatic telescope in 1758, prizes were offered for a good many years for the production of high-quality glass suitable for making it, but although awards were made in 1770 and 1771 to Abraham Pelling and Richard Russell, these were for what could only be described by the Society as "attempts". In the next century, however, the production of satisfactory achromatic objectives for the microscope, for which Chevalier in Paris and Tulley in London were independently responsible, led to a rapid development of the design of the whole instrument in which the Society played a leading part. Among those who were rewarded were Varley, Powell, Goodley and Ross; and Jabez Hogg, in *The Microscope* (1855), said that since 1831 the Society's *Transactions* had been "the vehicle through which nearly all the improvements in the construction of telescopes and microscopes have been made known to the world".

Besides the smaller tools and instruments which we have just been considering, most of which were used for a variety of purposes, the Society also took steps from time to time to encourage the design of those larger tools we call machines, which are generally made to fulfil a particular function in a particular trade. Most of the Society's efforts to promote industrial mechanisation were on behalf of the textile industry and will be discussed in that connection in the next chapter, but perhaps the outstanding example of a machine designed, or at any rate introduced into this country, as a result of the Society's offer of a premium was Stansfield's saw-mill, which was the first saw-mill ever erected in England, although such machines had long been in use overseas. Dossie, in explanation of their tardy development in this country, refers[1] to the fear (not without warrant, as we shall see) "that the populace might be incited to a violent opposition against it, under the notion that it had a tendency to take away the bread of those who lived by sawing with the hand". There was also, he said, an erroneous belief (denied by the Society in some of its public announcements) that for this reason the erection of saw-mills was prohibited by Act of Parliament. The Society, however, con-

[1] *Memoirs of Agriculture*, vol. I, p. 124.

cerned at the importation of large quantities of timber which had been sawn by foreign labour and foreign machines, offered what was for those days the substantial prize of £100 "to the person who should first erect a good saw mill and work it for one year".

The prize was successfully claimed in 1761 by James Stansfield, who erected a saw-mill in Yorkshire designed on principles which he had learned by personally travelling to Norway and Sweden and studying the saw-mills there. So important did the Society consider Stansfield's achievement that when he came to London in 1765 to present a model of his mill to the Society, they granted him a "bounty" of a further £100, and asked him to prepare another model, for which they paid him £60, to be sent to America for the information of the colonists. This model is known to have proved of very considerable practical benefit on the other side of the Atlantic. After a while things began to go poorly with Stansfield's own mill. Having worked it successfully for five years, he found that, as it was erected in "a corner of the country where there was not an adequate consumption of timber", the number of orders began to fall off. The Society, also, were disappointed because "in that distant corner it had no influence", and no other saw-mills were erected in England as a result of their efforts. Stansfield therefore decided to follow his second model to America, where his invention was so much better appreciated than in England, but as he passed through London on his way to the ship he was introduced by the Society to a timber merchant named Charles Dingley who had been greatly impressed by the model which he had seen in the Society's collection. The result was that Stansfield agreed to remain and assist Dingley in the building of a large new saw-mill at Limehouse, where there were excellent facilities for the transport of timber by river and canal. So successful was this plant that even an attack by a mob only put it out of action temporarily, and by its size and situation it drew that measure of attention to itself which the Yorkshire mill lacked. Having, therefore, amply rewarded Stansfield himself, the Society showed their final gratification by conferring a gold medal on Dingley for thus crowning their endeavours.

Another industrial process of which the Society secured the

mechanisation at an early date was the grinding of plate glass, a process which became largely redundant, of course, on the introduction of modern methods of manufacture. In 1762, premiums of £70, £50 and £30 were offered "for the best effectual mill or engine to be erected in London . . . to perform by horse, wind or water the grinding and polishing plate glass", and in 1765 the first premium was awarded to Mr. Jeremiah Burrows of Southwark for erecting what Dossie describes as "an excellent and curious machine of this kind", the first to be erected in London.

7

In assessing the part which the Society played in the Industrial Revolution, we are apt to overlook the fact that, even regarding the matter from the purely technical point of view, that movement was by no means entirely mechanical, and at the time when the Society was founded chemistry played so obvious and important a part in many industries that it must have seemed to many people that it was in the development of chemical science that the course of industrial advance lay. The Society of Arts was doubtless all the more inclined to this view because of the presence of a number of distinguished chemists among its members, and it is not surprising that in its early years the chemistry committee was one of the most important in the Society.

The chemicals then in greatest demand for industrial purposes were sulphuric acid and the alkalis, potassium and sodium carbonate. Joshua Ward (whose robust statue by Carlini is in the possession of the Society), Roebuck and others had by various improvements recently increased the supply and reduced the price of the acid. Greater supplies of alkali, however, were still a pressing need, which the Society tried to meet, as we have seen, by developing home vegetable sources and, as we shall see, by importation from the American colonies. Among the other industrial chemicals which figured prominently among the Society's early offers and awards were cobalt (which we considered in the last chapter) and its products zaffre and smalt, borax (required for glassmaking, soldering and the fusion of ores), saltpetre (for the making of gunpowder and nitric acid), verdigris (a pigment for paints and calico-printing), bismuth (required for solders and metallurgical purposes) and sal-ammoniac (used at that time in dyeing and metallurgy and also for medicinal purposes). The greater part of the national requirements of these chemicals was then met by importation from abroad, and during its first five years the Society made offers to encourage the home production of each of them.

Its chief success was with verdigris (basic acetate of copper), which was at that time a product of considerable importance. Not only does the Society appear to have been the first to suggest that in England the pulp of apples and other fruit might be used instead of the wine-lees used in this manufacture by the French, but as a result of its offers at least two people began to make verdigris in bulk, the second of them, John Bindley, on a considerable scale, for to win his award of £100 in 1764 he must by the terms of the offer have manufactured at least two tons. Dossie[1] also says that the quality of his product was actually superior to that of the French. Particularly determined efforts were made by the Society to establish the making of saltpetre, and at least one firm lost a considerable amount of money in the attempt, but all that was achieved was the definite proof that with British materials and with the British price of labour it could not be a commercial proposition in this country. The Society's part in connection with sal-ammoniac manufacture was a curious one. Several attempts, which ultimately succeeded, were being made at the time to establish it in Great Britain. Some of these were in Scotland, to which the Society's offers did not apply, and several English manufacturers who entered for the Society's prizes failed for purely technical reasons to qualify although their products were good, so that the only award actually made was to Mr. Faulconbridge of Bewdley, in 1769. Nevertheless, it is clear that the Society's offers acted as a stimulus, and that it can claim some share in the establishment of the industry.

Besides encouraging the production of these well-known chemicals the Society took a great interest in the discovery of a number of new chemical materials and processes, particularly dye-

[1] *Memoirs of Agriculture*, vol. I, p. 178.

stuffs, stains and pigments for enamels and paints. The chemistry committee tried very hard for several years to obtain really fast dyes ("in grain" as they were called) of various colours and for particular textile materials, and besides offering premiums for their discovery by people at home it co-operated with the committee of colonies in an effort to find new materials of this kind overseas. When various dyes were submitted to it, however, it put them through such searching tests, including boiling with an alkaline solution, that in only a few cases was it able to recommend an award. The most notable was for a process for dyeing cotton a fast "Turkey" red, which had not previously been achieved in this or other European countries, and for which John Wilson of Manchester in 1761, and Simon Spurre of Isleworth in 1764 received £50 and £100 respectively. John Wilson had sent a representative out to Turkey to find out the secret, and although the process was discovered in this way it proved to be too complicated for Wilson's particular purposes, for which madder was after all more suitable. Wilson did not therefore put his discovery to serious industrial use.[1] Another notable award in this field was for a process for staining leather red and yellow which a certain Mr. Philippo was persuaded by two zealous members of the Society to investigate in Asia Minor and report to the Society. The Society was so satisfied with the result of Philippo's process that in 1767 it gave him £100 towards his expenses, and a gold medal as well to mark its special approbation. These generous awards seem to have been well deserved, as Philippo had declined several remunerative offers for his secret and chosen to reveal it to the Society so that it could be published. The details are to be found in Dossie's *Memoirs of Agriculture*,[2] and several people established factories to work the process. Among these was a member of the Society, William Blake, of Aldersgate Street, who received a silver medal in 1773 and a gold medal in 1775 for improvements in Philippo's process. His two partners in addition received pecuniary awards on both occasions.

The Society also took a very great interest in the question of

[1] See Clow, *Chemical Revolution*, pp. 214 ff., for details.
[2] Vol. I, p. 400.

tanning materials. Tanners had for a long time been restricted by Act of Parliament to the use of certain prescribed materials, of which oak bark was the principal, but in 1765 John Eldridge of Battle, near Hastings, offered for a consideration to reveal to the Society a method of tanning with oak sawdust, which was not one of the permitted agents. This would have made use of a much cheaper material of which there were plentiful supplies. The Society agreed to pay Eldridge his expenses in coming to town and carrying on a protracted series of tests, and £100 if the results of the tests were satisfactory. The leather tanned by Eldridge in front of the committee was all that could be desired and he duly received his £100, but an attempt made in due course to obtain parliamentary sanction for the use of his prescription was quite unsuccessful.

Undeterred by this, the Society continued to make awards for improvements in Eldridge's process, and for entirely new tanning materials, such as mangrove bark and myrobolans, for which a gold medal was awarded to Dr. James Howison in 1804, and larch bark, for which the silver medal was awarded in 1813 to Thomas White of Durham.

Another industrial process of a chemical nature which the Society took up with considerable energy was the "edulceration" of "train", or whale, oil. The character of this oil is vividly indicated in the Minutes by a rich vocabulary including such epithets as "vicious", "stinking", "foetid", "putrid" and "disgustful", and in 1757, at the suggestion of Dr. Peter Shaw, the Society began to offer an award of 10 guineas for a method of refining the oil so as to make it suitable for such purposes as soapmaking, woolcombing and lighting. Only one method (and that, ineffective) was produced, and the offer was discontinued after 1760. Robert Dossie, however, felt that the matter should be pursued and himself produced two processes, one with the use of heat, and the other, a more elaborate one, without it, which he submitted to the Society in April, 1761, requesting that, if they were approved, he be granted a bounty of £100 to cover his expenses. Subsequently, he submitted an improved process without the use of heat, for which he requested a further £50.

Dossie's methods, which were quite simple and employed a few very ordinary chemicals,[1] soon came into general use and made life a good deal sweeter and brighter for large numbers of people. The investigations carried out by the chemistry committee, however, before they could make a recommendation to the Society, were a truly devoted service. Having purchased from John Baskerville three gallons of the "most stinking but genuine unmixed train oil", they tested out Dossie's processes with meticulous care, even repeating a number of these unpleasant experiments because the Society's housekeeper had technically invalidated the tests by failing to lock up the samples between experiments. Altogether thirty-five meetings were devoted partly or wholly to this nauseating business, and in due course Dossie (who, so far from being considered subject to the Society's rule debarring members of the Society from receiving prizes, was present at the meetings and actually in the chair at the decisive meeting) was awarded £100, and his process was published in the *Gentleman's Magazine* and the *Annual Register*. Fifty years later it was still "the last word" on the subject and was reprinted, by request, in the *Transactions* of 1802.

One of the great factors in the early development of modern industrial chemistry was the pioneer study of the constituents of coal and coal-tar. The Society did not stand far outside the beginnings of this movement. In 1768 we find it, probably for aesthetic reasons, offering a prize for "destroying smoke" from factory chimneys, and this led in 1791 to its publishing[2] an article by William Pitt, of Pendeford, near Wolverhampton, giving an answer to this problem, the collection of the solid matter, including the tar, by condensation on the walls of the chimney. This process was already going on in connection with coke ovens erected in at least three places in the Black Country, on lines which Pitt describes in detail, and the properties of tar, which thus began to be manufactured in bulk, were soon investigated. Winsor obtained his well-known patent for coal-tar distillation in 1804, and six years later the Society awarded a silver medal to B. Cook of Birmingham for his distillation process by which he obtained a

---

[1] Slaked lime, chalk, potash and salt.　　　[2] *Transactions*, IX, 131.

"volatile oil" and a "residuum" equal to the "best asphaltum". He had, moreover, found a use for these products which, employed together, had proved to be excellent for japanning.

Meanwhile the other great product of coal, coal-gas, was also being developed, and the Society honoured one of the pioneers, Samuel Clegg, the inventor of the modern type of gas-holder and later of the gas-meter, with a silver medal in 1808 (the year after the first gas street-lights in London were erected in Pall Mall) for an important paper[1] giving clear directions for the introduction of gas-lighting schemes in factories and public buildings.

Two further applications of chemistry in which the Society took an interest in its early days, the twin sciences of mineralogy and metallurgy, remain to be considered. We have already seen some of the first members busy in their laboratories over the assaying of cobalt in connection with the offers for that mineral, and in 1762 the Society's attention was drawn to a far more important metal by the famous Shropshire ironmaster, John Wilkinson. In a letter still preserved in the archives, Wilkinson stressed the need for a process applicable to British ores whereby high-quality pig-iron could be produced by the use of coke, for although at that time coke was already in use for producing low-grade iron, the secret of using it for high-grade pig had not been acquired and the quantity of charcoal required for that purpose was prohibitive. Metal of that quality was, therefore, all imported from Sweden. Acting at once on Wilkinson's suggestion the Society made two offers that same year, one for the production of at least 100 tons of high-grade pig, or cast, iron with coke, the other for at least 10 tons of bar, or forged, iron, also with coke. The importance of these objectives was marked by the offer of £150 in each case, but the premiums were not claimed. Dossie's explanation of this failure shows that even at that time the Society was aware of the limitations of its premium system. "None but the proprietors of considerable works", he says, "could possibly perform what was

[1] *Transactions*, XXVI, 202 ff. E. F. Armstrong (in his account of Clegg in *Journal*, LXXVII, 887 ff.) speaks of it as being "second only in interest" to Murdoch's paper to the Royal Society. One of the engravings illustrating the paper is reproduced in plate 17.

required to be done [by the terms of the Society's offer] and they have infinitely greater inducements than the sum offered." In any case, he added, the need for an improved process of smelting and refining was so well known that there was no need for the Society to draw attention to it.

But although the Society was unable to make any important award for the manufacture of iron, one outstanding award for the use of iron must be mentioned: this is the gold medal awarded to Abraham Darby (the third of that name) in 1788 for the famous iron bridge erected by him over the Severn at Coalbrookdale. This was the first all-metal bridge ever constructed in this country, and Darby presented a very beautiful model of it to the Society, which is now in the Science Museum.

The Society's metallurgical interests were not, of course, confined to iron. The offer which it began to make in 1765 for crucibles for assaying tin ore appears to have contributed to the revival of Cornish tin mining, and nearly twenty years later a gold medal was awarded to George Unwin for reviving the export of tin to India and China. In 1769, an offer was introduced (and an award made four years later) for making white copper, which was then wholly imported from China and Japan, and in the early nineteenth century there were offers for an improved method of refining copper and zinc and of preparing their alloy, brass.

Thus, in what were usually small but sometimes larger ways, we find the Society making its varied contributions to the mechanical, chemical and sometimes even the social development of the Industrial Revolution. In the next chapter we shall see its multifarious activity most fully exemplified in the case of a single industry, or group of industries: that concerned with textiles.

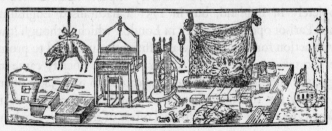

CHAPTER 7

The Textile and Allied Industries

1

ALTHOUGH we have already at various points considered some of the Society's early activities on behalf of the textile industry, the subject deserves a chapter to itself because of its comprehensiveness and importance. Throughout the hundred years we are now reviewing, in every annual list of premiums and in almost every section of each of those lists—mechanics, chemistry, manufactures, agriculture, colonies and trade, and polite arts—there were offers which were concerned directly or indirectly with textiles, and the Society's influence on the industry, affecting it as it did at so many points and over so long a period, must obviously have been very considerable.

The Society certainly lost no time in directing its activities in this direction. As we have already seen, one of the four offers which it made in the year of its foundation was for a dyestuff, and within four years, by an offer made from 1756 to 1758, it had actually contributed very substantially to the establishment, or at least the re-establishment, of an important branch of the industry, the manufacture of carpets.

This came about in the following way. In the first half of the eighteenth century the carpet industry appears to have died out completely in England, but in 1751 a naturalised Englishman named Parisot opened a factory in London which, although it was only in action for four years, was sufficiently successful to prompt others to take up the trade. At this point the Society came into the picture and, in each of the three years 1756 to 1758, it offered two prizes for the manufacture in England of carpets of the Turkey type. Few of the industrial offers of the Society ever met with so quick and satisfactory a response, for all six of the prizes offered during the period of the competition were awarded. Thomas Witty, of Axminster, was successful in each of the three years, Thomas Moore, of Moorfields (who later made some famous carpets for Robert Adam's buildings), received a prize in 1757,[1] Passavant, of Exeter (a Swiss who seems to have taken over Parisot's factory and workmen), in 1758,[2] and Jaffer of Frome in 1759. Of these four names the most interesting is that of Witty, for it was he who established the original Axminster factory in 1755. This factory, having made the name of Axminster world famous, was removed in the early nineteenth century to Wilton (somewhat as the original university at Cambridge is reputed to have been transferred to Oxford!) and still survives, merged in the Wilton Royal Carpet Factory. Witty's triple success with the Society, and the reputation which this brought to him, must undoubtedly have assisted in firmly establishing the Axminster factory and saving it from the fate of Parisot's, and the whole effort of the Society was neatly rounded off in 1760 when at the suggestion of Witty two of his carpets were exhibited for a fortnight in the Society's Great Room, together with two of Passavant's and two of Moore's.[3]

Writing therefore in 1768 Dossie[4] claimed that "the Society . . . may be justly deemed to have contributed, in a very great degree, to the introduction of those extensive and valuable manufactures of carpets established in various parts of Great Britain", and this claim was confirmed by a statement in the *Transactions*[5] that "by the Society's awards the manufacture of carpets is now established in different parts of the kingdom and brought to a degree of elegance and beauty which the Turkey carpets never attained". Dossie applauds this achievement not only because the home manufacture of what was previously imported saved foreign exchange and increased the consumption of English wool, but also

[1] Each pair of prizes was awarded in the year after its offer was announced.

[2] See plate 12 for what may have been Passavant's prize-winning carpet.

[3] For further details, see C. E. Tattersall *A History of British Carpets* and A. F. Kendrick *English Carpets*. Also *Journal*, LXVII, 136 ff.

[4] *Memoirs of Agriculture*, vol. I, p. 91.

[5] I, 28.

because it provided employment for labour, and particularly for "women and children, who are thus rendered profitable to the public and moral in their conduct instead of being burthensome or loose in their way of life which [he most unchivalrously adds] they otherwise would be".

2

Dossie's reference to a surplus of labour only refers to unskilled women and children. In general, the main hindrance to the progress of industry was a lack of labour owing to the wars. A committee of the Society laid it down in May, 1760, as the reason for offering an award for a more efficient loom, that "at this time in some branches the want of workmen is so great that some millionsworth of manufactures are imported from foreign countries, the rivals to our own". The branch of the textile industry in which the shortage of labour was felt most seriously was spinning, as Kay's invention of the fly-shuttle in 1733 had doubled the rate of weaving and therefore the potential consumption of yarn, while the first spinning-machine, that of Wyatt and Paul, which was patented five years later, was in advance of its time and had not established itself in the same way as Kay's shuttle. The Society did not, therefore, for the time being accept its committee's advice to assist the mechanisation of weaving, but decided to concentrate on the improvement of the spinning-wheel. Not only did it offer prizes for cheaper and simpler spinning-wheels of the ordinary type but it aimed at a much greater advance by offering a prize for a machine with which one worker could spin six threads at once. Twenty years later the Society claimed[1] that it had thought of the possibility of such a machine before any of the manufacturers, and although this offer achieved, directly, only slight success, part of the second premium being awarded in 1763 for what Dossie calls "an attempt towards such a machine", yet, whether as an indirect result of the offer or by mere coincidence, it was in the very next year that Hargreaves began to design his "spinning jenny", which in its original form spun eight threads, and later up to a hundred, at once.

[1] *Transactions*, I, 33.

The Society discontinued its offer after 1763 and concentrated on minor modifications of the ordinary wheel, which, being mechanically simpler, were more readily forthcoming and more immediately practical. There is a very understandable reason for this apparent retrogression. The Society was essentially practical in its aims and outlook and most great inventions have little practical value in their early stages. Dossie, for example, says of Wyatt and Paul's famous spinning machine that it was "now [i.e. in 1768] wholly laid aside as unprofitable, after sixty or seventy thousand pounds have been spent in various attempts to establish its use".[1] And Wyatt himself, in a plaintive letter which he addressed to the Society in 1762, complained that twenty years before he was "ruined by a scheme for improving spinning".

3

If the Society's contribution to the development of spinning machinery was small or hypothetical, its achievements on the weaving side were quite definite and substantial, though somewhat specialised. Its first success after the carpet competition was to establish an entirely new industry, that of "quilting in the loom", which had never before been produced in this country. It began to offer premiums for this object in 1761, and four years later, when a total of £410 had been expended on awards, it was able to discontinue the competition because "the manufacture appears to be sufficiently established". That this was in fact the case was confirmed in 1778 when it recorded[2] that "there are few persons of any rank, condition or sex in the kingdom (and we may add within the extent of British commerce, so greatly is it exported) who do not use it in some part of their clothing".

There were several other specialised textile products which the Society endeavoured with varying degrees of success to foster by its offers of premiums. A few, such as special types of drugget and light broadcloth, which were promoted during the Society's first decade, were for export to "the Lisbon market". Others were

---

[1] *Memoirs of Agriculture*, vol. I, p. 98.
[2] *Register of Premiums and Bounties*, p. 25.

encouraged for the benefit of particular social classes, such as the genteel cambric and lace which it was hoped to stimulate impecunious "women of the middling rank" to make, in contrast with the worsted hose, on which, as we saw in the last chapter, the masters of workhouses were encouraged to employ the female inmates of their institutions. Brocades, tapestries, ribbons, embroideries, all figure in the premium lists from time to time. For example, Messrs. Freestone, of Kidderminster, were awarded 25 guineas in 1773 for improvements in a loom for weaving tapestry and other figured work, while in 1809 the patrons and committee of the Flag Association were awarded a silver medal with gold border for "a matchless specimen of double brocade weaving". Women's mittens, milled caps, and crêpe bands for hats and mourning armlets were all manufactured for the first time in England because of the Society's offers, and in 1811, influenced perhaps by the vogue which followed the Waverley novels, the Society gave 10 guineas for an improved method of weaving tartan hose, an article which John Robertson of Edinburgh, the prize-winner, described with patriotic fervour as "essentially necessary in the *Highland garb*, the dress of the *Conquerors of Egypt*, and more than *match* for *French Invincibles*!"

Fifty years earlier the Society had made a contribution of more general importance (*pace* John Robertson and other Scots) to the hosiery industry, which was then in a very depressed state because it had lost most of its trade to France. Beginning in 1764 the Society offered a prize of £100 for improvements in the stocking-frame, and these provoked such valuable ideas from Unwin and Whyman, who were awarded £80 and £100 respectively in 1765 and 1766, that by their aid the stocking-weavers were able to regain much of what they had lost.

The ordinary loom[1] itself also was considerably improved as a result of the Society's offers, the loom for which John Almond received a prize of £50 in 1771 being so notable a development that many years later it was found after a long period of trial and error

[1] For the interesting story of the relations of John Kay, the inventor of the fly-shuttle, and his sons, with the Society, see Trueman Wood, *A History of the Royal Society of Arts*, pp. 259-62, and *Journal* LX, 73 ff.

that this was the most convenient form of loom for power-driving.[1] As for the power-loom, the Society first showed an interest in the idea in 1780 when it began to offer an award for "an engine for working looms", at least three looms to be driven at a time by the machine. The first award, however, was not until 1806 when John Austin, of Glasgow, received a gold medal for harnessing three hundred Almond-type looms to steam- or water-power. Subsequently, a number of other awards were made for power-looms and for numerous specialised developments. Particular attention was paid during the first decades of the nineteenth century to silk-weaving, and all the chief mechanical advances were so carefully and exhaustively described in the *Transactions* that its pages were claimed in 1830[2] as the best available source on the subject. At the same time as it fostered the progress of mechanisation, however, the Society continued to encourage improvements in the hand-loom, particularly by Spitalfields and Bethnal Green weavers, to whom "the Society have ever shewn themselves desirous of lending a helping hand, so far as their finances would permit".[3] A deserved tribute to this side of the Society's work was paid by G. R. Porter, who said in 1831 that it "had done more for the encouragement of ingenious artisans in this branch of industry than has been, or than could be, effected by the patent laws under the present system".[4]

But the Society's greatest achievement in connection with weaving was a curiously indirect one. Among the many textile products which it sought to encourage were fishing nets, and a prize was first offered in 1771 for a special loom for weaving them. The prize was awarded in 1775 to Messrs. Freestone, of Kidderminster, but as their loom was not considered a final answer the offer was continued, at intervals, until well into the nineteenth century and another award was made in 1806.

The real interest of the offer, however, lies in the fact that in

[1] Luther Hooper, *Journal*, LX, 995. Almond's loom is illustrated in plate 15 of this book.
[2] See *Transactions*, XLVIII, xxiii. ff., where an excellent review is given of the Society's publications on this subject.
[3] Preface to *Transactions*, LIV, viii.
[4] *Treatise on Manufacture of Silk*, p. 35.

1792 an English newspaper containing it fell into the hands of a Frenchman called Jacquard. Jacquard was at that time in a state of penury. He was a weaver and had inherited two looms from his father, but, having no work for them, was keeping himself alive by lime-burning. The offer of the Society of Arts somehow intrigued him and he set to work to invent a new type of loom. The machine he produced was destined to revolutionise the weaving industry of the whole of the western world. It was first made known at the Paris National Exhibition of 1801 where its value was immediately recognised, and shortly afterwards Jacquard was bought out by the French Government on very generous terms. In ten years there were 11,000 Jacquard looms in operation in France and, as was just, this country, which had provided the first incentive to the invention, soon benefited, in common with others, by the discovery, while the Society of Arts made a further contribution to this great advance in weaving by rewarding a number of improvements in the Jacquard machine in the 'thirties.

4

Another side of the textile industry in which the Society took an interest was dyeing and bleaching, which has already been discussed in some detail. Britain was lamentably behind other countries, particularly France, in this matter and almost wholly dependent on them for supplies of the necessary materials, or, more frequently, for the actual processing of British-made fabrics. More often than not the colour of English-dyed materials could actually be rubbed off. The problem therefore needed to be tackled from every possible angle, and the Society did not fail to make such an effort, with notably successful results, as we have seen.

Another very important aspect of textile manufacture which we have already had occasion to consider is that of design. In view of the present-day active interest of the Society in this subject and its annual offer of bursaries to promising students of textile design, it is interesting to find it doing almost exactly the same thing nearly two hundred years ago, and evidently with very appreciable results.

Before closing this chapter it might be well to consider the Society's work in connection with one or two industries which, although not concerned with textiles, deal in materials very closely related to them. One of these is the manufacture of straw hats. This industry seems to have been well established in its present home, the Luton district, by the beginning of the seventeenth century, but to have succumbed in course of time to the Italian trade in Leghorn and other kinds of straws. In 1760, however, the Society made a threefold effort to revive it. It offered prizes for the making of coarse straw, or "chip", hats and fine straw, or "Leghorn", hats, and also for importing from the colonies "straw-plait", the raw material for the latter. Unfortunately, the male members of the Society, unprompted, apparently, by their wives or the few lady members, overlooked the fact that Leghorn straw hats had just gone out of fashion, so that it was only the offer for "chip" hats which achieved any success. However, this small and passing effort did something to keep the industry alive and forty years later the Napoleonic Wars, by casting the country back on its own resources, fully resuscitated it, large numbers of women and children in the Home Counties finding much-needed employment in this way. To encourage this war-time revival the Society in 1805 awarded a gold medal to William Corston for making straw-plait equal to Leghorn plait from rye straw grown in Norfolk, and after the war, when the revival of trade flooded the market once more with the superior Italian product and threw many people out of employment, the Society took the matter up with some vigour. The aim, clearly, had to be to enable British workers to produce hats which could fairly compete with the Italian, and a possible solution was suggested by a fortuitous circumstance, the receipt from a Mrs. Wells, the daughter of a Connecticut farmer, of a straw bonnet of particularly good colour and exceptional fineness of material, which she had made from a native American grass. Feeling that British countrywomen could do what an American had done, the Society awarded Mrs. Wells a silver medal and persuaded her to send over, for distribution in this country, a supply of the seed of the grass (*Poa pratensis*) from which the hat had been made, and information as to the bleaching and other processes which she had employed. At the same time a reward was granted to a Mr. Parry who after considerable researches had discovered the secret of the Italian method of plaiting.

At this point the Society acquired a notable ally in the person of William Cobbett, who attempted with some success to put the industry on an entirely indigenous footing by making straw-plait from native English grasses and straws. The Society responded to Cobbett's efforts with a silver medal, whereupon, as Cobbett was particularly unpopular at the time, the newspapers came out with the head-line: "The Society of Arts humbugged at last." The Society, however, whether "humbugged" or not, continued its efforts on various lines. A premium of 20 guineas was offered and awarded for producing seed of *Poa pratensis* in this country, investigations were made as to the precise type of wheat used by the Italians, and small prizes were awarded for "the first rude attempts" to produce Leghorn-plait hats in this country. These activities met with very considerable success, and in fact put the industry once more on its feet, so that at last, in 1827, it was possible to report that English hats had "met with a ready sale as Italian". At this stage the Society decided that it could drop its part in the matter, "in full confidence that the ladies of England will do justice to their countrywomen" by purchasing English-made hats on their own merit—and even if advertised as English-made!

Another industry closely connected with textiles in which the Society took a considerable interest was the manufacture of paper, for which the growth of the Press, in particular, was constantly increasing the demand. Its main preoccupation was the development of alternative sources of raw material, a subject which became an acute, but fortunately temporary, problem after the recent war. Until the middle of last century and the introduction of esparto grass, and later of wood, the only paper-making materials normally used were cotton and linen rags, and the first unused source to which the Society turned was silk rags, which were neglected for what seemed an unaccountable reason. After several awards had been made, in 1758 and 1759, for some excellent paper made from silk rags, the practical difficulty was discovered: the majority of silk rags were dyed, and in spite of the offer of a special premium by the Society, no method of bleaching them could be found efficient enough to prevent every "making" being of a different tint, for chlorine was not discovered until 1774 and its use as a bleaching agent not until 1785.

The Society's attention was then drawn from various quarters to an entirely different solution to the problem, the manufacture of paper direct from fibrous vegetable matter without any intermediate textile process. This development began in 1768 with the receipt from a corresponding member, Dr. Schaffers of Regensburg (Ratisbon), of a specimen of paper "made from various vegetables" for which a silver medal was awarded. A few years later we find evidence that the subject was still in the minds of the committee of manufactures, who decided to send a specimen of "wild cotton down" which had been received from Jamaica to James Whatman (whose name still brands one of the best types of paper), asking him if it was suitable for paper-making. Whatman's reply (which is still preserved[1]) is interesting. While admitting that paper could be made of this or any other fibrous vegetable material, he disagreed with the Society's endeavours to encourage their use, because of the difficulty of making paper of a good colour from them. He therefore advised the Society rather to direct its efforts towards an improvement of the supply of rags by encouraging richer folk to sell their rags to the paper-makers instead of burning them. In this case, at least, it can fairly be claimed that the intelligent laity composing the Society's membership were more far-sighted than the leading specialist.

Then, a few years later, when Dr. Schaffers sent a whole sheaf of specimens of paper made from "thistles, potato haulms, poplar, hop binds, etc." it was decided to make a determined effort to foster the use of these materials, and a premium was offered annually over a period of thirty years. Several prizes were awarded for papers produced from various natural fibres. One of these, awarded in 1801 to T. Willmott, was for paper made from

[1] MS. *Transactions*, 1774–5, 79.

"paute" (i.e. jute), and a single page of Volume XIX of the *Transactions* (now very faded) was printed on paper made of this material, while Volume XLV, which is still in excellent condition, was entirely printed on paper made from flax.

Besides endeavouring to increase the general supplies of paper the Society also took active steps to establish the manufacture of two special types in this country. The first of these was a high-grade paper suitable for copper-plate printing, the secret of making which reposed at that time with the French. A number of awards were made for various specimens over a considerable period; but not until 1788, when a gold medal was awarded to John Bates, of Wickham Marsh, Bucks., could the Society declare that the paper it was rewarding was actually "equal to the French". Indeed, only the previous year a silver medal had been awarded to W. Lepard (of the firm of Lepard & Smiths, which supplies writing paper to the Society to-day), for "an attempt to make it equal to the French". But the sad thing is that no award seems to have been granted to, or indeed sought by, Whatman, who according to the *Gentleman's Magazine*, 1755,[1] was then producing and actually exporting paper of larger size, if not of better quality, than the French and with whom, as we saw above, the Society was in touch.

The Society's one complete success in connection with paper-making was the establishment in this country of a specialised, but not unimportant, branch of the industry, the manufacture of marbled paper, which had hitherto been largely imported from France, in spite of frequent attempts to produce it here. The Society's offers resulted in the establishment of "a considerable manufactory", sufficient to meet all internal requirements, and for this the proprietors, Messrs. Portbury & Smith, received the advertised prize of £50 in 1765. A further award, of a silver medal, was made to John Davis of Fleet Street in 1787, in recognition of the high quality of his productions.

[1] p. 269.

CHAPTER 8

The Encouragement of Commerce

1

MANUFACTURES and commerce go hand-in-hand (and not merely in the title of the Society), and the development of industry which the Society sought to foster could not properly proceed, nor could its benefits be distributed, unless there was a corresponding development of the means of transport. This was therefore another matter in the various aspects of which the Society took a practical interest.

At the time when it was founded the roads of this country, which were the basis of its inland communications, were in an appalling condition. As an example, the main road between Preston and Wigan (which, with its hard granite setts, is still not exactly a motorist's paradise) was thus described by Arthur Young: "They will meet here with ruts which I actually measured four feet deep, and floating with mud, only from a wet summer. What, therefore, must it be after a winter? The only mending it receives in places is the tumbling in some loose stones, which serve no other purpose but jolting a carriage in the most intolerable manner."

The Society was not very long in turning its attention to this problem, and, realising that it would ultimately have to be handled in a big way, its first step was to seek for reliable information. Beginning in 1759, therefore, it offered to make a grant of up to £100 to anyone who would undertake the accurate trigonometrical survey of a whole county and produce a map on a scale of at least one inch to the mile. The first award under this offer was made in 1765 for a map of Devon drawn by Benjamin Donn and engraved by Jefferys, the well-known cartographer, and this

137

was followed in 1767 by a grant for a map of Derbyshire by Mr. Burdett. Further awards, sometimes of cash, sometimes of medals, continued to be made at intervals for county maps until 1809, and it is clear that the Society's lead was followed by many who never claimed one of its awards. For example, Thomas Jefferys took up the subject, according to Gough's *British Topography*, in response to this offer, although he himself never received a premium,

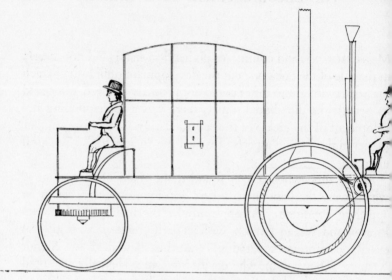

FIG. 3. DESIGN FOR A "GUNPOWDER CARRIAGE"

Submitted to the Society *c.* 1830

(Apparently, the powder was meant to be admitted gradually into the engine by the cord attached to the funnel at the rear)

and the Society claimed in 1788[1] that "in consequence of several rewards bestowed many maps of the different parts of the kingdom have been obtained". In this way the Society made an important contribution to British cartography.[2]

[1] *Transactions*, VI, 153.

[2] The Society's interest in maps was also shown, as we have seen, in the prizes offered for mineralogical maps, and in other awards such as a prize for the invention of contour maps (1806) (*Transactions*, XXII, 221 ff.), and prizes for a few particular maps such as that of London by Horwood in 1803, and Bouchette's map of Lower Canada in 1816.

Beyond encouraging the production of basic information about the existence of roads the Society did little during this period to assist in their improvement. It made a good many awards, however, for the improvement of the vehicles which used them, some for rather freakish inventions, such as a "machine cart" which could be manually assisted with cranks when it was "in a slough or going uphill", and a one-wheel chaise, for which R. Ford was awarded a gold medal in 1782. There were also numerous awards for particular parts of vehicles and for safety devices. For example, an award was made in 1800 for a method of preventing injury to the passengers when the horses took fright, and another in 1803 for preventing accidents when going downhill.

But the Society's biggest effort in connection with road transport, and, indeed, the most ambitious and expensive project in which it was ever involved, was a scheme for the supply of fresh fish to London. At that time fish was very scarce and expensive, partly owing to the great practical difficulties of speedy transport and partly to the existence of a monopoly of the Fishmongers Company who brought fish up the river in barges. In 1761, however, John Blake, who had recently been appointed chairman of the committee of manufactures, proposed to the Society a new scheme to break this monopoly by the transport of fish by land. Having gained excellent support for his idea he succeeded in persuading the Society to advance to him the sum of £3,500 as capital (only part of it on security) and also, as the basis of the whole scheme was to be the use of greatly improved fish carriages, to offer prizes for new designs. This offer evoked considerable competition and two awards were made for what proved to be excellent vehicles. Blake then went to Parliament and with the support of the Society obtained a grant of £2,000 and a reduction in the tolls on fish carriage.

Built on such excellent foundations the scheme soon met with success. A really effective supply of fish "in great variety and abundance" was instituted to the metropolis, and soon (Blake's example being followed) to other large cities, so that "the inhabitants were thereby furnished with a delicious and wholesome

food they were formerly in a great degree unfamiliar with".[1]
Blake received repeated formal expressions of thanks from the
Society, which were ordered to be published in all the newspapers
and the approbation of his fellow-members was confirmed by the
award of a gold medal. The success of the scheme is perhaps
attested even more effectively by the attitude of those whose
monopoly was broken by it. One of the Society's minutes of
February 1, 1764, speaks volumes by its sheer discretion:

> A Motion was made that the Letter from certain Fishmongers,
> order'd to be read, containing an indecent Expression in the
> Beginning of it, be burnt by the Porter.
> Agreed to, and the same was accordingly burnt.

But unfortunately, although Blake's efforts permanently established the supply of fish by land to our large cities, he himself
began to get into difficulties. This first became apparent in 1764
when he asked the Society for the return of his security without a
corresponding repayment by him of the loan, and a year later the
wording of the Society's annual vote of thanks, which had hitherto always spoken of his "disinterestedness, fortitude and assiduity"
in prosecuting the scheme, was amended by a special vote to a
reference to "his care and trouble in disposing of the money advanced to him by the Society". Shortly afterwards the Society
called upon him to sell his vehicles and hand over his cash balance
as apparently he had "with great justice offered", but, without
exactly refusing to do so, he temporised for so long that the
Society, making a virtue of necessity, finally decided to look upon
the loan as deliberate expenditure on an important public cause
and so the matter closed.

Important though Blake's scheme was to the food supply of
large towns, its indirect results were almost as valuable as the

[1] *Transactions*, I, 57 ff. An interesting sidelight is thrown on the widespread
effects of the scheme by a letter from Walter Stevens of Dartmouth, dated Jan
30, 1763, in which he states that as "the Society's agent" (Blake, presumably)
had made arrangements with only a proportion of the Brixham fishermen, and
others were still unemployed, a Mr. Floyd had made himself responsible for
putting another ten boats in commission and the writer had then raised a fund
of £1,700 in Dartmouth within forty-eight hours to finance the building of
fourteen more for the organised supply of fish for the London market.

direct, for it caused a considerable improvement in the design of vehicles for the carriage of all kinds of fragile goods. This was clear, the Society claimed in 1782,[1] "to everyone who compares the light and easy vehicles now made use of with those employed for the same purpose before the above-mentioned plan took place in London".

2

It is small wonder that, roads being what they were, alternative means of communication were strenuously developed. The eighteenth century witnessed a remarkable development of canals and other inland waterways, and this the Society assisted by several awards for improvements in the design and operation of locks, and for methods of keeping the waterways in a navigable condition. Its outstanding award in this connection, and one of the best deserved in all its long history, was the gold medal awarded to the Duke of Bridgewater in 1800 "for his great exertions in inland navigations".

Soon after the country had acquired this very fine system of canals, railways began to take their place as a means of conveying heavy goods, and before long to supplant the roads as the primary means of passenger transport. But although some of the most famous of the early railway engineers were members of the Society, the Society made few contributions to this great development. The Society's list, however, does include, among others, awards for improved "tram-plates" (i.e. rails) for iron "rail-roads" for the conveyance of minerals (1807), a carriage for Mr. Palmer's railway (1828), a cast-iron wheel for railway carriages (1836) and the use of vulcanised rubber in railway-carriage springs (1847). There were also a number of awards of a technical character relating to steam locomotives, including a gold medal awarded to Crampton in 1846 for his improved steam-engines. These engines, the "Namur" and the "Liège", made for the Liège and Namur Railway, were the two first of the long line of Crampton engines (particularly popular in France) some of which were running until the early years of the present century. This award

[1] *Transactions*, I, 57 ff.

illustrates once more the Society's constant interest in questions of public safety, for the main feature of Crampton's basic design was its low centre of gravity.

Before we leave the land for the sea a word must also be said regarding the Society's contribution to the development of the telegraph. The mechanical telegraph (still commemorated by numerous "Telegraph Hills") was invented by a Frenchman, Chappe, in 1794, but it was soon taken up by numerous inventors in this country, and awards were made by the Society for several such devices, the most important being the one invented by Admiral Sir Home Popham. This telegraph, which became the standard equipment of the Services until it was superseded by the electric and wireless telegraph, was a semaphore arrangement consisting of two masts with movable arms which could be set at any angle. Hardly less important, though simpler, was Knight Spencer's "anthropo-telegraph", the antecedent of the ordinary hand semaphore system on which the army and navy relied until quite recently, for which Spencer was awarded a silver medal in 1809.

But the Society's greatest contribution to the subject of telegraphy during its first century was in connection with the submarine electric cable. Through one of its corresponding members, Dr. Montgomerie of Singapore, the Society was the first to obtain and disseminate information about gutta-percha in this country, and at its meeting on March 19, 1845, when the properties of gutta-percha were being demonstrated, Michael Faraday remarked to William Siemens that this substance, being impervious to water, might be a useful insulator. This observation led before long to its being used to make the submarine cable possible.

3

The Society's activities on behalf of maritime transport were a good deal more numerous and substantial than its efforts for land transport. They began in 1757 when the Society first offered a prize for a preparation to prevent the destruction of the timbers of ships' bottoms by worms. The importance which the

Society attached to this object may be seen from the fact that the offer was increased by stages from the original £50 to £200; and by the care with which the entries were investigated. The timbers submitted to the Society were not just submerged in some convenient backwater of the Thames estuary. Arrangements were made for them to be sent for a prolonged test, against untreated controls, at such widely separated places as Chatham, Southwold, Ostend, Kingston (Jamaica), St. Kitts and North Carolina, where the waters were known to be infested with worm. Several compositions were tried out and a good deal of useful work was done, but unfortunately it proved impracticable to exercise an adequate control over the more distant experiments, and in the end no award was actually made.

In the year after the Society had begun to try to stop this serious wastage of ships' hulls, G. F. Tuffnell directed attention to the question of their shape and proposed that the Society should offer a prize for a "model of a ships' bottom which may soonest pass through a given space of water drawn by a given weight". This proposal was strongly supported by Sir George Savile, and later in the year it was announced that awards were offered for "ship's blocks", i.e. what we should call scale models of ships, the purpose being to "ascertain by experiments the principles on which a good vessel is founded . . . passing through the water with least resistance seeming to be the first quality necessary". The other quality under investigation was "stiffness", or resistance to rolling, it being assumed very naturally that stiffness was a good quality in a hull, although this view has been qualified a good deal in modern times.

It was not until 1761 that there was a "field" (to use a landsman's metaphor) for these prizes, but by then four models of 32-gun frigates and two of 74-gun ships had been submitted, and the Society therefore had to make preparations for testing them. A member of the mechanics committee named Joseph Gardiner invented the necessary apparatus. For the stream-lining test two "engines" were to be used, actuated by two equal weights, which by means of simple systems of two barrels[1] would convert

[1] Described in the minutes as "a compound of two axes in peritrochio".

this motive power into long-distance pulls of proportionate force. The "stiffness" apparatus, called "the Society's instrument of Ship balance", enabled the committee to measure the weight required to cause the blocks to heel over to an angle of 20 degrees, and for this test the blocks were fully rigged, at the Society's expense. A third piece of apparatus,[1] also for the streamlining

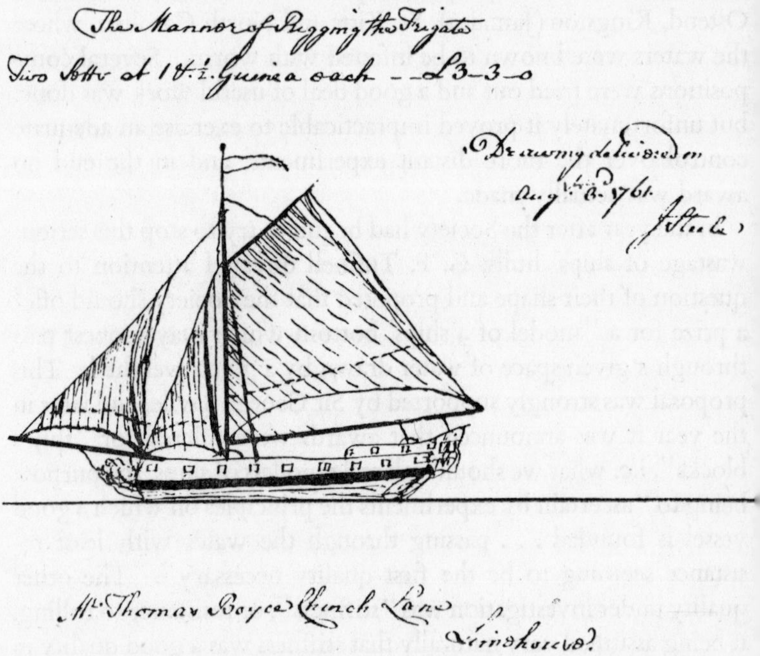

FIG. 4. MODEL OF 32-GUN FRIGATE, FULLY RIGGED FOR "STIFFNESS" TRIAL
Sketch from the Society's minutes

test, was devised by the committee and made by William Bailey at a cost of nearly £90 to the Society. It consisted of a 12-foot trough in which the resistance of the blocks could be measured by forcing water past them instead of by forcing them through the water: it was, in fact, the water equivalent of a wind tunnel, a device used at the present time by American ship designers.

[1] Fully described, with a drawing, in the Minutes of the mechanics committee, July 27, 1761.

The preparation of the apparatus took over a year, and the committee were not ready for the first trial until September 16, 1762. It was held on the sheltered waters of the 262-foot long fishpond at Peerless Pond, near Old Street, in the City, where every effort had been made to secure undisturbed and accurate trial. Both ends of the pond had been railed off to protect those who officiated from interference by sightseers, and a committee room was provided close by where proper records could be kept and disputed decisions threshed out in private. As there were only two "barrel engines", only two blocks could race at a time, and to ensure perfect fairness each block made two runs with each "engine", so that there was a pretty full day's sport. But there was more to follow. Next week the "stiffness" trials were held at the Society's House, and then arrangements had to be made for rough-water trials on Snaresbrook Great Pond, Epping Forest. Here there was a slightly longer run (105 yards) and greater wind resistance, but otherwise everything was much as it had been at Peerless Pond—except for the weather. Twice the committee made the journey out to Snaresbrook and settled the preliminary details in their committee room at the Spread Eagle, and then on going down to the pond, found that conditions had become unsuitable. However, two further efforts were successful and the trials were finally completed on November 6th in the presence of twenty members of the committee. After that it was quite understandably decided to dispense with any further tests on William Bailey's tank, and to make the awards, which were £100 for the better of the two 74-gun ships, £60 for the best frigate and £20 for the runner-up.

Next year some challengers made their appearance, and a further series of trials was held on the same lines as in 1762. But the original winners held their own, and after that no further prizes were offered for competition, and the contests terminated.

Unfortunately, these painstaking tests proved largely abortive as they were so far ahead of their time that the information which they brought to light could not at that stage in the science of ship building be converted accurately into modifications in the shape of full-scale ships. It will be agreed, however, that as a piece of experimental work they were highly creditable to the Society, as they not only elaborated what was for many decades the standard, and indeed the only, method of testing resistance to water—by weights—but also introduced what is now the most up-to-date, a method of doing so by water-resistance. Nearly seventy years later the large silver medal was awarded to Sir John Robison, Secretary of the Royal Society of Edinburgh, for a new method of performing the same kind of tests by towing the models from a bar extended in front of a canal steamer and observing the tension on the towing cords. By these means Robison made important discoveries as to the form which mechanically propelled canal boats (which were then, of course, just coming into use) should take.

Among the more immediately practical of the objects for which the Society made awards in connection with shipbuilding may be mentioned machines for driving and extracting bolts (regarding which the Society complained in 1801, after it had made several awards, of "the prejudice which workmen have in general for old modes of practice, however ineffectual and absurd"), the use of iron for "attaching the end of the beams of ships to their sides", an important development for which T. Roberts was awarded a medal in 1808, the suspension of ships in dock, for which the gold medal was awarded to the famous naval architect [Sir] Robert Seppings in 1804, and improvements in the propulsion of steamboats, for which a silver medal was awarded to John Dickson in 1816.

A good many awards were also offered, and more were made, for improvements in navigational instruments such as chronometers, telescopes, quadrants, sextants and compasses, for ships' pumps, for methods of preserving food and keeping water sweet on board ship, for improved port equipment such as cranes and capstans, and for new methods of clearing navigable channels (an award was made, for example, in 1804 for improving Rye Harbour).

In keeping with its general humanitarianism, the Society paid particular attention to life-saving and quite early on we find it considering devices which became very familiar in the hazards of the recent war. In 1763 two eighteenth-century equivalents of the "Mae West" were examined, a cork life-saving jacket designed by a Dr. Wilkinson and selling at 5s., and a more expensive inflatable leather affair designed by a Mr. Cobb. Both of these were approved and the Society was so impressed by the cheaper one that it advertised it in the newspapers and urged the Admiralty to adopt its use. Then, as already mentioned, a silver medal was awarded to William Shipley for a lighted buoy which could be thrown into the water to people who had fallen overboard and is reminiscent of the red lights which were issued to wartime seafarers of more recent days. This simple idea of Shipley's, which was first mentioned in the Minutes soon after the foundation of the Society, was again revived by the Society during the Napoleonic Wars by an article in the *Transactions*.

But the two outstanding life-saving devices which were recognised by the Society's awards were Greathead's lifeboat,[1] the first practical craft of its kind, the importance of which was marked by the award of a gold medal and 50 guineas in 1802, and Captain Manby's mortar apparatus for throwing a line from the shore to a stranded ship. The latter, which was invented in 1807, and awarded a gold medal the next year, subsequently came into general use along the coast, until it was superseded by the rocket. The Society also made awards for the same idea in the reverse direction, i.e. the throwing of a line from ship to shore. The first of these was a bounty of 50 guineas awarded to John Bell in 1792 for the use for this purpose of a shell from a mortar, and in 1820 the large silver medal and 30 guineas were awarded to H. Trengrouse for his use of rocket apparatus for the same purpose. Trengrouse was inspired to follow the line of research which led to his invention, and ultimately to the saving of many thousands of lives, by witnessing the drowning of hundreds of sailors from H.M.S. *Anson* on the shores of his native Cornwall in 1807.

The naval operations of the Napoleonic Wars naturally increased the Society's interest in these matters and in ideas for saving ships as well as lives, such as jury masts, temporary rudders and other salvage devices. Its interest in naval affairs even ex-

[1] See plate 18.

tended to ships' armaments, for which a very considerable number of awards were made. For example, the large silver medal was awarded to Captain Bagnold in 1812, for a gun and gun-carriage which could "by a discharge of 144 musket balls at every fire, clear away the men in the enemy's rigging in the close action". Such an award was quite understandable in wartime, and particularly, as the Preface to the *Transactions* points out, soon after "the loss of the great and gallant Lord Nelson", who was, of course, shot by a marksman in the enemy's rigging. But to read of the Society making an important award in the peaceful year 1831 for "a method of concentrating a ship's broadside, which is likely to shorten the time of naval actions and to render them more decisive", is certainly a little surprising, although it illustrates the breadth of the Society's interests, and emphasises the importance to the continuance of commerce, one of the Society's avowed objects, of the efficiency and well-being of the British navy.

Such thoughts may well lead us on to the consideration of the extension of the Society's influence and work overseas.

CHAPTER 9

Relations with the Colonies and Foreign Countries

1

It is hardly to be expected that an institution whose interests are so nearly universal in subject as those of the Society of Arts, and which is concerned, as we have seen, with the welfare of all classes of society, should restrict its activities within the confines of a single country, particularly as among its earliest members were scientists and traders whose outlook was inevitably international. It became the Society's practice, therefore, whenever it took up a subject to which it attached particular importance, to make inquiries about the progress which had been made in the same field in other countries, and in this way friendly contacts were made with important bodies and distinguished individuals overseas.

The system of electing honorary corresponding members, which was very early adopted, confirmed these relationships. The first to be so appointed was Dr. Pocock, Archdeacon of Dublin and a member of the Dublin Society, who was elected on March 12, 1755, at his own request, and in the course of a few years appointments were made in Russia, Germany, Sweden, Switzerland, France and Italy, as well as a number of British overseas possessions. Through these various connections, and on account of the store of information on a wide diversity of subjects which the Society rapidly accumulated, it soon acquired an international status itself, not only as a useful and friendly source of knowledge, but still more as a new type of institution peculiarly well suited to the practical needs of the time. It was even mentioned in the Dutch press some months before it was founded, for the

Amsterdam Gazette for January 4, 1754, contained the following paragraph:

> Several noblemen and others, being animated with the same zeal for the interest of their country, have concluded to establish a Society, the chief object of which will be to encourage those arts and sciences which are of the greatest consequence to the nation.

The Society's reputation abroad was greatly enhanced by the formation in foreign countries of national and local societies for the promotion of the practical arts, consciously based on the one in London. Among such may be mentioned the Patriotische Gesellschaft established in Hamburg in 1763 and still an active body, whose founder, in letters preserved by the Royal Society of Arts, acknowledged that society as "mother" of his own; the Free Oeconomical Society at St. Petersburg, founded in 1766 through the influence of the Empress Catherine after she had read of the London Society's activities in the English newspapers; and the Société pour l'encouragement de l'industrie nationale, founded by Napoleon in 1801 likewise on the London model, and still an important organisation.

2

But although the Society's relations with foreign nationals and foreign institutions were friendly and at times even parental, and although its sharing of knowledge with them was freely made in accordance with the usage of science, its ultimate objects were national rather than international. Indeed, in many respects they were essentially *not* international, for one of the chief motives underlying the choice of subjects for premiums, at any rate in the earlier years, was the building up of British industries in order to reduce imports—and therefore at the cost of foreign industry. The Society was also anxious, as we have seen, to assist in every appropriate way the defence of this country in war.

But there was one direction in which the Society could extend its activities beyond the limits of Great Britain and yet in a wholly patriotic manner. That was in the development of the British colonies, and as early as the third meeting of the Society, held less than a month after its foundation, a proposal was made "for extending the premiums to raw silk produced in our plantations". This proposal was implemented within a year, an offer for planting mulberry trees in the American colonies being included in the second list of premiums, published by the Society in 1755, and within a few years offers of awards relating to colonial development formed a separate section of the annual list.

Besides its offer and award of premiums the Society very soon began to do a great deal for the colonies by supplying information. Its archives contain many letters from colonial officials and others, putting forward problems which it was in a unique position to answer because of its peculiarly representative membership, including as it did distinguished botanists and chemists, and traders with a wide experience of the various markets of Europe. These diverse sources of information enabled the Society to gain a balanced view of the many problems which were put to it, the value of which is brought out by a letter it received from Dr. Dancer of Jamaica in 1792 in which he wrote, "It gives me sensible pleasure to find the opinion of the Society respecting our cinnamon confirmed by commercial gentlemen engaged in that branch of trade: this will have more influence in the minds of people in the colony, in exerting their attention to so important an object, than the decision of men of science to which they pay little deference."

Besides supplying the colonies with information the Society rendered them a valuable service—and to an increasing extent, as time went on—by supplying them with customers. This it did by publicising the products which the colonies could supply. Not only were many of the written communications received from the colonies published in the *Transactions*, but the specimens of colonial produce which accompanied many of them were placed on permanent exhibition in the Repository. Once this practice became established, many articles were sent from overseas specifically for the purpose of inclusion in this collection, and thus for a long time the Society's rooms fulfilled the function for which the Imperial Institute Galleries were formed many years later.

3

But the Society's main work in the colonies, as at home, was to carry out its premium system, and special difficulties arose in applying it to remote places overseas. There were administrative difficulties to begin with. It was no easy task, even at home, to conduct the competitions and make the awards entirely satisfactorily and free from any possibility of fraud. How much more was this the case when the competitors were all overseas!

The first arrangement was to appoint local agents in the colonies to make awards on the spot and actually hand over the prizes; but this soon proved impracticable, and the Society then had to fall back upon the same system of certification as at home. Unfortunately, as the committee of colonies and trade observed in a frank and penetrating report compiled early in 1762, "the manifest lack of precision in the method prescribed for ascertaining the claims . . . not a little contributed to render the premiums ineffectual". On the one hand, the Society, in ignorance of colonial conditions, required in many cases certification by the Governor, who by his very office was prevented from having first-hand knowledge of the circumstances he was to certify; alternatively, it offered vaguely to accept "some other attestation to the satisfaction of the Society". "This", the report goes on, "your Committee humbly apprehend does materially operate to render the premiums ineffectual, and the case speaks so strongly for itself and the impropriety is so glaring that your committee are unwilling to make any comment upon it"! Needless to say, so wise a body as the Society of Arts was ready to learn its lesson, and a practical system of certification by local officials, comparable with that in use at home, was duly instituted.

A more difficult problem in connection with these overseas premiums was the choice of the objects for which they were to be offered, for these offers, to be effective, had to be based on a sound and broad knowledge, not only of what was physically possible in the differing circumstances of the various colonies but also of what it was economically prudent to encourage. Such a decision was no easy task in the case of places so far distant. How was the Society to know, for example, what products most needed to be encouraged in the backwoods of North America or the newly conquered territories of the East India Company? The ground-nuts fiasco in East Africa during the nineteen-forties has shown how easy it is, even to-day, for knowledgeable and intelligent people to make grievous mistakes about colonial productive activities through lack of a complete understanding of all the local factors. Similarly, to take one out of numerous examples in the Society's experience, much of its work in introducing new crops into the West Indies was wasted, not because the crops were un-suitable for that part of the world, but, as the Society was warned in 1807 by Dr. Alexander Anderson, superintendent of the Botanical Gardens at St. Vincent, for the opposite reason that the planters feared that by their very success they would imperil the staple industry of the islands, the cultivation of sugar.

The Society therefore came to depend very considerably in its work for the colonies upon the information and advice of corre-sponding members residing and holding established positions there, and it was very fortunate in the men who were willing to collaborate with it in this way. The first colonial corresponding member to be appointed was Dr. Garden of South Carolina, a well-known botanist after whom the gardenia is named. Garden was proposed by the Secretary and elected on March 19, 1755, and he immediately began a frequent and detailed correspondence with the Society. In the following autumn Benjamin Franklin wrote to say he would like to be admitted as a corresponding member, and sent a gift of 20 guineas, the equivalent of a life composition, although, as he knew, no subscription was expected from those so elected. Franklin, indeed, was for a period able to do more than correspond, and during his temporary residence in this country he participated actively in the affairs of the Society and served as chairman of the committee of colonies and trade for some time. The first meeting at which he was present was on September 7, 1757, when the American generosity which attended his application for membership again showed itself, for he brought with him a letter from John Hughes, a merchant of Philadelphia, with the following message: "I herewith put into your hands

32 dollars, which I desire you will present to the Society you mentioned to me some time ago and be pleased to let them know I commit it to their direction to be laid out either for the good of Great Britain or America as they think proper." Another very active corresponding member in the American colonies was Mr. Carter, of Virginia, who was awarded a gold medal in 1763 "for care and industry to promote in Virginia the purposes of this Society in the British colonies".

As soon as it became the practice to establish botanical gardens in the colonies, primarily for the purpose of experimentation with new crops, the directors of these institutions were obviously suitable men to collaborate with the Society, some of them being very distinguished botanical scientists. Among them may be mentioned Dr. George Young and Dr. Alexander Anderson (referred to above) at St. Vincent, Dr. Dancer in Jamaica, Dr. William Roxburgh and his successor Dr. N. Wallich at Calcutta, and Dr. William Montgomerie at Singapore. It was through the last named, it will be remembered, that the Society can claim the credit of being the first to make the potentialities of gutta-percha known in this country.

Besides receiving the advice of these colonial scientists the Society was often assisted by colonial governors and other high officials, some of whom were members of the Society and many of whom were ready to use their influence in support of its efforts, while another fruitful source of information was found in local societies with kindred aims, such as a society at New York with which intimate relations were established in 1765.

In general, the function of these various consultants was to advise on proposals submitted to them by the Society rather than themselves to initiate proposals for action by the Society. Some of them, indeed, did take it upon themselves to make suggestions for premiums, but most of the proposals which resulted in actual prizes being offered originated within the Society. This is an important point, for it must be emphasised that, generally speaking, the Society's colonial activities were definitely Anglo-centric. This is not to say that the Society ever encouraged a selfish exploitation of the colonies: it often quite genuinely stressed that what it attempted to do was for the mutual benefit of the colonies and the mother country. But in almost every case the initiating motive was the desire to foster the supply from the colonies of raw materials and food-stuffs for which the United Kingdom was dependent on foreign countries. As the committee of colonies and trade put it in their report, referred to above, "the importation into this Kingdom of those articles for which premiums are offered is the primary object". Normally, therefore, the Society's premiums were offered for the actual importation into England of substantial quantities of the commodities concerned. In the case of entirely new crops, however, the Society had, naturally, to be content with rewarding the mere production of small quantities, or even simply the establishment of new plantations. There were exceptions to this principle, notably the offers made for the transplanting to the West Indies of the bread-fruit tree,[1] the produce of which was perishable and could only be consumed in the country where it was grown. But generally speaking the ideas for colonial premiums sprang from a perusal of the Board of Trade lists of imports into this country rather than from proposals by colonists of what would benefit their colonies.

4

We may now turn to consider these premiums in detail, and as their purpose was to foster specific products required in the home market, it will be convenient to conduct our survey on similar lines, rather than geographically.

The first offer actually made by the Society for a colonial object was, as has already been mentioned, for the production of silk. The original proposal, made in 1754, was not immediately followed up, but in April, 1755, Lord Romney produced to the Society a report from thirty-nine traders on a consignment of raw silk just received from Georgia, which said that the silk was of excellent quality and "well adapted to the weaver's use in most branches". No better commendation could be desired, and the Society at once decided to encourage this promising industry. At

[1] See pp. 165 f.

first it took the indirect course of offering prizes for the planting of mulberry trees, but after two years, on the advice of its agents, it changed to the more direct but far costlier method of offering a subsidy on the actual silk produced. The bounty amounted to threepence, twopence or a penny per pound of cocoons, according to quality, and in the course of a few years, during which it was extended to Pennsylvania and Connecticut, the scheme involved the Society in a total expenditure of nearly £1,400, representing about 12,000 lb. of raw silk.[1] Besides demonstrating the generosity of the Society, this effort throws an interesting light on its broad social sympathies, for one of its professed motives in adopting the subsidy was to give an equal opportunity to everyone, rich and poor, aboriginal Indians and white settlers,[2] alike, as every pound of cocoons brought to the appointed agents qualified for benefit.

The Society was not alone in its efforts to establish silk culture in America. The Government also granted a subsidy, and established a Public Filature at Savannah which it put in charge of Mr. Otolonghé, one of the Society's agents. Yet in spite of all this assistance the industry never stood on its own feet. The truth is that, as we have already seen, silk culture has normally had to depend on bounties in any of the western countries in which it has been attempted or established, and after the Government and the Society had withdrawn their subsidies the Americans themselves continued them for many decades.[3]

After the cessation of its efforts in the American colonies the Society made a few awards to silk producers in other parts of the Empire—in Minorca, during its British occupation in the seventeen-seventies, and in Malta and Mauritius, shortly after their acquisition in the Napoleonic Wars. A gold medal was also awarded in 1796 to Robert Wissett of the East India Company for having introduced into this country the throwing of Bengal silk.

[1] *Transactions*, I, 24.

[2] Minutes of the Society, March 8, 1755.

[3] It is interesting to find Benjamin Franklin, who presumably persuaded the Society to extend its scheme to Pennsylvania, occupied just before the War of Independence in establishing a Public Filature at Philadelphia.

But by contrast with its American efforts, these activities of the Society were spasmodic and ineffective.

A few years after the Society had begun to foster the production of silk in America, the stern necessities of war turned its attention to the much more utilitarian fibre of hemp, and in 1761, the year before it put forward its elaborate scheme for the production of hemp at home, it began to offer premiums for its importation from America. At that time the Americans had neither the labour nor the skill required for harvesting the crop, and the offer was withdrawn after a few years. But forty years later, when the Napoleonic Wars created the same urgent demand for the material, the Society renewed its attempt, and succeeded in establishing the culture of hemp as an important industry in Canada. Thus, in a small way, it had a share, however indirect, in the victory of Trafalgar.

The effort began in 1801, when two separate gold medals were offered in Upper and Lower Canada respectively: one for cultivating the greatest area with hemp and the other for importing the greatest quantity into England. The Canadians took to the idea at once, but were prevented from making an immediate start by lack of seed. However, the Government of the Lower Province voted a sum of £1,200 to assist the scheme, and with part of this grant a quantity of seed was purchased in the United States and distributed gratis to settlers who were willing to sow it, while the balance was used to enable the produce to be purchased by a Government-sponsored Hemp Society at an uneconomic price from the settlers. The whole thing was taken up with patriotic fervour, under the personal leadership of the two Lieutenant-Governors, and by the time that a number of awards had been made by the Society the crop was well established in the colony.

Another way in which the Society helped the movement was by encouraging the improvement of machinery for processing the fibre, which, as we have already seen, is the chief difficulty about hemp-growing. Four awards were made for this purpose, two to Canadians and two to British inventors.

Another rich source of hemp and hemp-like fibres is India, and the Society did a great deal to encourage their development there, though not so much by the award of premiums to the growers as by eliciting information for the benefit of potential users in the west. Several important reports on the subject were sent to the Society by Dr. Roxburgh and published in the *Transactions*, including detailed accounts of his experiments on the strength of a great number of eastern fibres. Among these fibres was "calooee hemp" or ramie, now important and well known, which was first introduced to the west by Roxburgh, and for the cultivation of which in Bengal a silver medal was awarded to Captain Cotton in 1815. The references to this plant in the *Transactions*[1] are probably the earliest accounts of it to be found in western literature.

The Society had little success with its offers of premiums for the cultivation of cotton, and it was not until 1820 that wool appeared in the list of colonial premiums; even then it was not so much to initiate as to crown a good work. In 1795, shortly after the occupation of the Cape of Good Hope by British forces, three or four merino sheep, which had been sent to the Cape from Spain as a gift to the Dutch governor, were transferred to New South Wales by Captain Kent, R.N., and disposed of by him to Captain (as he then was) John Macarthur. These few much-travelled animals were the foundation of one of the Empire's great industries. Carefully tended by Macarthur they increased, were added to by the importation of further merinos from George III's flock, and finally, by means of an annual sale established at Parramatta, became a source for populating various parts of the colony with a breed of animals which had by then been proved to thrive there, and indeed to do better in Australia than in Spain, their home.

In 1820, a year or two after the establishment of the Parramatta sale had begun to convert one man's hobby into a national industry, the Society began to offer a gold medal for the greatest quantity, and another for the finest sample, of fine wool imported from New South Wales, and two years later both medals were deservedly won by John Macarthur. The same year (1822) a silver medal was awarded to John Raine for introducing twenty

[1] *Transactions*, XXIV, 148, and XXXIII, 182.

Merino sheep into Tasmania (Van Diemen's Land), and in 1824 a third gold medal was awarded to John Macarthur and a silver medal to his nephew Hannibal for furthur importations into England.

The Society gave encouragement to Australian wool at the consuming as well as the producing end. A gold medal was awarded in 1822 to Messrs. Starkey, Buckley & Co., of Huddersfield, for manufacturing a piece of cloth from John Macarthur's wool, and two years later a medal was awarded for a similar reason to Messrs. Harris, Stephens & Co. Mr. Maclean, who submitted the latter claim, reported that "a gentleman who had a coat made of this cloth states that he has constantly worn it for two months and that it looks as well as it did the first day, although he has travelled some hundred miles in stage coaches". Truly a testimonial!

Another need of the home textile industry which the Society very early tried to supply from the colonies was dye-stuffs. Just as this need had induced the Society to take up the home cultivation of madder as one of its first and biggest projects, so the first additions, after silk, to the colonial list of premiums, were the two dye-stuffs, safflower (scarlet) and logwood, for both of which premiums were first offered in 1757. Logwood is a particularly important dark-blue and black dye, so useful, indeed, that it long survived the introduction of coal-tar and synthetic dyes. But apart from its special usefulness, an interesting historical circumstance underlay the Society's offer. The logwood tree is a native of Central America, and the forests of Honduras had been exploited by a settlement of British cutters since the seventeenth century. These men, however, came periodically into conflict with the Spaniards, and it was probably owing to a particularly bitter fight which took place in 1754 that the Society decided to encourage the planting of the tree in the islands, where it could be cut in safety. Dossie[1] strongly criticised this premium because, according to him, trees which had been planted in Jamaica before 1757 had become a serious nuisance, spreading like weeds but yielding very inferior dye. Judging from the lack of claims for the premiums,

[1] *Memoirs of Agriculture*, vol. I, p. 263.

Dossie need not have worried about the Society's action, and the offer was discontinued in 1765 because the position of the British settlers in Honduras had by that time been improved by a treaty with Spain, so that the chief reason for the premium no longer existed. Logwood did, however, become usefully established in the islands, and even in Jamaica it became, in spite of Dossie's condemnation, quite an important product for many years.

The year after the safflower and logwood offers were commenced, cochineal was added to the Society's list, and some years later the orange dye anatto and indigo, and these materials appeared in the list at intervals until well into the nineteenth century. The only awards actually made were the gold medals awarded in 1774 for the production of indigo in East Florida and in 1778 to John Robley for growing indigo in Tobago, but as with so many others of the Society's offers, the absence of awards must not be taken as an indication that they were without effect. In many cases, particularly where offers were long continued, it may be assumed that their publication induced people to try the crops although they may not have had the ambition to apply for the prizes.

5

The shortage of oil in Great Britain during the eighteenth century has already been referred to. This need was naturally in the Society's mind when it considered the potentialities of the colonies, and in 1758 it introduced a premium for the planting of olives in the American colonies south of the Delaware river. It was reasonable to suppose that somewhere in these territories conditions could be found similar to those of the Mediterranean home of the olive, and in response to the Society's offers a number of experiments were made. In 1763 Carter of Virginia sent over to the Society some olives produced in the colony, but these were pronounced to be "much less than the Lucca olives". Shortly afterwards we find the committee sending Carter for trial a box of Spanish olives presented to the Society by Jonathan Perrie; and another box to Governor Johnson, who was to "be desired . . . to try to cultivate them in West Florida". Dossie tells us the result:

the trees grew all right, but the yield of fruit was small and of poor quality. The Society's efforts were dropped, therefore, until the next century, when a premium was offered, but never awarded, for olive oil produced anywhere in the (by then far more extensive) British Empire.

Early in the nineteenth century the Society also became interested in coconut oil. This was on account of a report which it received in 1816 from Thomas Hoblyn, who claimed to have initiated the importation of this oil into this country from Ceylon. The Society gave Hoblyn a silver medal for starting this trade, and another the next year for an oil-press designed by him and manufactured by Messrs. Bramah. A few years later it offered further awards to those who would follow up Hoblyn's initiative by importing coconut oil from any part of the Empire.[1]

This offer had important results in Mauritius, where the Governor, Sir Galbraith Lowry Cole, who was a corresponding member of the Society, did his best to publicise it. A French planter, M. Barbé, successfully claimed a medal for exporting seventy-six tons of oil to England, and this award, and the encouragement of the Governor, resulted in the coconut, which was already being grown on a small scale in Mauritius, becoming recognised there as a great potential source of wealth, and being developed into one of the most important products of the island.

In the same year, 1758, in which the Society turned to the colonies to improve the national supply of oil, it also began to seek in them a much-needed source of an important industrial chemical, potash. Owing to failing supplies of wood in north-eastern Europe, this chemical was very difficult to obtain just at the time when increased supplies were becoming necessary to this country, for bleaching and other purposes, owing to the expansion of the textile industry. The obvious remedy was to encourage the manufacture of potash in the limitless forests of North America,

[1] The reason given for this offer is interesting in view of the development of coal-gas lighting just at that time. It was "to encourage the use of coconut oil for the purpose of illumination, such gas having been found much superior to those commonly in use".

and a certain Mr. Stevens, backed by the English Government, had gone out there in the previous decade to establish the industry. Stevens had devised a new method of manufacture which promised to make large-scale production possible, but unfortunately it proved to be so tricky in operation that in 1758, when the Society decided to support his efforts by offering premiums for the importation of potash in substantial quantities, his scheme was on the point of failing, and there was therefore little response to the offer.

At this point Robert Dossie came to the rescue. He persuaded the Society that the proper policy was to encourage as many colonists as possible to go in for small-scale production and, at the Society's request, he wrote an account of a simple method of home manufacture by which potash could be made even from the wood ashes of the domestic grate. This note was printed and circulated in the colony. The idea of manufacturing potash as a sideline at once appealed to the colonists, and in 1763 the Society abandoned its original offer for large-scale production and substituted for it a bounty of £4 per ton imported into London from North America, which it was within the reach of most colonial families to earn. There was an immediate response, and by 1768 Dossie could claim, in the first volume of his *Memoirs of Agriculture*, that English needs were now being fully met from America and that "an establishment of the manufacture of potash in America was wholly owing to the means used by the Society". Which was all the more a feather in the Society's (and Dossie's) cap as this success immediately followed the Government's failure. Certainly, Dossie well deserved the gold medal which he was awarded in 1766 "for effectually acting to establish the manufacture of potash in North America", and the Society could feel satisfied that the £900 which it granted in potash bounties was money well spent.

On the other hand, the Society's efforts to obtain the twin alkaline salt, sodium carbonate,[1] from America had no direct results, although they were ultimately successful in another direction. A premium for the production of barilla in any of the

[1] Called at that time "fossil (or mineral) fixed alkali", potash being "vegetable fixed alkali".

American colonies was offered in 1761 and continued for a good many years, while Dossie again obliged with a set of simple instructions for the preparation of the chemical; but the premium was never awarded. In 1774, therefore, the Society drew attention to the existence of deposits of sodium carbonate in the soil as a mineral, and began to offer premiums for the discovery anywhere in the United Kingdom or the American colonies and importation into London of "native fossil fixed alkali" or natron. In 1776, doubtless in view of the trouble with America, this offer was extended to the "East Indies" (i.e. the territories administered by the East India Company), and in 1785 a silver medal was awarded to Hellenus Scott, a surgeon in the East India Company's service, for the discovery of deposits of natron on the coast of Sind. These "pits" had long been known and exploited by the Indians, but Scott claimed to be the first to make them known in this country, and to have done so because his interest was attracted to them by the Society's offer.

6

Judged from the point of view of to-day, when we look largely to the Commonwealth to feed us, the Society did surprisingly little to develop food production in the colonies, but the reason was that in its earlier years the home country was more or less self-sufficient, at any rate in the basic articles of its diet. The only important exception was in the products of the vine, for which the climate of England was unsuitable, and two of these, wine and raisins, became the subject of offers in 1758 and 1759 respectively. Several colonists (including the worthy Mr. Carter) were induced by these offers to experiment with wine-growing, both with imported European and wild native types of grape, and a number of generous awards were made. But although the committee of colonies and trade was confident enough to record its opinion, on January 7, 1772, "that the production of wine in some parts of North America in considerable quantities is practicable, particularly from the native or wild grapes", the crop never established itself, and the offer for raisins appears to have had no effect at all.

A more practical line than the offering of premiums was

followed in the case of currants, in which the Society took a particular interest because, as it said in a letter[1] to Dr. Garden, "from these Corinths [sic] it is that sevl. of our national dishes are composed". In this case the Society actually obtained and sent out cuttings of the right type of vine, some of them given by the Duke of Argyle from his own garden, others specially obtained from their Mediterranean home on the islands of Zante and Cephalonia. What was the ultimate fate of these various cuttings is not recorded, but a letter from Dr. Garden the following July indicated that some, at any rate, had taken.

Many years later (1822), when great changes had overtaken the Empire, the Society began to offer premiums to encourage winegrowing in South Africa and Australia, and awards were made to Francis Collison at the Cape (1827) and to Gregory Blaxland at Parramatta (1823 and 1828). As viticulture was then in a purely experimental stage in Australia, and at the Cape had recently made a new start, after the British occupation, with new types of grape, these offers and awards undoubtedly helped to encourage the establishment of what are now very successful and important industries.

Spices, naturally, received a good deal of attention from the Society in connection with the colonies. It proposed as early as 1758 to establish the production of cinnamon in the British-occupied parts of Sumatra, but was dissuaded by the East India Company who feared that so valuable a product might entice the Dutch to raid the British plantations. Such are the interactions of politics and agriculture! Soon after this, the Seven Years' War brought to light the existence of cinnamon trees, apparently growing wild, in the French West Indies, and the Society therefore decided in 1760 to offer premiums for the planting of cinnamon trees in the neighbouring British islands. Several attempts were made in consequence of this offer to transplant trees from the French to the British islands, the most notable being those successfully made by Dr. Young to introduce the tree from Guadaloupe into St. Vincent.[2]

[1] Minutes of Colonies Committee, January 25, 1760.
[2] Dossie, *Memoirs of Agriculture*, vol. III, p. 198.

The Society also helped in various ways to establish cinnamon in Jamaica (where two young trees had been introduced in 1782 by Hinton East) by technical information supplied to Dr. Dancer[1] and by the premium instituted in 1790 for the importation of cinnamon into London from the British West Indies. The result of all this was, as Dr. Dancer informed the Society in 1792,[2] that "the attention paid by the Society to this interesting subject had the desired effect of awakening the public of the island to a sense of its importance", and already one planter, he reported, had put in 50,000 trees.

In 1775 the Society also decided to encourage the production of nutmegs in the West Indies, and in later years it offered premiums for mace, cloves, pepper and vanilla, in various parts of the Empire. A number of notable awards were made as a result of these offers, including a gold medal awarded in 1802 to Dr. Anderson for his work on cloves and cinnamon at St. Vincent, an award of 50 guineas in 1825 for a plantation of cloves in Trinidad, a gold medal in 1831 to David Lockhart, Botanical Gardener to the Government of Trinidad, for the cultivation of nutmegs in that island, and a gold medal to Dr. Montgomerie for the cultivation of nutmegs at Singapore (1842).

Reference has already been made to the Society's departure, in the case of bread-fruit, from its usual policy of fostering only those colonial products which were required in the home country. There are several claimants to the credit of being the first to suggest the transplantation of this tree to the West Indies. It may have been Captain Cook, and in 1772 Valentine Morris, Captain-General of St. Vincent, wrote a letter on the subject to Sir Joseph Banks. At some time prior to 1777 Mr. Ellis, an enthusiastic member of the Society's committee of colonies and trade, wrote a description of the tree and made suggestions as to where in the East Indies it might be most conveniently found and how it should be transplanted. It was, however, as the result of letters from an unknown correspondent that the Society, in 1777, decided to offer a prize for the successful completion of the operation, and copies of this offer, with Ellis's instructions, were distributed to all out-

[1] See p. 151. [2] *Transactions*, XI, 209.

going East Indiamen. How this prize was won by Captain Bligh, after the abortive attempt in the *Bounty*, is a matter of general history—and of the films—but the Society was not content with awarding a gold medal (in 1793) to Bligh.[1] When the initial transplantation was accomplished, it continued to offer prizes for the extension of bread-fruit cultivation in the West Indies, and a silver medal was awarded in 1799 to Samuel Mure of Jamaica and two gold medals (in 1802 and 1803) to Joseph Robley, President and Commander-in-Chief of Tobago, for their respective plantations, derived, of course, from the six hundred trees brought over by Bligh.

Having reviewed the various types of product which the Society endeavoured, with varying success, to foster in the colonies, one more general aspect of its work there remains for us to consider. This is the establishment of botanical gardens, in which it took a great interest. With some gardens, as we have seen, it maintained a close connection by appointing the director or superintendent an honorary corresponding member. The original purpose of these colonial gardens was not, of course, the delectation of the inhabitants with beautiful flowers and trees; they were intended for the very practical purpose of experiments with new crops. In the West Indies, in particular, where the line of agricultural development had for so long been the introduction of tropical plants from the East Indies, nurseries of this kind, under skilled supervision, were of the utmost importance.

The Society can claim not merely to have encouraged such gardens but to be the first to have publicly proposed their establishment,[2] for appended to its lists of premiums for 1760 and succeeding years was a declaration that if such gardens were established the Society would co-operate by offering premiums to encourage the general cultivation of crops which had been proved suitable by their means. As a result of this encouragement the

[1] Bligh's official report to the Society will be found in *Transactions*, XII, 305–17. An engraving of the *Bounty* is reproduced in plate 19 of this book.

[2] Only once did the Society actually offer a premium for this purpose. This was for establishing a garden in the Bahamas, but the premium of 100 guineas was offered from 1793 to 1802 without effect.

first botanical garden in America was established in St. Vincent in 1765 by General Melville, the Governor-General of the Windward Islands, who was a member of the Society, his agent being Dr. Young, an army surgeon, who became entirely responsible for the garden after the General's departure from the Caribbean. Inspired no doubt by Melville, Young made special efforts to raise plants, such as logwood, safflower and cinnamon, for which the Society had offered premiums, and in due course he became a corresponding member of the Society. Both men were rewarded in 1773 with gold medals, and Dossie published Young's report on the whole venture in his *Memoirs of Agriculture*.[1]

Considering how vast, changing and unknown a field of activity the colonies presented during this period to an organisation centred in the home country, it is remarkable how much the Society achieved there when it had so much to do at home at the same time and when "Colonies and Trade" naturally came at the end of the list of its varied activities.

In this brief account it has only been possible to record a fraction —the more successful fraction, of course—of the Society's many efforts overseas, but what is most to be praised is not so much the sum total of concrete achievement, although that was very considerable, as the fact that in a day when communications were so bad and such little interest was generally taken at home in the welfare of the colonies, the Society made so brave an effort to assist their development. It is clear that the circumstances and potentialities of every part of the Empire were brought constantly under review, and newly acquired possessions appeared so quickly in the list of premiums that it would be true to say of those days that, hand in hand with trade, the Society of Arts followed the flag.

[1] Vol. III, p. 196 ff.

CHAPTER 10

Men and Measures

1

IT is time, now that we have considered the various achievements of the Society during its first century in as much detail as our limits have allowed, to take up its domestic history at the point at which we left it in Chapter 2. What sort of men were the leaders and officials of the Society? How was its business carried on? And how far had the conduct of its affairs led to the Society's prosperity and stability?

We have noted how much the Society owed to its first three Presidents, Viscount Folkestone, Lord Romney and the Duke of Norfolk. It was equally fortunate in the two Presidents who followed them—the Duke of Sussex (1816–43) and Albert the Prince Consort (1843–61).

Augustus Frederick, Duke of Sussex, the sixth son of George III, was a liberal and progressive in politics, a freemason and a man of genial character with a real interest in art and science. It was not to be expected that he would play a large part in running the Society, but he never shirked the duties of his office. He enjoyed presiding on ceremonial occasions, and his amiability and dignity invariably made the best impression. We have already caught a pleasant glimpse of him in our third chapter, presenting a medal to the youthful Millais and patting him on the head in the friendliest manner.

The Duke of Sussex proposed Prince Albert as a member of the Society in June, 1840, and he was at once elected a life member. His fellow-sponsors were the Duke of Northumberland and Lord Radnor. When the Duke of Sussex died in April, 1843, Prince Albert was invited to succeed him as President. As he immediately signified his acceptance, he was duly elected on May 26, 1843, and entered on his memorable term of office (of which more will be said at the end of this chapter) by presiding at the annual distribution of awards in June.

The functions that in those days chiefly called for a presidential appearance were the annual distribution of premiums and the annual dinner. Originally the prize-giving was held in the Society's Great Room, but there was a period in the first half of the nineteenth century when it had become such an important social function, involving the presence of stewards, policemen and a military band, that it was necessary to arrange for accommodation elsewhere. Thus in 1816 the distribution was made in Freemason's Hall and in 1830 in the Argyll Rooms. From 1822 until 1829 either Drury Lane Theatre or the Haymarket Opera-House (now known as Her Majesty's Theatre) was used. During the eighteen-thirties the ceremony took place for four years in Exeter Hall and for three years at the Hanover Square Rooms. In 1839 the Society was compelled by lack of funds to bring the distribution back again to the Adelphi.

The Duke of Sussex was required to stand up to some preaching on these occasions, as well as to a good deal of eloquent flattery. The flowery language of the following quotations from one of the Society's scrapbooks may revive the elaborate courtesies of those days more vividly than a paragraph of description. Here, then, is Thomas Collett thanking the Duke of Sussex for a medal he received at the Opera House, Haymarket, on May 29, 1826, "for his improved Tagg Shears":

> In receiving this Token from the hand of your Royal Highness, Language cannot express the feelings of my Heart; Happy am I to see a Prince of Royal blood leave the Mansions of the noble and the Great, and condescend to mix with his fellow man, patronizing the Institutions of the Country, some of which are established for the rewarding of ingenious merit, and others for relieving the distress of mankind. You participate in the greatest felicity of an earthly nature that can be enjoyed here below, that of causing the sorrowful Heart to rejoice.
>
> If providence in its unerring wisdom should ever place you on the Throne of this Realm, you will have the pleasing satisfaction

of knowing that you not only reign over a People with the Sceptre of Power, but you will reign in their Hearts the object of their Love and Adoration.

O! Most noble Prince! think O! seriously think! the time will come, and shortly too, when all distinctions will cease, when we must meet in the presence of Him who is no respecter of Persons. Till then may the blessing of Him rest upon you:—Of Him, that is able to keep you from falling, and to present you faultless before His Glory with exceeding Joy. To the only wise God and our Saviour be all praise Glory Majesty and Dominion now and for ever more.

In the ode written for the annual dinner of the same year "by Mr. Logan" and "set to music by Mr. Barnett", patriotism is more conspicuous than piety:

> All hail to those whose aid hath thus combin'd
> To spread the seeds of Man's immortal mind;
> And watch where Science daringly explores
> The varied wealth of earth's unnumber'd stores:
> Or Art on wilder wing exulting strays
> To cull the scenes her mimic pow'r pourtrays.
> To those whose smiles dispel the doubt that shrouds
> The morn of genius 'neath a night of clouds;
> And bids her gathering radiance burst away,
> And kindle into glory's boundless day.
> All hail to him of England's royal tree
> Who deigns our Patron and our Friend to be;
> Fill high each glass, and drink, while echoes ring,
> The Patriot Offspring of a Patriot King.

These annual dinners were great affairs while they lasted, and the custom went on for many years. At the dinner held at the Crystal Palace in 1854, in celebration of the Society's centenary, 750 people sat down. In 1860 Disraeli was in the chair, and in 1862, when the dinner was held in one of the refreshment rooms of the 1862 Exhibition building, Mr. Gladstone presided. But this was the last dinner to be held, for the numbers of those attending had gradually fallen off. The Secretary's regulations of 1838 will indicate the high degree of organisation that the annual dinner required in its heyday, during the presidency of the Duke of

ussex, and may be read with some nostalgic melancholy in these
ess spacious times:

> RESOLVED, That the DINNER of the SOCIETY take place at Free-
> masons' Hall, in Great Queen Street, on Saturday, June 9, 1838.
>
> That the price of the Admission Tickets be 20s. each, to be had
> at the Society's Rooms, also at the Freemasons' Tavern—The
> Ticket includes Port, Sherry, Bucellas, and Moselle. It is to be
> understood that no other wines are to be allowed, unless ordered
> in writing by that Steward who sits opposite to, and attends to the
> wishes of His Royal Highness the President.
>
> That each Ticket be signed by the Secretary.
>
> That all Soda Water, or Spruce Beer, be paid for by the person
> ordering it.
>
> That no persons but the Stewards and Secretaries be admitted
> into the Dinner Room, previous to the Dinner being served up.
>
> That the Stewards confine themselves to one servant each.
>
> That no servant be admitted but those of the President, Vice-
> Presidents, Chairmen of Committees, Nobility, and Stewards.
>
> That a yard of White Ribbon be provided for each of the ad-
> mitted servants, to be given them by the Collector, on producing
> a Ticket with the name of his Master. Such ribbon to be worn on
> the left arm during the entertainment, to distinguish him from the
> Waiters.
>
> That no charge be made for servants' eating, and that each
> servant is to receive from the Collector 2s. 6d., to expend as such
> servant pleases, as no liquor furnished to them is to be charged in
> the Bill.
>
> That White Wands be provided for the Stewards, and delivered
> to them on the day of the Dinner. . . .
>
> That the Secretary wait on His Royal Highness the Duke of
> Sussex, the President, with a list of the Noblemen and Gentlemen
> proposed to be invited by the Stewards, and that his Royal High-
> ness be requested to signify to the Secretary such additions as his
> Royal Highness may be pleased to make to the list. . . .

The functions of the royal Presidents were necessarily limited to
state occasions and to informal but influential advice behind the
scenes, and the day-to-day control of the Society's affairs was in
the hands of a number of honorary office-bearers as well as paid
officials. At the end of the eighteenth century there were twelve
Vice-Presidents (later increased to twenty), nearly all great noblemen but including a few distinguished men who took a more

active part in the Society's affairs. The most effective authority, however, was in the hands of the eighteen chairmen of committees (many of whom also held the rank of Vice-President), two for each of the nine committees—the six premium committees (Arts, Agriculture, Manufactures, Mechanics, Chemistry, Colonies and Trade), and the three domestic committees (Accounts, Correspondence and Papers, and Miscellaneous Matters).

2

During this period the secretaryship passed through several hands. On the death in 1799 of Samuel More, who had held the office for thirty years, Charles Taylor was elected to succeed him in February, 1800. Taylor appears to have been a competent though by no means an eminent chemist, and he apparently made an efficient Secretary until his death in 1816.

Arthur Aikin, another chemist, who succeeded Taylor, was a man of more distinction. A son of Dr. John Aikin and a nephew of Mrs. Barbauld, he had been a founder of the Geological Society, established in 1807, and its honorary Secretary since 1811. In 1817, at the age of thirty-four, he became Secretary of the Society of Arts, and he held the office for twenty-three years. On his resignation in 1839 he was appointed chairman of the Society's Committee on Chemistry. He also became the first Treasurer and subsequently President of the Chemical Society, which was founded in 1841—largely through the efforts of himself and other members of the Society—at a meeting held in the Society's House.

Aikin's successor as Secretary, W. A. Graham, held office for no more than three years before giving place to Francis Whishaw, an engineer who was the author of a book on *The Railways of Great Britain and Ireland*. Whishaw was Secretary for two years only, but he is to be remembered for having sponsored the idea of holding exhibitions, first on a small scale in the Society's House and afterwards in the form of a national exhibition of industries. More will be said of his influential work in this connection in the next chapter.

John Scott Russell, F.R.S., who succeeded Whishaw in 1845

and held the secretaryship until 1850, was a man of remarkable scientific gifts who left his mark on his profession as a naval architect. While still young, he served as Professor of Natural Philosophy at Edinburgh. He advocated the ironclad man-of-war, built the *Great Eastern* steamship, and published books on shipbuilding. During his period as Secretary, the reconstruction of the Society, of which we shall soon come to speak, was completed, while his energy in helping the preparations for the 1851 Exhibition—to be discussed in the next chapter—led to his appointment as Secretary to the Royal Commission in 1850.

Scott Russell was succeeded in February, 1850, by another outstanding character in George Grove, who held the post for two years before leaving to become Secretary of the Crystal Palace on its establishment at Sydenham. Although qualified as an engineer, Grove's main interest, as he developed, lay in music, and he is best remembered as the editor of his famous *Dictionary of Music and Musicians* and as the first director of the Royal College of Music which succeeded the National Training School. Grove was the last Secretary to live during his term of office in the Society's House, as all the Secretaries had done since Templeman, and on his resignation the Secretary's apartments were added to the Society's offices.

The successor to Grove was Edward Solly, F.R.S., a distinguished chemist who had been an active member of the Council. He held office for a year only before giving place to Peter Le Neve Foster, who was Secretary from 1853 to 1879, and whose achievement and character will be best assessed in a later chapter.

Among the Assistant Secretaries of this period two may be selected for mention. Thomas Taylor, who was Assistant Secretary from 1799 to 1805, was an eccentric character known as the "Platonist", whose labours as a translator and exponent of the ancient philosophers earned him lengthy notice in the *Dictionary of National Biography*. Thomas Woodfall, who became Assistant Secretary in 1807, came of a family well known in Fleet Street. He was a son of the famous reporter "Memory" Woodfall, and nephew of Henry Sampson Woodfall, the printer of Junius's *Letters*, conductor of the *Public Advertiser*, and early member of the

Society of Arts. Thomas Woodfall held the post of Assistant Secretary for thirty-five years, from 1807 until 1842. He owned a printing business, and seems to have done some of the Society's printing.

But no account of the officials of the Society in the first century of its existence would be complete without some reference to the Registrars (whose title was originally spelt "Register"). We saw in Chapter 2 that there was a suspicion that this post was originally instituted to provide a comfortable job for William Shipley. The duties of the Registrar are duly listed in the Society's "Rules and Orders" of 1758, the first of them being "the Custody and Care of all Books, Papers, and other Things whatsoever belonging to the Society", but the office appears not to have been a strenuous one. It was held by Shipley from 1757 to 1760, and by E. G. Tuckwell from 1760 to 1766. Tuckwell was succeeded by William Bailey, the author of that excellent and useful work, already mentioned, whose full title reads: *The Advancement of Art, Manufactures, and Commerce, or Descriptions of the useful Machines and Models contained in the Repository of the Society*—a quarto volume published in 1772 with a collection of fine illustrations in folio. A second edition in two folio volumes was issued in 1782 by the author's son, A. M. Bailey, who succeeded to the office of Registrar on his father's death in 1773 and held it until 1779.

The next Registrar was that curiously interesting character George Cockings, who was associated with the Society as a loyal and respected servant from the date of his appointment as porter in 1765 until his death in 1802. Before he entered the Society's service he had held a small government appointment in Boston, America, and his authorship of certain inferior poems and dramas even procured him admittance to the *Dictionary of National Biography* under the very wide terms of reference allowed to compilers of the *D.N.B.*'s original volumes (many far more notable people than Cockings having been refused mention in the later supplements). Cockings was the author of one epic in particular that must be noted here, "Arts, Manufactures, and Commerce", written in 1766, "no doubt in the first flush of satisfaction at being appointed porter", as Trueman Wood observes. It is a rewarding quarry for students of bad verse and contains lines worthy of *The Stuffed Owl*. Two of these have already been quoted, on p. 112.

With the death of George Cockings in 1802, the office of Registrar fell into abeyance. It is not listed in the edition of the Society's "Rules and Orders" published in June of that year; but another office may be noticed as having virtually taken its place—that of Housekeeper. And the Housekeeper, a formidable lady, was none other than Cockings's daughter, Ann Birch Cockings, who held that office for forty-two years until her death in 1844. For some of the latter part of this period she was also styled Registrar and Librarian, but the title of Registrar does not appear thereafter in the Society's records.

Clearly the new office had been instituted to suit the special talents of this conscientious, masterful, but apparently somewhat truculent lady. Not only did she have charge of the effects of the Society, as her father had done, but she had "the direction of all the inferior servants", she was required to "keep an account of all stationary ware, printed books, coals, candles, and all other particulars sent in by tradesmen", and she was given £50 "to pay the servants, for cleaning the rooms and the furniture, and the boys that attend the meetings of the Society and committees."[1] Even this does not suggest the full scope of Miss Cockings's influence, for it is apparent that this strong-willed and quick-witted lady "during the later years of her life", as Trueman Wood put it, "practically ruled the Society". Her monument at Kensal Green records a "grateful remembrance of the perfect integrity and the constant and zealous diligence with which she performed the duties of her office".

These, then, were some of the paid officials of the Society during its first century, on the whole a wise and scholarly band, rich in the little mild eccentricities and touches of character that are becoming to antiquaries and philanthropists. It may be asked: how much were they paid? Even allowing for the decrease in the

[1] *Rules and Orders*, 1802, p. 11. It was for the paying rather than the cleaning of the boys that Miss Cockings was responsible, though she would have made a capable figure supervising the scrubbing beside the Society's official tub.

value of money, it was not—and could not be—very much. The "Register" in 1758 received £50 a year (and "an Apartment in the Society's House"); Miss Cockings got no more when she was Housekeeper. The Secretary's salary of £50 in 1758 had been increased by 1802 to £250, and the Assistant Secretary was then receiving £120 a year.

3

Despite what we have seen of the general competence of its officials and of the useful work achieved in the opening half of the nineteenth century, there is no doubt that the Society's influence and financial prosperity alike suffered a serious decline during this period, especially during Arthur Aikin's secretaryship from 1817 to 1839. The Society's revenues had been decreasing gradually for a long time. It was at its most prosperous in its first decade—in 1763 the record sum of £4,614 had been subscribed—but there had since been a gradual falling-off, until at the end of the century the income averaged no more than £2,000. An analysis made in 1803 showed that the annual receipts were then just balancing expenditure, with a small surplus. For the next twenty-five years income continued to fluctuate around the £2,000 mark, though it showed a tendency to fall below it. Then it began to drop more seriously. The account for the year ending June, 1837, revealed a total revenue of only £1,235—and a debt of nearly £300. The situation declined still further until a drastic reorganisation of the Society became essential to its survival.

There were various reasons for this unhappy crisis in the affairs of a body that had long been prosperous and successful, and True-man Wood in his *History* has listed several of them. The serious industrial depression that followed the end of the Napoleonic Wars must, as he pointed out, "have reacted on a Society whose main objects were industrial". Again, the Society in latter years had had to contend with the competition of many similar institutions in the sphere of the arts and sciences which were not in being when the Society was founded. But there was a more serious factor that directly involved the Society's objects and procedure—and therefore touched the very core of its existence. Enormous advances in industry had made obsolete the whole idea of encouraging industrial progress by the award of prizes. These prizes had been of great value in stimulating inventors at a time when help of some kind was of vital importance to their activity; but as industry itself became increasingly capable of rewarding its inventors, the distribution of prizes by the Society was being clearly shown to be ineffective. The pioneering days were past. The Society's energies had obviously to be diverted into a new channel.

Above and beyond all this lay the fact that the Society's constitution did not lend itself to the efficient conduct of its business. The Society lacked a council, a general committee of management, such as had been considered essential in all the younger societies with similar aims that had been established since 1754. The Society's affairs were debated in open meetings, which all members had the right to attend, and at which the numbers of those actually attending would be quite unpredictable. Hours were spent in wrangling over the elaborate "rules and orders". It is said that Lord Brougham, after visiting one meeting, was so appalled by the amount of time wasted in discussing procedure that he lost any interest he might have had in the Society's endeavours. If this is true, it was a blow to the Society of Arts, for, though Lord Brougham was a difficult man to deal with, the Society would doubtless have benefited from the energy which he devoted, instead, to the Society for the Diffusion of Useful Knowledge and the Social Science Association.

By 1841 the situation of the Society had become most serious. The committee of accounts then reported that it had practically used up all its available resources, that its revenue was insufficient to meet its expenditure, and that only about £400 was available from accumulated funds to meet future deficiencies. At this late hour a special committee was appointed, under the chairmanship of Thomas Webster, to consider the grave problem of the Society's future. At the end of the same year this committee produced a candid and far-seeing report outlining the measures that it considered necessary for the prosperity of the Society.

But reforms are not easily accepted in learned institutions that have established their own traditions. At a general meeting most of the proposals were rejected. Another committee was appointed, which in its turn presented proposals for drastic economies that would have killed the Society stone dead. When these proposals were seen to have increased rather than reduced the general feeling of insecurity and apprehension, Webster's committee was reappointed—and promptly prepared a second report almost identical with its first. This time the committee wisely submitted it immediately to the President, the Duke of Sussex, who warmly approved it and sent it to the general meeting with his blessing. As a result of this manœuvre, the report was adopted in April, 1843, the very month in which the Duke of Sussex died. It was his last but by no means his least service to the Society to have thus turned it firmly into the path of reform.

The outstanding improvement suggested by the Webster committee was one which we have already foreshadowed—namely, the appointment of a council or managing committee which should have full control of the Society's business. In December, 1845, new rules and regulations were passed establishing the Council—which was to consist of the chairmen of committees, together with a certain number of elected members—and laying down its powers. Substantially, the new body was the same in constitution and personnel as the existing committee of miscellaneous matters, which had for some time formed a select and influential inner circle and was the only committee which met in private. It now formally assumed the full responsibility for the Society's management.

4

It has been noted in an earlier chapter[1] that one of the first proposals made to the Society after its foundation was that it should apply for a charter for an Academy of Painting, Sculpture, etc. The proposal was not adopted, and, as everyone knows, the objects that it envisaged were later taken care of by the Royal Academy. The Society did not concern itself again with the question of a charter until 1843. Both in that year and in 1845 the committee of miscellaneous matters discussed the desirability of

[1] See p. 40.

applying for a Royal Charter, but nothing was done until the newly formed Council gave serious attention to the idea in February, 1846. A draft of the Charter was then submitted by the Society's honorary solicitor, William Tooke, and, after this had been passed, it was lodged in the Privy Council Office, together with a petition—both draft and petition having received the approval of the Prince Consort as President of the Society. In June, 1847, Tooke reported that the Charter had been granted, and that a sum of £400 would be required to pay the official charges and other expenses involved in obtaining it.

Strengthened by the acquisition of the Charter, and directed by the firm hand of the new Council, the Society now entered upon a new period of usefulness. The advantages of having a governing body were soon manifest. The committee of miscellaneous matters had been merged into the Council; eventually the six premium committees likewise disappeared; and the system was adopted of appointing *ad hoc* committees from time to time, as and when they were required. The swathes of red tape that had been strangling the Society for so many years were diligently cut away. One of the most important results of the appointment of the Council was that the ordinary meetings no longer had to occupy themselves with general business, which had led to much fruitless bickering in the past. Papers read to the Society, and discussions which followed them, now became the principal object of the meetings.

The change from a premium-giving to a paper-reading society had been foreshadowed for some time. Although the Society had undoubtedly fallen off during Arthur Aikin's secretaryship, it should not be inferred that he was in any way to blame for the decline. He had realised that a change in the Society's methods was overdue, and he himself complained, probably with justice, that he could never get his ideas properly supported by influential members. Indeed, it was Aikin who had seen, more clearly than anyone, that the best hope for the Society's future lay in its undertaking the dissemination of information about the industrial arts and sciences, and the publication of new discoveries and inventions of an industrial nature.

From 1829 onwards a series of lectures on manufactures had been given at the Society's House. This was Aikin's idea, and he delivered many of the lectures himself. He seems also to have envisaged the substitution of papers and discussions at the ordinary meetings for the mere consideration of inventions competing for prizes. Certainly it was in 1829, again, that a notice appeared in the *Transactions* inviting the submission of papers for reading and publication only. Soon these papers had become the most important contributions to the annual volume, and, with the reconstitution of the Society, the reading of papers gradually became its main function. Aikin richly deserved the testimonial and gold medal, the valuable microscope and the honour of life-membership, which were gratefully tendered to him as some recognition of his services. It was an unmerited misfortune that his term as Secretary should have coincided with the decline in the Society's fortunes, but his successors reaped the benefit of his foresight.

Mention must also be made of one unexpected benefit that accrued to the Society during his secretaryship, and might have given Conan Doyle the title for a Sherlock Holmes story, *The Strange Bequest*. Sometime in 1831 an unknown visitor appeared at the Society's House, put into Aikin's hand the will of one Dr. George Swiney, sealed up in an enclosure, and then immediately left. Aikin endeavoured to discover the doctor's address but without success. When he retired in 1839 he took legal advice as to what had better be done with the packet, and was advised to open it. He found inside it a note from Dr. Swiney to himself, asking him to take charge of his will. But the mysterious doctor could still not be traced. Aikin therefore handed the will to Tooke, as the Society's solicitor, who looked after it until January, 1844, when Aikin received a summons to attend at some lodgings in Camden Town where Dr. Swiney had recently died. On the will being read, it was found that Dr. Swiney had left £5,000 in Three Per Cent. Consols to the Society on condition that a sum of £100 contained in a silver cup of the same value should be awarded on every fifth anniversary of the testator's death as a prize to the author of the best published book on Jurisprudence.

It was a measure of the eccentricity of the doctor that he should

have chosen to discharge his bequest an institution that had no
particular connection with or interest in the law. He complicated
things still further by stipulating that the adjudicators should be
the members of the Society and the members of the Royal College
of Physicians, "with the wives of such of them as happen to be
married". This joint adjudication being quite impracticable, the
Society arranged with the College—as a mild gesture of compromise—that the award should be given alternately for Medical
and General Jurisprudence, and that on the occasions when it was
given for Medical Jurisprudence the College should be asked to
appoint the jury. The award is then formally made at a joint
meeting of representatives of the two bodies.

Dr. Swiney—an M.D. of Edinburgh—arranged rather a jolly
funeral for himself. He seems to have enjoyed an amiable weakness for the opposite sex, for his will stipulated that his coffin,
covered by a yellow velvet pall, should be followed by three girls
in gay dresses. These requirements were duly fulfilled, and the
procession attracted such a large crowd that there was some
difficulty in carrying out the burial at Pratt Street, Camden Town.

5

When the newly formed Council met for the first time at the
end of 1845, the Society was nearly bankrupt. A loan fund subscribed by members, and in particular a special loan of £1,000
from Henry Holiday, which was secured by a debenture, tided
over a difficult period. The Society then made such a spectacular
recovery that the balance-sheet for the year ending June, 1862,
showed a total of actual revenue of nearly £9,000 and a balance
of income over expenditure of more than £1,000. The prestige
accruing from the 1851 Exhibition, and the large influx of new
members resulting both from that exhibition and from the exhibition of 1862, were among the main reasons for the Society's
revival.

Of the part played by the Society in the organisation of these
and other exhibitions there will be much to say. Meanwhile,
some of the most prominent members of the Society during these

eventful years must be gratefully remembered. Chief among them was Henry Cole, Chairman of the Council in 1850 and 1852, who, Trueman Wood declared in his *History*, "ought to be looked on as the second founder of the Society". The Society had been rescued from the worst of its troubles by the time that Cole joined it in 1846, but from that moment his enterprise, energy and perseverance stimulated its proceedings and supplied much of the driving force that gave the Society a new importance in the land. An appropriate opportunity for considering Cole's life and character will be found in our next chapter, which will deal with the greatest single triumph of his career—the leading part that he played in conceiving and organising the Great Exhibition. Cole had, it must be admitted, the defects of his qualities—his judgment was sometimes at fault, he could be impatient and unscrupulous, and in matters of finance he was notoriously over-optimistic. But of his outstanding abilities there can equally be no question, nor of the gratitude and pride that the Society must take in his memory. He became in 1860 the director of the South Kensington Museum, which he had done so much to promote, and in 1875 was made K.C.B. for his public services. Cole died in 1882, aged seventy-three, and left behind him a characteristic autobiography.

With Cole must be remembered such outstanding members of the Society as C. Wentworth Dilke, Harry Chester, the Rev. Dr. James Booth, William Saunders, Colonel W. H. Sykes and Lord Ebrington, all of whom held office as Chairmen of the Council in the eighteen-fifties. Among the other members of the Council who were most assiduous in their attendance at meetings and most helpful in their contributions to the discussions, we may mention Dr. Lyon Playfair (afterwards Lord Playfair), the distinguished chemist; Richard Redgrave, R.A., and his brother Samuel, the art-historian; Robert Stephenson, the engineer; Sir Joseph Paxton, who designed the Crystal Palace; Joseph Hume, the Radical M.P.; and J. C. Macdonald, the manager of *The Times*.

But it was the President himself, Prince Albert, who stamped the proceedings of the Society most surely with the hall-mark of his own integrity for the greater part of twenty years. The Society was one of the first public institutions in his adopted country for which he worked, and at a time when he was mis-understood, and even actively disliked, by many Englishmen, he was accepted as a friend and valued at his true worth by his colleagues of the Society of Arts. For the Society obtained from him something far more than a benevolent patronage. From the moment that he assumed the presidency, in 1843, he impressed on the Society that the main object of its existence henceforth must be the application of science and art to industrial purposes; and the Society soon learned that it could expect from him, not merely a formal consideration of routine matters, but a quick and wise judgment on any important question that was submitted for his opinion. When he accepted the presidency, the Society's in-fluence was small; when he died, its prestige stood high. Not all the credit for this, by any means, belong to the Prince Consort, but that he deserves a large share of the credit is incontestable.

It is no wonder that, when he died in 1861, the Society wished to honour him to the limit of its resources. The subscription of £1,000 that the Council voted to the national memorial was a large sum for a small society to give. But in addition a special fund was raised to pay for the bust of Prince Albert, the portrait of him by Cope and the group of Queen Victoria and her children by Horsley, which are now in the Society's House. Yet another memorial—and perhaps the most appropriate of all—was the in-stitution in 1863 of the Albert Medal "for distinguished merit in promoting Arts, Manufactures and Commerce", which has been awarded, from that time to this, to a long succession of eminent men and women who have helped the advance of science and art for the good of mankind.[1] Appropriately enough, among its early recipients stands the name of Henry Cole. It is to his collabora-tion with Prince Albert in the Society's greatest triumph that we now turn.

[1] See Appendix B for list of recipients.

PART II

EXPOSITION AND EDUCATION

CHAPTER 11

Origination of the Great Exhibition

1

OUT of the thousand-and-one achievements of the Society which
are recorded in this book the present chapter is concerned with
only one, the Great Exhibition. Yet so full a treatment of a single
episode, or indeed, part of an episode—for the chapter is concerned
only with the earlier history of the exhibition—is not really out of
proportion, for the origination of the Great Exhibition of 1851 is
not only the Society's most famous enterprise, but also the most
far-reaching in its effects. It stands, too, at the opening of the
Society's second era, a public manifestation of the re-birth which
had taken place a few years before.

Although outstanding, this was not a mere chance effort unre-
lated to the general run of the Society's activity. Earlier chapters
have shown that the Society found in exhibitions one of the most
effective means for the "encouragement of arts, manufactures and
commerce". It used them first of all for the arts, and was responsible for the earliest organised exhibition of art in this country; it
used them next for industry and held the first industrial exhibition
in the world. But in fostering the "Great Exhibition of Industry
of All Nations" it not only gave encouragement to art and industry on a hitherto unheard-of scale, but also gave an enormous
fillip to the commerce of the whole world.

There was, however, no very direct connection between its
first pioneering of exhibitions in the seventeen-sixties and its
great effort eighty years later. During the intervening period art
exhibitions had been taken over by newer and more specialised
bodies and the Society's industrial exhibition had largely become
atrophied into a museum of dusty curiosities, while the exhibitions

which it continued to hold each year of the works of art, designs and machines for which its prizes had been awarded were quite informal and haphazard and reached only a very small circle.

Nor were there any industrial exhibitions of importance in this country outside the walls of the Society of Arts. It is true that a few progressively minded educationists gained the support of George IV for an annual industrial exhibition which they commenced to hold in 1828 in the Royal Mews in Trafalgar Square. But after a moderate success the first year this "National Repository", as it was called, steadily dwindled, and petered out in 1833, by which time it had shrunk to the dimensions of a small shop in Leicester Square.

Various foreign countries, on the other hand, were discovering that exhibitions, if held on a sufficiently big scale, could have widespread effects in disseminating new knowledge and stimulating progress. As a result of the obvious success of a series of great national exhibitions which the French government organised in Paris from 1798 onwards, many other countries of Europe and America began to hold national exhibitions, and at last, after fifty years, these events had their effect even upon this island.

The year 1844 witnessed two important exhibitions on the Continent, a French national exhibition in Paris and a Zollverein exhibition in Berlin, and these two displays set at least one Englishman thinking once more on the subject of an exhibition in England. This was Francis Whishaw, Secretary of the Society of Arts, who, towards the close of this year, took two preliminary steps towards establishing what he called a Grand Annual Exhibition of Manufactures. First of all, he offered from his own purse prizes amounting in all to £300 for various types of painting and "useful inventions", and he then arranged, under his own direction and at his own expense, a single evening's exhibition of pictures and mechanical inventions, which took place in the present Lecture Hall of the Society on December 6, 1844, and was attended by about one hundred and fifty people.

Whishaw thought it was a failure, but it so much interested some of the office-bearers of the Society that they asked him to repeat the experiment, at their expense. A second exhibition was accordingly held in the next month, and this succeeded a good deal better than the first. It was attended by eight hundred people, and it achieved Whishaw's immediate object, which was to set people talking about his idea of a Grand Annual Exhibition. The result was that the following May he persuaded his friend, W. F. Cooke, of electric telegraph fame, to propose formally to the committee of miscellaneous matters, that the Society should forthwith institute a national exhibition of industrial products. Cooke's proposal was well received, and after much discussion the following resolution was adopted at the next meeting, held on May 28, 1845:

That the experience of foreign countries has proved that great national advantages have been derived from the stimulus given to industrial skill by bringing the manufactures of different establishments into competition with each other, and by presenting Honorary rewards to those who have excelled in each department, cheapness of production and excellence of material, both in execution and durability, being assumed as the criteria of superiority. That by carrying out a similar principle in this country founded on the experience of the past, with more extensive views, still greater benefits may be anticipated.

That having regard to the objects promoted by the Society of Arts Manufactures and Commerce it would appear to be their peculiar province to attempt to carry out such an object in Great Britain, on a scale commensurate with the magnitude of the interests involved.

That immediate preparation be commenced for such a periodical Exhibition of Works of Industy, at which the producers shall be invited to display their various productions.

Now it so happened that, whether by accident or design (and it seems much more likely to have been by design), Cooke chose to put forward his proposal less than a fortnight before the annual visit of Prince Albert, as President, to present the Society's prizes, on which occasion it was customary, until a Council was instituted, for the Secretary to make a personal statement on the Society's progress. Whishaw made full use of this opportunity. He not only referred publicly in his address to the resolution adopted by the committee a few days before, but also spoke privately to the Prince afterwards on the same subject. It is hardly likely that Prince Albert, with his knowledge of Continental affairs, had not already considered the desirability of organising a large exhibition in this country, but his reply to Whishaw was a wise one. He "commanded me", said the Secretary in reporting the conversation to the committee, "so soon as the plan for carrying it into effect should be matured, to lay it before His Royal Highness". This instruction was a challenge to the Society to produce a practical plan, and was quoted throughout the years that followed as its authority for pursuing this great objective.

Meanwhile no time was lost in appointing a "National Exhibition Sub-Committee" and in getting down to the task. Funds were raised by way of loan or subscription, one of the most substantial offers, of £1,000, being made by Robert Stephenson, the famous engineer and son of George; the question of site was discussed, and with singular far-sightedness the committee were unanimous in thinking that the exhibition should be held in a temporary building in Hyde Park; finally, as it was realised that public opinion, and particularly that of manufacturers, was essential to the success of the project, a list was drawn up of places to be visited and canvassed.

Approaches were then made to a number of towns, but the result was most discouraging. To quote a report written in 1849 by John Scott Russell: "The public were indifferent—manufacturers lukewarm—some of the most eminent even hostile to the proposition. The Committee neither met with sufficient promise of support in money, sufficient public sympathy, nor sufficient co-operation among manufacturers, to see their way to success. The attempt was abandoned."

2

But only temporarily abandoned, for the ultimate objective was never given up, thanks largely to Scott Russell himself. His personality and character were not without their faults and in the future developments others played a more prominent part, but without his influence in the background at this time it is more than likely that this project, in which he took the keenest personal in-

18. GREATHEAD'S LIFEBOAT

Awarded a prize, 1802

19. CAPTAIN BLIGH LEAVING THE *Bounty*, 1789

Note the bread-fruit trees and other tropical plants at the stern of the ship

20. H.R.H. PRINCE ALBERT

President of the Society of Arts, 1843–61
From the obverse of the Albert Medal

21. PART OF THE MINUTES OF THE CONFERENCE ON JUNE 30, 1849,
when plans for the Great Exhibition were drawn up
Corrections are in the Prince Consort's own handwriting

terest, would never have come to fruition. It seems probable, for example, that it was he who initiated the new policy which the Society lost no time in adopting after this first setback. "The English people", he continued in his report, "were then very imperfectly acquainted with the value of such exhibitions—their influence on the character as well as the commerce of the nation. They required to be educated for this object, and education had to be provided." Accordingly, towards the end of 1845, it was decided to enlarge the prize competitions, which the Society had continued to hold annually since its foundation, by offering a number of special prizes—for which a fund was raised, and Scott Russell himself gave the nest-egg—for various industrial products embodying artistic design. The idea was that the competitions would provide material for small annual exhibitions which would prepare the way for the proposed national exhibition.

The entries for the first competition were so disappointing that for the moment a public exhibition was quite out of the question, and the organisers had to be content with merely displaying the few prize-winning entries on the day of the annual prize-giving, in accordance with custom. But the competition had one consequence of importance: it was the means of bringing into the Society Henry Cole, who was to share with the Prince Consort the chief credit for the Great Exhibition. Henry Cole was a typical product of the nineteenth century, a son of the rising middle class, industrious to a degree, versatile, cultured and (although a civil servant!) the embodiment of personal initiative and drive. At this time he was one of the assistant keepers at the Record Office (in the establishment of which he had played a considerable part), but his spare time was taken up with many other activities. He had already taken a leading place in the agitation for postal reform, had published the first Christmas card ever issued, and had for a number of years edited *Felix Summerly's Home Treasury*, a series of illustrated children's stories, and other publications. He was also an artist and a musician of some distinction, and the friend of many distinguished contemporaries, especially of Thackeray. His life and character could hardly be better summed up than by the quotation which appears on the title-page of his biography, *Fifty Years of Public Work*—"Whatsoever thy hand findeth to do, do it with thy might."

Cole's first known contact with the Society of Arts was when, at the end of 1845, he was consulted as to the subjects for which the special prizes should be offered, and becoming interested in this way in the competition, he decided to compete himself. Although possessing no previous experience, he specially designed a complete tea-set and entered it under his pen-name of "Felix Summerly". His tea-set was awarded a silver medal, and later that year he was persuaded by Scott Russell to join the Society. Besides introducing Cole to the Society the competition brought him into contact with the Prince himself, who inspected the tea-set at Buckingham Palace that summer, and finding it in accord with his views on design commissioned other goods from "Felix Summerly".[1] It is interesting also to note that Messrs. Minton, who had co-operated with Cole in the design of the tea-set, now put it into production, and sold it extremely well for many years (a few "F.S." pieces are still a stock pattern of the makers), while Cole himself, encouraged by his success, set up an organisation, rather like a present-day "design unit", which consisted of manufacturers, artists and designers, co-operating in the production of "Felix Summerly Art Manufactures" of various types.

For the Society, these developments were cheering first-fruits of its new movement for the improvement of design in manufactured goods, and it received a further encouragement from its great and far-seeing President, who received a deputation from the Society in June, 1846, and impressed upon them that this was the most important task to which the Society could set itself. "To wed mechanical skill with high art", he said, "is a task worthy of the Society of Arts and directly in the path of its duty." He therefore suggested to them further subjects in this field for which prizes might usefully be offered, and in accordance with his advice arrangements were made for a second competition in 1847. It was the entries received for this, together with the 1846 entries, which formed the nucleus for the Society's first "exhibition of

[1] Some pieces of this historic set are preserved at the Victoria and Albert Museum.

select specimens of British manufactures and decorative art", held during March, 1847, in the Great Room (now the Lecture Hall) of the Society's House. By themselves, the competitions did not provide sufficient material for an exhibition, and Cole and Scott Russell spent days in visiting manufacturers and persuading them to lend suitable articles. In the end, however, about two hundred pieces, some of them of purely historical interest, were got together.

The introduction to the catalogue of this first exhibition of industrial art summarises admirably the purposes of such an exhibition. After stressing its technical value to the designer and the manufacturer, it continues:

> It is a universal complaint among manufacturers that the taste for good Art does not exist in sufficient extent to reward them for the cost of producing superior works: that the public prefer the vulgar, the gaudy, the ugly even, to the beautiful and perfect. We are persuaded that if Artistic manufactures are not appreciated, it is because they are not widely enough known. We believe that when works of high merit, of British origin, are brought forward they will be fully appreciated and thoroughly enjoyed. We believe that this Exhibition, when thrown open gratuitously to all, will tend to improve the public taste.

But the object was to train, not to dictate to, the public taste. The introduction continued, therefore:

> The visitors of these objects will require not to glance at them merely but to study and examine and learn to appreciate them. These specimens are not all of the best, nor even all good, and the visitor must discriminate for himself. Let him praise in the right place, let him blame in the right place, and the object of our exhibition has been attained.

Some two hundred and fourteen objects are listed in the catalogue, covering such diverse fields of design as pottery and glass, cutlery, silversmithing, furniture, wall-papers and bookbinding, and it is interesting to note among the manufacturers several whose names are still well known, such as Wedgwood, Copeland, Minton, Longman, John Murray, James Powell (Whitefriars) and Osler.

In spite of its small size the exhibition was a great success, being visited by upwards of 20,000 people, and the Society, doubtless under the inspiration of Henry Cole, who was not long in exerting his influence, now felt that it was justified in seriously planning the national exhibition which, since 1845, had remained its ultimate goal. Henry Cole therefore drew up a new scheme. It was proposed that the Society of Arts should continue its series of annual exhibitions, that the contents of these should be circulated to the Government Schools of Design, the first of which had been established in 1840, and that selections from this material, together with special exhibits, should be formed into periodical national exhibitions. These larger exhibitions, like the annual exhibitions, would be organised by the Society of Arts, but held on a site, and, it was hoped, in a building, provided by the Government. Trafalgar Square was now suggested as the site.

Early in January, 1848, Cole had occasion to write to Prince Albert regarding some of his "art manufactures" and he took the opportunity to send him privately a copy of this plan and ask his advice. The Prince, evidently after most careful inquiries, informed Cole that it did not seem that the Government would give it any assistance—at any rate, for the present; but nothing daunted, Cole persuaded the Society to approach the Government direct. On March 12, 1848, a deputation waited on Mr. Labouchère, the President of the Board of Trade, who appeared to be warmly sympathetic, and a few weeks later the same deputation approached the Chief Commissioner of Public Works regarding a site. Here again they met with considerable success. The Commissioner would not agree to Trafalgar Square, but he offered to grant the use of the courtyard of Somerset House or some other site on Crown property. This promise was a very definite step forward, and accordingly the Society found an opportunity to announce it that summer when it published the particulars of its 1849 competition and exhibition.

But meanwhile the Society's second annual exhibition had been held from March 9 to April 30. The success of the first exhibition had evidently greatly impressed manufacturers, and in 1848 they were almost falling over one another to get in. Some seven hundred exhibits were shown, of which a considerable proportion were newly designed and produced, and the attendance of visitors reached a total of 73,000, an enormous figure for so small a building, although all its public rooms, and even the main staircase, were brought into use for the display of exhibits.

The demand for space at the third exhibition in 1849 was even larger, and, as the limits of accommodation in the Society's House had now been reached, it was necessary to limit the scope of the exhibition to a few special sections. Of these the most important was the display of gold- and silversmithing, exceeding in magnificence anything seen even in the French national exhibitions, and the loan by the Queen of a gilt centre-piece designed by Prince Albert himself[1] was taken by the Society as setting the seal of royal approval on the Society's enterprise. The exhibition was announced to last for seven weeks and was extended for an eighth, and during that period some 100,000 passed through it. Admission was by tickets signed by a member, or on payment of sixpence (reduced to twopence during Easter week for the special benefit of "artisans"), and there were two evening "promenades" which were rendered additionally notable by the electric lighting, especially hired for each occasion from the Electric Light Co.

With the opening of the 1849 display it was at last felt possible to announce a definite date for the national exhibition. Influenced probably by the French practice at that period, the Society's leaders decided that the British national exhibitions should also be quinquennial, which meant that, counting the first of the Society's annual exhibitions as the beginning of the cycle, the first national exhibition would fall in the fifth year, 1851. This date appears to have been first publicly mentioned in an address of Council incorporated in the exhibition catalogue that year. Taking advantage also of the enthusiasm of the public while the exhibition was on, signatures were invited from visitors to a petition to Parliament seeking formal support for the project and the grant of a building.

[1] See plate 23.

The presentation of this petition marked the end of a distinct stage in the story. The Society had by now fully succeeded in arousing the interest of the public and of manufacturers in the idea of industrial exhibitions, it had gained the general support of the Government for a national exhibition and their promise of a site, and it had even gone so far as to fix a date for it. All this had been achieved by the ordinary members of the Society without any open support from the President. But a stage had now been reached in the campaign which called for the active participation of the commander-in-chief. He had instructed his staff to work out a plan; he had watched while his subordinate commanders had successfully carried out the preliminary skirmishes for position, and had occasionally given them important advice on the details of these tactics. Now he must take over command in person.

The intervention of the Prince was accompanied by a great expansion in the objective. Hitherto the intention had been to establish a *national* exhibition, exactly on the model of those held in France; but the glory of 1851 is that it was the first *international* exhibition ever held, although it must be admitted that the French were the first to suggest such a display. Early in 1849, only a few months before the French national exhibition of that year was due to open, M. Buffet, the newly appointed Minister of Agriculture and Commerce, had sent a circular to all the French Chambers of Commerce advocating that other European nations should be invited to participate in the display. But French industrialists did not take kindly to the idea of competing with foreigners in an exhibition, and the attempt had to be abandoned. Thus, in June, 1849, an international exhibition was still a dream, and it remained for Prince Albert and the members of his Society to make that dream a reality.

The decision of the Prince which led to these great developments, like his original instruction to the Society to "mature a plan", was occasioned by a speech by the Secretary at the Annual Distribution of Prizes. Addressing the Society on June 14 in the presence of Prince Albert, Scott Russell concluded by referring, with the Prince's prior approval, to "the probability of a large National Exhibition of specimens of Manufactures and Art taking place in 1851". The definiteness of this pronouncement convinced the Prince that at last his Society had "matured their plan". On June 20, therefore, he sent for Scott Russell to explain to him at length the grounds for his statement; and he in turn confided his own views to Scott Russell. A few days later he summoned the historic conference at Buckingham Palace at which the Great Exhibition of Industry of All Nations 1851 was born.

Besides the Prince himself and Scott Russell, the three other members of the Society who attended this meeting, which took place on June 30, were Henry Cole, Francis Fuller, who had been a member of the original committee set up in 1845 to plan the national exhibition, and Thomas Cubitt,[1] the founder of the famous firm of builders. Now it happened that Cole had gone to Paris at the beginning of June with Digby Wyatt, another member of Council, who had been sent over by the Society to prepare a report on the Paris exhibition. While there they had learned of Buffet's proposal to make the Paris exhibition an international one and, inspired by this, they had discussed at great length the desirability of inviting foreign participation in the British exhibition. On his return to England and shortly before the Buckingham Palace conference, Cole had had an opportunity of reporting all this to the Prince. In his autobiography he says:

> In consequence of a letter received from Colonel Phipps [the Prince's Private Secretary] about the exact day of a meeting appointed by Prince Albert to discuss the exhibition of 1851, I called at Buckingham Palace [on the 29th]. He said that the Prince was at home and would like to see me. [At that moment the Prince came into the room] and entered fully into the ideas of the Exhibition so far as they had been developed. He thought the Exhibition should be a large one and suggested that a permanent building might be erected in Leicester Square. . . . I observed that there appeared to me to be an earlier question than the site, and I asked

---

[1] Not to be confused with (Sir) William Cubitt, the civil engineer later engaged on the erection of the Exhibition building, and Chairman of the Royal Commission Building Committee.

the Prince if he had considered if the Exhibition should be a National or an International Exhibition. . . . The Prince reflected for a minute and then said, "It must embrace foreign productions", to use his words, and added emphatically, "International, certainly." Upon which I said, "Do you think, Sir, Leicester Square would be large enough?" He replied, "Certainly not, for works of all nations. Where do you think it should be?" I answered, "In Hyde Park."

After some discussion of the possible appointment of a Royal Commission, the interview closed with the Prince asking Cole to find the most suitable site in Hyde Park and report it to the meeting next day.

Francis Fuller had also been to the Paris Exhibition, and returning on June 12 (two days before the Prince's visit to the Society) full of enthusiastic ideas, he happened at Southampton to meet Cubitt, who was an old friend of his and was at that time carrying out some alterations for the Prince at Osborne House. The two friends talked hard about exhibitions all the way to London, about the Paris exhibition and about the exhibition proposed for London which, Fuller excitedly told Cubitt, could far surpass the French one, and when they parted, Fuller urged Cubitt to report their conversation to the Prince. Cubitt did so, and, according to Fuller, influenced him considerably.

Thus, before the crucial interview on the 30th, the Prince had held personal discussions with three out of the four men whom he had summoned, and he had heard the views of the fourth. When, therefore, all five finally met, it was possible, as the Prince clearly intended, to take most of the vital decisions there and then, and he instructed Scott Russell to act as secretary and take formal minutes of the meeting. These Minutes, which were very substantially amended by the Prince in his own hand, are still in the possession of the Royal Society of Arts and form one of the most interesting and important manuscript records of the Exhibition.

Six fundamental issues were discussed at this meeting and "settled" (to use the excellent word of the Minutes). First of all the Prince raised the question of the kind of exhibits to be included, and "considered" that there should be four divisions, viz. raw materials, machinery, manufactured products and "sculpture and plastic art generally". It was next agreed that a temporary building would have to be used, and Somerset House, Leicester Square and other earlier suggestions for the site were all carefully discussed and ruled out. Finally, as a result of Henry Cole's speedy investigations, and under the Prince's prompting, it was agreed that "the vacant ground in Hyde Park on the South side, parallel with and between the Kensington drive and the ride commonly called Rotten Row, afforded advantages which few other places might be found to possess". Next to be settled was the scope of the exhibition, and on this vital point the Minute was almost wholly drafted by the Prince. It reads: "It was a question whether this Exhibition should be exclusively limited to British Industry. It was considered that, whilst it appears an error to fix any limitation to the productions of Machinery, Science and Taste, which are of no country, but belong, as a whole, to the civilised world, particular advantage to British Industry might be derived from placing it in fair competition with that of other nations."[1]

After this it was agreed that substantial prizes should be offered to induce manufacturers to produce for exhibition goods which might be risky as commercial propositions. (Here it is evident that the traditional method of the Society was being introduced.) Then it was "settled" that "the best mode of carrying out the execution of these plans would be by means of a Royal Commission, of which His Royal Highness would be at the head". Some suggestions were made regarding its composition and it was proposed that the executive committee should be formed of "some of the parties present who are members of the Society of Arts and have been active in originating and preparing for the execution of this plan". To follow out this decision it was agreed that a draft of the proposed Commission should be prepared and submitted privately to the Government "in order that no time be lost". Finally, the question of finance was discussed. It was realised that little if any help could be expected from the Government and that, therefore, funds would have to be raised "on a large scale" immediately in the form of voluntary subscriptions. It was decided that the Society of Arts, having, through the influence of its

[1] The last two sentences are reproduced in plate 21.

President, been incorporated by Royal Charter two years before, would be an appropriate agent for collecting these donations.

It is a remarkable testimony to the statesmanship of the Prince that as soon as he agreed to take up this great enterprise it was possible to make six such fundamental decisions at a single meeting, and that except for important modifications to two of them—the substitution of medals for monetary awards and the handing over of financial responsibility by the Society to the Royal Commission —they all stood the test of time.

4

These decisions having been taken, the Prince lost no time. He spoke to the leading members of the Government, and to his friend Sir Robert Peel, and he arranged for Mr. Labouchère, the President of the Board of Trade, who had given such a favourable reception to the Society's deputation a year before, to represent his ministerial colleagues at a second meeting at Osborne on July 14 when Scott Russell, Henry Cole and Francis Fuller were again present. This meeting went far to prepare the way for the application which the Prince, as President of the Society of Arts, forwarded to the Home Secretary at the end of the month for the issue of a Royal Commission. It was, however, wisely suggested by Labouchère that as, owing to the holidays, it would be some time before the Government could make a decision, the Society might in the meantime sound the chief manufacturing centres of the country regarding their attitude to the exhibition.

Then followed a period of tremendous effort. Armed with credentials from the Prince the three enthusiasts, who were joined a little later by other members of the Society commissioned by the Prince, conducted a whirlwind campaign. Manufacturers and authorities were called upon in some sixty-five towns in England, Scotland and Ireland, and Scott Russell also visited a considerable number of places in Germany. The reconnaissance was carried out under very difficult conditions, for the Prince, being anxious that the plan should be considered freely on its own merits and that judgment upon it should not be influenced by his personal association with it, would not commit himself publicly except as considering the matter in his capacity as President of the Society of Arts. The visits were therefore supposed to be regarded as unofficial and largely private; but, in fact, the interest taken in the project was such that, much to the concern of the Prince, the meetings took on more and more of a public character. Finally, after the encouraging reports which he received from his emissaries, and when he learned that the powerful East India Company, and even the Prince President of France (later Napoleon III), had promised support, the Prince himself asked for arrangements to be made for a great public meeting at the Mansion House in London on October 17. This formed the climax of the whole series and Cole outlined the scheme to a highly influential audience as the Prince's accredited spokesman.

At all these meetings views were invited on specific points, including the proposal to make the exhibition an international one, and the reactions were uniformly good. Opportunity was also taken to set up local committees to foster interest in the project.

While Cole and his friends were busy on their fatiguing but exciting task, the Council of the Society were grappling at a series of special meetings with the less attractive but equally urgent problem of finance, urgent because an assurance of money was just as essential a condition of the Prince's publicly committing himself—and also, as Labouchère made clear, of the Government's agreeing to the issue of a Royal Commission—as an assurance of public approval.

When they were first called together at the end of July to consider this question it was still impossible, for the Prince's sake, to inform them of the great decisions which had already been reached, and it is of interest, therefore, that, quite independently, one of their number proposed that foreigners should be invited to participate in the exhibition, and that this was unanimously agreed. All that the Council could be told for the time being was that the Prince wanted them to find money, and money they had not. Clearly, there was only one thing to do now and that was to raise another loan. But the amount required was then estimated as at least £75,000, and they had absolutely no security to offer for the advance which they had to obtain so quickly.

The task seemed impossible, and probably, had it not been for Francis Fuller, it would never have been achieved. Fuller, however, after ceaseless inquiries and much persuasive talk, was able to introduce to the Society two "contractors", or speculators as we should term them, an uncle and nephew of the name of Munday, who made a generous offer which solved the whole problem. They were prepared to provide all the needed funds as and when required, and to take the whole risk of the enterprise (which when they first made their offer was a very great one), in return for five per cent interest on the sums advanced and two-thirds, not of the net profits, but of the balance of receipts left after the deduction of the prize fund and the cost of the buildings. From this two-thirds all the administrative costs were to be met, while the Society was to retain the other third as a fund for financing future exhibitions.

In the course of the negotiations the contractors made a concession which was fraught with great consequences. One day in September, Cole and Fuller took a day off from their propaganda campaign to visit Stephenson's Britannia Bridge across the Menai Straits, the work on which was now at a most interesting stage. While they were there it occurred to Cole that if the Government were only offered an opportunity to take over the financial responsibility for the exhibition they might not agree but would be better disposed through such an invitation at least to support the exhibition in a general way. Fuller agreed, and so did the Society when Cole told them his idea on their return, but hardly a member seriously believed that the Government, which had hitherto been so careful not to get involved in the finances of the scheme, would ever take advantage of such an opportunity. The Messrs. Munday also agreed when the suggestion was put to them, perhaps sharing the Society's well-founded scepticism, and a clause was accordingly added to the contract providing that if, within a prescribed period, the Treasury might be willing to take the risk, the Society might determine the contract, paying to the contractors due compensation. The contractors, for their part, claimed a right, subject to arbitration, to abandon the contract if a Royal Commission was not ultimately issued.

Upon the signature of a contract embodying these various provisions the prize fund of £20,000 was paid over, as a guarantee to intending exhibitors, to trustees appointed by the Society, and the executive committee, with Robert Stephenson as its chairman and Digby Wyatt as its secretary, moved into offices provided by the contractors at 1 Palace Yard, Westminster, and began its work, which for the moment mainly consisted of mobilising the local supporters of the project throughout the country. The signatures of many of these "promoters and subscribers" were collected in a small book still preserved by the Society.

Meanwhile, the Government, fully satisfied by the concrete advances made by the Society, had indicated at last that a Royal Commission would be granted. After a long period of drafting, most of which was carried out by Henry Cole, the Commission was finally issued on January 3, 1850.

Yet it was still in effect the Society of Arts' exhibition. The Society's contract with Messrs. Munday was still the functional mainspring of the whole project, and the execution of the terms of that contract was the immediate responsibility of a committee appointed by the Society. The function of the Royal Commission, on the other hand, according to the terms of its appointment, was merely to "make full and diligent enquiry" regarding the best way of carrying out the exhibition: it was not to take action.

But it was soon clear that this arrangement could not work. One body must be responsible for both policy-making and execution, and, once appointed, only the Royal Commission could be that body. Moreover, a feeling had been expressed that, now that the project had acquired a national status, it should not be financed by private speculators. At the very first meeting of the Commissioners, therefore, held on January 11, it was decided to take advantage of the loophole so prudently proposed by Cole, and to terminate the contract—or to be precise, to ask the Society to do so.

The Society for its part immediately concurred in an act which meant surrendering not merely its official connection with the 1851 Exhibition, but also its potentialities for initiating further great exhibitions by means of the third share of the profits which was to have come to it for this purpose under the contract. The Mundays, on the other hand, were greatly put out, when it came to the point, at losing now, when the chances of success had so greatly improved, an undertaking of which they had borne the entire risk when it had been a very chancy affair. They proceeded to delay, by a whole series of difficulties, settlement of the compensation due to them under the contract, and it was not until the summer of 1851, more than a year later, that the matter was finally settled by Robert Stephenson as sole arbitrator. Stephenson then awarded them compensation amounting to £5,120, and he rewarded the unfortunate Society for its public spirit in terminating the contract by making it liable for the payment within ten days of the Mundays' legal costs of £587 and his own out-of-pocket expenses! The Council, of course, appealed to the Royal Commission to pay these expenses, which the Commission immediately agreed to do.

5

With the termination of the contract, the Society's official task was done, a task which is perhaps best summed up in a paragraph of the speech which was made by Prince Albert at the closing of the Exhibition on October 15, 1851.

> To the Society of Arts, which, by its exhibitions of works of national industry, prepared the way for this international Exhibition, the Royal Commission and the public feel that their acknowledgments are specially due, and the Commission have to thank that body for having carried out the preliminary arrangements to an extent which justified me, as their President, in the application which I made to the Crown for the issue of a Royal Commission.

But the detailed work continued in the hands in which the Society had placed it. The Trustees, Treasurers and Executive Committee appointed by the Society from among its members all continued to serve, except that Robert Stephenson resigned his chairmanship of the Executive Committee to become a Royal

Commissioner. Scott Russell became one of the two joint secretaries of the Commission on behalf of the Society of Arts, while Henry Cole and Wentworth Dilke as members of the Executive Committee, and Digby Wyatt as its secretary, continued to devote their whole time to the affairs of the exhibition.

Nor was the Society itself allowed to drop out of the picture completely, although it was undoubtedly eclipsed by the grandeur of its prodigious offspring. The Royal Commissioners found a few simple chores for it: they entrusted to it, for example, the sale of the season tickets and, more appropriately, the conduct of the competition for the design of the Exhibition medals. The Society was also kept well informed about the progress of the Exhibition building. Paxton, who was a member, offered to come and lecture on his design actually before the Royal Commission had adopted it, although his lecture was not delivered until November; and the contractors gave members of the Society the unique privilege of a private view of the works on the last day of 1850, a month before the building was handed over to the Royal Commissioners. When the time for the opening arrived the Society, in common with other learned bodies, offered special facilities and hospitality to the foreign commissioners and exhibitors, and after its close it arranged, at the express suggestion of Prince Albert, a special course of lectures, which was opened by Dr. Whewell, Master of Trinity College, Cambridge, on the results which it could then be seen to have achieved.

But the Society's reward for its vision and enterprise in pioneering this great national achievement lay not so much in official recognition, which then, as on so many other occasions, seemed grudging and meagre, as in a general enhancement of its prestige. In its stature before the public eye it grew a hundred-fold, and emerged from the exhibition year as an institution which had to be reckoned with in the public life of the nation. Above all the Society then, as now, felt fully rewarded by the knowledge that by its sole initiative and drive it had rendered an outstanding service to the nation, and, indeed, to the world.

CHAPTER 12

Later Exhibitions—and Museums

1

THE Society had an even more intimate connection with the International Exhibition held in London in 1862 than it had with the Great Exhibition of 1851. The initial preparations for both exhibitions were undertaken by the Society at its own risk, but in addition the exhibition of 1862 was managed by a Commission officially nominated by the Society.

Although the exhibition of 1862 was relatively a failure, it was not nearly so complete a failure as is generally believed. Fate was unkind to it. It took place during a very wet summer and in the subdued atmosphere of mourning for the Prince Consort. And yet the total attendances slightly exceeded those of 1851, and the number of exhibitors was far greater. The personal generosity of Sir John Kelk, a member of the contracting firm of Lucas and Kelk, ensured by a gift of £11,000 that the accounts were balanced and that no call had to be made on the guarantors.

The history of the exhibition begins in the early months of 1858, when the Council of the Society resolved, after discussions in which Henry Cole and Wentworth Dilke were moving spirits, that it was desirable that international exhibitions should be held in this country every ten years, beginning with 1861, and that steps should be taken to form a guarantee fund for the next exhibition, this being the method ultimately adopted by the Royal Commission to finance the 1851 Exhibition. It was decided that the exhibition should deal with art and industry, and should be mainly an exhibition of progress, showing the advances made during the past ten years. The intervention of the Franco-Austrian War delayed the project, and it was not until November, 1859, that the

23. GILT CENTREPIECE, DESIGNED BY PRINCE ALBERT

Lent by Queen Victoria to the Society of Arts exhibition, 1849

(Reproduced by gracious permission of Her Majesty the Queen)

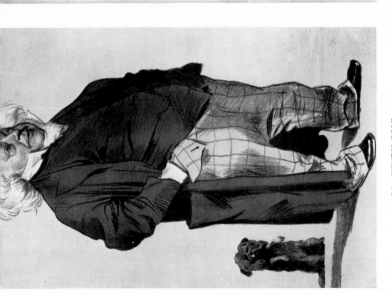

22. HENRY COLE

Vanity Fair caricature, 1871

24. THE GREAT EXHIBITION, 1851

The western, or British, nave looking east

25. OPENING OF THE INTERNATIONAL EXHIBITION, 1862

Council again proceeded in the matter. They then postponed the proposed exhibition until 1862 and resolved to aim at a guarantee fund of £250,000. They also appointed a committee which in its turn nominated five trustees—Earl Granville, original Chairman of the Royal Commission for the 1851 Exhibition, the Marquis of Chandos (afterwards Duke of Buckingham), Thomas Baring, M.P., C. Wentworth Dilke and Thomas Fairbairn. On February 14, 1861, a charter was granted to the Society by which these trustees were incorporated under the title of "Commissioners for the Exhibition of 1862" and given full powers of management.

This conclusion was not reached without prolonged negotiations (a detailed account of which may be found in Trueman Wood's History of the Society) between the Society, the trustees, and the Commissioners of the 1851 Exhibition, who eventually agreed to appropriate a portion of their estate at South Kensington, approximately on the site of the present Natural History Museum, rent free, for the exhibition. The Society had hopes of obtaining for itself some tangible results from the success—and they perhaps rather too hastily assumed there was going to be a success—of the 1862 Exhibition. The form signed by intending guarantors stipulated "that one-third at least of the sum expended on buildings should be employed on erections of a permanent character, to be used by the Society for holding decennial or other periodical exhibitions, and for other purposes tending to the encouragement of arts, manufactures and commerce". But in the long run, as there was a loss on the whole undertaking, the Society received no benefit whatever.

It was a most disappointing result, especially so because of the success which had attended the Society's efforts to raise the guarantee fund, which by June, 1860, had already passed the total originally aimed at and stood at £308,350. A further goal of £370,000 was then set up, and guarantors continued to enrol, though there were some set-backs. A typical snub from Edward Bulwer Lytton may be quoted:

Sir,

I beg to acknowledge your letter requesting me to join in a Guarantee Deed for £370,000—to provide Funds for an Exhibition of Works of Art, &c, in 1862 &, with full sense of the honor proposed to me, I must beg to decline making that Exhibition of myself.

I have the honor to be, Sir,

Your serv^t.

E. B. LYTTON

Nice, Feb. 28 1861

Fortunately this was a minority view. The guarantee fund was eventually raised to £451,070, contributed by 1,157 subscribers; and, as we have seen, Sir John Kelk's gesture ensured that they were not called upon.

Besides the weather and the death of Prince Albert, a further reason for the relative failure of the exhibition may have been a certain over-confidence and dangerous complacency engendered by the success in 1851. "Oh! for the opposition of 1851," said Granville to Dilke, "that's a stimulant wanting now!" Although Henry Cole again employed his robust energy to the full—and this time had the title of "consulting officer", which enabled him to stimulate and encourage on all sections of the battle-front—it must be admitted that his chief contribution was disastrous. For it was he who secured acceptance of young Captain Francis Fowke's lamentable design for the exhibition building itself. This was considerably larger in superficial area than the Crystal Palace, and had two huge domes which seemed out of proportion to the commonplace low buildings from which they sprang. No one was sorry when it was demolished.[1]

Yet the exhibition had points of merit. There was the art gallery, not included in 1851, and a section devoted to educational equipment. There was the useful emphasis on progress made since the last exhibition, and the friendly support from foreign exhibitors, notably the French. The Society's final service in 1862 lay in its publication of the Jury Reports, a duty which had been undertaken eleven years earlier by the Commissioners of the 1851 Exhibition and which had resulted in a volume that industrial historians have found exceedingly valuable. The Commissioners

---

[1] The building is illustrated in plate 25.

lacked the funds, this time, to enable them to publish the Reports. But the Society was anxious that this record of industrial progress since 1851 should not be lost and therefore sponsored the volume, edited by Dr. Lyon Playfair, which appeared in January, 1864. The book proved a costly undertaking and left the Society more than £1,000 out of pocket.

2

It was consistent with the Society's interest in the welfare of the working classes that it should have done what it could to ensure that representative British workmen were able to visit the Paris exhibitions of 1855, 1867 and 1878. In 1855 the Society secured a reduction in railway fares, free lodgings and other privileges. In 1867 the project was more ambitious. Not only were eighty artisans, representing various industries in different parts of the country, selected to make the journey to Paris, but they were encouraged to write reports of what they saw at the exhibition and in the French factories and workshops which they also visited. These reports made an unusual and valuable book which was published by the Society in the same year.

In order to forward this scheme, the Society assembled a committee of distinguished people who were known to have the welfare of the working classes at heart. The correspondence of a busy philanthropic society does not readily lend itself to publication, letters tending to be either brief and formal or long and detailed in their discussion of a particular point at issue. But occasionally a series of letters in its archives, however trivial in content, will throw a light on the great mass of work done by successive Secretaries; on the care given to what may appear, in historical perspective, to be only a minor incident; and also, not least, on the traditional patience with which prominent men much in the public eye have been wont to receive appeals for public service. Here, then, are three short letters of acceptance addressed on this particular occasion to the Secretary of the Society, Peter Le Neve Foster:

GAD'S HILL PLACE,
HIGHAM BY ROCHESTER, KENT.
Saturday Fifth January 1867.

Sir,

I beg to acknowledge the receipt of your circular letter, honoring me with an invitation to become a member of the Committee for promoting the study of the Paris Exhibition by artizans of the United Kingdom.

While I readily place my name in this connexion, at the disposal of the Council of the Society, I deem it right to inform you that my engagements will oblige me to be constantly occupied in various parts of England and Scotland during the next three months, and that I shall be quite unable to attend any meeting during that term at least.

I am Sir
Faithfully yours
CHARLES DICKENS.

P. Le Neve Foster Esquire.

ST. GILES'S HOUSE,
CRANBOURNE,
SALISBURY
Jan. 9. 1867

Sir,

I heartily approve the plan of facilitating the visit of skilled Artisans to the Exhibition at Paris; and I shall be very happy to be on the Committee.

Your obed. Servt.
SHAFTESBURY

P. Le Neve Foster Esq.

8, YORK PLACE, W.
Jan. 11. 1867

Sir,

I have to acknowledge the favour of your letter of the 3^d instant respecting the Society for the encouragement of Arts &c; & in reply to express my readiness to become a member of the Committee referred to in the Resolution.

I remain, Sir,
Your obed^t Servant,
✠HENRY E. MANNING
Archbishop, &c.

P. Le Neve Foster Esq.

And by way of contrast, here is a letter of refusal:

ROCHDALE
Jany 7. 67.

Dear Sir,

I have so many engagements, that I cannot hope to be of any use on your Committee, & therefore I prefer that my name should not appear upon it.

I thank your Council for their wish that I should join the Com^{ttee} & am

my dear Sir, yours

JOHN BRIGHT.

In the end this visit of the "artisan reporters" to Paris in 1867 was financed as to £500 by the British Commissioners for the Exhibition and as to £350 by the Society of Arts, while the remainder—rather more than £500—was obtained by subscriptions. The same plan was carried out at the French Exhibition of 1878, when even more artisans were sent over and still more of their reports were published, though this second volume of reports is perhaps not quite so interesting as that issued in 1867.

3

In view of the relative failure of the 1862 Exhibition, it is not surprising that the idea of holding large decennial exhibitions did not receive much support when it was again mooted as the twentieth anniversary of the Great Exhibition drew near. Instead, Henry Cole put before the Commissioners of the 1851 Exhibition a scheme for holding a series of annual international exhibitions of "selected works of fine and industrial art" to cover the decade from 1871 to 1880, the exhibits in any one year being limited to a certain group of subjects. The Commissioners accepted the proposal and the programme was announced in the *Journal* of August 6, 1869. A sum of £100,000 was guaranteed by the Commissioners, who also provided for the purpose of the exhibitions a part of their land at South Kensington just to the south of the Albert Hall. The Royal Horticultural Society then occupied a portion of this area, and in the first year (1871) their charming gardens were included in the exhibition and contributed largely to its success. This exhibition had more than a million visitors, its total receipts exceeding £75,000. But the attendance at the exhibitions in the three following years (for the experiment was not continued after that) declined steadily, so that the Commissioners were ultimately faced with a loss of £150,000. The Horticultural Society's refusal of their gardens after the first year certainly contributed to this disappointing result, but another reason was that the exhibitions, excellent in their way, were too specialised and too highly technical to appeal to a wide public.

The Society co-operated with the Commissioners in organising all four exhibitions. Certain sections were placed under its special charge, and the *Journal* was made the official organ of the exhibitions, its volumes for 1870 to 1874 containing much information about them. The cost to the Society of its work for these four exhibitions was less than might have been expected; it amounted to a little more than £300.

The lesson of the 1871–4 exhibitions was turned to good account in the series of exhibitions held on the same site between 1883 and 1886. These four exhibitions were devoted, respectively, to Fisheries, Health and Education, Inventions and Music, and the British Colonies and India. Here, again, the Society co-operated with the Exhibition Executive, and the Society's House was used for many of the committee meetings that preceded the exhibitions. Care was taken to make these shows attractive to the general public, with the result that sixteen million people came to see them, and they not only paid their way but earned a profit. Old differences were forgotten; the Royal Horticultural Society did not now refuse the use of their grounds, which were the scene of evening fêtes made beautiful by coloured fountains and strings of fairy lights. In each of these years, one evening was set aside for a conversazione held by the Council of the Society in the exhibition buildings or the gardens. The conversaziones in 1885 and 1886 were each attended by about 10,000 people.

As in the 'seventies, these exhibitions of the 'eighties were greatly assisted by the publicity given to them in the *Journal*. In the case of the Education exhibition of 1884 the Society assumed charge of the valuable series of hand-books issued by the exhibition authorities and continued their publication after the dissolution of the Exhibition Council. In the case of the Colonial and Indian Exhibition, the Society undertook to superintend the publication of the Reports on the Colonial sections. This final exhibition was the most successful and the most influential of the four; and it was also the first serious attempt to interest the people of Britain in their Empire. A direct result was the establishment, on a site in the neighbourhood, of the Imperial Institute, a body with which the Society has always maintained a close connection, and towards the foundation of which its members contributed a special fund of over £2,000. The Society was represented by the Chairman of the Council on the Governing Body of the Institute during its early years.

4

This record of the way in which the Society furthered the impetus given to international exhibitions by the Great Exhibition of 1851 may be concluded by a reference to a large-scale American achievement, the World's Columbian Exposition held in Jackson Park, Chicago, in 1893, in which the Society had a particular share.

It was in June, 1891, that Sir James Fergusson, the Under-Secretary of State for Foreign Affairs, applied to Sir Richard Webster, who then held the office of Attorney-General, and was Chairman of the Council of the Society of Arts, to know whether the Society would undertake to organise the British section of the Chicago Exhibition if a Treasury grant of £25,000 was made available for the purpose. The Council agreed to do so on condition that a charge, proportional to the space occupied, should be made to the exhibitors, in order to supplement the grant. On this understanding, a Royal Commission was issued to the Society on August 26, 1891. But in April, 1892, the Chancellor of the Exchequer intimated that the Government were willing to increase the grant to £60,000, if it was understood that space should be provided free for British exhibitors. This was much more satisfactory, though it did involve the Society in a lot of trouble in returning the deposits and dealing with the greatly increased number of applicants, of whom only a carefully selected proportion could be given space—and then not always as much space as they had asked for.

The Council of the Society constituted the Royal Commission, but consultative committees were established for the various departments into which the work was sub-divided. Thus Sir Frederick Leighton, P.R.A., became chairman of the Fine Arts Committee; Sir Saul Samuel, chairman of the Colonies Committee; the Earl of Feversham, chairman of the Agriculture and Food Products Committee; Sir Frederick Bramwell, chairman of the Engineering, Architecture, etc., Committee; Sir Henry Doulton, chairman of the General Manufactures Committee; and so on. The thoroughness with which the Society carried out its duties can be gauged by a study first of the *Handbook of Regulations and General Information* which it issued in May, 1893, and then of the *Official Catalogue of the British Section* published later in the year.

It was a most comprehensive collection. The total area allotted to Great Britain and the British possessions within the exhibition buildings was about 500,000 square feet, of which more than 300,000 were occupied by Great Britain. Few aspects of British industry and commerce can have gone unrepresented. The Fine Arts section contained works by Frank Brangwyn, George Clausen and Wilson Steer, as well as a quantity of pictures by Leighton, Millais, Watts and other older artists. Nor was the black-and-white drawing of Keene, du Maurier and Tenniel neglected. And one of the most interesting departments of the British Section was that devoted to the varied achievement of British women.

The Commission's offices were situated in Victoria House, a building intended to represent "an ordinary half-timber country house in England of the Elizabethan period". Alas, the style has been debased by speculative builders since 1893, and to an irreverent modern eye a photograph suggests nothing so much as a fashionable hostelry on one of the by-pass roads near London. It could not, certainly, have stood comparison with the elaborate

Rathaus set up by the Germans. But the interior was sumptu-
ously decorated, containing, among other features, plaster ceilings
copied from those at Haddon Hall, Crewe Hall, Campden House
and elsewhere.

The World's Columbian Exposition was intended to celebrate,
though a year late, the four-hundredth anniversary of Columbus's
discovery of America. The lavish memorial volume of the exhibition found room for photographs of several of his descendants,
among them the Duke and Duchess of Veragua; His Excellency
Christopher Columbus, the Duke's son, in an Eton collar; Pilar
Columbus, dark-eyed daughter of the Duke; and His Excellency
Peter Columbus, son of the Marquis of Bariboles, wearing a
splendid stock. No effort, in fact, was spared on this occasion to
show that the United States had assimilated all that was to be
learnt from Europeans of the technique of exhibitions, and—in
point of size and attention to detail—could beat them at their own
game. But the British nation had reason to be pleased with the
careful display that the Society of Arts devised to represent them,
in such competitive circumstances, at Chicago.

5

The Society has sponsored or assisted in organising a number of
smaller exhibitions in the past hundred years. Perhaps the most
notable of these have been the series of Inventions Exhibitions
(1848–61); the first Photographic Exhibition (1852); the first
Educational Exhibition (1854); the exhibitions of Lithography
(1898–9), of Modern Illustration (1901), of Etching and Engraving
(1903), and of Photogravure (1904); the Exhibition of British Art
in Industry (1935); and the Exhibition of Humorous Art (1949).
These exhibitions will best be dealt with when we come to consider the particular subjects with which they were concerned. But
there is one particular exhibition that may fittingly be mentioned
here, if only because it harked back to the Great Exhibition of
1851 (which was at once the Society's proudest achievement and
its chief inspiration)—and that is the Society's contribution to the
Festival of Britain, 1951, the "Exhibition of Exhibitions".

The Festival of 1951 was born of the proposals of the Ramsden Committee, of Sir Gerald Barry, and of the Royal Society of Arts that the centenary of the Great Exhibition should be suitably commemorated. (The Council of the Festival held its first meeting at the Society's House and Princess Elizabeth attended it as President of the Society.) In view of its particularly intimate connection with the 1851 Exhibition, the Society felt it could best celebrate the centenary by organising an exhibition which would demonstrate the pioneering work accomplished by the Society in the whole sphere of exhibitions. Accordingly Mr. Hulme Chadwick devised a display in the Great Room which centred upon five pioneer exhibitions held by the Society: the first exhibition of contemporary art (1760), the first industrial exhibition (1761), the first exhibitions of industrial design (1847–50) and of photography (1852) and the first international exhibition (1851). Some indication was also given of the way in which these achievements were followed up, and of how in the case of industrial design exhibitions the campaign of Victorian days was resumed in recent years.

The "Exhibition of Exhibitions" had a special interest because the Society's lecture-hall in which it was held had itself been the scene of some of the exhibitions it commemorated. Mr. Hulme Chadwick employed to the utmost the limited area available; a feeling of additional space was given to the room by staging the exhibition on two levels; and by a skilful use of colour and concealed lighting the essentially modern design of the display stands was made to blend harmoniously with the eighteenth-century setting. Some of the Barry paintings were specially lighted, and were seen to great advantage from the raised dais on which part of the exhibition was staged. Altogether, this exhibition, which included a Reynolds portrait shown at the exhibition of 1760 and the gilt centre-piece (designed by Prince Albert) lent to one of the Society's exhibitions in 1849, was one of the most unusual and attractive ever sponsored by the Society. Unfortunately it had to contend with intense competition from the many other attractions of Festival year. The attendance was disappointing and the exhibition involved the Society in a considerable loss.[1]

[1] A photograph of the exhibition appears in plate 39.

Princess Elizabeth opened the "Exhibition of Exhibitions" at twelve noon on May 1, 1951—a hundred years to the day and hour since Queen Victoria had opened the Great Exhibition. The Society had further undertaken to mark the site of the Crystal Palace in Hyde Park with flagstaffs at intervals round the original perimeter, and at the moment that King George VI declared the Festival open from the steps of St. Paul's, on May 3, 1951, the flags were unfurled by members of the Society's staff under the direction of the Assistant Secretary—a nostalgic salute to 1851.

6

The great interest that was aroused in temporary exhibitions through the Great Exhibition was accompanied by a corresponding interest in permanent exhibitions, or museums. The Commissioners of the 1851 Exhibition, in their second report, announced their decision to use part of the proceeds in establishing a permanent museum at South Kensington—and in this important enterprise the Society of Arts had a large share. Not only must the sum of £200,000 which was available to the Commissioners for this and other purposes be traced ultimately to its initiative, but the Society was able to assist in preparing the plans for establishing the museum and to contribute in various ways to its collections.

The Commissioners invited the Society, in particular, to help in forming a trade museum. The Council thereupon offered, as a first step, to undertake to form a collection of animal products used in manufactures, and to devote to it a sum of £400 if the Commissioners would provide a similar amount. This being agreed, the Society proceeded to get together a comprehensive collection which was shown in the Society's House in May, 1855. It was afterwards made over to the Science and Art Department, was placed in the South Kensington Museum on its opening in 1857, and eventually found its way to the Bethnal Green Museum. This was not the only instance in which the Society contributed to the enrichment of the newly established museums, for we shall see that the Society's educational exhibition of 1854 provided the nucleus of the educational collection and library of the South Kensington Museum, and that many of the models from its Repository were given to public museums, where some of them still exist.

The Society's preoccupation with the education of the working classes gave it a special reason for taking an interest in museums. We shall see that the Society assumed the initiative in linking the numerous mechanics' institutes up and down the country in the Union of Institutions, and one of the Society's aims was to encourage the formation of local collections of a practical and educational value in connection with them. In a memorandum of 1852, the Society emphasised that "A museum, properly considered, is not a collection of curiosities, monstrosities, antiquities and artistic works grouped together in glass cases in a species of native confusion, but, if it deserves its name, is a place in which instruction is to be gained, and consequently in which order, arrangement and method is evident throughout." A list of twenty-eight centres was appended where collections of this kind had already been established. Three examples may be given. Bacup, Lancashire, had "illustrations of the various stages of the cotton manufacture, from the raw materials to the finished article, and collections in illustration of the geology of the district". Bridgwater, Somerset, showed "specimens of the entire series of the rock formation of the county, with selections of organic remains, and specimens in illustration of the manufacture of Bath brick and scouring brick". Newbury, Berkshire, offered "samples of wool selected so as to show the various qualities and the points of chief importance in connection with the wool trade".

The Society had a special opportunity to press its case for the encouragement of local museums when the Science and Art Department decided in 1866 to remove some of the surplus material at the South Kensington Museum to Bethnal Green and to found a new museum there. The Council made a substantial grant towards this museum, and when it was successfully opened in 1872 the Society published a declaration signed, among others, by twenty-three peers and sixty-six Members of Parliament who were members of the Society, pointing out that in three months more than 700,000 people had visited the museum and urging the Government to make the development of museums a matter of policy and to apply for an increased grant in pursuance of it. As nothing came of this first move, the Society formed a standing committee in the next year to further what amounted to a national scheme for museums. Among its principal aims were the assistance of local museums by the loan of objects from national museums, the placing of control of all national museums under a Minister of the Crown, and the granting of increased powers to local authorities for the improvement of the museums in their charge. Under the auspices of the committee a public meeting was held at the Society's House, at which resolutions embodying these and related objects were moved by Mr. Joseph Chamberlain and communicated to the Prime Minister, Mr. Gladstone, by the chairman, Lord Hampton. The matter was brought before the House of Commons soon afterwards, and petitions were presented to Parliament; but though these efforts proved partially successful in course of time, not all the Society's objects have, even now, been attained.

The Society also concerned itself at this period with advocating the evening opening of museums, a step which it considered of vital importance because without it working people were in so many cases unable to visit these places. Most of the small museums associated with the local institutions were already open in the evenings, and so were the Geological Museum and the South Kensington Museum, but in 1859, when further buildings were added to the South Kensington Museum to house the Vernon and Turner collections belonging to the National Gallery, no provision was made for their lighting and they were closed in the evening, although the rest of the building remained open. After unsuccessful correspondence with the Trustees of the National Gallery, the Society persuaded Lord Shaftesbury in the House of Lords, and the Right Hon. Mr. Cowper in the House of Commons, to move for copies of the correspondence, with the result that a Select Committee of the House of Commons was appointed to inquire into the matter.

Lord Overston, on behalf of the Trustees, had previously raised in the House of Lords the question of the effect of gas-light on paintings, and accordingly a commission of scientists, including Michael Faraday, was appointed to inquire into this aspect. They reported that, with suitable precautions, the use of gas-light would not be deleterious to the pictures, and had not been proved to be so in the case of the Sheepshanks Gallery at South Kensington Museum, which, being under different control, had been illuminated at night when the Vernon and Turner Galleries were closed. The House of Commons Committee then inquired into the general principles, and concluded that institutions such as the British Museum and National Gallery ought to be open on week-day evenings to the public. The British Museum Trustees accordingly made careful inquiry, but found that in their case there were many special risks in the use of gas and decided to open only on summer evenings when no artificial light was necessary. The National Gallery Trustees also agreed to open the Vernon and Turner collections three evenings a week, and thus the Society's original point was won, but no action at all appears to have been taken with regard to the National Gallery in Trafalgar Square. The Society can claim, however, to have been the first to make the evening opening of museums and galleries a public issue.

With the formation of the Society's standing committee in 1873 and its various agitations in the years immediately afterwards, its main efforts on behalf of museums came to an end. But Sir Henry Cole, speaking in 1877, urged the importance of an annual conference that would keep the movement alive, and twelve years later there was held the first of the series of yearly conferences of the Museums Association, whose activities henceforth made it unnecessary for the Society to continue its pioneer work in this field. At the Jubilee Conference of the Association in 1939, Lord Amulree, the Chairman of the Council of the Society, delivered an informative address[1] on the part the Society had played in the museum movement. Not that it has ceased to interest itself in a subject which touches so closely on its essential activities. The Society is still officially connected with the Soane Museum, to which it nominates a representative trustee, and, of course, papers

[1] Published in the *Journal* of October 13, 1939.

bearing upon the subject of museums are read from time to time before the Society. Among these special mention must be made of a series which was read in 1949 and subsequently published by the Society as a book under the title of *Museums and Modern Life*. In this form these valuable lectures have found their way all over the world.

CHAPTER 13

Miscellaneous Activities

1

A variety of matters occupied the Society's time during the period after the Great Exhibition. They range from postal reform, the reform of the patent law, and the question of copyright in works of art, to the provision of public lavatories in London and the placing of memorial tablets on houses in which celebrated persons had been born or lived. It was not for nothing that E. V. Lucas once referred to the Society as England's Fairy Godmother. A versatile fairy, she has been benevolent always, a little sentimental sometimes, and on occasion sternly practical.

It was as early as 1851 that the Society took up the question of cheap international postage, and in 1852 that a deputation waited on the Foreign Secretary (Lord Granville) to discuss the matter. A parcel post was first proposed in 1855, when a committee was appointed and much discussion ensued. More demonstrably useful was a paper read by Edwin Chadwick in 1867 urging the purchase of the telegraphs by the State, which had a powerful effect on public opinion and helped to influence the passing of the telegraph legislation of 1868. The Society's exertions in the cause of postal reform were largely inspired by Chadwick and by Henry Cole, who kept up a steady pressure on the Post Office, year after year, for cheaper postal charges, the development of a parcel and sample post, savings banks, the reduction of telegraph rates, the improvement of colonial and foreign postal communications, and so on. The Society even sponsored a short-lived but voluminous journal called the *Postal Reformer*, which weighed more than 1 lb. and was primarily intended to demonstrate the absurdity of the newspaper charges. Deputations were sent to successive Post-masters-General; conferences were held—such as that on March 13, 1871, with Lord Henry Lennox in the chair; and petitions were presented to the House of Commons.

Owing to the Society's persistence, many of the improvements it advocated eventually came to be adopted. For example, the institution of a newspaper post of $\frac{1}{2}d$. per 6 oz. in 1871 was directly due to its action. The Society might well have appeared an intolerable nuisance to the Post Office at this time; so that it was gratifying for it to learn in 1910 from Sir John Cameron Lamb, a former Secretary of the Post Office, that its efforts had on the whole been appreciated as useful and judicious.

2

From an early stage in its history the Society had held strong views on the subject of patents. In the Rules and Orders for 1765 it was expressly stated that "No person will be admitted a candidate for any premium offered by the Society who has obtained a patent for the exclusive right of making or performing anything for which such premium is offered." This was a restriction that prevented the Society from recognising many valuable inventions, but it was a restriction that was felt less in 1765, when only fourteen patents were granted, than it was in later years when the number of patents had greatly increased. The rule was eventually abolished after it had been in force for eighty years, and from 1845 onwards patented inventions were no longer disqualified from the competitions.

Soon after this, the Society turned its attention positively to the amendment of the patent law. In 1849 the Council, which had in the previous year shown its interest in the subject by holding an exhibition of inventions, was instigated by Henry Cole to appoint a Committee on the Rights of Inventors. Cole's was the driving force behind the committee, which in its turn stimulated public opinion by issuing several reports, the process being assisted by the appearance in 1850, in *Household Words*, of Dickens' "Poor Man's Tale of a Patent". The Committee's reports tended to favour the French system of simple registration without a government guarantee, but this view was not adopted when the Bill, which in 1852 became an Act, for the reform of the Patent Law was introduced into the House of Commons. Many parts of the Act were however, based on the Society's suggestions.

The Act of 1852 greatly improved the system of granting patents, and in general it now worked well, so that the question of further reforming the Patent Law was not again considered by the Society for more than twenty years. But in 1875, the Government, urged on by admirers of the American patent system, introduced a Bill in which it was proposed to establish a system of examination in this country similar to that which had always been favoured in the United States. The Bill attracted considerable opposition from those most versed in the mysteries of Patent Law, among whom was Sir Frederick Bramwell, F.R.S. (1818–1903), the distinguished engineer and authority on the legal side of his profession, who was an active member of the Society and held in succession every office on the Council. Under his leadership, the Society took a prominent part in opposing the Bill, and petitions against it were presented by the Council to the House of Lords— in which the Bill was introduced in 1875—and in the following year to the House of Commons. A special meeting was held to discuss the Bill in March, 1877, at which Sir Henry Trueman Wood, then Assistant Secretary of the Society, read a paper. The general feeling of the meeting was against the proposed measure. Probably this was an accurate reflection of public opinion as a whole. At all events, the Bill was dropped; and a different Bill introduced two years later met the same fate.

When Sir Frederick Bramwell became Chairman of the Council in 1880, he soon made it clear that he believed the Society could usefully pursue the matter of patents a little further. It was decided that the best way in which the Society could exert its influence would be by drafting a Bill embodying certain amendments to the Act of 1852 which time had shown to be necessary. A committee was appointed, and, on its instructions, a Bill was drafted by a Parliamentary draftsman. After being considered by a special meeting of the Society, this Bill was introduced into the House of Commons in March, 1882, and again in 1883, by Sir

John Lubbock (later Lord Avebury) and others. The attention it received led to the Government's introducing and carrying through the Patents, Designs, and Trade Marks Act, 1883, which exceeded the Society's Bill in scope but embodied many of its main provisions.

The Society's interest in patents was closely paralleled by its concern over the question of copyright in works of art. For more than a century the only Act that gave any protection at all to artists was Hogarth's Act (as it was called) of 1735, which had been obtained by William Hogarth, largely at his own expense, in order to secure to himself the rights in his own engravings. There had been several amending Acts, but none of these had given the author of an original work of art the power to prevent its reproduction or the sale of copies. This was the position when in 1858 the Society appointed a committee under the chairmanship of Sir Charles Eastlake, P.R.A., to inquire into the subject.

The committee drafted a Bill to establish copyright in works of Fine Art which was introduced to Parliament in 1860. But this Bill encountered heavy opposition and was not passed until two years later—and then only in an altered form, having been shorn of many of its more important provisions. The existence of copyright in works of art was established, but it was left uncertain to whom the copyright should belong in cases in which the artist had executed the work for a valuable consideration, and there were other serious ambiguities. Nevertheless, the Act of 1862 represented a great step forward at the time. Its main provisions were preserved in the Copyright Act of 1911, by which all previous statutes were repealed and the whole law was consolidated and in many respects assimilated to that in force on the Continent.

We have seen, then, that both in regard to patents and to copyright the Society was able to make useful contributions towards safeguarding the rights of inventors and artists. Its efforts in these respects have long been merged in the general stream of legal progress; but they deserve to be remembered, for they accorded well with the aims of a society that set out to encourage "Arts, Manufactures and Commerce".

3

The Society might well have adopted as its motto Terence's *Homo sum; humani nil a me alienum puto*: "I am a man, I count nothing human indifferent to me." And this seems an appropriate thought with which to approach its pioneer endeavours to establish a system of public lavatories in London. It may be granted that mankind in general—for some psychological reason beyond the scope of this History—has difficulty in contemplating the subject of public lavatories with a straight face; but there is no doubt whatever that, for reasons of health, this is one of the most important causes that the Society has ever taken up. Indeed, what the Society was mocked at for advocating in 1851–2 has now come to be regarded as one of the necessities of civilisation.

It was the Great Exhibition that first turned the Society's attention to the matter of public conveniences. They were, of course, provided on that occasion, and the charges made for their use resulted in a considerable profit, the receipts being £2,470 and the expenses about £680. That they were going to "pay their own way" must have been apparent to the organisers from the start, for we find a resolution among the Council Minutes as early as May 14, 1851, only a fortnight after the opening:

> Resolved that the following Noblemen and Gentlemen be requested to act as a committee for the purpose of establishing some model Water Closets on the self-supporting principle:—The Earl of Carlisle, the Earl Granville, S.M. Peto, Esq., M.P., Henry Cole, Esq., C. W. Dilke, Esq.

Ten days later, the committee had ready a printed list of regulations which they proposed should govern their attempt to prove that "Public Conveniences, so much wanted, may be made self-supporting". They began by coining a euphemism that might seem to have disguised, all too effectively, the nature of the new premises: the conveniences were to be termed "Public Waiting-Rooms" and they were to be "established on a moderate scale, in connexion with shops, in some public thoroughfares". Next, the committee decreed, with a hint of firmness in their benevolence, that "the Public Waiting-Rooms for Men and Women be established in distinct shops, on opposite sides of the street". They went on to describe the "Waiting-Rooms", as they envisaged them, in some detail. Each was to have "a Superintendant and two Attendants", and the charges were to include their services. There were to be "two classes of Water-Closets and Urinals" in each establishment, "for the use of which a penny and twopence should be charged"; and there was also to be "a Lavatory for washing hands, clothes' brushes, &c., at a charge of twopence and threepence". The final clause again showed a disciplinary touch: "That the Police should be requested to cause these establishments to be visited from time to time."

The committee urged that there should be no delay "in inviting respectable persons holding Shops in public thoroughfares, who may be desirous of connecting the proposed Public Waiting-Rooms with them", to inform the Secretary of the Society. And they added, no doubt after mature consideration (and one hopes after consulting their wives): "The Shops which appear to be most suitable for Waiting-Rooms for Ladies are Staymakers', Bonnetmakers', Milliners', &c. Those most suitable for Gentlemen's Waiting-Rooms are Hairdressers', Tailors', Hatters', Taverns, &c."

Mr. Peto, who was a famous contractor and a member of the firm which put up the Nelson Column—he became, not long after this date, Sir Samuel Morton Peto, Bt.—at once undertook to bear the expense of two experimental "Waiting-Rooms". And there were other offers of help from the commercial world. Mr. Minton promised "twenty-four Earthenware Urinals and a number of Encaustic Tiles", and Mr. J. Ridgeway was willing to present "some of his new Fountain Washhand-stands". All seemed set for a successful enterprise. By the beginning of 1852 the two "Waiting-Rooms" were ready—that for ladies at 51 Bedford Street, Strand, and that for gentlemen at 95 Fleet Street (no doubt considered a suitably tavernous district for the experiment). A Council meeting held on February 24, 1852, agreed that the two addresses ("Entrance 2d") should be advertised in *The Times* three times a week for a month, and it was ordered that 50,000 handbills be distributed. The wording of the advertisement struck a rather solemn note of social responsibility: "Public Waiting Rooms and Water Closets on the self-supporting system as at the Exhibition under the direction of a special Committee of the Society of Arts consisting of the Earl Granville, the Earl of Carlisle, S. M. Peto Esq. M.P., Henry Cole Esq., and C. W. Dilke Esq. . . ." To those who have seen the French film *Cloche-merle*, it conjures up visions of a top-hatted opening ceremony; but this is not recorded.

It is disappointing to have to state that the experiment was a complete failure. Throughout February, 1852, only fifty-eight people used the Gentlemen's Waiting-Room, while the Ladies' Waiting Room, which was not opened until February 11, attracted only twenty-four visitors between that date and the end of the month. Nor did the attendances improve. In April we observe the Council desperately reducing "the terms of the Water Closets in Bedford Street" from twopence to a penny. But after six months the total receipts at both establishments were only £15 13s. 11d., while the costs of the whole experiment amounted to £492 17s. 4d. Mr. Peto paid up the substantial balance, and the "Waiting-Rooms" ceased to offer their hospitality to an unappreciative London.

In retrospect this conclusion must appear startling. We have been so long accustomed to an extensive system of public lavatories in London that it is very hard for us to imagine how its citizens ever got on without them—and indeed a thorough examination of that problem is not an inviting piece of research. Though the Society's experiment was limited in scope, it sufficed to disprove the theory that public conveniences could be "self-supporting". It drew attention to the need for such places and led to the whole matter being taken up by the City Corporation, largely owing to the recommendations of William Haywood, who was the City engineer from 1846 to 1894 and who originated the system of underground lavatories.

4

It is appropriate that, as we have just reviewed an attempt by the Society to introduce a necessary reform into the streets of

London, we should now go on to consider the pioneering part that the Society played in originating the practice of placing memorial tablets on London houses which have been the home of famous people—a practice which has added so much of interest to the City and in the inauguration of which the Society may take particular pride.

Although the Society first began to consider this matter in the eighteen-sixties, it had since its foundation occasionally interested itself in the commemoration of outstanding individuals. This may therefore be the best place in which to quote a vigorous letter written in 1847 by Thomas Carlyle to Henry Cole, and preserved in the Society's archives. It refers to a project for a Caxton memorial, set on foot, presumably, by the Rev. H. H. Milman— who became Dean of St. Paul's in 1849 and who in 1847 was still Rector of St. Margaret's, Westminster, the church in which Caxton is buried. The letter reads as follows:

CHELSEA. *7 June* 1847

My dear Sir,

You certainly do well in assisting Mr. Milman in his Caxton enterprise; which is rational, patriotic, praiseworthy, instead of fatuous, false and deplorable, as most enterprises for "public monuments" now are! Old Caxton, tho' not much of a hero to my knowledge, does deserve to have a little stone of memorial set up for him, to mark his transit among us; the Art of Printing (tho' the theme of infinite twaddle in these poor days) does deserve to have its date and place notched down, since there is opportunity:— and I, in common with all good citizens, will gladly do my small part in that service.

Mark me down, therefore, as a subscriber of a guinea; expect that (for my own sake), if I can, I will attend your Meeting; but do not ask me to move any resolution, or otherwise open my mouth on the matter. "Unaccustomed as I am to public speaking";— besides in an epoch presided over by the "Testimonial *to King Hudson*", I do not think I should succeed well in comforting men's minds on the subject of "public monuments"!

Believe me

Yours always truly,

T. CARLYLE.

Henry Cole Esq.

The Society's minute-books have little to say of this Caxton scheme, except that the Society considered offering a gold medal for a design for a monument and decided not to do so. It may perhaps have ultimately borne fruit in one of the many memorials to Caxton in Westminster (the stained-glass window given to St. Margaret's by London printers in 1862 was destroyed by enemy action during the Second World War). If Carlyle liked the idea of a memorial to Caxton, he would surely have equally approved as "rational, patriotic, praiseworthy" the Society's proposals for tablets on houses. His own house in Ampton Street, St. Pancras, was one of those eventually marked by the L.C.C., who succeeded the Society in the discharge of this duty.

An anonymous letter published in the *Journal* in 1864 first directed the Society's attention towards this matter of memorial tablets. In the same year a similar proposal appeared in the *Builder*. It was probably as a result of these suggestions that the Council appointed a committee to consider "the erection of statues or other memorials to persons eminent in arts, manufactures, and commerce". In May, 1866, George Bartley—Henry Cole's son-in-law, who later became M.P. for Islington and received a Knighthood—proposed to the committee that the Society should affix memorial tablets to houses in London which had been inhabited by famous men. The committee at once approved the idea; a list of suitable houses was prepared; and in 1867 the first memorial tablet was placed on the house in Holles Street, Cavendish Square, where Byron was born. The work, once begun, was continued steadily until 1901, by which time tablets to the following thirty-five persons had been set up by the Society: Joanna Baillie, James Barry, Elizabeth Barrett Browning, Robert Browning, Edmund Burke, Lord Byron, George Canning, George Cruickshank, Fanny Burney (Madame D'Arblay), Charles Dickens, John Dryden, Michael Faraday, John Flaxman, Benjamin Franklin, Thomas Gainsborough, David Garrick, Edward Gibbon, George Frederick Handel, Sir Rowland Hill, William Hogarth, Samuel Johnson, John Keats, John Milton, Napoleon III, Lord Nelson, Sir Isaac Newton, Peter the Great, Sir Joshua Reynolds, John Ruskin, Richard Brinsley Sheridan, Mrs. Siddons, William

Makepeace Thackeray, John Thurloe, Sir Harry Vane, Sir Robert Walpole.

The Society loyally took this opportunity of commemorating James Barry, whose masterpieces adorn its Great Room; and, among the more famous, there are other names that reflect the history of the Society. It is an interesting list, catholic but discriminating, though it does include one or two people who are hardly of first importance. We must remember, however, that many owners of houses, especially in the early days, were reluctant to give permission to have a tablet put up, and that a willing owner may sometimes have turned the scale in favour of a

FIG. 5. COMMEMORATIVE TABLET TO PETER THE GREAT

minor celebrity. Yet, by any standards, the great majority of this mixed but splendid company deserved to have their abodes distinguished by a plaque.

Apart from a sum of £50 presented to the Council in 1872 by Benjamin Whitworth and H. D. Pochin, the cost of erecting the tablets was always borne by the Society. It was never a very expensive business, although from the start the Society took pains to see that its tablets were well designed. An offer of a £10 prize appears to have been unproductive, but various designs were prepared for the Society in the offices of the Science and Art Department, South Kensington, under the supervision of Godfrey Sykes and his assistant. Working on these, Messrs. Minton of Stoke-on-Trent eventually produced the circular tablet which was approved and adopted by the Council of the Society. One of the objects in designing it was to embody the name of the Society as unobtrusively as possible, and this was achieved by a decorative border, ingenious though to some tastes rather fussy in effect, incorporating the words "Erected by the Society of Arts". They must have been painfully deciphered by thousands of Victorian Londoners who gazed admiringly upwards from the pavements at these novelties.

In 1901 the Historical Records and Buildings Committee of the London County Council proposed to advise the County Council to undertake the duty of indicating houses and localities of interest in London, but as a preliminary step they courteously applied for the Society's views. The Council of the Society readily agreed to hand over the work to the L.C.C. and offered all possible assistance. From that time to this the L.C.C. has carried out the task with great efficiency. By the end of 1951, the L.C.C. had erected a further 189 tablets since 1901. Many of the Society's original tablets have now disappeared altogether owing to the demolition, sometimes through enemy action, of the houses on which they were placed—the tablet to James Barry is one of those that have gone—but the L.C.C. list shows that more than twenty of the Society's tablets have survived. When Mrs. Siddons' house, 27 Upper Baker Street, was demolished in 1904, the original tablet was refixed by the L.C.C. on the new premises (now 226 Baker Street). Similarly the Society's plaque commemorating Thomas Gainsborough, at 82 Pall Mall, was replaced by the L.C.C. in 1951. But in some cases, such as the tablets to Canning and Hogarth, the houses have been either demolished or so seriously damaged by enemy action that the L.C.C. has had to remove the tablets altogether.

In this matter of memorial tablets on London houses, as in other matters, the Society was content to lead the way and to retire as soon as it saw its enterprise successfully launched. By initiating the practice, it clearly gave a considerable stimulus to the average citizen's interest in his country's history and achievement. The Society continued to follow the progress of the work, and in 1950 the Council suggested that memorial plaques should be erected to

Thomas Chippendale and William Caslon, both former members of the Society. As a result, the L.C.C. decided to affix tablets to the sites of Chippendale's workshop at 61 St. Martin's Lane, Westminster, and of Caslon's foundry in Chiswell Street, Finsbury. Few craftsmen had hitherto been commemorated in this way.

CHAPTER 14

The *Journal* and Education

1

THE Society's volumes of *Transactions* came to an end in 1851, after having been published only at irregular intervals since 1830. Meanwhile, the issue of a weekly publication called the *Abstract of Proceedings* had been started in 1845. To begin with, this had consisted of no more than a few pages of notices and general information about the Society, but from 1848 onwards it had contained abstracts of the papers read. The title was soon changed to *Weekly Proceedings*, and in the number for June 12, 1852, there was an announcement that the Council were considering the publication of a "a stamped weekly Journal". A few months later, on November 26, 1852—a memorable date in the Society's history—the first number of the *Journal* appeared.

It is interesting, in the retrospect of the century that has since passed, to read the following paragraph concerning the institution of the *Journal* that was included in the Council's annual report presented to the general meeting on June 8, 1853:

> A very important change has been made in the form and publication of the weekly proceedings, the Council having, after due consideration, determined on the regular publication of a Weekly Journal, which should at the same time include reports of the ordinary meetings of the Society, the proceedings of Committees, correspondence, and memoranda respecting all subjects coming within the range of the Society's operations. In some respects this change has been attended by most valuable results; and from the more varied character of the publication, and its regular appearance once a week, it has gradually become an organ of considerable importance; so that the Council feel fully justified in continuing its publication, and may perhaps even endeavour still further to

extend and improve it. As a means of disseminating the information collected by the Society; as an organ for acquainting the members with the proceedings and reports of particular meetings and Committees; and as a medium of communicating with the associated Institutions and their members, the Journal has already proved to be of much value. The Council hope that the organ of correspondence thus offered to practical men will be frequently made use of by the members, because, bearing in mind the very large circulation which the Journal commands, it is evidently a most excellent medium both for collecting and for disseminating information. Its utility as as organ of Technical correspondence will probably be more fully appreciated when the members become more accustomed to its appearance.

A long line of bound volumes in the Society's Library, and also in other libraries, testifies that the hopes of the Council in 1853 have been substantially fulfilled. In the course of a century the intervals of publication of the *Journal* have not greatly varied. Weekly publication was continued until March 22, 1940, since when publication has been fortnightly. During the First and Second World Wars the size of the *Journal* was limited, but not even the General Strike of 1926 prevented its regular appearance, and the only issue in the whole series that is missing is that for February 28, 1947, when publication was prevented by the fuel crisis. The *Journal*'s chief aim has remained constant—namely, the publication of that vast mass of information contained in the authoritative papers read to the Society, and of the often most interesting and sometimes entertaining discussions which they provoke. For example, the first thirty volumes of the *Journal* contain reports of more than seven hundred meetings on the most diverse topics—industrial, mechanical, commercial, hygienic. . . . There has been virtually no limit to the range of subject-matter, provided only that there was, in each individual exposition, some germ of progress, some new line of approach that tended to an advancement in human welfare. To the published papers there have been added reports of the Society's activities; illustrations in the shape of photographs, drawings, maps and diagrams; book reviews; obituaries; miscellaneous notes likely to be of interest to members; and—a characteristic feature—the announcement of

"Some Meetings of Other Societies". As long as it maintained weekly publication, the *Journal* was registered as a newspaper and it has from the beginning contained advertisements—more now than ever in the past, for, with its present circulation of about six thousand copies, the *Journal* is an attractive medium for advertisers.

In addressing the Society as Chairman of the Council in 1890, Lord Alverstone, later Lord Chief Justice, spoke of "the mine of wealth as to the history of invention and scientific research which lay stored up . . . in the pages of the *Journal*". And, when Lord Bennett, the former Prime Minister of Canada, addressed the Annual General Meeting of the Society as its President in 1946, he said: "You wonder how I came to join this Society? I recall one evening in the House of Commons in Canada an old friend of mine, Senator Cantley, then a member of the Commons, coming and sitting beside me and saying to me, 'Have you ever seen the *Journal of the Royal Society of Arts*?' I told him that I had not much time to read magazines and he said, 'It is the best magazine in the world for it contains more information than any other and it is so useful; I constantly look at it for guidance in my own business.' (He was the Chairman of a steel corporation at New Glasgow.) I looked at it often after that. . . ."

Such praise, coming from two men of such distinction, at an interval of more than fifty years, is enough to show the continuing value of the *Journal*, and the esteem which it has won for itself, not only in these islands but all over the world.

2

The credit for suggesting the initiation of the *Journal* belongs to the Rev. Dr. James Booth, F.R.S., who at that time was Vicar of Wandsworth. He made the suggestion in a letter to the Council in June, 1852, setting out his scheme in such careful detail that it was adopted a few months later with very few modifications. The main reason for Dr. Booth's advocacy of the *Journal* was that a newspaper would serve as an excellent means of communication between the Society and the members of the mechanics' educational institutions all over the country which had recently allied themselves to the Society in what was called the Union of Institutions. It is time to say something of this important movement, which occupied much of the Society's energy in the eighteen-fifties and contributed powerfully to the progress of educational advance in Britain.

The pioneer of popular education in our country was Dr. George Birkbeck, who established in 1800 those cheap courses of lectures on science for Glasgow working men which developed into the Glasgow Mechanics' Institution, which in its turn inspired the London Mechanics' Institution (later known as the Birkbeck Institute). Many similar institutions came into being after this, and in 1848 the Society of Arts resolved that any institution established not less than fifty miles from London might join the Society for the same subscription as an individual, so that its members could enjoy, under certain conditions, the advantages of membership of the Society. A few institutions accepted the offer, but it was not until Harry Chester, later Chairman of the Council, took up the matter with his usual vigour that a conference was held, in May, 1852, under the presidency of Lord Lansdowne, which led to the formation of the Union of Institutions by a resolution of the Council in the following July.

The Society provided a central organisation for the Union, from which information could be made available, lists of lecturers distributed and so on. The number of member institutions increased from 71 in the first year to 270 in the second year, and 368 in 1855. Annual conferences were established, and in 1854, the year of the Society's centenary, a large exhibition of educational apparatus and appliances, plans and models for school buildings, books, maps and so forth, was held in the ill-fated St. Martin's Hall, Long Acre (a building completed for John Hullah, at great expense, in 1850, and burnt down in 1860).

This educational exhibition, though it involved the Society in a loss of £363, was a great success. Many eminent lecturers were engaged, and some of their papers were published in a volume by Routledge (1855). A direct outcome of the exhibition was the foundation of the educational collection and library at South Kensington which now forms part of the Victoria and Albert Museum.

From the Society's point of view, the most far-reaching result of the establishment of the Union of Institutions was the beginning of the Society's system of examinations, which has continued with ever-widening scope and increasing success from that day to this, and which will merit a chapter on its own account. But the Union also had the advantage of establishing educational organisations in provincial towns, which, in turn, provided centres for local science and art schools, and eventually became a basis for the system of scientific, artistic and technical education which grew up around those schools. The work of the local institutions varied widely in efficiency when the Society took them in hand, but the Society provided a standard to which they had to conform and a central organisation which was ready to back them with information and advice.

The Annual Conference of the Union of Institutions was held each year until 1875. The Union had by then outlived its usefulness, and when the examination system was remodelled in 1882, so that the examinations, which had originally been introduced for the benefit of its members, were thrown open to everybody, another reason for its continuance disappeared. It had, however, exerted a very valuable and encouraging influence at a difficult period in our educational history, and in 1951 the Society decided to take steps towards re-establishing this useful link with local learned bodies. The Festival of Britain in that year was made the occasion for inviting a number of societies which formerly belonged to the Union to rejoin.

3

The Society's work for education at this period was diverse in its scope and far-reaching in its effects. It was greatly concerned with technical education from 1867 onwards, when Dr. Lyon Playfair, returning from a visit to the Paris Exhibition of that year, where he had been acting as one of the jurors, commented in a letter to Lord Granville on the superior progress made on the Continent in technical or industrial education. As a direct result of Dr. Playfair's initiative, the Council appointed a committee on the subject in the latter part of the same year, and by this committee an important conference was organised which met at the Society's House in January, 1868. Shortly after, a further committee was appointed which in due course published a thorough report.[1] This report mainly envisaged the education of managers and superintendents, rather than of operatives, and included an appendix suggesting courses for students who had already acquired a certain amount of general and scientific education. The Council followed up the publication of the report by presenting a petition to the House of Commons in May, 1869, urging the necessity of technical education and asking for legislation that would encourage scientific training in secondary schools. Another result of the concentration on technical education at this time was the introduction of the technological examinations, which, as we shall see in a later chapter, were carried on by the Society for a number of years until they were handed over to the City and Guilds of London Institute in 1879.

4

The Society's chief educational work had always lain in furthering industrial education, whether general education for artisans or specific technical training, but in 1869 and 1870 it was drawn into the movement for improving national education generally. Its main contribution here lay in its publication, during the year 1870, of some remarkable reports on the educational needs of certain districts of London.

The most sensational of these reports was painstakingly prepared for the Society by George C. T. Bartley and dealt with "the educational condition and requirements" of one square mile in the east-end of London, including the worst portion of Bethnal Green, Shoreditch and Hoxton, a part of Kingsland, Hackney, and the whole of Haggerstone. The achievement of Henry Mayhew had

[1] *Journal*, XVI, p. 627.

already familiarised the Victorians with the possibilities of this type of investigation, but the Society's close study of numerous homes and schools in the district equally reminds the modern reader of the subsequent work of Rowntree and Lavers—and, indeed, represents an important advance in the progress of sociological research.

It is not surprising that Bartley's report attracted shocked attention when it was published as a supplement to the *Journal* for March 25, 1870. On the very first page appeared the startling statement: "In this square mile there are 165 public-houses and 166 beer-houses, and the estimated amount spent in them by these very poor people is not less than £450,000. If one penny out of every eight now spent in drink were put by for one year, the amount raised would more than build the schools required, and one penny out of every twenty-eight would keep them up efficiently, without any government aid or assistance from charity." The second page included the information that the houses in the southern half of the area "are composed chiefly of four or five rooms, and usually contain the same number of families. An old inn which, some sixty years ago, was a sort of Sunday excursion house on the Cat-and-Mutton-fields, now called the London-fields, contains twenty-six rooms, and has no fewer than twenty-six families residing in it." When the investigator turned his attention to individual families, there were many very sad, not to say tragic revelations to be made, but there was also evidence of honest and respectable living, especially in the religious homes, and of abundant Cockney spirit. "The character of this part of London", wrote Bartley, "may be judged from the opinion of one of its inhabitants who, on being asked by the writer the way to the 'Ragged School', replied, 'The Ragged School? I don't know; we are all ragged here.'"

Bartley's report was followed by inquiries into "the existing state of education" in Richmond, Twickenham, Mortlake and that neighbourhood, and in Battersea. Both these reports, which were published as supplements to the *Journal* of April 8, 1870, and August 12, 1870, respectively, were undertaken for the Society by T. Paynter Allen. In sponsoring and publishing these investigations the Society was stimulating the national conscience in the best tradition of the higher journalism, and its efforts left their mark on W. E. Forster's Elementary Act of 1870. Before this Bill was introduced, a conference was held, and afterwards a petition was presented to the House of Commons and a memorandum to the Prime Minister embodying the Society's views. The Society was not successful in its far-sighted demand for a Minister of Education, but some of its other suggestions were fruitful.

At the end of 1868 the Society began a vigorous campaign for the encouragement of drill in schools, which met with considerable success. As a result, in June, 1870, three thousand boys from metropolitan schools drilled at the Crystal Palace in the presence of the Prince of Teck. In 1871 Prince Arthur (later the Duke of Connaught) watched a similar review at the Horticultural Gardens; in 1872 the Prince of Wales was present and afterwards gave to the winners in the Albert Hall the flags that the Society had provided for them. More than four thousand boys attended on that occasion. Further reviews were held in 1873 and 1875, but in the latter year the Society decided that the time had come for the movement to be put on a national basis and expressed the hope that the London School Board would continue the reviews which the Society had inaugurated.

The London School Board accepted the suggestion and arranged for all the schools to be represented at a public review held in Regent's Park in 1877. Over ten thousand boys then took part, and the Society provided an elaborate challenge-banner, for the winning team, which was embroidered by the School of Art Needlework and cost nearly £100.[1] But this mammoth feat of organisation seems to have been too much for the London School Board to sustain indefinitely, and in 1879 we find them informing the Society that they proposed to direct their drill instructor to select each year ten of the schools, where the boys were most efficient in drill, to compete for the Society's banner. Accordingly, forty boys from each of the ten schools appeared in the

[1] The banner was returned to the Society in 1951 by the Education Officer of the London County Council. One of these parades is illustrated in plate 27.

grounds of Lambeth Palace on October 11, 1879. In the words of the *Journal*, "the proceedings commenced with a march past the 'saluting post'—where the banner occupied a prominent position —in open column of companies, and after various evolutions, performed with considerable steadiness by all concerned, the banner was presented by the Hon. Lyulph Stanley to the Limehouse School".

These drill reviews had always been subjected to some criticism from those who believed they would encourage "militarism", and it appears to have been partly for this reason that they were not longer continued. The Society's object had, of course, been otherwise; it had thought primarily of the advantages to health and discipline (although it is true that Henry Cole's interest in Army reform had provided part of the inspiration). Anyway, beyond doubt the Society's initiative was largely responsible for the greatly increased attention that has been given to drill in our schools since 1870.

One further example of the Society's achievement as a pioneer in education may be given before we close this chapter. In June, 1871, Mrs. Maria Grey read a paper on "The Education of Women", as a result of which a committee was appointed by the Council "to promote the better education of girls of all classes". A proposal to form a "National Union for the Improvement of the Education of Girls" was carried out under the name of the "National Union for the Higher Education of Women", and although this Union only lasted until 1884, from it something more enduring emerged—the establishment of the Girls' Public Day School Trust, which is still in successful operation to-day.

That the Society has by no means lost its interest in education in the twentieth century is sufficiently shown by the remarkable series of twelve lectures on "Education To-day and To-morrow" given to the Society in 1943–4 and later republished from the *Journal* in book form under the editorship of R. W. Moore.[1] Miss E. Strudwick, Hugh Lyon, Basil Yeaxlee, Sir Richard Livingstone and Dr. Moore himself were among the authoritative lecturers, and Dr. R. W. Holland in the concluding paper

[1] Michael Joseph, 1945.

provided an able summary of what they said. Incidentally, this book was published in Japanese in 1951.

With this continuing interest in our minds, we may well turn next to consider the Society's main claim to recognition in the educational field—its flourishing system of examinations: after which, in coming again to the fine arts, we shall also have to consider its important work in establishing two educational institutions, the National Training School for Music and the School of Art Wood-carving.

CHAPTER 15

The Society's Examinations

1

WE now approach, therefore, a branch of the Society's work which occupies a unique place in its history. Alone of the countless projects which it has initiated, its examinations organisation has grown to maturity under the parental roof, and still remains very much a member of the family, although it has now set up house on its own. Indeed, there are probably many thousands of people who know little of the Society except as an examining body, and to them it stands as the oldest and largest examining body in commercial subjects in the country.

The Society's examinations date back to the years immediately succeeding the Great Exhibition, an event which, as we saw, not only provided a great fillip to education generally, and particularly to adult education, but also started a positive fever of examinations (which are, after all, a kind of intellectual exhibition) throughout the country. A few years before, the Union of Lancashire and Cheshire Institutes had begun to hold examinations for students of its member institutes, and the College of Preceptors had just started its system of examinations for schools. But the decade immediately following the Exhibition saw the start of several examinations systems of a more open and general character. The earliest was that of the Society of Arts, and this was soon followed by the Oxford and Cambridge "locals", the Science and Art Department examinations and the public examinations of the University of London.

The Society's examinations were initiated specifically for the benefit of the working classes, but as with so many other of its activities on their behalf, its interest in their education arose to some extent from a sense of their importance to the general economic prosperity of the nation, as well as from true philanthropy. Nevertheless it is certainly impressive to find its early Council, a body composed largely of aristocrats and men of culture, devoting a good deal of the Society's resources and of their own time to the educational interests of those whom they termed "artisans", particularly during a period when there was considerable opposition among the upper classes generally to such a development, for fear of the psychological and social effects which they rightly forsaw it must ultimately have.

The Society's first great effort in this direction was, as we have already seen, the establishment of the Union of Institutions, whereby it sought to assist the spread of good literature, to provide openings for popular lectures, and to circulate instructional exhibits of various kinds among these educational centres. But all this, although quite valuable in its way, was not enough. Many of the institutions, having gone in rather half-heartedly for this vague kind of "uplift", were degenerating into mere recreational clubs, and if they were to serve their real purpose, something had to be done to induce their members to get down to real hard study. One of the stated objects of the Union therefore was that "without ceasing to be places of amusement, the Institutions should be encouraged to become places of systematic instruction, with systematic examinations, and certificates of the results of the studies".

Nor was the Society's concern limited to the members of the institutions, for it set up a committee to inquire into the whole subject of industrial workers' education, and an important report[1] resulted. This report set out the need only too clearly, and the Society, acting upon it, began to plan further steps.

2

It was Harry Chester who again took the lead. In December, 1853, two years after he had initiated the Union, he proposed to

[1] *The Report of the Committee appointed by the Council of the Society of Arts to inquire into the subject of Industrial Instruction, with the evidence on which the Report is founded.* (London: Longman & Co., 1853.)

the Council that they set up a committee to consider the provision of "class examinations" for the members of the member institutions, and their report, after much discussion, was adopted by Council. In the following April a notice was accordingly issued in the *Journal* giving an outline of the scheme decided upon, which was on similar lines to the system still used by the Society. Question papers were to be set by a Board of Examiners in London and distributed by post to local committees which would be responsible for the proper conduct of the actual examinations. The worked papers would then be returned to London and certificates issued by the examiners there.

Meanwhile, the Society was still further strengthening its position as an educational body by holding the first international educational exhibition already described, and the conferences and lectures on educational questions which were arranged in connection with that exhibition formed an appropriate background to that year's annual conference of the Union of Institutions, when the examinations scheme, including the list of proposed subjects of examination and the names of the proposed Board, was put to the Conference and approved. At the suggestion of Lord Ebrington, Chairman of the Council, an arrangement was also agreed to which would enable students in rural areas to benefit as well as those attending classes at town institutions.

In the following November it was duly announced that an examination on the lines agreed upon would be held in March, 1855, but it was hardly to be expected that with only four months' notice of these entirely new examinations many entrants would present themselves. In fact there was only one—a chimney-sweep—and the examination was cancelled.

This setback caused a change of policy which nearly wrecked the whole scheme, for serious thought now had to be given to ways and means of attracting more candidates, and the Chairman of the Board of Examiners, the Rev. Dr. Booth, F.R.S., whose origination of the *Journal*, and then his enthusiastic leadership of the Society's newest interest, had brought him rapidly to the Chair of the Council, suggested that the appeal of the examinations would be enhanced if they were conducted partly by interview as well as by written papers. Others felt very strongly that candidates would be attracted by the privilege of meeting the distinguised panel of examiners, that an examination conducted in this way would be fairer and more thorough, and that consequently the certificates based upon it would carry greater weight with employers. Dr. Booth's proposal was therefore agreed to, and in order still further to increase the value of the certificates the Society published a form of declaration on which people and firms of standing could state that they would regard them as "testimonials worthy of credit". Some four hundred signatures were obtained to this declaration, mostly of firms, but headed by that of the Archbishop of Canterbury, and the list was published with the syllabus for the 1856 examination.

This time, although the candidates were again given very short notice, fifty-two presented themselves. Papers were set in Mathematics, Book-keeping, Mechanics, Chemistry, Physiology, Botany, Agriculture, Geography, English History, English Literature and Composition, Latin and Roman History, French, German and Freehand Drawing, and each candidate had to take at least two of these subjects and also a preliminary and qualifying examination in handwriting and spelling. Two of them were ploughed in the latter, but one wonders what would be the effect of such a test to-day.

Because of the oral nature of the main examinations all the candidates had to attend at the Society's House in London, and in the case of provincial candidates this meant considerable expense. Some of them were fortunate, however, for institutions in Leeds and Liverpool raised funds to assist a few suitable students from those cities. There were also numerous offers of prizes from members of the Society, and one of the leading examiners, the Dean of Hereford, presented each successful entrant with a copy of his book, *Lessons on the Phenomena of Industrial Life*. But the crowning generosity was the gift of their services by the examiners, all of whom were men of standing and some of whom devoted four gruelling days, each of nine hours' actual examining, to the task.

The 1856 examination, small though it was, was large enough to start a movement which soon showed signs of spreading. The

Conference of the Union of Institutions that summer devoted much of its time to discussing how the benefits of the examinations might be extended as widely as possible, but it soon discovered how great were the difficulties imposed by the oral examination introduced by Dr. Booth. Some delegates to the Conference discussed ways and means of bringing Mahomet to the mountain and of assisting deserving candidates to come to London after the excellent example set by Leeds and Liverpool. Others were for taking the mountain on tour and asking the learned examiners to visit a number of provincial centres and conduct separate examinations in each. The Board of Examiners decided in favour of the latter course and recommended that there should be four centres in 1857, but the Council of the Society, out of pity for the peripatetics, reduced the number to two, one in London and one in Huddersfield.

At the same time, however, they proposed that local unions of institutions should be formed (where they did not already exist), which, besides providing a liaison with the Society's headquarters, would conduct preliminary tests for weeding out the weaker candidates and arrange local prize—and certificate—distributions for those who passed the Society's final examination. Thus was introduced what is still one of the main features of the Society's examinations system. The extension of the examinations throughout the country still depends on local co-operation, through the voluntary service of local committees which receive and transmit the entries although they do not any longer hold a preliminary examination. Correspondingly, the certificates granted to successful candidates bear the signatures of local education officials as well as of officials of the Society and are in most cases presented at local functions.

The local distribution of the Society's certificates goes right back to the 1857 examination, and the reports of the prize-givings that year in London and Huddersfield, as recorded in the *Journal*, invite an intriguing comparison between metropolitan dignity and provincial enthusiasm. The London proceedings, held at the Society's House, consisted merely of two formal speeches and the presentations to the eighty successful candidates. The Huddersfield ceremony, on the other hand, which was preceded by a sale of work in aid of the institutions from which the 140 local candidates came, was conducted in the Riding Schools, "tastefully decorated for the occasion", and packed out, with a "highly-respectable company" in the front rows and the galleries "filled with perhaps humbler persons". The chairman, Lord Granville, was in good form, having just dined with the other members of the platform party, and as he warmed to his subject his remarks were interrupted by "several workmen breaking some of the windows for the purpose of ventilation". "I believe this is only a practical illustration", commented Lord Granville (whereupon "his voice was again rendered inaudible by the falling glass"), "of what it is our duty to try to effect this evening—to throw as much light as possible upon the subject and to ventilate it thoroughly. I trust that we shall go on in this course but that our agitation may not be of so destructive a character!"

3

After the 1857 examinations the Society's experiment was considered to have succeeded, and it was felt that the project must now be put on a permanent basis. It was decided accordingly to add a series of bye-laws to the constitution of the Society, regulating the appointment of the Board of Examiners and delegating to it the necessary authority. A most respectable proceeding, yet it led, strangely enough, straight into one of those bitter disputes from which even so benevolent an institution as the Society of Arts cannot remain entirely immune. Dr. Booth, who, as has already been mentioned, was Chairman both of the Council and of the Board of Examiners, took it upon himself in the course of that summer to prepare a programme for the 1858 examinations which embodied regulations quite contrary to the general views and in some cases even to the formal decisions of his Council. What was worse, he announced these changes in public addresses and published letters and he even went to the printers of the *Journal* (by-passing the Secretary) and published in the advertisement pages a syllabus of his programme which indicated clearly enough the irregularities which it contained. Although the Council had decided the previous winter that it was impossible to conduct oral examinations at more than two centres, the syllabus made it clear that the programme would announce quite a number of centres. Above all, it implied that the Society had adopted a pet idea of Dr. Booth's to which the greatest exception was taken by the Council. This was the establishment of something tantamount to a degree—an "Associateship of the Society of Arts"—in connection with the examinations.

When the Council met again in the autumn they persuaded Dr. Booth to drop the associateship proposal, but when they also passed by twelve votes to his one a resolution calling upon the Board of Examiners to draw up a scheme of examinations by written papers only, he advised, and persuaded, the Board not to comply with the instruction. The climax came in November when he summoned a special meeting of the Council to establish a fund, consisting of the subscriptions to the Society of the institutions in union, which would be set aside purely for examinations purposes and be administered by a joint committee representative of the Council and the Board. It was pointed out to him that this was contrary to the terms of the Charter granted to the Society ten years before, which had placed full control over all the Society's funds in the sole hands of the Council, and he was therefore asked by his colleagues to withdraw his resolution. When he refused, the ten other members present signed a requisition calling upon him to resign, which he did there and then. There can seldom if ever have been so tense a moment in the Council Chamber of the Society.

There still remained the recalcitrant Board to deal with and the new bye-laws provided the occasion for this. These bye-laws provided that the Board should be annually reappointed each November and that the nominations for the new Board should be made by the retiring Board, and not by the Council, which only had the power to veto a name and not to propose one. Furthermore, the Chairman of the Board, who was elected by the Board, and need not even be a member of the Society, was given the right to attend all Council meetings. These bye-laws violated the terms of the Charter even more patently than the proposed fund, for they entrusted part of the Society's work to a largely independent body. Dr. Booth's resignation came at a critical moment, for a week later the retiring Board was to nominate the first new Board under these bye-laws. The Council took the strongest possible line. It forbade the retiring Board to meet, so that they could not nominate their successors, and then, at a special general meeting later that month, gained approval for revised bye-laws which brought the status of the Board into line with the Charter by transferring the executive functions of the Board to the Council and its officers and leaving to the Board the duties simply of setting and correcting the papers.

No opposition was raised at the meeting to these changes, but a spirited debate followed regarding the system upon which the examinations should be conducted in future. There was a general feeling that the continuance of the oral examinations was desirable, Samuel Morley and Henry Cole being among those who spoke in favour of it, but a very large majority felt equally strongly that the Council should not be tied to that system if they found it impracticable. Accordingly, in the revised announcement of the regulations for the 1858 examinations which was hastily issued a few days later, oral tests were eliminated altogether from the examinations, and this permitted the establishment not merely of the five centres which Dr. Booth had tried to establish but of as many more as there was need for. Fresh encouragement was accordingly given to the institutions to form centres, and the response to the appeal was excellent, fifty-eight centres being formed in time for the 1858 examinations, although, owing to the short notice only forty of these centres, in thirty-two different towns and cities, were actually able to submit entries. This time there were over 1,100 candidates, but less than half of these passed their local preliminary examinations and not more than half of those thus qualified took the final examination. Of the 288 candidates who actually sat the final examination, 197 were successful.

A considerable amount of confusion occurred at first in the conduct of these more dispersed examinations. Heartburnings were created in many breasts by the lists of results as first published because the wrong names had in some cases been attributed by the local centres to the successful candidates' numbers. What was far worse, all the candidates at the Oldham centre had to be disqualified through no fault of their own on account of irregularities committed by their supervisors. On the whole, however, the Society was satisfied, and as soon as those concerned became familiar with the controls (which were identical in most details with those in use to-day) the scheme worked admirably.

Having broadened the basis of the examinations geographically, the Society began to widen their scope with respect to the class of candidate for which they catered. Originally they had been confined to members of mechanics' institutes, and this restriction was not due merely to administrative convenience. The Society had founded its examinations specifically for the "artisan class", and even gave a detailed definition of those for whom the examinations were intended as being "commonly mechanics, artisans, labourers, clerks, tradesmen and farmers not in a large way of business, apprentices, sons and daughters of tradesmen and farmers, assistants in shops, and others, of various occupations, who are not Graduates, Undergraduates, or Students of a University nor following nor intending to follow a learned profession nor enjoying nor having enjoyed a liberal education". However, insistent requests were made by and on behalf of candidates outside these categories, and the Council finally relented. They agreed to admit such students to the 1861 examinations, but imposed upon them an entrance fee of half a guinea, whereas the ordinary candidates, entering through their institutes, paid none.

There was also the question of age. The examinations were meant for those who had left school and were actually in employment, and to ensure this a minimum age limit of sixteen was instituted. But it must be remembered that at this time, as the Newcastle Report of 1861 shows, most children of the working classes left school before they were twelve. A table compiled from questionnaires issued to candidates for the Society's examinations in 1858 shows that the average school attendance of these candidates was six years. The Society was anxious to preserve the serious character of its examinations and the solid worth of its certificates by maintaining its sixteen-year age limit, and yet to do something to encourage youngsters who had left day school to continue with their studies at night schools or in other ways until they reached this age. It therefore stimulated the local boards and unions of institutions, which were already conducting the preliminary tests for the Society's examinations and in some cases also holding examinations of various types of their own, to provide local elementary examinations, with local certificates, for these children. The Society refused to become responsible for these examinations itself, but, in response to many requests for active help, it agreed to provide uniform question papers, and marked copies of these papers for the guidance of local examiners, to such bodies as cared to make use of them.

4

Meanwhile, the State was at last coming to realise its supreme responsibility for the education of the people. Even before the Education Acts of 1870, 1876 and 1882 had provided and imposed an elementary education for all, the importance of doing something for members of the industrial classes who had already left school was realised, and the Science and Art Department, which had been established in 1853, began a few years later to establish local examinations throughout the country on lines based upon those of the Society of Arts and in many of the same subjects. The Department's system, with all the resources of the State behind it, developed rapidly and soon far outstripped that of the Society. By 1869, therefore, it seemed to many that the time had arrived to discontinue the Society's examinations. The Society had, after all, now completed its traditional task as a pioneer. Not only were the Science and Art Department and, as it claimed, the Oxford and Cambridge Local Examination Boards following directly in its footsteps, but it had stimulated adult educational institutes in all parts of the country to organise courses and conduct examinations of their own. In the programme for the Society's 1870 examinations, therefore, all those subjects were omitted which were included in the Science and Art Department's examinations. This meant cutting the Society's list of thirty-six subjects by half, and it is not surprising that after taking so drastic a step the Council decided next year to abandon the examinations altogether.

But this decision never came into effect. At the selfsame meeting as that at which the Council came to this conclusion they considered a proposal by Captain (later Sir John) Donnelly that the Society should open up an entirely new field of examining. A new word, "technology", and with it a new aspect of technical education, was coming into prominence, and Captain Donnelly proposed that the Society should supplement the Science and Art Department examinations in general scientific and technical subjects by inaugurating "technological" examinations dealing with the scientific background and actual practice of specific trades.

For a body instituted specifically "for the encouragement of . . . manufactures" this proposal at once commended itself to the Council, and it received the full support of a public conference convened at the Society's House under the chairmanship of Prince Arthur in July 1872. It was accordingly decided to hold the first technological examinations in 1873, and the trades to be included that year were to be cotton and paper, together with three industries which formed the basis of the London international exhibition of that year, viz. carriage-building, silk and steel. To ensure that students taking these very specialised tests had an adequate background, all candidates had, in addition, to take certain of the more general papers of the Science and Art Department examinations in order to gain the Society's certificate.

There were only six candidates for the first technological examinations and no candidates at all in two out of the five trades advertised. But the Society was not discouraged, particularly as it was gaining considerable public support for its new experiment. A number of City Companies contributed prizes, and a few years later the Clothworkers Company gave a great fillip to the scheme by a grant of £200 to provide bonuses to the teachers of successful candidates. This "payment by results" brought the Society's examinations into line with the Science and Art Department examinations and with what was at that time the basis of the State education system.

26. THE FIRST PHOTOGRAPHIC EXHIBITION
Held by the Society of Arts, 1852

27. SCHOOL DRILL PARADE BEFORE THE PRINCE AND PRINCESS OF WALES, 1872

28. HEADQUARTERS OF THE NATIONAL TRAINING SCHOOL FOR MUSIC
Now the headquarters of the Royal College of Organists

29. EDISON'S "PHONOGRAPH"
An improved version of the instrument demonstrated to the Society in 1878

But while assisting the Society's scheme in these ways the City Companies had begun to consider what they themselves could do to provide training for the trades from which, after all, they derived their names, and in the summer of 1878 their scheme for the foundation of a City and Guilds of London Institute was announced. The Society had made it clear long before this that it regarded its conduct of technological examinations as a purely temporary measure, and as soon, therefore, as the opportunity presented itself, it lost no time in handing over its whole scheme to the new Institute, in time for the latter to conduct the 1879 examinations. Thus was completed another brief but important chapter in the Society's remarkable record as a pioneer.

5

There had been developments, in the meantime, regarding examinations in other subjects. At the conference which was convened to launch the technological examinations, some of the institutions in union took the opportunity to register such strong and influential protests against the Society's decision to drop these other examinations that the Council felt compelled to rescind the decision and to continue what, in order to distinguish them from the new technological series, were termed the "General" examinations of the Society. They might more accurately have been described as "Miscellaneous", for their only *raison d'être* was that they were concerned with subjects not considered appropriate by other examining bodies. The Council were very conscious of this and in 1875 attempted to mould them into a systematic scheme by dividing them into four clear groups—applied art, technological, commercial (these three groups corresponded with the three primary objects of the Society) and domestic economy. But such tidiness could not long survive with so opportunist a body as the Society of Arts, and soon the list of groups had grown from four to eight and lost any semblance of logic or balance.

The answer was to lie, not in classification but in concentration, on one group only, that of commerce, and a move in this direction was made in 1876 by the introduction in connection with the commercial subjects of an entirely new principle. Hitherto, a separate certificate had been issued for each paper in which a candidate passed, but the Council now decided to discontinue the issue of these single-subject certificates for the subjects in the commercial list and instead to issue a group "Commercial Certificate", for which a candidate had to pass in Arithmetic, English and at least one other subject out of a list of ten.

Educationally, the scheme was very sound, but in practice it proved a complete failure and the Society again lost heart. It had given up many of its most popular subjects in favour of the Science and Art Department and had handed over its technological examinations to the City and Guilds Institute. It now saw the examinations of both these other bodies prospering, while the commercial examinations with which the Society was left made no appreciable progress. It was clearly best, therefore, now that the major pioneering work was done, to close down the Society's examinations altogether and to free the Society for new activity in other directions. "The Society of Arts", reported a special committee, "held science examinations before the Science Department, examinations in literature before the Universities went a-field to meet the classes who could not go to Oxford or to Cambridge. It has seen the system it established develop, with the aid of Government funds, as it could never have grown without such help, and the time has now arrived when it may cease to compete with the agencies it has done so much to foster." On the committee's recommendation, therefore, the Council decided for a second time to give up all its examinations after 1880, except in Music, Domestic Economy and Political Economy.

This time its decision took effect, but for only two years, for again the institutions in union raised their voices in protest and again the Council gave in, although with considerable reluctance, and upon terms. If the institutions wanted the examinations, said the Council, they must justify their request by producing the candidates and the money. Examinations would only be authorised in subjects for which there were at least twenty-five entries, and they must be self-supporting so that the Society's limited funds might be freed for other objects. An entrance fee of 2s. 6d. was therefore instituted for all candidates and the scope of the examinations was limited to commercial subjects, music and domestic economy, and then only if the minimum twenty-five candidates in each subject were forthcoming. Incidentally, as has already been mentioned, the imposition of a uniform entrance fee for all candidates removed any special advantage previously enjoyed by members of the institutions in union.

6

Thus began the present series of commercial examinations, which in the course of seventy years have expanded to proportions which would have seemed fantastic to the originators. During the 'eighties progress was slow, but by 1890 the number of candidates had risen to 2,315, a little in excess of the top figure reached in 1869, before the process of concentration upon commercial subjects had begun. During the 'nineties the yearly increase accelerated, so that by 1900 the number of candidates had risen to nearly 9,000 and the papers worked to nearly 10,000. Surprisingly enough, this increase was due in large measure to the passing of the Customs and Excise Act of 1890, for that Act, by allowing the newly created county councils to use the proceeds of the spirit duty for purposes of technical and commercial education, enabled them to put into effect the powers conferred upon them by the Technical Instruction Act of the previous year to establish classes in these subjects. These new classes naturally produced many candidates for the Society's examinations.

Another factor which contributed to the growing popularity of the examinations was the introduction of bronze medals in 1891. Prizes had been instituted in connection with the examinations from the start and had from time to time been contributed by many notable persons and institutions. The Sovereign herself had annually maintained a prize of 25 guineas, instituted by the Prince Consort a few months before his death, for the candidate who obtained the largest number of first-class certificates in four consecutive years. Then, in 1883, in accordance with the Council's generally "tougher" attitude, the offer of prizes was discontinued, but it was revived in 1891, when a new and carefully thought out system was introduced. At least one bronze medal was awarded in each subject in which an examination was held, additional medals being awarded according to the number of candidates. This is similar to the system still in operation. In addition, money prizes were awarded to medal winners in a number of subjects, through the generosity of various city companies, but this practice was discontinued during the First World War.[1] The intention of the medals was not so much to attract a greater number of candidates as to attract a greater number of *good* candidates, and, as time went on, and the Society's examinations became nationally known, its medals became a certain passport to a good appointment.

With the turn of the century there came another important development in the Society's examinations system, the introduction of three stages. For nearly half a century the Society had examined at only one level in any one subject, but in the year 1900 it was decided to institute three entirely separate grades, the existing standard becoming "intermediate", with new "elementary" and "advanced" grades below and above it. This decision was implemented by stages. The elementary grade (for which there was an immediate clientele in the new day continuation schools) came into effect the next year, but the advanced stage, regarding which there were considerable doubts at first, was not introduced until 1905.

Together with these new grades, or "stages", the Council reintroduced the group certificates which had so poor a chance to establish themselves in the 'seventies. By encouraging the acquirement of a wide and ordered range of knowledge, these certificates are of great educational value, but unfortunately they have never attracted as many students as the Society could wish.

Now followed a period of astounding expansion. In 1900, the number of papers worked had been 9,808, but by 1905, when the three grades were in operation, it had risen to 23,803, and thereafter there was a steady increase until a new level of about 30,000 was reached in 1911. In 1914, on the eve of the First World War, the way to another important advance was opened by the intro-

[1] The Clothworkers' Company still continues its annual grant, which is now devoted to providing medals instead of prizes.

duction of a second series of examinations each year, one series continuing as before to be held in the spring, and a new series being added at Whitsun. When the war was over this change naturally had an effect on the number of entries, which again began to rise rapidly. The papers worked in 1919 numbered 31,000 and by 1925 they had risen to 71,000. The introduction in 1926 of a third series, to be held in July, which was established particularly in the interests of day schools, gave a still further "boost", and the figure of 100,000 entries was passed for the first time in 1929. A fourth annual series, in November, was introduced in 1938, but this, although it at once justified its institution, did not—for obvious reasons—attract so large a number of new candidates.

The Second World War, with the evacuation of schools and the "blitz", had a profound and widespread effect on education, but the number of students who actually succeeded in preparing and sitting for examinations in such conditions was remarkably high. By encouraging these young people to persevere with their studies the Society felt that it was rendering a real service to the nation, and as time went on it was able to undertake several special war-time examination tasks. At the request of the Treasury it organised a scheme of shorthand and typewriting proficiency tests for civil servants which had a marked effect in improving the standard of these "office arts" in the Civil Service. In both the wars the Society conducted examinations for British prisoners of war, and an amusing incident occurred in 1917 when the German Censor not unnaturally stopped the English papers because the examiner in précis-writing had selected for his test "Correspondence with the United States Ambassador respecting the treatment of British Prisoners of War in Germany"!

Since the Second World War the Society has been invited by Government departments, local education authorities and other bodies to undertake a number of other special examining tasks, some of them of very considerable importance, and the Society's examinations department is, in fact, entering upon a new phase. Besides maintaining its own regular commercial examinations on an ever-increasing scale, it is now becoming generally recognised as a maid-of-all-work to be called in by other bodies wishing to have internal examinations of a commercial character conducted by an outside organisation. All this has of course meant a further expansion in the work of the department and an increase in the number of papers which it handles, and since the war the total number of entries has in some years been in the region of 150,000. The present record is 154,100 in 1949.

Although this vast number of entries and of worked papers passes through a single office in London, the Society's system also depends, as has already been emphasised, upon a great network of local centres. For the 1953 examinations there were nearly 800 centres of examination in Great Britain and Ireland, almost all of which were under the control of the local education authorities; those not under the local authority were supervised by a special local committee approved by the Society. Because of the difficulty of exercising due control over the supervision of examinations overseas few centres have been opened outside the British Isles, but, with the approval of the Colonial Office and under the control of the local government officials, there are centres in East and West Africa, the West Indies and other parts of the Empire. The Society's certificates are, in fact, much sought after in these rapidly developing colonies, and the following letter from the Gold Coast, evidently composed with the aid of an excellent phrase-book, is typical of many inquiries received from ambitious young Africans:

Dear Sir,

I will be in fied of an interesting thing, if you will have a paramount consideration about me, as though you will send me one of your prospectuses.

My heart will be expanded more and more with an exalted gladness if you will your best to have the same opinion as and then sending it by leaps and bounds to me.

I am looking very pleased at the result,

my dear Sir,

With the good compliments to you,

I am,

Yours faithfully

The Society has also sought, and very readily obtained, both local and national co-operation in the central organisation of its examinations. In 1919 the Council reorganised the Examinations Committee to include representatives of the Board of Education, local education authorities, the teaching profession and various professional bodies concerned with commercial subjects. The establishment of this large and representative body set a seal—if such were needed—upon the national status of the examinations.

7

A brief word must be added regarding the officials who, under the Council and Secretary, have been responsible for the execution of this very important work, and who personally deserve so much of the credit for its successful accomplishment. For a considerable proportion of the period during which the examinations have been in operation the executive work was carried out by the ordinary staff of the Society and combined with their other duties. In 1869 it was felt that a special appointment was required, and the Assistant Secretary, Charles Critchett, was made Examinations Officer and held this appointment until the handing over of the technological examinations to the City and Guilds of London Institute made it redundant. But the late J. H. Buchanan, whose name is outstanding, on the staff side, in the history of the examinations, and who was made responsible for the examinations in 1900, was not formally entitled Examinations Officer until 1917, and although during his period of responsibility the number of entries rose from 10,000 to 100,000, even at the time of his retirement in 1938 he still combined with his examinations responsibilities the post of Accountant of the Society. It was not until the war enforced a complete segregation of the examinations staff that their duties became entirely specialised.

J. H. Buchanan was succeeded as Examinations Officer by the late C. D. Cassidy, and from 1942 by Mr. H. T. Broad, who was eminently successful in the task of restoration from the disruptive effects of the war and in leading the Society into several new fields of educational service. On his retirement at the end of 1951 he was succeeded by Mr. F. A. Wheeler.

Of recent years the Examinations Officer has also been assisted by an adviser of high academic standing and wide experience in the field of commercial education, whose counsel has ensured that the examinations machine should be properly geared to constantly varying external conditions. In 1928 Mr. A. Kahn, on his retirement as H. M. Inspector, was appointed to this post. He was succeeded by Dr. F. H. Spencer, formerly Chief Inspector of Schools to the London County Council, who acted for many years in this capacity, and who was followed in turn by Mr. T. C. Scadden, formerly Principal of Westminster Commercial Institute, and the present Adviser, Mr. J. P. Ivens, formerly the Principal of Chiswick Polytechnic.

Tribute should also be paid to the rest of the staff of the Examinations Department, who, though few in numbers for much of this period, have been characterised by an exemplary team spirit which enables them to conduct a remarkable volume of work with the reliability and efficiency which its special nature demands.

CHAPTER 16

The Fine Arts: 1854–1954

1

IN Chapter 3 an attempt was made to summarise the Society's services to the Fine Arts during its first century. It is now time to consider its achievements in the same sphere during the second half of its existence. The principle that directed the Society's initiative—and is still the mainspring of its activity—did not alter as the Society moved into its second century. That principle has always been to respond to the needs of the hour, to search for and to choose the field in which its gifts of encouragement and leadership could be most usefully deployed, to devote its full energies to the chosen object over a period of intense creative organisation, and finally, more often than not, to retire once again into the background, leaving the good work (where success had attended the Society's pioneering endeavours) to be carried on by those best qualified to further it.

We would not therefore expect to find in the second century any attempt to repeat the characteristic achievements of the Society in the realm of the Fine Arts between 1754 and 1854. The Society that had held the first art exhibition in England, that had played a decisive part in the movement leading to the foundation of the Royal Academy, that had done so much to encourage British artists by the award of no less than three thousand medals and prizes, and that had sponsored in 1852 the first public exhibition of the new art of photography, was entitled to feel that the major part of its vigilance in this sphere could now safely be left in other hands.

But its general interest in the Fine Arts did not slacken. At the outset of the second century we see the Society interesting itself in the Fine Arts in miscellaneous ways, some of which have been touched on already in this narrative. The Society's concern over the question of artistic copyright, for example, has been mentioned as an extension of its interest in the reform of the patent law: it occupied the attention of the Society, off and on, from 1858 to 1866, with results that, though somewhat disappointing at the time, left their mark on the Copyright Act of 1911. There were also one or two minor art exhibitions sponsored during the decade 1854–64, such as those of the works of John and Alfred Chalon and of Sir William Ross. In 1861 the Society was associated with the Company of Painter Stainers in promoting an exhibition of the work of artisans in decorative arts, and in 1862 it offered 100 guineas towards the funds required for executing two large mosaic pictures as decorations on the outside walls of the picture galleries of the International Exhibition building in Cromwell Road—a project which elicited working designs from W. C. Cope, R.A., and J. C. Hook, R.A.

An undertaking that was more far-reaching in its consequences was the Society's collaboration with the Society of Wood Carvers, in 1863, to hold an exhibition of wood-carving in the Society's House. The Society agreed to offer a silver medal and to make a grant of £30 towards the prize-fund. The success of this exhibition led to the Society's instituting a series of art-workmanship prizes for modelling, *repoussé* work, hammered work, carving, chasing, enamel and porcelain painting, and so forth. The scheme was further developed in 1864, when a more extended list of subjects was drawn up, and the competitions were continued annually, with a fair amount of success, until 1870.

This year was the last in which the Society offered its art-workmanship prizes as a regular annual practice. In the Council report of 1870 it was announced that the prizes would be discontinued "for the present", but that special prizes would be offered for objects of art-workmanship to be exhibited at the International Exhibition of 1871. Seventy-five articles were sent to the Society's House in response to this invitation. They were awarded silver medals and money prizes, and many of the articles were subsequently shown at the exhibition. But the annual report of 1871 confirmed the Society's decision to discontinue the art-workman-ship prizes, and gave the following reasons for it:

These competitions have now been carried on for several years, but the Council regret to observe that, in spite of the large amount of prizes offered, there is still wanting anything like an adequate response on the part of either manufacturers, designers, or work-men. The result is, that although no doubt the articles rewarded are of a very satisfactory character, showing great skill and taste, yet the competition is small, and the amount of money awarded is far less than that which was offered, and which it was hoped would be claimed. The Council have for some time past felt that it was doubtful how far, in face of so small a response to their offer, it was right to continue these prizes. In this state of things, and looking at the fact that Annual Exhibitions of Industry are now established, where an opportunity is afforded to any one to send articles for admission, and where such admission stamps them for excellence, the Council have thought it right to suspend this offer of prizes, for the present at least, in the belief that a sufficient stimulus is given by these Exhibitions, and that the money prizes are no longer needed. . . .

In fact, the annual exhibitions did not by any means take the place of the Society's prizes. There is no doubt that the prizes, with their accompanying small exhibitions, had served a useful purpose. The workers had certainly appreciated them, and there was some disappointment at their discontinuance. They were temporarily revived for a further short period in 1887.

2

"In compliance with a request from the Directors of the Royal Academy of Music, the Council have appointed a Committee to consider, in conjunction with that body, what measures should be taken to place that Academy in a position to realise the hopes of its founders, by subserving the purposes of a National School of Music." This announcement appeared in the report presented to the Society's annual general meeting held on June 26, 1861, and there was a concluding sentence: "The subject is still under con-sideration." In fact, the Academy's request had been received as early as June, 1860, and the Society's committee had already

(May, 1861) recommended rather sweeping alterations in the constitution and management of the Academy—alterations which, if carried out, would have amounted to the creation of a new institution. It is clear that the proposals did not appeal to the Academy, for nothing came of them.

The Royal Academy of Music had known startling ups and downs since its foundation in 1822, but at this time its fortunes were at a particularly low ebb. In 1864, the board of management was compelled to resign, and, before doing so, drew up a memorial to the government, praying for an annual grant. The prayer was successful, Mr. Gladstone, as Chancellor of the Exchequer, allowing a grant of £500 a year, which—despite its temporary withdrawal by a Conservative Government in 1867—was largely instrumental in securing the survival of the Academy. The events of 1864 had, however, drawn attention to the precarious state of music-teaching in England, with the result that in the same year the Society appointed a further committee to consider the whole problem of musical education.

Sir Henry Cole became chairman of this committee, and it may be assumed that he was the moving spirit in its proceedings, as he was in any campaign in which he was actively interested. A mass of information was collected about the working of Continental music academies, much of which was published in the *Journal* and embodied in two reports to the Council. The committee expressed the opinion that a National Academy of Music should not only provide free education for a limited number of persons having great musical gifts, but should also be open to the public at large on payment of adequate fees. It urged the Royal Academy of Music to broaden its basis of action and drew attention "to the fact that the Royal Academies of Music of Paris, Brussels, and Naples, being instances of highly successful institutions, present useful suggestions for the re-organisation of the Royal Academy of Music". Having considered the reports, the Council expressed their willingness to establish experimentally, in connection with the Academy, for a limited period, four free scholarships of £50 a year for the study of vocal and instrumental music, provided that the Royal Academy was placed in a permanent and efficient position, in accordance with the committee's reports.

This offer was made in 1867, and for the next four years intermittent discussions took place with the Royal Academy of Music. The discussions were not successful and showed no prospect of leading to the development of a national institution such as the Society envisaged. The Society therefore decided, in 1871, to take its own steps towards "the establishment of a National Training School for Music". At first there was a depressing setback, for a series of six concerts organised by the Society at the Albert Hall in 1871 (the first to be given in that building), so far from raising funds for the foundation of the School, as had been hoped, resulted in a loss of over £87. But in 1873, sufficient promises of help having been secured, a meeting was held at Clarence House, with the Duke of Edinburgh (who was a Vice-President of the Society and had joined the Society's committee the previous year) in the chair, at which it was resolved that "it is desirable to erect a building at a cost not exceeding £20,000 for the purposes of a Training School for Music at Kensington, in connection with the Society of Arts". A site on the west side of the Albert Hall was granted by the Commissioners of 1851, and C. J. (afterwards Sir Charles) Freake, a member of the Council of the Society, generously undertook to provide the building at his own expense. The Duke of Edinburgh laid the first stone on December 18, 1873. In the years immediately following, meetings were held at the Mansion House, at Marlborough House (under the presidency of the Prince of Wales), and at Manchester, Liverpool and other provincial centres, all with the object of procuring an adequate endowment of scholarships for the new institution. Eventually, eighty-two scholarships, of £40 each tenable for five years, were provided, of which thirty-three were founded by provincial towns, ten by the Corporation of London, fourteen by the City Guilds and four by the Society of Arts.

The building (illustrated in plate 28) was opened at Easter, 1876, and the school carried on a very successful career until 1882, when it was reconstituted and became the Royal College of Music. The College then took over the building, furniture and fittings, organ, and music, and a balance at the banker's of £1,100. When the accommodation in the original building became insufficient for the needs of the College, a new building was erected in Prince Consort Road, and this was formally opened in 1894, the former building becoming the headquarters of the Royal College of Organists.

During the six years of its existence the National Training School for Music had done very well. For five of these years Arthur Sullivan was its principal, and for the final year John Stainer. The professors, besides Stainer, included Ernst Pauer, and among the examiners were Sir Michael Costa, Sir Julius Benedict, Charles Hallé and John Hullah. The instruction in the Training School was systematic and thorough. One hundred and eighty students passed through the school, and such well-known musicians of their time as Eugene D'Albert, Frederick Cliffe and Annie Marriott were educated there. In 1880 the pupils of the school gave a concert to members of the Society in the Society's Great Room.

The Society not only spent £2,000 in establishing the school but also devoted a great part of its energies, over a period of twelve years, towards stimulating public interest in the project. Probably sufficient credit has never been given to the Society for its efforts. At least, however, the Society has the satisfaction of knowing, as it observes the continued progress of the Royal College of Music, that its labours in the cause of musical education have borne good fruit.

Unfortunately the same cannot exactly be said of another educational institution founded by the Society, the School of Art Wood-Carving, which is no longer in existence. It was established in Somerset Street, Oxford Street, in 1878, as the result of the application to this purpose of a sum of money offered to the Society by the Drapers' Company for the promotion of some branch of technical education. Subsequently the school was at various times accommodated at the Albert Hall, at the City and Guilds of London College in Exhibition Road, at the Royal School of Art Needlework, and at premises of its own in Thurloe Place. In 1901 the London County Council made the school a grant, which was increased in 1903, and again in 1912. Under the leadership of Thomas Armstrong, it prospered throughout the Edwardian years and obtained the recognition of the Board of Education. Although it eventually failed, this school had to its credit the training of many teachers and of many fine carvers whose work has benefited the trade.

3

The Society's well-meant but not particularly happy efforts to obtain a uniform musical pitch now require consideration. And, for the convenience of the uninitiated, it may be desirable to explain at the outset that pitch is the exact height (or depth) of any musical sound according to the number of vibrations that produce that sound. When we speak of one sound being "higher in pitch" than another, we mean that the vibrations producing the former are more rapid than those producing the latter, so giving what is recognised as a higher sound. Pitch is also the standard by which notes, with the A above middle C as a starting-point, are to be tuned, a standard which determines at how many vibrations to the second that A is to be taken, as well as the other notes in relation to it.

One would naturally have assumed that there ought to be some general agreement among musicians as to what musical note should be indicated by a certain musical sign, but unfortunately this agreement has been slow in coming, and the question has been much debated. Nevertheless, from early in the seventeenth century down to about the death of Beethoven, the pitch in use was fairly uniform; and this is known as the "classical pitch". Early in the nineteenth century the pitch was gradually raised, especially by the makers of wind instruments to secure more brilliant effects; but the change altered the character of compositions and tended to ruin the voices of singers, besides throwing musicians everywhere into confusion. In 1834 a "Congress of Physicists" at Stuttgart adopted a proposal to fix the A at 440 (true C = 528), but this seems to have had no practical results. Twenty-five years later, a French government commission fixed A at 435 (true C = 522), and this French standard pitch, since known as the Diapason

Normal, became legal in France on July 1, 1859. As a consequence of the French decision, the Society of Arts, acting on the suggestion of Wentworth Dilke who was then Chairman of the Council, called a meeting of musicians to discuss the matter, and then appointed a committee which produced a valuable report drawn up by Dr. Hullah.[1]

Following the committee's recommendations, the Society proposed a standard of 528 vibrations for the middle C, thus reverting to the Stuttgart standard, although instead of making A = 440, which would have been the natural consequence, it made A = 444 vibrations, on the "equal temperament" system. It was unfortunate that the Society's committee did not sponsor the "just" A = 440, for this would have been near enough to the French pitch to have led, in all probability, to its early adoption in this country. And the question was further complicated by the misfortune that the musician entrusted by the Society with the tuning of the standard forks was incorrect in his determination. The Society's efforts were therefore ineffective and its suggested pitch was never adopted to any extent.

Many years later it was brought to the Society's notice that the existence of this pitch, which had become known as the Society of Arts' pitch, might actually be considered an obstacle in the way of those who were endeavouring to secure the adoption of a uniform pitch. In 1885 a well-attended meeting of musicians, convened by the Royal Academy of Music at the St. James's Hall, resolved that it was desirable to conform to the French pitch; and in the following year the Society, accepting the advice of a special committee, formally abandoned the Society of Arts' pitch and published its reasons for so doing.[2]

That this decision did not please every musician is shown by two letters in the Society's archives from Dr. John Stainer (later Sir John Stainer) to the Secretary, Trueman Wood. In the first, dated January 29, 1886, he writes:

> I feel sure that the English nation will never adopt the French pitch—I hail with satisfaction, therefore, the effort to establish

[1] See the *Journal*, VIII, 572 (June 8, 1860).
[2] *Journal*, XXXIV, 265 (February 12, 1886).

30. DESIGN FOR LABOURERS' COTTAGES

Awarded a prize in 1864

31. CROP DRYER DESIGNED BY W. A. GIBBS

Awarded a prize in 1867

a "medium pitch" which I am confident would be accepted by orchestral and other players, by singers, by makers of instruments, and by military bands—the wood-wind instruments of which could be modified to a medium pitch at a comparatively small cost.

And in a letter of February 16, 1886, he still maintains this point of view, saying:

Of course I shall not in any way attempt to throw obstacles in the way of the adoption of the French pitch; but I am absolutely certain the attempt to establish it will fail; we *cannot* ask the government to throw away as useless £100,000 worth of military instruments.

On the other hand an English National Pitch of C = 528 would be adopted by all our colonies, I am sure; and would I believe be some day adopted on the Continent.

However, in the long run Stainer's prediction proved false. In 1896 the French pitch, or something closely approximating to it, was generally adopted in England. It is true that, as Stainer had feared, the military bands did not lower their pitch until some time afterwards, owing to the cost of altering the instruments; but in 1929 they too conformed, thus enabling British bands to play with British organs and British and French bands to play together.

Although the Society's examinations have been dealt with generally in another chapter, it may be desirable to refer specifically to its music examinations at this point. Music was included among the examination subjects almost from the first. Theory of music appears in the 1859 programme, the examiner being John Hullah. After Hullah's death W. A. Barrett, Sir Joseph Barnby and Dr. W. G. McNaught were among those who conducted the examination, which in 1893 was divided into two parts: "Harmony" and "Rudiments of Music". The Theory examinations were not continued after 1914.

Practical examinations in music were established at Dr. Hullah's suggestion in 1879 and were continued annually for thirty-six years until they also came to an end in 1914. The examiners already mentioned in connection with the Theory examinations officiated for the practical tests also, and in the later years John Farmer, Dr. Ernest Walker and B. W. Horner examined. The highest number of candidates recorded was 557 in 1904: from that point there was a gradual decline. It was intended that these examinations should apply to a less advanced class of candidate than those who entered for the examinations of the Royal Academy of Music when the Society's system was started, or for the examinations of the Associated Board which took their place. They undoubtedly fulfilled a useful purpose in their time.

4

Throughout the late Victorian and Edwardian years, the Society continued to concern itself with the Fine Arts over a wide field. A curious by-product of its activity was the committee appointed in 1878 which advised the British Museum on the printing of its catalogue of books. In 1881 the Society sponsored an Art Furniture Exhibition at the Albert Hall, in respect of which the committee appointed by the Council recommended an award of nineteen medals and thirteen certificates. In 1882 two interesting and successful exhibitions were held in the Society's House—the first an exhibition of the progress of photography from its early stages, and the second an exhibition of modern English pottery which contained contributions from the principal manufacturers. In 1888 a paper read to the Society by T. R. Ablett on Drawing as a means of education, and advocating the inclusion of drawing as part of the curriculum of the ordinary school, led to the establishment of the (Royal) Drawing Society, whose annual exhibitions of children's drawings (encouraged in their early years by the award of medals by the Society of Arts) have continued ever since 1890. In 1889 the Society offered £150 in money prizes and twenty bronze medals for objects in an exhibition organised by the Arts and Crafts Exhibition Society in that year.

An important undertaking of this period was the Exhibition of Lithography initiated by the Society and held at the South Kensington Museum from November, 1898, until the end of February, 1899. This exhibition was the result of a suggestion by

Joseph Pennell that the Society should commemorate the centenary of the invention of lithography by Aloys Senefelder, an invention which the Society had been the first to recognise in this country by the award of its gold medal in 1819. After a committee had been formed, it was discovered that the exhibition would require far more space than was available on the Society's premises. The Stationers' Company then agreed to lend its hall for the purpose, but it was found that even with this assistance the cost of the exhibition would be considerable, and the Council therefore proposed to the Science and Art Department that they should take charge of the exhibition. The department acceded to this request and the Society's committee, with some additional members, continued its labours on behalf of the department. This admirable exhibition not only included a large and widely representative collection of historical and artistic lithographs but also a small set of examples of modern industrial lithography: in all, there were over 2,250 examples, and the number of artistic lithographs was greater than had ever been publicly shown before.

The Exhibition of Lithography proved to be the first of a series of exhibitions of the graphic arts in which the Society successfully collaborated with the Board of Education (as the Science and Art Department now became). The Society next proposed an Exhibition of Modern Illustration, and the Board of Education consented to organise such an exhibition, on the understanding that the Society would make itself responsible for the catalogue. As before, a committee of the Society, with some co-opted members, acted in an advisory capacity. The exhibition, which was opened at the Victoria and Albert Museum in January, 1901, was designed to illustrate the progress which had been made in the typographical reproduction of drawings for book illustration since 1860—a date selected because, photography having been made available for reproductive purposes in that year, the original drawings had henceforth been for the most part preserved and were available for comparison with the prints. The exhibition was restricted to illustrations capable of being printed with the text, i.e. woodcuts and process reproductions.

This was a most stimulating exhibition, for artists and book-

273

designers no less than for the general public, because the original drawings were shown side by side with the reproductions. Students could see the work of Millais, Thackeray, Tenniel, du Maurier, Keene, Birket Foster, Beardsley, Phil May, Caldecott, Kate Greenaway and Walter Crane, among many others who contributed to this golden age of British illustration. There were also representative collections of work done in foreign countries. Dalziel, Swain and other leading firms assisted, and so did many of the illustrated papers.

As an outcome of this exhibition, the Council of the Society next proposed that the series should be completed by a display of the various methods of illustration which had not been dealt with in the previous exhibitions, i.e. engraving, photogravure and the various photographic processes other than those applicable to typographic work. An Exhibition of Etching and Engraving, comprising a fine representative collection of engravings, etchings and mezzotints from the earliest times, was therefore opened in May, 1903, and an Exhibition of Photogravure in March, 1904, the Society advising the Board of Education as before. The processes represented in this last exhibition included photo-engraving, photo-lithography, collotype and three-colour process work.

Thus the Society and the Board of Education between them had completely covered, in these four exhibitions, the whole range of graphic art as applied to illustration. The exhibitions were extremely popular and provided salutary instruction for artists and the general public alike. In retrospect, they stand as a landmark recording a revolution which has enormously affected—for the better—both the public taste and the artist's chances of employment. It was another feather in the cap of the Society that it had initiated and collaborated in these significant displays.

5

It is arguable that, despite the various special enterprises and achievements that we are considering, the Society's chief service to the Fine Arts during its second century has lain in the long series of papers that it has commissioned for reading to the Society and has preserved for posterity by publication in the *Journal*. It is impossible to do justice to the great variety of artistic subjects that were treated by experts under the Society's auspices. There were many such important occasions as Seymour Haden's paper on Etching in 1883 and A. J. Ellis's on Musical Scales in 1885. And in 1887 a section of Applied Art was inaugurated which flourished until 1908, largely under the inspiration of H. B. Wheatley, who was its secretary for the whole of that period. During every session between 1887 and 1908 from four to six papers were read, dealing with subjects coming more or less within the scope of the application of Art to Industry. The definition was liberally construed, however, and some of the papers dealt with artistic matters in a more general sense. In the first year we find Walter Crane (who was, incidentally, one of the very few artists to receive the Albert Medal) arguing strongly for the "Importance of the Applied Arts, and their Relation to Common Life", and the section gave hospitality to such practical interpretations of his thesis as were contained in Joseph Pennell's paper on lithography in 1898, or in the papers by Edward Johnston and Graily Hewitt on "Calligraphy and Illumination" in 1905, or in Louis N. Parker's paper on "Historical Pageants" in 1906.

After the abolition of the Applied Art Section, all artistic subjects were dealt with at the ordinary meetings of the Society, as they always had been before the section was instituted. Indeed, it may be noted that, even while the Applied Art Section was in being, such important papers as Arnold Dolmetsch's on "The Chamber Music of Purcell, Handel, and Bach" in 1897 and Douglas Cockerell's on "Leather for Bookbinding" in 1900 were given to the ordinary meetings. From that day to this the Society has been most fortunate in attracting to its lecture-lists the leading authorities on their special subjects. Who would not feel pride and confidence in a society that could present, as it did in 1930-1, the views of D. S. MacColl on Alfred Stevens, W. G. Constable on Italian Art, Mrs. Arundell Esdaile on "The Portrait in our Later Monumental Sculpture", and Laurence Binyon on Persian Painting?—or sponsor Sir Walford Davies's lecture on "Melody in English Music" in 1936, or the lectures by Peter Ustinov, Sir

Ralph Richardson and Tyrone Guthrie on "The Modern Theatre" in 1952?

The Society's relations with its lecturers have been, almost without exception, extremely cordial. It will, however, be consistent with the aims of this History to refer to one occasion when the artistic temperament of a distinguished lecturer precipitated an angry letter to the Society. In 1888 Hubert Herkomer gave a special course of three lectures on "Etching and Mezzotint Engraving" which were of a practical nature, and were intended to offer the audience some information on the nature of the manipulations required for the various processes. They were fully illustrated by examples of finished and unfinished work, plates in various stages, tools and appliances generally. The lectures were attended by very large audiences and were greatly appreciated, so that the Society naturally looked forward to printing in the *Journal* as full an account of them as space permitted. Accordingly, the reports were duly set up in type and proofs were sent to Professor Herkomer. It was not long before the following letter reached the Secretary:

July 22. '88.

My Dear Sir,

I must stoutly refuse to have these ridiculous reports of my lecture published in your journal. They are consistently *wrong* throughout and there is no excuse for such abominable style & English in a published lecture. I *"talked* the thing out" with my actual materials to illustrate my words. Such a hash of a report is likely to be of lasting injury to me, & I cannot & *will not* consent to its publication. Nor will I ever lecture again at the Society with this sort of nightmare to follow.

I am worn out with work— & cannot attempt to *correct what cannot be made even decent reading by correction.* It is beyond it; & I am extremely surprised that such a hash should have been sent me. As it reads there is neither *sense* nor form of any kind.

These Reports *must* be kept back until you can get somebody to give a *summary* of the lectures—that is all that would be possible. A note to this effect should be entered in your journal—I do not think I talked *such nonsense* as the reports give, or the audiences would not have been so happy.

Yours sincerely,

HUBERT HERKOMER.

In face of this broadside, the Society obviously could not maintain its intention to publish the reports, and in fact the lectures were not recorded in the *Journal*. Fortunately, the proofs of the reports were preserved and bound up into a small book. From them a reader can obtain a vivid idea of the way Herkomer "talked the thing out" as an impromptu performance. One might hazard an opinion that the shorthand-writer had not done too badly, though there are undoubtedly some mistakes and probably a few things that Herkomer himself (assuming he said them) would rather have said differently. The editor of the *Journal* has the comfort of knowing that, now as always, the great majority of the papers given to the Society are read from a manuscript; the services of a shorthand-writer are normally only required to take down the discussions at the end.

Sir Hubert Herkomer forgave the Society, and was offered a rather piquant form of revenge against the Secretary, Trueman Wood, whom he had reproached so bitterly. He was asked to paint Trueman Wood's portrait, which was presented to the Society by the members of the Council in 1902 and now hangs in the Council Room (it is reproduced in plate 33). The portrait was a success: Herkomer not only achieved a good likeness but also a life-like impression of character.

6

Mention should be made of several comparatively routine matters touching the Arts for which the Society has made itself responsible. In 1875 the Society accepted the balance of a sum collected for a memorial to William Mulready and made itself responsible for the upkeep of the tomb, an erection of considerable interest and artistic merit in Kensal Green cemetery.

There are also several trusts of an artistic nature the duties of which are carried out by the Society. One of these, the John Stock Trust, was mentioned in an earlier chapter. Another, with a much larger income, was accepted by the Society in 1928 and provides for the periodic award of an Art Congress Studentship for the promotion and encouragement of Art. This fund was the balance remaining after the winding-up of The National Association for the Advancement of Art in its application to Industry, a body founded in 1888 for the purpose of holding an annual congress in different parts of the country for the discussion of problems relating to industrial art, and the income has been used for the award of studentships in connection with the Competition of Industrial Designs and the Industrial Art Bursaries Competition, which will be described a little later in this chapter.

Similarly, after the death in 1874 of Owen Jones, the joint-director of the decoration of the Crystal Palace, a sum of £400 was presented to the Council on condition that the interest should be expended in prizes to "students of the Schools of Art who, in actual competition, produce the best designs for Household Furniture, Carpets, Wallpapers and Hangings, Damask, Chintzes, etc., regulated by the principles laid down by Owen Jones". The prizes were awarded from 1878 to 1915 on the results of the annual competition of the Science and Art Department and its successor, the Board of Education. After 1916, when the Board of Education decided to suspend the "National Competition", the Society arranged competitions in collaboration with the Director of the Victoria and Albert Museum, until 1924, when they were merged in the Society's own competition.

7

During the nineteen-twenties and nineteen-thirties the Society undertook a campaign for the preservation of ancient cottages, which was carried on energetically and, within its limits, successfully. A work that aimed both to cherish the beautiful and to safeguard the remnants of an ancient craft may surely be described most appropriately in a chapter devoted to the Fine Arts.

The campaign was opened at a special meeting in May, 1926, when Sir Frank Baines read a paper entitled "The Preservation of Ancient Cottages". After sketching the conditions in which our village craftsmen grew up and evolved almost unconsciously their admirable arts, he showed a series of slides of delightful cottages representative of all parts of the country. Many of the most beautiful had already been demolished, and others were doomed to early destruction unless practical steps were taken to save them. Sir Frank was able to announce that the Society had undertaken "to initiate and endeavour to organise a movement, directed towards the final preservation of the cottage architecture of this country", and that the Society would "call to a conference all those anxious to help and devise a scheme to accomplish our aims".

That conference was held on January 26, 1927. The Prime Minister, Stanley Baldwin, was in the chair and proposed a resolution approving the action of the Society and signifying the intention of the meeting "to assist in the establishment of a substantial fund for application on the broadest national lines in furtherance of this movement". The resolution was supported by Lord Crawford and Balcarres, by the Speaker of the House of Commons (J. H. Whitley), and by Sir Alfred Mond, M.P., and was carried unanimously.

The conference was followed by the publication of an illustrated booklet in which Mr. Baldwin explained that the Society had "decided to do what they can to save these cottages—not for the week-ender, who may be left to look after himself, but for the benefit of those classes of local workers for whom they were originally built. Further, as the Speaker of the House of Commons put it, the aim of the Society is to preserve those cottages 'not as museums but as homes'". Thomas Hardy added an interesting note in which he emphasised the comfort and practical convenience of the old cottages of mud-wall and thatch. He remembered seeing one of the last of them being built when he was a child, and said that he had "never heard of any damp coming through these mud-walls, plastered and lime-whitened on the outside." "I can with pleasure support the appeal of the Royal Society of Arts for assistance in its plan towards preserving the ancient cottages of England," wrote Hardy, "having been, first and last, familiar with many of these venerable buildings in the West of England, and having also seen many of them vanish under the hands of their owners, through mistaken views not only on their appearance, but on their substantiality and comfort."

The Worshipful Company of Carpenters gave a luncheon in

aid of the fund, at which the Lord Mayor and Sheriffs attended. By July, 1927, the amount received had reached just over £4,500, and eventually it advanced to about £15,000. In 1929 a further conference was held, at which another Prime Minister, Ramsay MacDonald, took the chair and was supported by G. K. Chesterton, Sir Arnold Wilson, Sir Fabian Ware and others. In the early days of the campaign, the Society was successful in saving the three beautiful Thomas à Becket cottages, near Worthing, and it also purchased and reconditioned—by means of a special fund of £1,200—the group of cottages known as Arlington Row at Bibury, Gloucestershire (it was made over to the National Trust in 1949 after being in the care of the Bristol and Gloucestershire Archaeological Trust during the intervening period). Thanks largely to the energy of P. Morley Horder, the chairman of the executive committee of the Fund, more than thirty half-timbered cottages near Shrewsbury were saved and put into order. The Society also became the owner of Charles Lamb's cottage "Buttonsnap", West Mill Green, Hertfordshire, which was handed over to it by Mrs. T. T. Greg (the cottage was sold in 1949 to the Charles Lamb Society). Two more cottages, at Drayton St. Leonard, Oxfordshire, were bequeathed to the Society by James Cranstoun, K.C.

In the hope of attracting greater public attention and support, the Society decided in 1929 to purchase in its entirety the lovely old village of West Wycombe, Buckinghamshire, which was then about to be put up for sale in sixty lots. West Wycombe is an excellent example of an ancient English rural community, including about fifty dwellings dating from Tudor to Georgian times, and two inns, the gem of the village being the fifteenth-century "Church Loft". The presence at West Wycombe of an ancient but still vigorous furniture industry, centred in two factories, was another reason for selecting the village for a practical example of rejuvenation.

The village was then in a very poor condition, repairs had been neglected, there was hardly a decent garden in the place, the water supply was inadequate and dangerous, and there was no drainage system. But in the course of a few years West Wycombe was put into first-rate order and every cottage was provided with a fenced garden. The Society then entered into negotiations with the National Trust, with a view to their taking charge of the property, and in February, 1934, a reception was given by the Trust at Goldsmiths' Hall when West Wycombe was formally handed over for permanent preservation.

The adventure—as it may well be called—at West Wycombe had involved the Society in alarming responsibilities but in the long run had resulted in a triumphant success. This was largely due to the generosity of James H. Hyde, an American gentleman resident in France, who contributed substantially to the Fund; to the labours of John Burrow Hill, the Society's agent at West Wycombe; and to the skill of William Weir, to whom the architectural work was entrusted. The completion of the task at West Wycombe was greeted by a chorus of congratulation from the Press, which showed that the action of the Society had been keenly appreciated all over the country. The Society took no further important action in this connection until 1953, when it decided to expend the balance of the fund, which by that time had accumulated to an amount of over £1,000. It again approached the National Trust and offered assistance towards the restoration of suitable cottages on the Trust's estates, and as this offer was naturally welcomed, the Society was enabled, as its final act in connection with this Fund, to make itself largely responsible for the thorough overhaul and repair of the roofs of the famous and beautiful group of cottages (with its inn) at Chiddingstone, in Kent.

If the results, as a whole, of the campaign for the preservation of ancient cottages were less far-reaching than had been hoped, several substantial achievements lay to its credit, and the Society could be satisfied that it had brought the problem to general notice in a manner impossible, perhaps, for any other public body.

8

It was towards the close of 1917 that the Council decided that, in order to carry out the object of their charter, "the Encouragement of Arts, Manufactures and Commerce", they would be well

advised to resume their efforts to promote the union of Industry
and Art in Britain, with the idea both of improving the artistic
and workmanlike qualities of British manufactures and of maintaining the national trade throughout the world. Accordingly the
Council appointed an Industrial Art Committee which included,
in addition to persons nominated by the Society, representatives
of the Arts and Crafts Exhibition Society, the Design and Industries Association, and the L.C.C. consultative committees on
silversmithing and allied trades. The committee drafted a scheme
for the promotion of industrial art, and arrangements were made
to hold a meeting on October 28, 1918, at which the chair was
taken by the President of the Board of Education (H. A. L.
Fisher).

At the same time a scheme for the establishment of a British
Institute of Industrial Art was being promoted under the joint
auspices of the Board of Trade and the Board of Education. As
the two schemes were considered to be mutually complementary,
it was decided that the Industrial Art Committee of the Society
and the authorities of the Board of Trade and the Board of Education should work in close co-operation. At the meeting in 1918, a
joint appeal was made on behalf of the two schemes. But the
work did not prosper. An executive committee appointed by the
Council in January, 1919, came to the conclusion that the Society's
scheme was too indefinite to attract public support and sought to
formulate more specific proposals. Accordingly, a conference on
house furnishings was held in connection with the Ideal Home
Exhibition at Olympia on February 19, 1920, with the President
of the Board of Trade (Sir Auckland Geddes) in the chair. As a
result of this conference, the Industrial Art Committee entered
into communication with Sir Frank Baines at the Office of Works,
which required a considerable quantity of furniture for various
purposes. Sir Frank believed, with the committee, that furniture
of good but simple modern design, and of fine workmanship,
would prove better and more economical than anything that
could then be obtained at reasonable prices. He invited the committee to submit specimen designs to the Office of Works.

The Design and Industries Association then prepared five designs for dining-room furniture (a chair, an elbow-chair, a dining-table, a side-board and a side-table) in accordance with specifications supplied by the Office of Works. The designs were not only useful as illustrations of the arguments put forward by the committee, but they were found suitable for adoption by the Office of Works, which invited tenders from manufacturers for supplying furniture made to these designs.

Here was a practical achievement in which the Society could take pleasure. But it was an isolated success at the time, for the cause of good design required steady advocacy over many years before any substantial progress was made. The Society continued its campaign by making propaganda whenever it could; by including in its programme papers and lectures on Industrial Art; and by instituting an annual competition of industrial designs.

This competition, which incorporated the Owen Jones Prizes, was begun in 1924 at the suggestion of Sir Frank Warner, the well-known silk manufacturer, who was impressed alike by the difficulties of young designers in making their work known to manufacturers, and of manufacturers in knowing where to turn for fresh designing talent. Firms and individuals were approached and asked to offer prizes; programmes of prizes and scholarships were drawn up and freely circulated by the Society; joint juries nominated by the Society and the prize donors were appointed, and everything was done to see that the competitions were efficiently conducted. In the first competition the Society was able to offer over £1,000 in prizes and travelling scholarships. After the awards had been made, selected designs were exhibited, in London and elsewhere. Queen Mary three times visited these exhibitions and took a great interest in the work.

The total number of competitors in the ten annual competitions was 10,269 and prizes and travelling scholarships of the value of £11,550 were awarded. But all this was not achieved without a cost to the Society of £5,000, and the state of its finances in 1934 made it impossible for the Society to continue to bear expenses on this scale. It was compelled to bring the competitions to an end—with great regret, for they had been the means of discovering and rewarding a number of promising designers whose ability would otherwise have remained unknown; and the Society had also helped to find posts for many of the successful competitors. As a small compensation the Society in 1934 offered three prizes to art-teachers for an essay on "Training Art Students for Industry and Commerce".

The discontinuance of the competitions enabled the Society to devote all its energies to the Exhibition of British Art in Industry[1] which it held in 1935 at Burlington House, in association with the Royal Academy. The exhibition was the Society's idea, and the Society's approach was welcomed by the President (Sir William Llewellyn) and Council of the Academy. It was a most appropriate collaboration; for the Society, by holding the pioneer exhibition of pictures in this country, could claim to be the parent of the Royal Academy, whose first president (Sir Joshua Reynolds) had been a very early member of the Society. And by allowing this exhibition to take the place of the usual "Winter Exhibition", the Academy was recognising the importance of industrial design as a branch of art; it was conceding that a thing could be beautiful even though its purpose was functional and machinery had been used in the making of it. The illustrated souvenir of the Exhibition revives, for those who turn its pages, the grace and beauty of pottery and glass, of silver and metal-ware, dress materials, furnishing fabrics, carpets. The exhibits ranged from furniture to commercial printing, from jewellery to plastic mouldings. Everything on show was British. It had taken two years of organisation to fill the rooms at Burlington House, and the active interest of the Prince of Wales (now the Duke of Windsor), who served as President of the General Committee and opened the exhibition, had been of the greatest value. It may be noted that there was a return to the practice of the Society in its original exhibitions of design, in that no manufacturer was charged for space and the inclusion of his products depended solely on the selection committees.

The success of the exhibition—the first important British exhibition of design in modern times—was shown not only in the impression that it made on foreign visitors, and the closer cooperation between artist and manufacturer that followed, but

[1] See plate 38.

also in the enhanced reputation at home and abroad of British design, and the increased interest that the public has shown in industrial art from that time onwards. The establishment of the Council for Art and Industry, and of its successor, the Council of Industrial Design, was largely inspired by the exhibition, and so was that of the Faculty of Royal Designers for Industry, which, as we shall see, was directly due to the Society's initiative. Mr. J. A. Milne, who was Chairman of the Council at the time of the exhibition and took a leading part in its origination and organisation, eventually read a paper to the Society on "The 1935 Exhibition and After", in which he cited numerous instances of the great encouragement which the Exhibition had given to industry. In particular, he stressed the marked improvements that had been effected in the textile, glass, pottery and cutlery trades—as also in the art of display.

In November, 1936, for the first time in its long history, the Society gave a dinner in its own House—it was held in the library —to distinguished guests and leading representatives of the Press. This unusual step was deliberately taken to emphasise the importance of the occasion, for Sir Henry McMahon, the Chairman of the Council, then announced that the Society had decided, again at Mr. Milne's suggestion, to establish a new and high distinction to be conferred on designers in industry. He stressed the fact that there had hitherto been no hallmark of distinction in this sphere, and maintained that the Society now stood in the same position to the industrial arts as the Royal Academy did to the Fine Arts, and was therefore the proper body to grant a distinction of this kind which was bound to enhance the status of industrial designers as a whole. It was at first decided that the letters "D.I." should be used to indicate this new honour, but a few months later permission was obtained for the letters "R.D.I." to be employed to designate the distinction of "Designer for Industry of the Royal Society of Arts". Finally, the Royal approval was granted for the use by the holders of the distinction of the abbreviated title of "Royal Designer for Industry".

The Duke of Gloucester visited the Society's House in February, 1938, to present diplomas to the first recipients of the new dis-

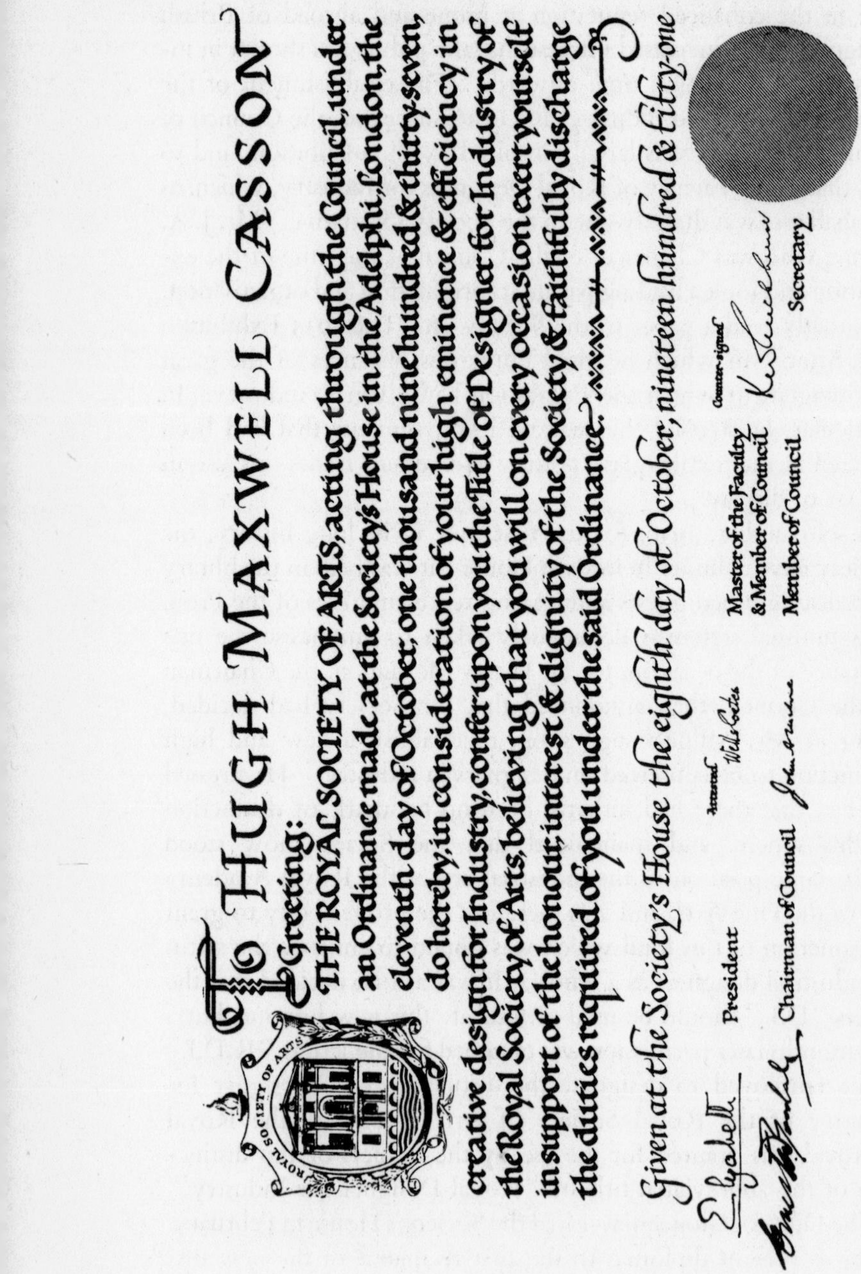

To **HUGH MAXWELL CASSON**

Greeting:

THE ROYAL SOCIETY OF ARTS, acting through the Council, under an Ordinance made at the Society's House in the Adelphi, London, the eleventh day of October, one thousand nine hundred & thirty-seven, do hereby, in consideration of your high eminence & efficiency in creative design for Industry, confer upon you the title of Designer for Industry of the Royal Society of Arts, believing that you will on every occasion exert yourself in support of the honour, interest & dignity of the Society & faithfully discharge the duties required of you under the said Ordinance.

Given at the Society's House the eighth day of October, nineteen hundred & fifty-one

		Counter-signed
E. Goodall	*Webster*	*K. Luckhurst*
President	Master of the Faculty	Secretary
	& Member of Council	
Ernest Pooley	*John Irwin*	
Chairman of Council	Member of Council	

FIG. 6. R.D.I. DIPLOMA

286

tinction. They were Douglas Cockerell (bookbinding), Eric Gill (typography), James Hogan (glass and stained glass), J. H. Mason (printing and typography), H. G. Murphy (goldsmithing and silversmithing), Keith Murray (glass and pottery), Tom Purvis (commercial art), George Sheringham (stage and interior decoration, costume design and textiles)—he had died since the announcement of the honour—Harold Stabler (pottery and silversmithing), Fred Taylor (commercial art), and C. F. A. Voysey (interior decoration, furniture and fabrics). E. McKnight Kauffer, an American citizen, received an honorary distinction for eminent services to commercial art. Another R.D.I. appointed later in the year was Edward Gordon Craig, who was honoured for his work in the theatre.

The value of the distinction was immediately recognised, and has been enhanced in the years since it was instituted—not least by the decision to limit the number of holders at any one time to forty, this deliberate restraint providing an assurance that the highest standard would be required and maintained. In 1939 the R.D.I.s, with the full approval of the Council, formed the "Faculty of Designers for Industry of the Royal Society of Arts" with the term "Master" for its active head. Through this Faculty the holders are able to act corporately for the furtherance of industrial design and the welfare of the designing profession. The Faculty appointed as its President, *ex officio*, the Chairman for the time being of the Royal Society of Arts; and the Master for the time being becomes, *ex officio*, a member of the Council of the Society, while the Secretary of the Society acts in that capacity for the Faculty also. H. G. Murphy was elected the first Master of the Faculty. Work by R.D.I.s provided the chief exhibits of the "Design at Work" exhibition held at Burlington House in 1948. The prestige of the distinction has been greatly enhanced by the inclusion in the diploma granted to its recipients of the signature of the royal President of the Society; and the present Queen, when holding that office, showed a most practical interest in the Faculty by attending its first evening reception, in November, 1950, and talking informally with every one of its members who was present.

The Society's competition of industrial design, which had been conducted so usefully between 1924 and 1933, was revived in 1938 on new lines, directed to the award of scholarships and travelling studentships to a few promising students, instead of the adjudging of a large number of miscellaneous prizes. A scheme was worked out, with the assistance of the Board of Education and other interested bodies, together with representatives of the manufacturing and distributing trades included in the competition, and a permanent Bursaries Board was established. An appeal for funds met with an excellent response, and the Council was able to offer one scholarship and one travelling studentship in 1938, not exceeding £100 in value, in each of the three groups, furnishing textiles, dress textiles and pottery. This was repeated in 1939 and, on a smaller scale, in 1940, but the Council was reluctantly compelled to suspend the competition in 1941, owing to war-time difficulties. Prizes for essays in industrial art were substituted, and the Council also organised a competition in design for the W.R.N.S. and a literary competition for the W.R.N.S. and the W.A.A.F. The industrial art bursaries were reintroduced in 1946, and scholarships of £150 were then offered from a fund to which the Society had been annually contributing during the war. In 1948 the scope of the competition was extended and eleven bursaries, of a total value of £1,400, were awarded to successful candidates that year. Since then the size of the competition has steadily increased, and in 1952 there were 233 candidates, coming from sixty-four different art schools, and seventeen bursaries of a total value of £2,300 were awarded. In addition to the bursaries the Sir Frank Warner Memorial Medal, which commemorates the initiation of the original Competition of Industrial Designs by Sir Frank Warner, is awarded for the best individual textile design submitted in the competition.

9

At the close of the Second World War, the Society was privileged to play an important part in guiding the nation's thought on the subject of its war memorials. On April 27, 1944, the Society called an all-day conference at which the speakers included Sir Fabian Ware, the Dean of Westminster, Sir Noel Curtis Bennett and others, and, as a result of this meeting, the Council was invited to institute a War Memorials Advisory Council. As many as fifty societies placed their resources and experience at the disposal of the Advisory Council, of which Lord Chatfield became the president and Mr. A. R. N. Roberts the Hon. Secretary, but membership was not limited to the representatives of societies; it included many distinguished people, from the spheres of Parliament, letters and the arts, the Church, industry and education.

The Society's action was widely appreciated, for it was generally felt that this time an advisory body had been created early enough to influence public opinion and ensure that the memorials of the Second World War should show an improvement on those of the First World War. Ten thousand copies of the Council's survey of the problem of memorials were distributed to Government Departments, Lords Lieutenant and local authorities throughout England and Wales. There was an immediate response; many requests for practical advice were handled by the associated societies, the schemes varying from playing-fields and Books of Remembrance to memorial hospitals; and it is probable that others among the United Nations were aided by the early attention which the Society had given to the subject.

Another interesting and important task undertaken by the Society during and immediately after the war years was the holding of a competition for the design of a new Anglican cathedral at Colombo. This was carried out by the Society as the agents of the Colombo New Cathedral Committee, Sir Giles Gilbert Scott, R.A., being the assessor. The result was announced in 1947, the first prize of £500 being awarded to Messrs. Pinckney & Gott, and the second and third prizes (of £200 and £100) to Messrs. F. X. Velarde and J. B. Wride respectively. Owing to its size and cost the prize-winning design was unsuitable for execution, but the successful architects were appointed by the Cathedral Committee and have begun work on definite plans for the new building.

Two other competitions, similar though less important, were

conducted by the Society during the same period. The first, undertaken on behalf of the Cement and Concrete Association for the design of a concrete fence, was held in 1945, and the second, sponsored by the Metropolitan Drinking Fountain Association for the design of a new standard type of drinking fountain for parks, in 1946. Both competitions received a very good entry.

A reference to the Society's Exhibition of Humorous Art, held at the Society's House in the summer of 1949, will make a fitting —though perhaps to some readers of this History an unexpected— conclusion for this chapter. "I never cease to be astonished, and impressed, by the versatility of the Royal Society of Arts," said Princess Elizabeth (as she then was), when she opened the exhibition, "but I frankly admit that one of the last things I expected to do here was to open an Exhibition of Humorous Art." However, she went on to add: "It is an enterprising undertaking, and a valuable one too, because there are few things in life more important than a sense of humour."

And yet was it, after all, such a surprising exhibition for the Society to sponsor? Mr. H. M. Bateman, reading his paper to the Society on "Humour in Art" in February, 1949, which directly inspired the exhibition that followed it, spoke of humorous draughtsmanship as "a fine art and a big industry", and asked: "Is it not high time that some official recognition of the worth of comic drawing was made?" Mr. Bateman was thinking, primarily, of his own idea of a National Gallery of Humorous Art, but what he said was pertinent to the Society's exhibition also: "The original drawings of many masterpieces of the art lie hidden away in back offices, or tucked into a corner of the studio of the artist, to whom they have been restored after publication. A few are prized and hang on the walls of collectors, which is all to the good; but they cannot be seen by the public when privately owned, nor until they are conveniently brought together." In fact, we may look on humorous art as an especially congenial and widely popular aspect of Art in Industry, and therefore well suited to the attention of the Society founded to encourage "Arts, Manufactures and Commerce".

The Society's exhibition,[1] which was on view from July 11 to August 13, 1949 (an extension of the original time-limit), owed much to the help of Mr. Kenneth Bird ("Fougasse"), the editor of *Punch*, who served on the exhibition committee with Mr. Bateman, Miss Anna Zinkeisen and Mr. Peter Le Neve Foster. One hundred and sixty-two drawings by more than fifty artists were shown, ranging from the work of Rowlandson and Gillray, by way of Tenniel, du Maurier and Keene, to Osbert Lancaster, Emett and Giles. Many of the artists were personally presented to Princess Elizabeth when she came to open the exhibition. The speeches made on that occasion, together with a notice of the exhibition by Mr. Nevile Wallis and Mr. Bateman's paper on "Humour in art", and numerous illustrations, provided material for a particularly rewarding issue of the *Journal*.[2]

This entertaining exhibition was the most successful held on the Society's premises for many years. It was visited by about 14,000 people and attracted press notice all over the world. The Council was able to arrange for the exhibition to travel, and during the seven months from October, 1949, to April, 1950, it was shown at Hove, Coventry, Salford, Preston, Liverpool, Glasgow, Aberdeen, Lincoln, Hull and Leicester. Probably another 40,000 people saw it in the course of this tour.

Even here, perhaps, we have not said the last word on the Society's work for the Fine Arts in its second century. But the exact scope of that elusive phrase is hard to define, and it has seemed more appropriate to follow the course of the Society's encouragement of the new art of photography, for instance, and its attention to certain purely technical aspects of painting and bookbinding in a later chapter, where references will be found at pp. 336–7 and at pp. 340–1.

[1] See plate 40.
[2] XCVII, No. 4799, July 15, 1949.

CHAPTER 17

Food and Health

1

THE story of the Society's work during its second century for the promotion of science and technology naturally offers striking contrasts to the record of its earlier work in this field. Its later efforts were actuated by the same humanitarian spirit and characterised by the same qualities of reliability and authority, but in keeping with the times the character of its work changed fundamentally. Formerly, the essence of the Society's handling of these practical subjects had lain, as we have so often seen, in the meticulous and detailed precision with which the improvements required by the terms of its competitions were specified and tested. During the second hundred years, on the other hand, it normally concerned itself mainly with broad developments and inventions of really fundamental importance.

Its method changed correspondingly. The offers of prizes for specific objects which characterised the earlier period were not, of course, dropped all at once; indeed, the Society occasionally awards prizes for practical improvements even to-day. But this method fell increasingly into disuse, and the present-day system of lectures and papers of a general character (which is still incidentally a system of reward, for an invitation to read a paper before such a society is highly prized) took its place as the Society's chief mode of operation, and in 1855 the two methods were in effect fused by the introduction of the present practice of awarding a silver medal for a few of the outstanding papers of each session.

The list of those who have lectured to the Society on scientific and technical subjects includes many famous names. In this chapter it is only practicable to single out for special mention a number of noted scientists (most of whom were incidentally brilliant lecturers) who became frequent, and sometimes almost annual, lecturers on the Society's platform. Among these may be mentioned F. Crace Calvert, Silvanus Thompson, Sir William Preece, Thomas Bolas, Sir Ambrose Fleming, Vivian Lewes, Sir William Abney, W. Worby Beaumont and Sir Leonard Hill. To this list of departed scientists in whose debt the Society so particularly finds itself it is a pleasure to add the names of two who are still with us and who, in their earlier years, also lectured to the Society on numerous occasions and on very varied subjects—Mr. Noel Heaton and Mr. Thorne Baker. Both of these gentlemen had addressed the Society several times before the First World War, while Mr. Baker's most recent lecture was in 1951, more than forty years after his first.

During the 'seventies it was not found possible to provide space within the limits of the programme of Wednesday meetings for the discussion of all the topics of applied science which that busy period was throwing up. A special section, at first dealing only with Applied Chemistry, but later also with subjects related to Applied Physics, was therefore set up, with a separate organising committee and a different day of meeting. This section, under the secretaryship of Dr. Mann, conducted a spirited programme until, in 1887, it was decided that the foundation of the Society of Chemical Industry and of the Institute of Chemistry made these special meetings of the Society of Arts redundant. The section was therefore discontinued and the section of Applied Art instituted in its place.

Not long after the lecture system was firmly established the Society received the munificent bequest of Dr. Cantor and decided to expend its income on fees for courses of lectures on industrial technology. This was a double innovation, for no fee is paid for the papers read at ordinary and sectional meetings, and these papers are all single and separate. The courses of paid lectures provided out of the Cantor bequest, however, enable technical subjects to be dealt with more exhaustively than is possible at a single meeting, and being in the nature of *ex cathedra* utterances (many of them have stood for years as the "classic" on their subject) they are not normally discussed by the audience. Their original restriction to subjects of industrial technology, however, has long been relaxed. Since the Cantor bequest the Society has received numerous other endowments providing for lectures on scientific subjects, to which reference will be made in due course. Mention must also be made of the Juvenile Lectures which have been delivered in the Christmas holidays since 1874 (in recent years provided for out of the Dr. Mann Trust). Many of these—and certainly many of the most successful—have been on scientific subjects, and amply illustrated by spectacular experiments.

At the same time as the old premium system was being largely abandoned, another of the Society's earlier expedients, its permanent exhibition of machinery, was also given up. This collection of mechanical and other models had gradually accumulated ever since the Society had held, in 1761, the first industrial exhibition in the world. From time to time the older models had been sold, given away or destroyed—a regrettable necessity, no doubt, but they soon became, for all practical purposes, obsolete and uninteresting, while there was no space on the Society's premises to keep them until such time as they might acquire an antiquarian value. Delighted therefore though the Society would now be to possess the whole original collection that was shown in 1761, it cannot really be blamed for this dispersal. The majority of the models were presented to Bennet Woodcroft. who was then Professor of Machinery at University College, London, the trustees of the College having agreed to repair and preserve them. Some of these, after being exhibited for a time in the Patent Office Museum at South Kensington, passed eventually into the collection of engineering models at the Science Museum. Others were given to the South Kensington Museum on its foundation in 1857.

While this dispersal of old models was going on the Society began to hold an annual exhibition of new inventions. The first of this series was held from December 26, 1848, to January 30, 1849, and the practice was continued regularly until 1861. During the earlier years a great variety of interesting and sometimes important exhibits was included, consisting in some cases of models and in others merely of drawings. No charge was made for either space or admission, and well-illustrated and well-annotated catalogues were produced. The exhibits ranged from heavy engineering down to simple household gadgets. Two of the most important and regular sections were devoted to railway and telegraphic apparatus, while scientific, navigational and medical instruments, building and sanitary appliances and agricultural machinery were also well represented. Most of the exhibits were serious and highly technical, but each year a few more fanciful articles crept in, such as an "automaton mouse trap" in which each unfortunate entrant reset the spring for the next victim, and a magnetic apparatus for turning over pages of music. There were also plenty of simple devices such as propelling pencils, fountain pens, washing machines—and velocipedes.

Until the end of the 'fifties the size of the exhibition and the number of visitors steadily increased, but when, in accordance with the Patent Law of 1852—on which the exhibition had a definite bearing, of course—facilities had been provided at the new Patent Office for the public to obtain full information regarding all new patents, the point of the Society's exhibitions was largely lost. By 1861 their character had deteriorated, so that Sir Thomas Phillips, the then Chairman of the Council, felt it necessary to point out that the series had "not kept pace with the progress of science" and was not "worthy of the present position of the Society". The planning of the international exhibition of 1862 provided an excuse for interrupting the series, and it was not resumed. It had always been the Council's intention, however, that the series would pioneer the way for a permanent museum of inventions, preserving a record of scientific progress, and in this sense the exhibitions may be truly regarded as a fore-runner of the present-day Science Museum.

2

Let us now consider some of the practical subjects with which the Society has concerned itself and which it has endeavoured to foster during the past hundred years by the organisation of lectures, the offer of prizes or in other ways suggested by circumstances.

Throughout almost the whole of the first century of the Society's work the subject which consistently took pride of place among its activities was agriculture, but by the time its second century began, Britain, as the leading industrial power of the world, had learned to look mainly to other countries to feed its population, and British agriculture had ceased to be of vital economic importance. Thus, until the Second World War permanently altered the country's economic situation, an occasional paper was sufficient to keep the Society abreast of the few important developments which took place.

During the early years of this period the inclusion of agricultural machinery in the Society's annual exhibition of inventions gave back to the Society's Repository something of its old rustic appearance, and J. J. Mechi of Tiptree Hall (a manufacturer-farmer with ample capital for experiments), and J. C. Morton (springing from a family of noted agriculturists) contributed to the Society periodical reviews of progress. There were also two notable prizes for essays on agricultural subjects. The first, instituted in 1858, concerned the possibilities of increasing mechanisation through the application of steam-power to tillage and was awarded to Algernon Clarke. Then, in 1867, the Society created a real stir by offering a substantial prize for an essay on the problem of harvesting corn in wet weather. This prize, which consisted of a gold medal and 50 guineas, was awarded to W. A. Gibbs, of Gilwell Park, whose essay included a description of an apparatus on which he had been quietly working for some years. This machine[1] enabled sheaves of corn, and also loose hay, to be dried in a shed by a current of hot air, and, brought to public attention by the Society's award, it created widespread interest. It was awarded a further gold medal shortly afterwards by the Highland and Agricultural Society of Scotland and received great attention from the government of the day; but it unfortunately failed to satisfy the Royal Agricultural Society. Altogether, Gibbs created a considerable furore, and the account of his experiences which he gave the Society in a paper which he read in 1882 shows that the Society's offer had far-reaching if not alto-

[1] See plate 31.

gether desirable consequences. Fifty years later, both he and the Society were proved to be right, and modern developments in grass-drying were fully described in a paper read in 1937 by Lieut.-Colonel Pollitt.

In 1883, a few months after Gibbs's paper, Professor Thorold Rogers, M.P., dealt with a very different, and at that time very new, way of treating wet and green crops, in a paper on American experiments in ensilage. Ensilage (or at any rate its modern revival) originated in France in 1877, and it was some years before it was taken up in this country, but the Society took a great interest in the method and encouraged its adoption by publishing in the *Journal* periodical reports of various experiments and of the impressive opening ceremonies with which the completion of some of the first silos was celebrated.

Perhaps the most important changes in agriculture during this period were those arising from the fundamental researches which were going on at institutions such as the one established at Rothamsted by Sir John Bennet Lawes. Lawes himself lectured twice to the Society. His first paper, read on March 9, 1855, contained a detailed scientific analysis of the potentialities for agricultural purposes of London sewage, while the second, which was delivered in 1877, showed how the Rothamsted experiments on artificial fertilisers had made nonsense of most covenant restrictions on farm cropping. Lawes never addressed the Society directly on his work at Rothamsted, but each of his successors there, Sir Daniel Hall, Sir John Russell and Sir William Ogg, has kept the Society informed of the progress of the work, while the series of five Cantor Lectures on artificial fertilisers which were delivered by Sir Daniel Hall in 1907 became a classic on their subject. While giving due prominence to the work done by leading scientists on the subject of fertilisers, the Society has very properly heard both sides of the present-day controversy on this subject, and the two papers by Sir Albert Howard, read in 1934 and 1936, on the manufacture of humus, aroused much interest and found their way into practice in many parts of the world.

The recent renaissance of British agriculture has naturally been reflected in a renewed interest in the subject on the part of the

Society. The change was foreshadowed by a striking paper read on the eve of the outbreak of war by Mr. S. J. Wright on "Recent Improvements in Agricultural Machinery", and when it became apparent that the promotion of British agriculture would be a vital matter not merely for wartime but in the peace that would follow, the Council decided to devote nearly half the ordinary meetings in the session 1942–3 to a series of papers under the title "Agriculture To-day and To-morrow".[1] Wartime forecasts of the post-war importance of home agriculture proved to be right, and when in 1951 the Council resolved, as one form of celebration of the centenary of the Great Exhibition, to offer a substantial prize in the old manner for some practical object, it was decided that the subject of competition should be some proposal for the improvement of British agriculture, as being the most important practical need of the hour. A prize consisting of £500 and a gold medal was offered, and it was awarded, on the unanimous recommendation of a very strong jury, to Dr. R. E. Slade for a new system of farming grass and arable land whereby he had greatly increased his output. What is perhaps the most important innovation in recent years in agriculture, the practical application of biochemistry, has also received due attention by the Society, notably in the admirable survey contained in Professor Harland's Fernhurst Lecture on "Plant Hormones" (1953).

3

As has already been emphasised, the slackening in the Society's interest in agriculture in the last century must be chiefly attributed to the introduction of Free Trade and the policy of looking abroad for the bulk of the nation's food supplies. But although bread soon became plentiful and cheap, no satisfactory means existed in the middle of last century for importing the more perishable articles of essential diet such as meat, or of distributing efficiently to the vast populations of the new towns the even more perishable commodities of milk and fish. In consequence, the bulk of the industrial population was seriously undernourished, and the gravity of the situation was brought home by a series of reports which

[1] Subsequently published as a separate book by Michael Joseph.

were published by a committee of inquiry appointed by the Privy Council in 1863, as well as by two papers read to the Society that year by Dr. Edward Smith, F.R.S.

Several members of the Society's Council had already indicated one possible solution. Harry Chester, in his Inaugural Address in 1853, pointed to the waste of good meat in Australia, where only the wool, fat and bones of the great flocks of sheep were made use of in trade. "Is it impossible", he asked, "to preserve the flesh and to export it in a satisfactory condition to this country, where butcher's meat is not overabundant?" His challenge was supported ten years later by Sir William Trevelyan, who gave the Society a sum of £70, subsequently increased to £100, to offer as a prize "for the discovery of an improved process of preserving fresh meat in countries where it was then almost valueless so as to render it an article of commerce". Finally, in 1867, the way being prepared by the Privy Council reports, Harry Chester persuaded the Council to appoint a "Food of the People" Committee, to which at its first meeting he put forward four quite definite and practical problems for consideration, viz.: (i) the discovery of a means of importing meat, if possible in a fresh condition, and failing that, preserved nutritiously and palatably, (ii) the increase and improvement of milk supplies, (iii) the increase of fish supplies, and (iv) the improvement of cooking among the working classes.

It was in connection with the first- and last-named problems that the Society made its most notable contributions. When the committee began its labours, only three methods of preserving meat, apart from salting it, had reached a practical stage. These were canning, drying, and extracting the "essence". The Society had awarded a gold medal as early as 1845 for the preparation and importation from Australia of an essence of beef in tablet form, and since then liquid extracts by Liebig's process had become a fairly common culinary article. Methods had also been found of keeping meat sweet and fresh by drying, but although the committee tried and approved numerous preparations of both types, they knew that their value was limited to certain purposes and that neither could take the place of meat in its natural condition. The public attention which was drawn to the problem by the

Society's campaign also evoked scores of proposals for treating carcases with various chemicals, many of which were very carefully tried out by the committee. The following quaint record is therefore a typical entry in the minute-book of the period:

Food Committee

8 May 1877

The Committee met this day at 4 O'clock. Present: Lord Alfred Churchill in the chair, Major General Cotton, R.E., J. A. Youl, C.M.G., and B. C. Tufnell.

The Committee had before them the leg of mutton which had been treated once a week and which had been hung 8 weeks.

The joint had been cooked the previous day and was served cold to the Committee.

The joint was pronounced absolutely without taint arising from decomposition, and being tested with a joint of fresh mutton cooked at the same time bore favourable comparison with it.

But from the first the committee pinned their faith on canning and, although it was at that time not far beyond the speculative stage, on refrigeration. It is not claiming too much for the Society to say that it established tinned meat as an article of diet in this country, by the publicity which it gave to the product and the improvements which were made in it as a result of the committee's recommendations. Innumerable samples were tested and tasted—some of them being submitted officially by the Australian governors through the Colonial Office—and the reports were published in the *Journal*, in order to keep up a running stream of propaganda. In this way the tonnage of tinned meat imported increased in a few years from a negligible total to an important item of commerce. The completion of the task was seen in the varied display of preserved foods at the International Exhibition at South Kensington in 1873, which came within a sub-section for which the committee had been made responsible.

The first successful refrigerating machine was patented in 1834 by Jacob Perkins,[1] and various improvements followed, such as

[1] Two apprentices who assisted in making Perkins' model were named Frederick Bramwell and T. R. Crompton. Nearly fifty years later Bramwell (then Sir Frederick) wrote a letter to the *Journal* pointing out that he, Crompton and Perkins' grandson, Loftus Perkins, were now colleagues on the Council !

the machine patented by James Harrison of Melbourne in 1857. But the first serious work on the application of refrigeration to the preservation of meat did not begin till the late 'sixties, when J. S. Mort, a prominent citizen of Sydney, put the development of the idea on a public basis by opening a subscription fund. The Society's committee kept in close touch with Mort's campaign and also with the efforts which were being made at the same time by several engineers at home, whose processes they submitted to careful and thorough testing. Meanwhile James Harrison, in Melbourne, hearing of what was afoot in Sydney, began to apply his own machine to this important purpose, and having given a successful demonstration of his process at the Melbourne Exhibition of 1872–3, he decided to try to bring over to London by means of it 20 tons of beef and mutton. The Society had its flags out for the arrival of his steamer, the *Norfolk*, but alas! the apparatus had been installed so hurriedly that a leak developed. By the time the ship was off the Azores, refrigeration ceased and, in the delicate words of the *Journal*, "the meat became subject to the usual process of decomposition". But in spite of this setback Harrison was given the welcome he deserved, and appeared before the Food Committee to present a detailed report.

Meanwhile, the Americans were getting busy on the same problem, and in 1876 the Anchor Line began to convey carcases weekly from New York to Britain by means of refrigerating chambers cooled by a current of air from an adjoining chamber filled with ice. Samples of meat conveyed in this way were tasted and approved by the committee. Then, three years later, the problem was finally solved when cargoes of meat were successfully brought both from America and Australia without the use of ice by means of a machine invented by J. J. Colman of Glasgow.

Unhappily, by this time the Society's committee, deprived by sudden death of its energetic chairman, Benjamin Shaw, seems to have lost its grip, and now that the problem for which the Trevelyan Prize had for so long been offered was solved, and on a commercial scale, they found themselves unable to choose between the various people who had contributed to this important result, particularly as none of the most important of them saw fit to put in a claim. In the end the prize was divided into five prizes of £20 which were offered and awarded in connection with the International Health Exhibition of 1884. One of these smaller prizes was appropriately given for a refrigerating machine, of the type invented by Giffard.

Before we finally leave the subject of refrigeration, reference must be made to the important lectures upon it which were delivered before the Society at various times, such as the paper by B. H. Paul in 1868 on "Artificial Freezing and Refrigeration" and the six Howard Lectures by Ewing in 1898 on "The Mechanical Production of Cold". With these and other formal papers, and with the detailed reports of the proceedings of the Food Committee, the *Journal* forms one of the most important sources for the early history of this subject.

The results achieved in connection with the three other objectives set before the Food Committee by Harry Chester can be summarised more briefly. All aspects of the milk problem were considered: production, purity, preservation and distribution, but the only definite results were achieved in connection with the last two. In November, 1867, L. P. Merriam, a director of the Anglo-Swiss Milk Company, appeared before the committee to demonstrate samples of condensed milk prepared by his company, and this seems to have been the first official introduction, as it were, of this product into England, although it was by then well known in America as well as Switzerland. The committee were impressed by what was shown them and were quick to appreciate the great superiority for most purposes of condensed over dried milk. As to distribution, the committee were perturbed by the condition in which country milk reached the London dairies and decided to recommend the Council to offer a prize for the design of an improved milk churn for its conveyance up to town. This prize was won by the Aylesbury Dairy Company in 1868.

The problem regarding fish was seen to be enormous, involving as it did the promotion of increased production, the improvement of distribution (one speaker pointed out the irony of the fact that while 23,000 people were at that time dying annually in

Britain of starvation, many tons of fish were regularly destroyed at Billingsgate Fish Market as no longer fit for consumption) and the popularisation of fish as an article of diet. The first step which the committee took was therefore to persuade the Council to set up a special Piscicultural Committee, and this committee in its turn could see only one solution—the organisation of a great international Fisheries Exhibition as a means of propaganda. This proposal, although not immediately given effect to, ultimately bore fruit in the very successful Fisheries Exhibition held at South Kensington in 1883.

The answer which the committee found to their fourth problem, that of the improvement of popular cooking, was also propagandist. In addition to experiments with novel cooking apparatus and investigations of commercial kitchen schemes they concluded that one reform which particularly needed advocating was the addition of cooking to the curriculum of elementary schools. This came about with the inclusion of Domestic Economy in the Revised Code of 1876, in support of which the subject was added to the Society's programme of examinations, and scholarships were offered by the Council to enable students to attend the newly founded school for the training of Domestic Science teachers at South Kensington.

In spite of these efforts, however, little progress was made with the actual teaching of the subject in the schools. One reason for this was felt to be the formidable term by which it was known, which terrified School Boards, teachers and pupils alike, and the Society began to press for the adoption of straightforward names such as Cookery and Needlework. Other detailed reforms were also felt to be necessary before it could have a proper chance, and in order to stimulate public interest and to secure the adoption of the proposed reforms the Council decided to hold an annual Domestic Economy Congress until the Government met their views. The first of these congresses was held, with great success, in Birmingham in 1877, and at the third, held in London in 1881 under the Presidency of H.R.H. Princess Christian, it was claimed that "very few important female minds were absent". A very extensive and valuable programme of papers was arranged on each occasion, but the avowed object was simply to put pressure on the Government and when, in 1882, a New Code was adopted for the elementary schools, meeting most of the Society's points, the series was terminated and the organising committee disbanded. Perhaps it cannot be claimed that the Society's victory had all the beneficial effects which were hoped for it. Nevertheless, there must have been many families in after years who all unwittingly owed it at least in some measure to the Society of Arts that their "inner man" was well cared for and their socks neatly darned.

Among the various papers and lectures which have from time to time been devoted to subjects relating to food, particular mention may perhaps be made of the series of ten Cantor Lectures on "Food" delivered by Professor Letheby in 1868, of the Trueman Wood Lecture on "Nutrition" delivered by Sir Frederick Gowland Hopkins, the discoverer of vitamins, in 1935, the series of Cantor Lectures by Sir Robert McCarrison in 1936 on "Nutrition and National Health", in which the remarkable results of his thirty years' Indian researches on mice and men were set out, and the many lectures by Sir Jack Drummond, whose brutal murder in the South of France is a recent memory while these words are being written. Nor has the Society been afraid to give a selected few of the host of nutritional "cranks" the opportunity to use its platform: in particular, several papers have been read on various types of what might be termed "back-to-nature" bread. Special mention must also be made of the series of seven Cantor Lectures delivered by C. Graham in 1874 on the Chemistry of Brewing for these "classic" lectures were the first effective attempt to put the brewing industry on the scientific basis which it occupies to-day. They exerted a remarkable influence upon the brewers and induced them for the first time to adopt a measure of scientific control over their industry.

4

Numerous other aspects of human physical welfare have, of course, been studied by the Society from time to time. One of these was housing, another problem which became gravely pressing on account of the phenomenal increase of population in the last century. Although the moving force was supplied by humanitarian principles the Society's approach to this problem was, typically, on essentially practical lines. For example, the Earl of Shaftesbury, who presided at one of its early discussions on the matter (1858), put his finger on what is still the crux of the problem when he stressed the economic difficulty, at any rate in towns, of erecting proper dwellings to let at a rent within the reach of poor people and yet adequately recompensing the builder. The only hope of a solution, he pointed out, lay in improved designs and cheaper methods of construction. Nearly thirty years later, Cardinal Manning, who, like Lord Shaftesbury, was a realist as well as an idealist, pointed out, when presiding at a similar meeting, that the great slum clearance schemes of that period were creating almost as many hardships as they remedied by their violent displacement of the population. He was reminded by them, he said, "of a county meeting at which three resolutions were passed—(1) that a new lunatic asylum be built, (2) that it occupy the site of the old one, and (3) that the patients remain in the old one until the new one be finished"!

The Society's chief efforts in the last century in connection with housing were both the result of gifts by members. In 1863 the Council agreed to offer for competition two prizes, given by J. Bailey Denton, for designs for a labourer's cottage not costing more than £100,[1] and the same year, at the instigation of Thomas Twining, it appointed a committee to collect statistics of model dwellings. These two efforts were followed up by the holding in May 1864 of a two-day conference at which the whole subject was methodically reviewed, and two years later the conclusions then reached were embodied in a Bill introduced into Parliament by Charles Buxton. Nearly twenty years afterwards, in 1884, another member, William Westgarth, enabled the Council to offer prizes totalling no less than £1,200 for essays on "Dwellings for the

---

[1] The prize-winning design is reproduced in plate 30. An earlier competition for the design of workmen's dwellings costing less than £300 was held, doubtless under the inspiration of the Prince Consort, in 1848.

Poor" and the "Reconstruction of Central London". Out of twenty-seven essays submitted (some from America) for these extremely generous prizes twelve obtained awards and three were published, but none of them reached the standard hoped for or received the full advertised amount.

Coming now to the present century, we find the renewed pressure of the housing problem after the First World War reflected in the paper on "Housing after the War" read by Mr. Seebohm Rowntree a month after the Armistice and, even more poignantly, in Sir Leonard Hill's paper a few months later on "Infant Mortality and Housing". Even two years before the Second World War the problem recurred in a paper on "Housing and Planning" by Sir Raymond Unwin, whose name is now so closely connected with the post-war Town and Country Planning Act, and in 1942, when the devastation caused by bombing had again rendered the problem as acute as ever, the Society looked forward to the period of reconstruction in a notable series of twelve lectures on the Post-war Home.

Some years after the war a member of the Society's Council, Sir Alfred Bossom, Bart., M.P., who was one of the pioneers of skyscraper construction, gave the Society an endowment to provide for periodical lectures on architectural developments, and the first lecture given under this Trust, delivered in 1952 by Mr. Hartland Thomas on the subject of "Modular Co-ordination", had an important result in the foundation of a new society. The theme of Mr. Thomas's lecture was the desirability of establishing agreed moduli as bases of dimensions for building units and materials, and in concluding his lecture he suggested the establishment of a special body to foster such a scheme. His proposal was warmly received by the audience and the first meeting of the new body, the latest of the numerous offspring of the Royal Society of Arts, took place a few weeks later in the Society's House.

Closely allied to the subject of housing are the twin problems of sanitation and water supply, and it is hardly surprising that a Society which numbered among its members such men as Edwin Chadwick and John Simon should pay particular attention to them. As is well known, the earliest Act dealing with the health of the whole of this country was the Public Health Act of 1848 which set up the Board of Health. The Government were at last driven to take action in this field by the cholera epidemic of that year, the circumstances of which demonstrated inescapably the close connection between insanitary conditions and disease, for in at least two towns in Scotland the cholera epidemic of 1848 started in the same house, and in one case in the very same room and bed, as the similar epidemic of 1832. A series of individual Acts after 1848 was digested into the first comprehensive Public Health Act in 1875, but the successful implementation of that Act was in a considerable measure due to the Society of Arts, through a series of national conferences which it convened between the years 1874 and 1884.

These conferences had been preceded by the appointment by the Council in 1873 of a committee to investigate the problem of water supply, particularly in towns, and it so happened that for entirely separate reasons a committee was also set up at about the same time to inquire into the question of fire-fighting. The two committees soon found themselves brought up against the same problem, and from their joint discussions it emerged that the two great causes for the inadequate supply of water, at any rate in the metropolis, were the appalling waste of water, caused mainly by leaking household installations, and the lack of co-ordination and co-operation between the various local companies.

The first of the conferences, held in 1874 under the chairmanship of Lyon Playfair, was primarily concerned with the serious problem of the pollution of rivers by sewage and industrial effluents, which had for years been under investigation by a Royal Commission, and it succeeded in prodding the Government into action long contemplated but continually deferred, resulting in the passing of the River Pollution Prevention Act of 1876. In that same year the first of a series of five annual conferences on Sewage and Water Supply (each accompanied by an exhibition of sanitary and water-supply apparatus) was held at the Society's House under the chairmanship of Sir James Stansfield, who had been the first President of the Local Government Board. In 1878, at the express request of the President of the Society, H.R.H. the Prince of Wales, a separate two-day session was held, immediately before the sewage conference, to consider questions of water supply, especially in rural areas, and in 1884, four years after the end of the main series, a further water-supply conference was held at the request of the Executive Committee of the International Health Exhibition of that year.

These conferences were attended by technical and administrative representatives of many important local authorities and were conducted under a strict rule limiting them to the discussion of practical experience and barring untried schemes and theories. In the course of the annual series (1876–80) a methodical and thorough investigation was made of the whole problem as it affected every part of the country and of all the various rival sanitary systems which were then being experimented with, and so detailed and complete was the resultant survey that over sixty years later, when enemy bombing interfered with normal sanitation and water services, frequent recourse was had to these records by government officials in the formulation of emergency schemes.

Of all the many problems which emerged in the course of the conferences perhaps the most serious was the dangerous weakness, and in many cases the complete absence, of connection between the expensive main sewers laid down as a result of recent legislation and the houses which they were installed to serve. There was, therefore, considerable irony in the fact, pointed out by the Chairman of Council in his inaugural address in 1877, that the residence of the Society's President, the Heir Apparent, had been found to be "undrained and unventilated and built over a nest of old drains and cess-pools that rendered it unfit for habitation". Worse still, in 1881, a few months after announcing a competition for "Plans showing the best sanitary arrangements in Houses built in the Metropolis", the Council had to confess that it had been "thought desirable to examine into the condition of the drains of the Society's House and the examination revealed so defective a state of things that it was determined to amend the system".

Nevertheless, in spite of these shocking examples in the Society's own highest places, very important results were achieved by the conferences. During a vigorous experimental period the exchange of information and experiences between the technical experts was obviously of the greatest value. But even more important was the general propagandist effect. The Act of 1875 gave the local authorities the administrative and financial means of putting their sanitary arrangements in order, but most of them needed the strong pressure of public opinion to push them into action. The collective action of the Society and its conferences, however, had just this effect, and in 1884 the Council felt that the Society could "fairly claim the credit of having taken a very leading part in drawing public attention to the unhealthy conditions of modern life, especially of modern town life", and that "the Sanitary Conferences held by the Society were, if not the cause, certainly the first indication, of a change in public sentiment as regards the need of healthful life".

The Society's interest in these subjects was, of course, in no way confined to this series of conferences. For many years the twin topics of sewage and water supply were discussed at meetings of the Society almost every session. To begin with, stress was repeatedly laid on the point raised by Lawes, the agricultural value of sewage, which could help to offset the cost of its disposal (an important point when the expenditure of public funds on such an object was still a novelty). But as water supplies improved and the water-borne disposal of sewage became more universally practised, this aspect of the matter, which it will be remembered was first raised by the Society in the eighteenth century, was dropped until, in the light of new methods of sewage treatment, it was revived before the Society in recent times by such lecturers as Sir Albert Howard (1935), Lieut.-Colonel Temple (1941) and Mr. J. C. Wylie (1952).

In the various papers contributed on the subject of water supply a similar change of emphasis is to be detected. To begin with, the primary object was to point out the chief sources from which increased supplies might be drawn; then, concern was repeatedly expressed regarding the impurity of many of the sources then in use (often resulting in epidemics); and finally, methods of purifying water became the main interest, culminating in a series of papers and lectures contributed by S. Rideal at the turn of the century on bacterial methods of purification. Thereafter, the whole subject fell into abeyance, as far as the Society was concerned, until, in the 'thirties, alarm spread in the metropolis regarding the rapidly shrinking sources of water. This change is reflected in an important series of Cantor Lectures delivered in 1935 by Dr. Bernard Smith on Underground Water Supplies.

Bad drains are not the only source of pollution of the atmosphere. Inside buildings it can be caused merely by the absence of fresh air, and a considerable number of papers read to the Society have recorded the progress of ventilation during this period. Out of doors there are the twin evils of fog and smoke, and the Society, which, it will be remembered, sought a remedy as soon as the Industrial Revolution began to fill the atmosphere of towns with the smoke of factory chimneys, continued to pursue this great problem assiduously in the nineteenth century. For this work it was inspired from time to time by orations such as that delivered in 1855 by G. M. Muir (obviously a "guid Scots Presbyterian") entitled, "The Smoke Nuisance considered morally, aesthetically, scientifically and historically".

Shortly after Muir's discourse a prize of £25 was offered for an essay on smoke prevention, which was won by C. W. Williams with a new system of furnace construction. The field of battle was now being extended, however, to the domestic grate, and the year before, another careful Scot, Dr. Neill Arnott, F.R.S., had showed the Society how to eliminate the smoking house chimney, and, at the same time, save fuel and avoid draughts, by the use of simple devices controlling the entrance of cold air to the combustion and the exit of heated air up the chimney, and by an arrangement, based on an idea of Benjamin Franklin's, for feeding new coal from *below* the blaze so that the smoke from it had to pass through the flames and so be consumed. The whole affair cost 45s. to make and install, and some months later Sir Edwin Chadwick forwarded to the *Journal* a testimonial from a friend who had tried it out throughout the winter and found that it did all that was claimed for it. Yet all but a century later only the first-named of Arnott's principles is beginning to come into popular favour, and we find another noted scientist, Dr. A. Parker, Director of Fuel Research in the Department of Scientific and Industrial Research, when speaking to the Society on what (for England) are still visionary "Cities without Smoke", admitting that "the problem of devising appliances [for the smokeless burning of bituminous coal] at a reasonable cost has not yet been solved". One wonders whether Neill Arnott's ideas, which, even then, were not particularly original, were given a fair trial, or whether they were really found wanting. Meanwhile, we still have the alternative, mentioned by Lyon Playfair when he took the chair for Arnott, of burning smokeless fuels such as gas and coke, into which, as Playfair pointed out, Arnott's stove virtually converted the coal supplied to it.

5

The unhealthy atmosphere created by the smoke of industry is only an extension of the more direct threat involved in specific industries to the health of their own workers. We have already seen that the Society concerned itself from its earliest years with this problem, and it returned to it with renewed vigour at the opening of its second century. As the result of a paper read by Dr. T. K. Chambers in 1854 it appointed an Industrial Pathology Committee to make a methodical investigation of the whole field. The committee's first annual report, published in 1855, covered, in a useful, if not profound, manner, the subject of eye diseases and eye injuries, but its work was discontinued, apparently because the production of a Government report was anticipated. When this also failed to materialise, the Society took the most practical line and, aided financially by Benjamin Shaw, appointed an individual, Dr. B. W. Richardson, to make an inquiry and present a report in the form of lectures. The result was a series of six special lectures, delivered by Dr. Richardson in 1876, in which the whole field was investigated with thoroughness and understanding. They were subsequently published as a parliamentary paper.

Following upon the success of Dr. Richardson's lectures,

Benjamin Shaw determined to endow a Trust to enable the Society to make an award every five years "for the most successful invention for preventing loss of life or promoting health in connection with any industrial occupation". This endowment has perpetuated the Society's interest in these subjects, and under its terms a number of prizes have been awarded for safety devices such as improved mining cartridges, diving suits and respirators. An important award was made under the Trust in 1908 to Professor Galloway for his researches on the effect of coal-dust in causing coal-mine explosions, which led to the institution of very valuable preventive measures. Another notable prize-winner was Henry Fleuss, who was awarded a gold medal in 1883 for a self-contained diving-suit with oxygen apparatus and another medal in 1911 for an improved form of the same apparatus produced by Messrs. Siebe, Gorman & Co. for the use of rescue parties in mines.

The Society's interest in respirators goes back a long way, as we saw in an earlier chapter, and the most interesting apparatus, historically, which was brought before it during the hundred years under review in this chapter was the first charcoal respirator, invented by Dr. Stenhouse (as a protection against disease) and demonstrated to the Society in 1854. Not only was its efficacy proved to the meeting by submitting several members of the audience to tests with chlorine and ammonia, but Stenhouse also demonstrated to everyone present the power of charcoal to absorb odours by exposing in the room, without unpleasantness, a tub containing, under an inch of charcoal, the corpses of a cat and two rats "in a highly putrid state".

The Society did not confine itself to surgical apparatus, such as respirators, with definite industrial applications. It will be remembered[1] that in the years preceding the Great Exhibition it made a number of awards for surgical instruments of a more general kind, and when the exhibition was over it appointed a large and authoritative committee to continue this work. The committee's main achievement was to extend the list of surgical exhibits which had been shown in the exhibition into what was

[1] See p. 109.

claimed to be the first complete and scientifically classified catalogue of such apparatus ever published. A few years later the committee was also entrusted with the task of preparing a list of suitable exhibits for the successor of 1851, the 1862 exhibition.

The progress of medicine has often formed the subject of lectures read to the Society, and some of the most important discoveries in this field have been described to the Society by those who had shared in making them. Among such papers may be mentioned that on "Rabies and its Prevention" by Dr. A. Ruffer of the Pasteur Institute, read under Lister's chairmanship in 1889; Sir Ronald Ross's lecture on "Malaria and Mosquitoes", delivered in 1900, two years after the lecturer had succeeded in transferring malaria from one bird to another by means of mosquitoes, and the Peter Le Neve Foster Lecture delivered in 1944 by Sir Howard Florey, with Sir Alexander Fleming in the chair, on the discovery and use of penicillin, which stands as a *locus classicus* on this subject.

There is, perhaps, no field of science which is more beset by conservatism and controversy than medicine (doubtless largely because so much is at stake), and the Society has sometimes rendered a valuable service, needing considerable courage, in giving a platform to those who, while occupying positions of authority in their profession, were frowned upon by their colleagues because of unpopular or unorthodox views or other circumstances. Among the Society's more controversial medical papers may be mentioned the lecture by N. Lawrence and Dr. Harries in 1891 on "Electricity in relation to the human body" (with which may be compared two papers read in more recent years by Mr. G. G. Blake), Sir Aldo Castellani's account of the remarkable health record, under his direction, of the Italian army in the Abyssinian War (which, delivered in 1938 and awarded a silver medal, obviously invited fierce criticism for political as well as professional reasons), and Sir Leonard Hill's outspoken condemnation of the radium therapy of cancer in 1939. Another case, in which the Society's willingness to give the unorthodox view a chance was well justified by the event, was that of F. W. Edridge-Green, who persisted for many years in his theory of colour-blindness and his method of testing for it, and was allowed to expound them more than once to the Society, before he won his case against much opposition.

6

Naturally, the Society has continued to concern itself with the prevention of the accidents as well as the diseases induced by industrial occupations. Various papers have been contributed to it from time to time on such subjects as explosions in coal mines, factory accidents (under the Shaw Trust), life-saving at sea and fire prevention and fire fighting. A number of important prizes have also been offered and awarded in connection with these subjects. In 1870 a competition was announced for the design of ships' lifeboats, and after the preliminary round full-scale models of five boats were called for and tested exhaustively in Regent's Canal Docks, a gold medal being awarded to Messrs. Woolfe & Son for their wooden boat and another to Messrs. Hamilton & Co. for an iron boat. Then, in 1878, a prize was offered for the best means of saving life when a vessel has to be abandoned suddenly (a problem which presented itself with tragic frequency during two world wars). The gold medal in this case was awarded to Messrs. J. & A. W. Birt for a set of buoyant articles, but the most important outcome of the competition was the exhaustive report drawn up by the panel of judges, under Admiral Ryder, which was so full of valuable information and comment that it was subsequently published as a parliamentary paper. One of the Society's members who was an official leader in this field at that time was Thomas Gray, Assistant Secretary at the Board of Trade and formulator of the "rule of the road" at sea, and many years later his son endowed the Thomas Gray Memorial Trust (of which more is said in the next chapter) under which prizes are still awarded for similar objects.

Finally, there is fire prevention. The Society's attention was particularly drawn to this subject by a series of great conflagrations in this country and America in 1873, which led the Council to appoint a special committee to discover if possible a means of preventing these disasters. It was further encouraged to take this step by a promise given by the Premier and the President of the Local Government Board that they would promote a Bill embodying the committee's findings. Much authoritative and varied evidence was taken, most of which, as we have already seen, led to the conclusion that the pre-eminently weak points were the inefficiency of the water supply and the lack of hydrants. Encouraged as it had been by the Government, the committee lost no time in seeking to have its findings put before Parliament. They were embodied in a Bill introduced by Colonel Beresford, but were at first frustrated by the influence of the water companies, and it was only as the result of cumulative efforts that these urgently needed reforms were finally made.

The Society also paid particular attention at this time to the subject of fires in theatres. A committee was appointed in 1882, and the following May their report was put before a public meeting, from which certain proposals were forwarded to the Home Secretary. This meeting was followed up by the offer and award of a special Fothergill prize for an essay on the subject.

Just as the Society's work for industrial health became embodied, as it were, in the Shaw Trust and its work for life-saving in the Thomas Gray Trust, so its work in connection with fire became centred round the Trust endowed by Dr. Fothergill in 1821.[1] Among those who have been awarded prizes under this Trust are Messrs. Nobel Brothers (1883), Messrs. Chubb & Sons (1884) and Sir William Crookes (1885), while those who have lectured under it include that gallant and aptly named former head of the London Fire Service, Lieut.-Commander Sir Aylmer Firebrace.

[1] The terms of Dr. Fothergill's will do not limit the use of the endowment to the subject of fire, but this is the principal activity of the Trust.

CHAPTER 18

The Amenities of Life

1

IN the previous chapter we have considered some of the Society's contributions to the betterment of mankind by the application of science to such closely personal matters as diet, housing and health. Let us now examine its activities in connection with some other elements of modern life which though less personal are considered almost as essential.

One such matter is artificial light. In the eighteenth century the Society tried strenuously, but quite unsuccessfully, to improve the supply of wax for candle-making either from bee-keeping at home or by the importation of myrtleberry wax from the American colonies. When gas-lighting came in, on the other hand, it was rather slow to take action, thinking that the appalling smell of the new illuminant outweighed its advantages. But the coming of the electric lamp brought the Society a blaze simultaneously of light and glory.

As has already been mentioned, one of the fundamental inventions of modern electrical engineering, the soft-iron electromagnet, was first announced by Sturgeon in a paper read to the Society in 1825, and six years later Faraday made his great discovery of the production of electric currents by the movement of conductors relatively to magnets. These discoveries opened the way to both the dynamo and the electric motor, but the development of the former lagged behind that of the latter, and it was not until early in 1867 that the dynamo first appeared in a practical form almost simultaneously from Varley, Wheatstone and the Siemens brothers. Even then there was very slow development, partly because, as Sir William Siemens pointed out in 1882 in his

316

inaugural address as Chairman of Council of the Society, the absence of a patent deprived commercial companies of an incentive for developing it. A few years later, however, that incentive was supplied by the sudden emergence of a new kind of use for the current which dynamos could supply—electric lighting.

During the 'seventies numerous arc lamps (an invention of long standing) were installed in this country and on the Continent, each light being supplied with current by its own dynamo. But such arrangements were only suitable for public places, and it was not until the production of the incandescent carbon lamp, originally invented by Swan as early as 1860 but only brought forward by him in December 1878, after the development of the dynamo, that the two discoveries, joined together, had immediate and sensational results. Edison, also, working independently in America, had announced a platinum lamp in December 1878 and applied for a British patent for a carbon lamp eleven months later.

The Society took a leading part in all the exciting developments which followed. Its building had on December 4, 1878, been lighted for the first time by dynamo-produced electricity, when, in illustration of a paper by J. N. Shoolbred, a Gramme dynamo in the library, driven by a Crossley gas-engine, worked a Hallé lamp in the entrance hall and a Suisse lamp in the anteroom, while the lecture hall was lighted by a Siemens lamp supplied by a Siemens dynamo in the backyard driven by a Brotherhood steam engine.[1] The first appearance of incandescent lamps in the building was on March 28, 1881 when, to accompany the last of a series of Cantor Lectures by W. G. Adams, Swan personally demonstrated his "glow-lamp". Two days later a lecture on the same subject by Sir William Preece was lighted by arc lights and incandescent lamps and further illuminated by a brilliant audience which included Sir William Siemens (as chairman), Varley, Swan and Crompton, while in December of the

[1] The lighting of the building in 1849 (see p. 195) was of course operated by chemical batteries. In the discussion following Shoolbred's paper Sir William Preece mentioned that he had heard of Edison's experiments with an incandescent lamp but added sceptically, with regard to Edison and his "269 patents", that "it was said of an American infant that he would improve his cradle, get out and patent it, and get back again!"

same year, at another lecture by Preece, the complete Edison system of lighting was for the first time demonstrated to an English audience, the Society's room being lighted by Edison lamps energised by an Edison generator.

By this time the heavy equipment necessary for such displays was so often being demanded at the Society's meetings that a group of members of Council decided to present to the Society a Crossley gas-engine, which was installed in a cellar. Soon afterwards a Siemens generator was purchased, and a general lighting system was permanently installed in time for the inaugural address by Sir William Siemens in November, 1882, the House therefore being one of the first in London to be so equipped. The system was improved in 1886 by the purchase of a storage battery and remained in use until, in 1899, it was possible for the building to be supplied from the mains.

Space forbids more than a reference to the spate of papers and lectures on electrical subjects by Preece, Oliver Lodge, Sylvanus Thompson, Forbes, Fleming, Crompton, Kapp and others which followed those just mentioned. These contributions kept the Society well informed of the rapid developments then taking place in the production and distribution of electricity and in its use for power and heating as well as lighting. But one other activity of the Society in this field during the pioneer period cannot be allowed to pass unnoticed. Until mains electricity became generally available—and there was considerable delay over starting to provide it even in towns, owing to the hampering effect of the first Electric Lighting Act (1882)—householders wishing to install electric lighting had to do so in the same way as the Society and generate their own current. The Council, therefore, decided in 1886 to hold a competition for the best prime movers, and offered four gold and two silver medals for engines of any type which would drive a dynamo. Only four engines were ultimately submitted, but these, an Atkinson, a Crossley and a Griffin gas-engine and a Paxman steam-engine, all received a gold medal after very extensive trials of which a full, technical report was published in the *Journal*.[1]

[1] *Journal*, XXXVII, 213.

When electric lighting suddenly caught the public imagination in 1878 it was at first assumed that gas-lighting would immediately become outmoded, and gas shares slumped heavily. But in the event the opposite happened. The gas industry was stimulated by the threatened competition from electricity and rapid development followed, even before the Welsbach incandescent mantle, which revolutionised the use of coal-gas as an illuminant,[1] came into common use in this country. The renewed interest in gas is reflected in the frequent papers dealing with it which appeared in the Society's programme during the latter part of the century, particularly by Vivian Lewes, who continued for many years to be a regular lecturer to the Society on gas and kindred subjects.

Perhaps the most important and interesting of the papers read to the Society by Lewes, however, was not on coal-gas but on another illuminating gas, acetylene, in the making of which coal is only one constituent. This paper, entitled "The Commercial synthesis of illuminating hydrocarbons", which he read in January, 1895, was the first public announcement of a process for the manufacture of calcium carbide on a commercial scale, and Lewes followed it a few years later by a series of Cantor Lectures on the same subject. The generation of acetylene is not, of course, without its dangers and in 1898 the Imperial Institute, having decided to hold an exhibition of acetylene generators, applied to the Society's Council to appoint a committee to test the safety of the apparatus which was submitted for exhibition. This the Council agreed to do, and Vivian Lewes and Sir Boverton Redwood, with others, having approved twenty-six models as not endangering the public, their guarantee was endorsed by the opening of the exhibition by the Chairman of Council, Sir Owen Tudor Burne. Subsequently the committee were asked to continue their investigations and to submit all the accepted lamps to a month's trial, these further tests being incorporated in what is presumably the first comprehensive report on this subject to be published.[2]

---

[1] The incandescent gas-mantle was the subject of a series of Cantor Lectures by Vivian Lewes in 1898.

[2] *Journal*, XLVII, 289.

Meanwhile another fuel, petroleum, had already made its debut, and had been the subject of numerous papers to the Society, of which the earliest was by William Marcet in 1864. At first, petroleum was used only for illuminating purposes,[1] for although the petrol-engine was suggested by Siemens as early as 1860, it remained in an experimental stage until the 'nineties because of the lack of an efficient carburettor. Thus Sir Boverton Redwood, in his well-known series of Cantor Lectures on "Petroleum and its products", said, in 1886, that "by far the most important of the uses to which the products of petroleum are as yet applied is that of illumination", and three years later Graham Harris, in his Cantor Lectures on "Heat Engines other than Steam", had little to say of the petrol-engine except to prophesy that its "use will without doubt be at once largely developed". Even in 1891 William Robinson, reading a lengthy paper on "The Uses of Petroleum in Prime Movers", declared, "I am strongly of opinion that such dangerous and highly volatile hydrocarbons as benzoline, gasoline and petroleum spirit ought not on any account to be used as fuel in gas engines but only for the production of steam", but in February, 1892, less than twelve months afterwards, this same lecturer, delivering a series of Cantor Lectures with the same title to the same Society ate his words and spoke of "the recent important advances" which had been made since the reading of his paper "in the application of oil as fuel, instead of coal gas, in the cylinder of the internal combustion engine"! Thus can the turning-point in the history of one of the greatest mechanical developments of modern times be almost dramatically traced in the Society's records.

Upon the subsequent evolution of the petrol-burning internal-combustion engine, as described in the Society's lectures, we cannot linger here, but reference must be made in passing to some of the lectures dealing with other types of combustion engine, such as the Howard Lectures on the diesel by A. R. Sankey (1912), Harry Ricardo (1932) and Alan Chorlton (1932), Major Halford's lecture on "Jet Propulsion" (with Sir Frank Whittle presiding)

[1] One of the earliest paraffin lamps, called "the poor man's candle", was included in the Society's exhibition of inventions in 1857.

(1946) and Sir Claude Gibb's lecture on the gas-turbine (1947). Nor has the harnessing of atomic energy, complex though the subject is and therefore largely outside the Society's scope, been entirely unrepresented in its proceedings. A number of notable lectures, all by pre-eminent authorities, have recounted some of its broader, and particularly its industrial, implications. These lectures are "Sources of Power: known and unknown" by Sir Oliver Lodge (1919), "The Stability of the Atom" by Lord Rutherford (1923) and, after a long interval, "Nuclear Energy and its Peace-time Applications" by Sir Charles Ellis (1946), and "The Industrial Applications of Atomic Energy" by Professor Oliphant (1950).

It happens that these last-named lectures were all delivered under the Trueman Wood Trust, but the encouragement of developments in motive forces of all types is specifically provided for within the Society by the Howard Trust, established by a bequest received in 1872, under which awards are made to the authors "of treatises on the properties of steam generally, or any of them particularly, as applied to motive power, or it may be of air or permanent gases, or vapours, or other agents so applied or . . ." (But that, perhaps, is enough of this delightful piece of legal drafting!)

2

It is, however, with the applications rather than the theoretical origins of power that the Society is mainly concerned, and no such application is of greater or more obvious importance than in the improvement of transport and communications. In every significant development in this direction a society founded "for the encouragement of arts, manufactures and *commerce*" has naturally been deeply interested.

When the Society's second century began, the first phase of the railway stampede was over and the iron road and the iron horse were well established as vital elements in the country's communications; while a network of lines, bearing rapidly improving services of trains, was beginning to cover the land. Throughout the Society's long series of exhibitions of inventions, railway improvements of all kinds formed an important part of each display, but in its general proceedings its attention was devoted less to mechanical improvements than to broad national issues in relation to railway development, such as nationalisation and the general principles of railway economics. There were, however, several technical subjects in which it took a definite interest. One of these was the application of electric traction to railway trains, which was first brought before the Society by Alexander Siemens in 1881. Another which was particularly taken up because it directly affected public safety, was the efficiency of brakes and couplings, on which, among others, Sir Henry Tyler, Sir Frederick Bramwell and T. A. Brockelbank lectured; and a third, a comparatively minor matter but yet greatly affecting the comfort of passengers, was the improvement of carriage lighting.

This latter was the subject of a competition, announced in 1874 but only completed three years later, in which, after exhaustive laboratory tests by Professor Barff, six lamps, five for oil and one for gas, were selected for further trial and fitted to different compartments of a coach lent for the purpose by the Metropolitan Railway and attached to a train running between Baker Street and Swiss Cottage. The committee then spent a very smoky afternoon riding backwards and forwards through the tunnels between these stations watching the behaviour of the lamps, and they came to the conclusion that the solitary gas-lamp submitted (Pintsch's), which used compressed gas, was the only one suitable for the purpose, the light it gave being "equally diffused and quite sufficient to read small print in any part of the carriage". Finally, the further co-operation of the Metropolitan Railway was obtained in much more extended practical trials, as a result of which the reliability and efficiency of Mr. Pintsch's lamp and its economy as compared with the gas-lamps then in use (which employed uncompressed gas) was definitely established, and the gold medal was duly awarded to its inventor. It is satisfactory to record that the Society's efforts and choice were well justified by later experience, for after the prominence given to it by the Society's investigations and award the Pintsch lamp came into extensive use.

Long after mechanised transport, in the form of the railway train, had become the accepted mode of long-distance travel, horse-drawn vehicles, by now considerably accelerated, and improved in comfort, were still the only means of transport by road, and were so greatly increasing in number that in 1873 the mass production of horse nails was considered an important enough subject to occupy one of the Society's meetings. G. V. Hooper, whose family name is still well known in connection with Rolls Royce cars, kept the Society informed of developments in carriages at all the big exhibitions, and it is gratifying to find in his review of the carriage section of the Paris Exhibition of 1889 that, although the British showing at these exhibitions was not very good, Hooper could record at the end of the horse-carriage epoch that "the best carriages now produced in England excel all others in elegance of outline, suitability and comfort for their intended use, durability and easy running".

By that time many experiments had been made on the roads with steam rivals to the horse, but in this country they were largely frustrated by the foolish restrictions of the "Red-Flag Act" and its successors, and it was not until 1895, when the Government, in view of the rapid developments taking place on the Continent, began to think of introducing amended legislation, that the Society found it worthwhile to take up the subject of "horseless carriages" at all seriously. Towards the end of that year Sir Henry Cunnynghame read a paper on "Locomotive Carriages for Common Roads", and a few days later W. Worby Beaumont began a series of Cantor Lectures on "Mechanical Road Carriages". At the suggestion of the Self-Propelled Traffic Association (whose President, Sir David Salomons, one of the chief pioneers of motoring in this country, was a member of the Society of long-standing), the Council also prepared a petition to Parliament praying for certain amendments, which were duly embodied in the Locomotives on Highways Act of 1896.

Worby Beaumont lectured again to the Society in November, 1896, and it is interesting to note that whereas, at the end of his

1895 Cantor Lectures, he was inclined to fancy the chances of the steam-engine as against the petrol-motor as the best prime mover for the road, he had reversed this impression by the end of 1896. But Sir David Salomons, who owned the second petrol-engined car ever brought into this country, surprisingly concluded a paper which he read in 1897 with the words:

> The best existing motor the world has yet seen, for its power, method of fueling, suspension springs and travelling long distances before re-charging, is one which is likely to remain with us for many a long year to come, and is known under the name of the horse!

Of subsequent lectures to the Society on the subject of the motor car there is only space to speak of one. That is a paper read by Colonel Crompton in 1924 in which he reminded his audience that he had built a steamcar and driven it on the road sixty-one years before—and he then concluded by looking forward to cars driven by the gas-turbine!

The coming of the bicycle was noted by the Society as well as that of the motor car. A paper on bicycles and tricycles was read in 1884 by C. V. Boys, and in 1898 "The Evolution of the Cycle" was recorded by W. K. Starley, the inventor of the first bicycle of the present "safety" pattern, the "Rover". The subject was finally rounded off by a series of Cantor Lectures on "Cycle Construction" delivered by Archibald Sharp in 1899.

In general, however, the Society has very properly devoted more attention to the broader questions of road transport than to its more abstruse technical aspects, and to public more than to private vehicles. There were, for example, its efforts to improve the London cabs. This subject was first brought to the Council's notice by the complaints made by foreign visitors to the 1862 exhibition, and in 1867 Henry Cole, in an address to the Society, quoted the Commissioners of Inland Revenue as saying that "our four-wheeled cabs are a disgrace to the metropolis of a great empire" and suggested that the reason was the high duties imposed on the vehicles and the extremely low fares allowed by law. The Government now began to move, and in 1869 the Council sent a deputation to the Home Secretary and convened a conference of cab proprietors and others at which many practical suggestions for improvement were elicited. The deputation and the conference doubtless had some effect in hastening and assisting in the drafting of the legislation which was introduced later in the same year.

In order to encourage the provision of better vehicles once the amendment of the law made it economically possible, the Council then offered gold and silver medals for open and closed hackney carriages built to hold two or four persons; and a silver medal was promised for an instrument which would indicate the fare (in fact, a taximeter). These offers failed to produce anything useful, although a number of the indicators submitted were worth serious consideration; but other money prizes, totalling £120, for improved cabs, sponsored by the Society in 1872 in connection with the international exhibition held in the following year, called out a stronger entry, for the cabs showed novelty in design and a great variety of construction. A committee appointed by the Council selected two hansoms and two four-wheelers as specially deserving of notice, and after they had been modified in certain ways suggested by the committee £30 was awarded to each of their makers. A specimen of each type was also taken to Marlborough House for inspection by the President, whose approval was shown in the most practical way by his ordering one of them for use at Sandringham. Henceforth the character of the London hansom was greatly improved, and the prizes also had some influence for the better on the four-wheelers, though not so much.

And then there was the tram. As early as 1857 W. Bridges Adam read a paper on "the application of rails for horse transport in the streets of London", in which, after sketching the history of public transport up to that time, and particularly stressing the social results of the introduction of the omnibus, he advocated the laying down of tram-lines. Three years later the first of several unsuccessful experiments in road tramways was made in Birkenhead, but in 1870 the Tramways Act opened the way for widespread development. Early in that year Adams had again addressed the Society with detailed technical proposals, and in a third paper on the subject, read in 1872, shortly before his death, he urged the substitution of mechanical for horse motive power. This latter subject the Society took up with some enthusiasm and the next year offered a Howard Prize of £25 for an engine using any type of motive power, suitable for being built into and drawing a tram-car. This prize was awarded in 1875, on the recommendation of Sir Frederick Bramwell, for a steam-engine designed by John Grantham.[1] Before many years had passed, however, the electric motor and the central production of electricity had become accepted facts and provided the answer to the need of the trams, as was indicated as early as 1885 in a report made by Sir Douglas Galton, the Chairman of Council, on the competition held in connection with the international exhibition at Antwerp in 1885. Electric traction, which of course affected not only trams but trains, was discussed in several lectures to the Society during the next twenty years.

The next advance in public road transport was the introduction of the mechanically propelled omnibus, the appearance of which was at once hailed as a challenge to trams, tubes and railways alike. In the event tubes and buses have become allies, not rivals, but it is extraordinary that it has needed nearly fifty years to put into effect the principles enunciated in a paper by Thomas Clarkson in 1904 (when the petrol-engine was still so unreliable that the steam-engine had to be advocated), and reiterated in a paper by Lord Montagu of Beaulieu in 1907 (when after many initial failures the motor bus was beginning to establish itself), that the mechanically propelled road vehicle was better for traffic reasons than the tram and for economic reasons than the small railway branch line.

The development of mechanical means of traction, permitting the haulage of increasingly heavy and rapid vehicles, very soon brought with it the problem of constructing road surfaces capable of carrying them. The Society's attention was first attracted to this subject, however, by the widespread introduction of tramways in 1870, when there were many proposals for laying down novel types of surface, particularly asphalt, on either side of the

[1] Grantham's steam-car was afterwards set to work at Wantage, Berks. *Proc. Inst. C. E.*, LXXIX, 129.

tramlines. A "traction" committee was therefore appointed in 1873 to investigate the effect of these new surfaces on the ease of running of the vehicles, and a new dynamometer was devised with which to carry out the tests, which were conducted with a specially loaded omnibus in the early hours of the morning. Macadam, asphalt, wood and stone pavings were tested, and the committee's terms of reference also included the sanitary aspects of the question—a subject we are apt to forget now that horse traffic has almost disappeared from the roads. They were so greatly appalled by what they discovered when they investigated this latter side of things that in the end they concentrated their attention upon it, their main recommendation being that arrangements should be instituted wherever possible to clear streets by washing instead of sweeping—a far-sighted proposal to which effect was given in due course.

It is hardly surprising that the committee came to no very definite conclusions on the technical side. Even with the new dynamometer it did not, and could not, obtain precise results with horse-drawn vehicles. In a paper read to the Society in 1900, however, Professor Hele-Shaw called for a new attempt on the problem in view of the more accurately measurable motive force of the automobile, and the remarkable developments which took place in that line of research in more recent years and the extraordinary pieces of machinery which have been devised to carry it out were well described in Major R. G. H. Clements' paper on "The Evolution of Modern Road Surfaces" (1927) and Sir Reginald Stradling's Peter Le Neve Foster Lectures on "The Problems of Road Research" (1936), while a most comprehensive and informative survey of all the aspects of road development is contained in the Trueman Wood Lecture delivered by Sir Henry Maybury in 1931.

The improvement of the roads and of the vehicles using them has, like any other development, however good, created new problems, to two of which the Society has devoted considerable attention. The first of these is the overburdened condition of the roads in the great traffic centres such as London, and a lead was given on this subject by Sir John Wolfe Barry (son of the famous

Sir Charles), who was Chairman of Council in 1898 and 1899 and whose two inaugural addresses both dealt with this problem. These addresses had considerable effect at the time, and still make interesting reading because of the bold engineering proposals which they contain, particularly for the use of cross-overs at the intersection of the north–south and east–west arteries. Since then a number of interesting papers have been contributed on this subject, none of them more remarkable, perhaps, than that by Frank Pick in 1935 in which he succeeded in raising the drab topic of "The Organisation of Transport" into the realms of philosophy without losing touch with reality.

A further consequence of the improvement of the roads of this country, and still more of the establishment of railways, was the pitiable condition into which they brought the country's canal system—one of the most remarkable in the world. This also is a subject to which the Society has faithfully and persistently called attention at fairly regular intervals, but its most important effort on behalf of the canals was made in 1888 when a national conference was convened and an important series of papers, covering most aspects of the problem, was read and discussed.

4

The mention of canals leads us to the consideration of ships and shipping, a subject to which the Society made such notable contributions during its first century. During the earlier part of the period with which we are now concerned a number of papers were read to the Society on the revolution in ship propulsion which was then taking place, and some of these, such as John McGregor's paper on "The Paddlewheel and the screw propeller from earliest times" (1858) and "The rise of steam navigation in the Port of London", by P. L. Simmonds (1860), are of considerable historical value.

But before long the Society settled down once more to its main interest, the human aspects of sea-faring. We considered its work in connection with life-saving in the last chapter, but it concerned itself equally with the prevention of accidents—with improvements in lighthouse illuminants (on which, among others, Lord Kelvin contributed a paper in 1881), the testing of cables and anchors, the use of sound signalling and gale warnings. It also endeavoured to assist safe navigation by promoting the invention of a revolution indicator which would enable a navigating officer to read the speed of the ship's engines directly from a dial on the bridge. A gold medal was offered in 1874 for an instrument of this kind, and from eighty-four entries five "strophometers" were selected to be tried out on H.M. gunboat *Arrow*, that of T. A. Hearson, which afterwards came into practical use, being ultimately selected for the prize.

The Society very properly did not stop short at questions of safety: it was concerned also to promote comfort at sea. A number of papers were read before it on the working and living conditions of seamen, and the interest which this subject evoked is illustrated by the fact that in 1875 no less than four additional meetings were found necessary to thresh out thoroughly the points raised in a paper read by Captain Bedford Pim, R.N., M.P., on "The Merchant Marine of Great Britain". A report was also prepared in that year by a committee of the Society and forwarded to the Board of Trade in connection with the discussion of the Merchant Shipping Bill.

Not unnaturally, however, the Society was still more concerned about the conditions for passengers, and the efforts which it made between 1869 and 1872 undoubtedly resulted in a material improvement in comfort in the crossing of the Straits of Dover. The difficulty in this passage was that the harbours on either shore only permitted the use of small, shallow-draught vessels, and though the steamer companies did all that they could to reduce the duration of the agony by increasing the speed of the boats, the passengers usually had, as Henry Cole graphically pointed out in a letter to the *Journal* in 1865, a choice between being stifled down below in the saloon or half-drowned on the shelterless deck. In these circumstances Cole made the very sensible suggestion that suits of waterproof clothing should be available on hire to enable passengers to remain in the fresh air without getting soaked through, but nothing appears to have been done about this idea, and in 1869 the Council decided to encourage a more radical solution by holding a competition for the design of cross-channel steamers with better accommodation. Unfortunately, none of the entries merited the award, and the competition merely served to prove that without larger boats—which meant better harbours—nothing could be done. By this time, however, a new pier had been built at Dover, and the Society's competition, and further investigations made by a committee of the Society in 1871 and the following year, aroused so much feeling on this side of the Channel that pressure was successfully brought to bear on the other. Thus the way was opened up for the long overdue improvements.

The Society's campaign had other results of an intriguing but less permanent kind. Sir Henry Bessemer, who was at that time a Vice-President, had for some time been thinking over this problem and had planned a ship in which the passengers would be independent of the rolling of the hull by sitting in a saloon suspended like a gigantic hammock. Stimulated by the Society's efforts, and keeping in close touch with the Council, he now got a company formed to produce an actual ship, the *Bessemer*, on these lines, and this remarkable vessel went into the cross-channel service in 1875. Unfortunately, it did not prove a success. The swinging saloon did not operate very successfully, and there were two serious collisions with the pier at Calais. Another unusual type of boat which was devised to meet the special difficulties of the crossing was the double-hulled *Castalia*, designed by Captain Dicey, which ran on the cross-channel service for a number of years. But to many, of course, the only real answer to cross-channel discomforts seemed to lie in the making of a channel tunnel, and to this idea also the Society devoted considerable attention.

In 1925 the Society's interest in the sea was secured in perpetuity by a legacy of £10,000 from Thomas Lowe Gray, £7,000 being received by the Society in that year and the residue becoming available in 1949, the purpose of the endowment being to perpetuate the memory of the testator's father, Thomas Gray (formerly Assistant Secretary to the Board of Trade and author of the rhyming "rules of the road at sea"), by promoting "the advancement of the science of navigation and the scientific and educational interests of the British mercantile marine".

Thomas Lowe Gray suggested several means of furthering these objects, all of which, with other projects falling within the basic terms of the Trust, have been successfully adopted since the Trust was established, the Council being of course advised both in matters of policy and the general administration of the Trust by a special committee, largely composed of experts. On the more technical side valuable prizes have been awarded in most years for navigational inventions, of which the "talking beacon" of C. A. and D. A. Stevenson, for which £100 was awarded in 1930, has perhaps the greatest interest for the layman. This ingenious device, which was installed at the Cumbrae lighthouse in the Clyde, enabled pilots automatically to ascertain their distance from the lighthouse by comparison between the reception of blasts on its fog horn by sound and wireless respectively. Another outstanding award, although, owing to the necessity for secrecy, its precise object could not be revealed in 1944 when it was made, was that received by Professor J. T. Randall and Mr. H. A. A. Boot "for their valuable invention in connection with radiolocation", which was, in fact, the magnetron. In 1946, when security regulations had been relaxed, Professor Randall read a paper to the Society describing his discovery, with Sir Robert Watson-Watt in the chair.

Since 1942 the Society has also made an annual offer of a prize for an outstanding "deed of professional merit", and the list of recipients, short as yet, has the making of a remarkable gallery of heroes of the sea. The first award was made to Mr. J. Wylie, Chief Engineer of the *Ohio*, whose courageous and brilliant handling of the tanker enabled it to reach Malta in the face of determined German attacks. Mr. Wylie was also one of the first members of the merchant service to receive the D.S.O. The first award of this prize therefore set a very high standard, but the stories which lie behind subsequent awards, both in the war years and after, are no less striking.

A third means of encouraging members of the seafaring pro-

fession has been the offer of prizes for essays on various set subjects, the object being the double one of stimulating thought and
bringing new knowledge and useful experience to light. A
number of the essays rewarded in these competitions have been of
a sufficiently high standard to merit publication, in the Society's
Journal or otherwise.

Finally, there are the many activities of the Trust to help and
encourage those still in training. For many years prizes were
awarded on the results of a special examination held in schools
with navigational courses, but these have been superseded by a
system of Thomas Gray Memorial Trust awards in connection
with the annual examinations of the Merchant Navy Training
Board. Perhaps the most interesting of the educational activities
of the Trust has been the scheme originated and financed by it,
but administered by the Seafarers Education Service, for providing
scholarships for deck boys and seamen wishing to study for the
third mate's certificate. Since the scheme was started in 1938,
forty-six of these students, most if not all of whom would never
have attempted to gain officer status without its stimulus, had by
1952 completed their courses and gained their "ticket".

5

Before we leave the subject of the Society's connection with
transport development there remains that newest means of travel,
the aeroplane. No outstanding contribution can be claimed for
the Society in this field, although a number of interesting papers
have been presented to it, probably the most remarkable being
the account given to the Society in 1894 by Sir Hiram Maxim of
his great steam-powered flying machine and of the flights (if so
they can be termed, for he certainly cleared the ground for some
distance) which he took in it. Among more recent lecturers may
be mentioned Sir Sefton Brancker, who spoke on Commercial
Aviation (1925), Kronfeldt who gave a fascinating account of the
rise of gliding in Germany (1938) and Sir Alan Cobham who
lectured on flight refuelling (1940).

6

Much though travel has been speeded up during the past hundred years, communications have accelerated even more, and the Society has played a notable part in their development. The first important paper which it received on this kind of subject during that period was one read to it in 1858 by Sir William Siemens on "The progress of the Electric Telegraph", and the following year H. Hyde described David Hughes's teleprinter (which was also shown in the Society's Exhibition of Inventions that year) and S. A. Varley introduced the problems of submarine telegraphy. As has already been pointed out, the Society itself had prepared the way for the development of the latter by its announcement in 1845 of the properties of gutta-percha,[1] and the subject appeared prominently in its programme of lectures for the next five years—until, in fact, the attempts to link America with Europe by cable had finally succeeded.

Leaving the technical side of telegraphs the Society then took up its administrative aspects and in 1867 invited Sir Edwin Chadwick to read a paper on "The economy of telegraphy as part of a public system of postal communication." According to Sir John Cameron Lamb, who was for many years Secretary to the Post Office, this paper, and a number of letters by Chadwick published in the *Journal*, "had a powerful effect on public opinion and helped materially to pave the way for the telegraph legislation of 1868"[2] which provided for the purchase of telegraphs by the State, as advocated by Chadwick. Not content with the nationalisation of land telegraphs the Society then began to press for the nationalisation of ocean telegraphs: but that was a far more complicated matter and the effort was wisely abandoned. Finally, in 1880, the Society took up the question of telegraph tariffs, and after a peti-

[1] A special gutta-percha committee was appointed in 1858 and, assisted by the Government, the East India Company and several firms, it continued researches and inquiries for a number of years. After the committee had discontinued its labours the Society long maintained a particular interest in this material, and the Cantor Lectures by E. E. A. Obach in 1897 are a standard work on the subject.

[2] *Journal*, LIX, 12.

tion had been sent to the Postmaster-General a deputation waited upon him to point out the advantages to the public and to the Post Office of a reduction to a sixpenny minimum charge. The deputation appears to have gained the Postmaster-General's immediate agreement, but unfortunately the Chancellor of the Exchequer also had to be persuaded, and the reduction did not come into effect until 1885.

Meanwhile a new medium of communication, the telephone, had made its appearance, and the Society was fortunate enough to have it explained and demonstrated in November, 1877, by Graham Bell himself. As might be expected, the meeting was crowded out, and Bell agreed to give a repeat performance three weeks later at the Freemasons' Tavern—a quite unprecedented procedure for the Society. Bell's paper, naturally, was concerned solely with his own particular invention, but eighteen months later C. W. Cooke gave a valuable supplement in a paper which surveyed all the various forms of telephone invented up to that date.

The telegraph and telephone were revolutionary enough inventions, but already pioneers such as Preece were opening up the way for the still more amazing discovery of wireless communication. The Society did not, however, receive any account of these developments until 1894, when Preece described to it results obtained over considerable distances with the inductive effects occurring between sets of parallel wires. Six years later, when true electro-magnetic radiation was beginning to be successfully harnessed, Sir Ambrose Fleming, the close associate of Marconi, delivered a series of Cantor Lectures on "Electrical oscillations and electric waves", which covered the theory of radio as it was then conceived, and in the following spring, in a paper entitled "Syntonic Wireless Telegraphy", Marconi himself gave the Society his first personal account of his achievement of tuned wireless circuits, one of the milestones in his career of invention.

Thereafter Fleming contributed several further series of Cantor Lectures, and a Trueman Wood Lecture, on radio developments, from which the Cantor Lectures delivered in 1919 under the title of "The Scientific Problems of Electric Wave Telegraphy" may perhaps be singled out because they gave him an opportunity to describe his own great invention, the thermionic valve. Marconi also read two further papers to the Society, both of them in 1924, when he was Chairman of the Council. In these he gave his account of what might be called his last great practical achievement, the development of the beam system, which made possible direct wireless communication with the Antipodes. The reading of the earlier of these papers, which took place a few weeks after the first direct exchange of intelligible speech signals between England and Australia, was a truly historic occasion. Finally, mention should be made of the concise but authoritative survey of Marconi's work contained in a paper[1] read by his old colleague shortly after his death in 1939. This also proved to be the last of Fleming's many valuable contributions to the Society's proceedings.

The past century has witnessed a number of interesting visual extensions, as it were, of the three new basic forms of long-distance communication which we have just been considering. One of these has already been mentioned, the teleprinter invented by David Hughes quite soon after the introduction of the electric telegraph itself. It took rather longer to apply wireless telegraphy to the same purpose but in 1920, in connection with an inaugural address by A. Campbell Swinton, Mr. F. G. Creed gave the first public demonstration of teleprinting by wireless, and messages were received in the Society's Lecture Hall direct from the Eiffel Tower.

Eleven years before, Mr. Thorne Baker had lectured to the Society on an even greater marvel, the wireless transmission of pictures, which he had experimentally effected by a development of Korn's process. Of the logical climax of such research, however, television, not a great deal is to be found in the Society's records, which is the more to be regretted as Campbell Swinton, who served the Society no less than four times as Chairman of Council and several times discoursed brilliantly to it, never seems to have mentioned to it the idea which he conceived as far back

---

[1] "Guglielmo Marconi and the development of radio communication", by Sir Ambrose Fleming. *Journal*, LXXXVI, 42.

as 1908 and which is at the foundation of every modern television receiver, the use of the cathode ray tube for "scanning".

7

From television we may perhaps pass naturally enough to forms of communicating sound and sight which transcend time as well as space—the various aspects of technical recording.

In the history of sound recording the Society occupies a proud place as the body responsible for the first public demonstration of the "phonograph" in London, which was given to its members in 1878 by Sir William Preece, assisted by representatives of Edison.[1] It is appropriate therefore that the specialised society in this field, the British Sound Recording Association, should have held its first meeting in the Society's House, and in fact still regularly meets there.

As has already been mentioned, the Society has a somewhat similar standing in the history of visual recording, for not only did it organise the first public exhibition of photographs,[2] which was held at the Society's House from December 22, 1852, to January 30, 1853, but it also provided house room for the first meetings of the (Royal) Photographic Society. These important developments came about in the following way. A collection of photographs had been included in the Great Exhibition itself, but there had hitherto been insufficient material for a separate exhibition, owing to the heavy charge made by Fox Talbot for the use of his patent. Fox Talbot, however, was so much impressed by the public interest shown in the photographs at the Great Exhibition that in July, 1852, after an appeal by the Presidents of the Royal Society and the Royal Academy, he decided to present his patent rights to the nation. The spread of photography then became rapid. Within six months it was possible not only for the Society's exhibition to be held but also for the Photographic Society of London to be established, and for its first meeting to be convened on the Society's premises while the exhibition was still in progress.

[1] An improved version of Edison's phonograph is illustrated in plate 29.
[2] Plate 26.

The Royal Photographic Society (as we now know it) was one of the earliest of all photographic societies and the parent of many similar bodies in this country and elsewhere. Roger Fenton, that brilliant photographer of the Crimean War, had been the first to propose its formation, in April, 1852, and Robert Hunt, F.R.S., had written to the Society of Arts in the same month to request the use of the meeting room for an inaugural assembly. The request was granted at once, but the meeting did not take place until January 20, 1853, when Sir Charles Eastlake, P.R.A., became the first president. One hundred years later, to the day—and indeed to the hour—the Royal Photographic Society, by a charming thought which was warmly welcomed by the parent body, returned to its birthplace for its centenary meeting.

The Society of Arts has always taken a pride in its association with the early days of the art of photography. And this first exhibition—which consisted of 397 photographs produced by all the varied processes then in use—set a further precedent, because in view of its great success three selections of photographs were sent on tours of the country and were shown in twenty-four towns for a week at a time. The Arts Council and other bodies, who brought such skill and enthusiasm to their task of organising travelling exhibitions during the Second World War, might be surprised to learn that they had been anticipated by ninety years.

After the exhibition the Society of Arts left the new body to carry on the good work, and paid little further attention to the subject for over twenty years. Then, picking up the threads in 1875 with a paper by Spiller which reviewed the developments that had taken place in the interim, the Society stepped right into the forefront again in 1880 with another review by Sir William Abney of the important progress made during the intervening five years. Thereafter photography remained for many years a constant interest of the Society, Abney himself being its most frequent as well as most distinguished exponent. It was in connection with a series of Cantor Lectures delivered by him in 1882 that the Society arranged the further exhibition of photographs, recent and historical, which has also been mentioned, and this proved to be so successful that it led to the formation of a historical photographic collection at the South Kensington Museum.

During the next three decades every important aspect of photography was covered. The use of films and paper instead of glass was described by Leon Warnerke in 1886, shortly after the completion of his long researches on this subject; photographic chemistry was discussed by numerous authorities, including Watkins, the inventor of time-development, and photographic optics by Beck, Dallmeyer and others. But the subject which seems to have attracted the Society most was colour photography, to which a considerable number of papers were devoted from 1896 onwards. The first of these, by one of the well-known pioneers, F. E. Ives, described the complicated apparatus known as the photochromoscope, and four years later Sanger Shepherd reviewed the theory underlying the subject in a series of Cantor Lectures. Thereafter many of the processes devised for making colour transparencies, and in due course the extension of colour reproduction to cinematography and ultimately to television, may be traced in the Society's proceedings.

Cinematography, indeed, is the branch of photography in connection with which the Society's record is most distinguished. Its association with the subject began in 1882 when Eadweard Muybridge, lecturing on the movement of animals, illustrated his talk by showing true photographic moving pictures of animals on his "praxizooscope". Each series of photographs, consisting of twenty-four pictures, had been obtained by twenty-four separate cameras, the shutters of which were operated by the animals themselves, as they passed, by means of an intricate network of strings and electric circuits. The true cinematograph was first shown to the Society somewhat belatedly in 1898, by Jules Fuerst, but the next two great steps in the progress of cinematography both received their first public announcement before it. The first of these was the production of colour films by a two-colour process, which was demonstrated to the Society by the inventor, G. A. Jones, in 1908. The other great advance was the "talkie", or the "phonofilm" as it was first called, in which sound and sight recording were finally brought together on a single film, and the Society may well be proud of the fact that the first public demonstration in England of this extraordinary invention, by the De Forest process, took place in its lecture hall in November, 1924, following a paper by C. F. Elwell. The secret of the present-day type of "talkie", and of its close synchronisation of sound with sight lies, of course, in the photographic recording of the sound in the sound-track, and ten years later Dr. Kenneth Mees went more deeply into this aspect of the subject in a notable Trueman Wood Lecture.

The Society has, naturally, been at least as much concerned with the many applications of photography as with the progress of the science itself. One of the earliest of these was its use in spectroscopy, which was discussed in important lectures delivered in 1885 and 1886 by Sir William Abney and Sir William Hartley: nowadays the applications are almost limitless, as may well be appreciated from the admirable surveys given by Dr. Olaf Bloch in 1937 and Dr. D. A. Spencer in 1947. The most familiar application, probably, is to printing, and thought was given to this possibility almost as soon as photography itself was invented. Several of the Society's lectures made notable contributions to the advancement of this subject. The first of these was the account given to the Society by Paul Pretsch in 1856 of the process invented by him (and by others at about the same time) for the use of gelatine treated with bi-chromate of potash, and this was followed by several papers, of which the first, in 1857, was by Christopher Dresser on the so-called "nature-printing" process. Next, in 1878 we find Thomas Bolas discussing what is now known as "process-engraving" in the course of a series of Cantor Lectures delivered in 1878 on "The application of photography to the production of printing surfaces and pictures in pigments." These lectures, which explained all the then known processes, and were delivered on the eve of a period of great progress, became a standard work and were followed by further important courses by Bolas in 1884 and 1890, and by other lecturers. Finally, in 1898, Sir William Abney introduced the subject of three-colour printing, which then became the Society's chief interest in this field. Besides arranging these various lectures the Society held a competition in 1895 for process blocks, and for negatives suitable for block making, and in 1898 it induced the Science and Art Department to commence the important and comprehensive series of exhibitions of reproduction processes which has already been described.[1]

8

Besides providing these various mechanical means of recording sight and sound, science has important contributions to make in connection with the permanence of certain less mechanical types of record, and in these the Society has shown a particular interest. One of the curious phenomena of our "scientific" age is the deterioration which has taken place in the purely technical aspects of the art of painting. This is a matter to which the Society has faithfully devoted attention. The earliest of many communications which it received on this subject during our present period was a series of Cantor Lectures delivered in 1871 by F. S. Barff on "Artists' Colours and Pigments", which had the notable effect of causing the Royal Academy to devote some of the proceeds of its exhibitions of Old Masters to the establishment later in the same year of its Chair of Chemistry, Barff, rightly enough, being the first to be appointed to it. Nine years later it was the turn of the artists to lecture to the Society on the subject when Holman Hunt read his famous paper on "The present system of obtaining materials in use by painters, as compared with that of the old masters", in which he impressively described the impermanence of the paintings of his day and laid the blame for it firmly at the door of the artists themselves. Since Holman Hunt the subject has been taken up before the Society by numerous chemists, including J. M. Thomson, A. P. Laurie, Sir William Abney, Sir Sidney Harmer and, most recent of all, Mr. Noel Heaton, but in spite of the efforts of the chemists through well over half a century Giorgio de Chirico, in a Selwyn Brinton Lecture delivered in 1949, condemned the artists as roundly as Holman Hunt for their complete loss of technique as far as the choice of pigments and paints was concerned.

[1] See pp. 272–4.

If the artists of the past century have been slow to make use of the gifts of science, the same cannot be said for the textile industry, which was revolutionised by the discovery of coal-tar dyes. On this subject the Society was fortunate enough to have Sir William Perkin himself twice as a lecturer. In 1868 he delivered a course of Cantor Lectures on "Aniline and Coal Tar colours" and eleven years later read a paper on "The History of alizarin and allied colouring matters and their production from coal-tar". Another noted lecturer to the Society in this field during the last century was Raphael Meldola.

But to return to our immediate subject. Just as the Society lamented the fading away of works of art and sought to find a remedy from the chemists, so it also took up the twin problems of the decay of paper, and of the leather-binding of books, both of which matters were investigated by specially appointed committees. The deterioration of paper was gone into in 1897 and the outcome of the committee's researches was the conclusion that, although large quantities of inferior paper were then in use, grade for grade there had been no deterioration.[1] A standard of quality was, however, suggested for papers required for publications of permanent value.

A different story was given by the committee appointed three years later, at the suggestion of Douglas Cockerell (subsequently one of the first R.D.I.s), to examine the problem of the decay of bookbinding leather. This committee, of which the chairman was Viscount Cobham, found that a serious deterioration of quality had in fact taken place and recommended methods for the proper preparation of durable leather. In making their investigations they devised a very successful means of simulating the effects of age upon the material. The committee's report was published in 1901 and had such widespread practical effects that a second edition was called for and was produced (with financial assistance from the Leathersellers' Company) in a considerably improved form in 1906. This second edition still remains one of the most valuable sources of information on the subject. Incidentally, the stock of this book which the Society still holds is wonderfully

[1] The full report may be found in *Journal*, XLVI, 597.

preserved, and the volumes look as fresh as when they were first produced. But they are bound in buckram, not leather!

Wide though our net has been cast in these last two chapters, there is many a noble prey which has escaped its meshes. But a detailed list of all the important communications contributed to the Society would have been tedious, and it seemed preferable to follow a few definite lines of activity which have been "encouraged" by the Society. There is a further chapter, also, which ought to, but never could have been written, on the practical effects which have followed the wide dissemination of so much knowledge. There is no doubt, however, that many of the papers read before the Society during the past century, and still more its positive efforts, have stimulated, guided and assisted activity in many parts of the world, and over considerable periods of time. The bread scattered upon the waters has returned after many days.

CHAPTER 19

The Society and the Commonwealth

SOMETHING has been said in a previous chapter of the remarkable work for the colonies undertaken by the Society during its first century. It is now time to consider how far this useful association has been maintained in all the altered circumstances of the Society's later years. And, great as were the practical benefits flowing from the active colonial policy in the late eighteenth and early nineteenth centuries, an historian has seriously to consider whether they have not, in fact, been exceeded by the Society's entirely different achievement in the same field since the date of its incorporation.

It must be admitted that the record is not one that provides any abundance of picturesque detail for the historian. The Society's method has changed; instead of offering prizes for the production of silk or coconut oil or bread-fruit, it has offered a long series of lectures and papers, delivered by men of experience and authority, over the greater part of a century, touching on every conceivable aspect of colonial development and administration, and made available for careful study by publication in the *Journal*. A mere chronicle of these regular occasions in the Society's lecture hall would, if we had space to attempt it, make only a dry and formal impression. But to the imaginative reader they will have a deeper meaning, for they must be considered in terms of the welfare and progress—to which they were dedicated—of millions throughout India and the Commonwealth.

It was the 1851 Exhibition, and the important colonial visitors which it brought to London, that inspired the Society to resume its efforts on behalf of the colonies. In 1852 the Society proposed to hold an exhibition of the products of India. A committee was formed and got together a remarkable collection with contributions from Queen Victoria, the Dutch Government, the East India Company and so on. But there was a difficulty about finding a suitable place in which to show it in London, and on the suggestion of Prince Albert it was resolved to offer the collection to the Great Dublin Exhibition of 1853. This gesture was fully appreciated in Ireland and there is no doubt that the "Eastern Court" was one of the most interesting features of that Exhibition.

At the Society's suggestion, the Secretary of State, in April, 1852, circulated a despatch inviting the formation of colonial associations in connection with the Society; and in response to this appeal some, though not many, of these associations were established. In 1952, a hundred years later, only one could be traced. That one, however, the Malta Society for the Encouragement of Arts, Manufactures and Commerce, is still in a prosperous condition and has done a vast deal of good, particularly by encouraging the simpler artistic crafts in the island, and at its centenary celebrations an illuminated address of congratulation was presented by the Governor, Sir Gerald Creasy, a Fellow of the parent body, on its behalf.

A few years later, the Society attempted to include colonial institutions in the Union of Institutions that was then being formed, and the *Journal* for December 21, 1855, set out the terms on which they could be admitted and the advantages that they would derive from membership. The colonial institutions that joined the Union were never more than sixteen, and from 1860 the numbers fell away.

A more hopeful line of approach, and one which ultimately proved successful, was suggested in a proposal made to the Council in 1857 by Hyde Clarke. His idea was that "a special section should be formed for India, another for Australia, one for English America, and so on", and that the Indian section should meet once a fortnight, and the Australian once a month, for the reading of papers on commercial and industrial topics. Clarke also emphasised the need for "a colonial centre in London". Nothing was done at that time, but ten years later, in 1868, Hyde Clarke renewed his proposal, with the result that the Indian Section then came into being. At the first Indian meeting, on March 12, 1869, a paper was read by C. H. Fielder; appropriately enough it dealt with that universal beverage, Indian tea. There were eight meetings in 1869 and four in 1870. Henceforth the meetings of the Indian Section, averaging between five and seven in each year, have been continued regularly up to the present time, but since 1951 they have been included in the programme of the newly established Commonwealth Section.

Throughout the whole period the subject most often considered by the Indian Section seems to have been that of population, which under one heading or another was dealt with in about twenty papers. Commerce, communications, public health, education, industries and art were the subjects next most frequently reviewed; then forestry and irrigation, currency and finance, administration, mining and metallurgy. During the latter part of the nineteenth century India's frontier problems were of acute interest; at least one afternoon in practically every session between 1886 and 1900 was devoted to a frontier question, Afghanistan and the Russian problem giving place in course of time to the problem of the Chinese frontier. Between 1886 and 1907 famines were given serious attention. Moreover, the Society has always taken an interest in other societies working for India, whether by arranging joint meetings with them (as in the case of the East India Association) or giving them publicity through special lectures—for example, the papers on the Imperial Institute read in 1916 and 1926, and that on the Imperial College of Tropical Science read in the latter year.

The success of the Indian Section led to the formation in 1874 of the African Section, and this, again, was largely due to the zeal of Hyde Clarke. The African Section became, in 1879, the Foreign and Colonial Section: in 1901 its title was altered to the Colonial Section, and in 1921, to the Dominions and Colonies Section. Together with the former Indian Section, it now forms part of the Commonwealth Section.

The Indian and Colonial sections have both done most valuable work, and by attracting to the Society many members from the Commonwealth have been instrumental in widening its influence immeasurably. In the historical advance of India, in particular, the Society can claim to have played an important part, not only by spreading information throughout India as to the directions in which Indian manufactures and products could most usefully be developed, but also by making generally known in this country the extent of India's resources and of her industrial progress.

Among the many valued servants of the Society who have been responsible for the activities of the Indian and Colonial sections, one name is outstanding, that of Samuel Digby, C.I.E., (1853–1925), who was appointed Secretary of the Indian Section in 1890 and held the post until his death thirty-five years later. In 1898 the Colonial Section also came under his charge, and in 1918, on the accession of Mr. Menzies to the secretaryship, he assisted him in his duties, though he was never actually styled Assistant Secretary.

Digby was a native of Wisbech and was one of four distinguished journalists from the Fen country who were honoured by the Crown for services in and for India. Another was his elder brother, William Digby, a fervent advocate of Indian political advancement, whose best-known book was sarcastically entitled "*Prosperous" British India*. The others were the late Sir Thomas Jewell Bennett and Sir Frank Brown, both with a long record of service on the Council of the Society. Samuel Digby had none of his brother's fiery Radicalism, but wrote chatty, non-propagandist London letters by the weekly mail to the *Bombay Gazette* and the *Indian Daily News* (of Calcutta), at a time when Press telegrams were few and costly and air transport was yet to come. His devotion to the Society was complete, and he avoided no labour, however prolonged, difficult or minute, that could contribute to good papers and discussions and to large attendances at meetings of his sections. With regular clear-cut features and hair immaculately brushed, Digby, in his neat black coat, was for many years a familiar and distinguished figure on the platform of the Society's lecture hall. The Society was greatly in his debt, for he was responsible for substantially increasing its membership, not only by recruitment from overseas, but also by bringing into the Society former residents in the Commonwealth who had returned to England.

No one who looks through a list of the papers read to the

Dominions and Colonies Section since 1874 can fail to be struck by the wide range of subject-matter and the authority of the lecturers. To the African Section (as it was known between 1874 and 1879), besides population, trading and mining, Livingstone's travels and the problem of slavery were of chief interest. Of the foreign countries considered in papers read to the Foreign and Colonial Section between 1880 and 1900, China, Japan, Russia, Siberia and Egypt were given most prominence; but British territories supplied the majority of the subjects, the papers dealing with questions of commerce, health, art, emigration and immigration, communications, land settlement, agriculture and forestry. Between 1901 and 1921 two outstanding papers read to the Colonial Section may be singled out for special mention—those by the Countess of Aberdeen on "Women in Canada" (1903) and by A. B. Keith on "The Development of Colonial Self-Government in the Nineteenth Century" (1908). The Dominions and Colonies Section heard a great variety of important papers between 1922 and 1951. The British Empire Exhibition at Wembley was considered in papers in 1923 and 1925, "The Work of the British Association in relation to the Empire" in 1930, and the Empire Marketing Board in 1931. Other public institutions dealt with were Kew (1935), Imperial Institute services to South Africa (1937), Fairbridge Farm Schools (1938), the Public Schools Exploration Society (1939), the International African Institute (1945), the Colonial Geological Survey (1945), and the Rhodes Trust (1947). In 1945, 1948, 1949 and 1951 came papers read by the Dominions scientific liaison officers.

As the years go by, speakers like Sir Bartle Frere, Commander Lovett Cameron or Sir Charles Dilke give place to Herbert Samuel (as he was in 1903) or to Lady Lugard (Flora Shaw). And, coming nearer to our own day, we notice, among the many eminent people who have addressed the Section, Lord Lovat, Lord Olivier, Sir Wilfred Grenfell, Margery Perham, Lord Bledisloe, Lord Hailey, Sir Bernard Bourdillon and Sir Frank Stockdale. The best was demanded, and the best has been given.

It is the same with the list of lecturers in the Indian Section. Many of the most interesting contributions made in our time to the study of ancient and modern Indian art have been given, since 1920, in the form of the Sir George Birdwood Memorial Lectures, which were founded in memory of a passionate and understanding lover of India who was for more than forty years a valued member of the Society. It was well said of Sir George Birdwood that "there was nobody quite like him—quaint, crotchety, generous and liberal to a fault, often wise, generally humorous, frequently eccentric, and especially of late years, inevitably outspoken". Being a great admirer of Lord Beaconsfield, he was a pioneer in the observance of Primrose Day; and he was also a great patriot whose faith in India and Britain never faltered in the darkest days of the First World War. The Society treasures a bronze bust of Sir George Birdwood by Alfred Gilbert, R.A., a replica of one presented in 1900 to the University of Bombay by some of his Indian friends.

The first of the Birdwood lectures was delivered in 1920 by Sir Valentine Chirol. Those who have followed him have included Sir Edward Grigg (now Lord Altrincham), Sir Michael O'Dwyer, Sir E. Denison Ross, General Sir George MacMunn, Sir George Schuster, Sir William Rothenstein—who spoke on "The Genius of Indian Sculpture" in 1937—Lord Hailey, and Sir Leonard Woolley. Among the most interesting of the lectures in recent years have been those of Major-General Sir John Megaw on "The Health of India" in 1946, and of Sir Alfred Watson on "The Growth of the Press in English in India", in 1948.

It will be appropriate to refer here to the R. B. Bennett Empire Prize of 100 guineas which was endowed by Lord Bennett in 1944 on the understanding that it should be given by the President of the Society every third year for the most outstanding contribution from the Dominions, India and the Colonies to the promotion of the arts, agriculture, industries and commerce of the Overseas Empire during each intervening period. The Prize was awarded in 1945 to Dr. C. Camsell, Deputy Minister for Mines, Canadian Government, in recognition of the work of exploration and mineral survey which he carried out in the North-West Province of Canada. In 1948 it was awarded to Sir Frank Stockdale, who was then development planning adviser to the Secretary of State for the Colonies, in recognition of his outstanding contribution to the promotion of agriculture and social welfare in the Colonial Empire. In 1951 the recipient was a New Zealander, E. Bruce Levy (now Sir Bruce Levy), Director of the Grasslands Research Division of the New Zealand Department of Scientific and Industrial Research, who was honoured for his important work on grassland farming, which has had great influence not only in New Zealand but also in Great Britain and the Empire generally. The awards are made on the recommendation of the Council and the Commonwealth Committee. Another important award made under the supervision of this committee was the prize for a design for Colombo Cathedral, referred to elsewhere.

Looking back to the time, nearly a hundred years ago, when Hyde Clarke first made his proposal that special sections should be formed within the Society for India, Australia, English America and so on, we may be tempted to regret that his scheme for creating separate departments that would interest themselves in the various portions of the Empire was not carried out. But we must remember that in 1868 the Royal Colonial Institute was established with aims that more than covered the aspirations of Hyde Clarke, especially so far as concerned the formation of a colonial centre in London. The Society of Arts could not have hoped to undertake so large a task successfully without sacrificing its own aims and objects, and with them its unique freedom of action. In practice, however, it has made its characteristic contribution to research and improvement within the Empire and Commonwealth in its own way, and can be as proud of it as of anything it has achieved in its long history. The volume *British Commonwealth Objectives*,[1] edited by Sir Harry Lindsay and containing a dozen papers read to the Society in the preceding few years by Lord Bennett, F. L. McDougall, Lord Hailey, Sir Angus Gillan, F. H. Andrews, Dr. Charles Camsell, Guy B. Gresford, A. L. Poole and Dr. I. E. Coop, A. P. van der Post, Sir Frank Noyce, Sir Bernard Bourdillon and the Rev. H. M. Grace, is perhaps the most striking evidence of this work.

[1] Michael Joseph, 1946.

CHAPTER 20

Domestic History: 1854–1954

1

NOT least among the reasons for the continuing prosperity of the Society has been its long and fruitful association with the Royal Family, which was begun, as we have seen, by the Duke of Sussex in 1816, and was strengthened so notably by the historic presidency of the Prince Consort. On the death of Prince Albert, William Tooke became the Society's President for a short period, until in 1863 the Prince of Wales, responding to an Address presented by the Council of the Society, intimated his willingness to accept the office "that he might be better able to promote the great and beneficent objects which his dear father had so much at heart, and in which he was so zealously supported by the Society". Accordingly, on October 22, 1863, he was elected first a member of the Society and then its President, and he continued to hold office until his accession to the throne in 1901. In that year he was awarded the Albert Medal in recognition of his aid "to Arts, Manufactures and Commerce during thirty-eight years' Presidency of the Society of Arts, by undertaking the direction of important exhibitions in this country and the executive control of British representation at International Exhibitions abroad, and also by many other services to the cause of British Industry". He himself had already, in 1887, had occasion to present the Albert Medal to his mother, Queen Victoria, "in commemoration of the progress of Arts, Manufactures, and Commerce throughout the Empire during the fifty years of her reign".

The Prince of Wales did not look upon his office as anything of a sinecure. By his wish, no new action of any importance was ever taken by the Council without his being consulted, and he

34. THE VILLAGE OF WEST WYCOMBE, BUCKS.

Restored by the Royal Society of Arts, 1929–34

35. A MEETING IN PROGRESS IN THE SOCIETY'S LECTURE HALL, 1953

36. PRESENTATION OF THE ALBERT MEDAL TO THE RIGHT HON. WINSTON CHURCHILL, 1945
The presentation is being made in the Society's library by Dr. E. F. Armstrong,
supported by Viscount Bennett

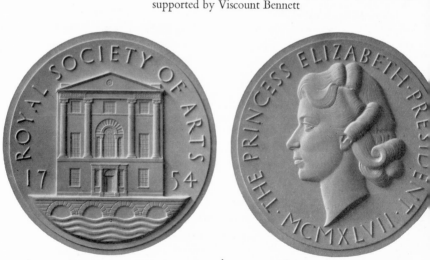

37. THE SOCIETY'S MEDAL, 1948–53
Designed by Percy Metcalfe, C.V.O., R.D.I.

could be relied on for shrewd and sensible advice. Often he made practical suggestions that affected the course of action pursued by the Society; he did so, for example, in connection with the National Training School for Music and the conferences on water-supply organised by the Society in the 'seventies. When he ascended the throne as King Edward VII in 1901, he necessarily vacated the presidency, but consented to become the Society's first Patron. It was in the capacity of Patron that in 1908 King Edward granted the Society permission to prefix to its title the term "Royal".

When his father became King, it was the Society's hope that the Duke of Cornwall (afterwards Prince of Wales and later King George V) would accept the presidency, but, as he was then absent on a journey round the world, a temporary President, Sir Frederick Bramwell, was chosen. On the Duke of Cornwall's return, in the autumn of 1901, he was duly elected and he continued to act as President until his accession in 1910, when he in turn became Patron. He had already been associated with the Society for some years; the first reference to him in the records occurs in 1893, when an address of congratulation from the Council and members was presented to him on his marriage, and in 1894 he had been elected a Life Fellow and nominated a Vice-President. During his tenure of the presidency, the Prince watched over the Society's affairs with the wisdom and good sense that was later to win him the affection of his subjects as King. It was he who was instrumental in bringing into the Society several of the Crowned Heads of Europe as honorary Royal members, and the Society has in its archives letters addressed to him by the Kings of Norway, Sweden and Denmark, among others, speaking in high terms of appreciation of the Society and of the honour thus done to them.

On the death of King Edward VII and the accession of King George V, the same procedure was followed as on the death of Queen Victoria. King George became Patron, and received the Albert Medal "in respectful recognition of His Majesty's untiring efforts to make himself personally acquainted with the social and economic condition of the various parts of his Dominions, and to promote the progress of Arts, Manufactures and Commerce in the United Kingdom and throughout the British Empire". For a period of less than a year Lord Alverstone then held the presidency. He was succeeded, in February, 1911, by the Duke of Connaught.

In accepting the Society's suggestion on the Duke's behalf, his Comptroller, Colonel Malcolm Murray, said that the Duke "will be pleased to accept the position of President of the Royal Society of Arts, but he trusts that this will not entail his attendances at the Council's Meetings, as his time is already so fully occupied". Any fears that the Duke may have entertained that he would be drawn into the day-to-day business of the Society were, of course, unfounded. But in fact, as the years wore on—and the Duke was President for thirty-one years—the Society retained a continuing hold upon his interest. The personification of dignity, graciousness, courtesy and natural charm, he was ever alive to the great services that his father, the Prince Consort, had rendered to the nation through the Society, and with the same high sense of duty he showed from the outset an active personal regard for its work. His advice and assistance were never sought in vain and he maintained the closest touch to the end.

Of all the many ceremonies in which the Duke of Connaught played a leading part there was probably none that gave him more pleasure—because of it origin, as well as of its importance—than the presentation of the Society's Albert Medal. Those who attended on those occasions at Clarence House could not fail to be impressed by the simple dignity with which the ceremony was performed and by the Duke's invariable affectionate reference to the fact that the medal had been "instituted in memory of my beloved father". The Duke's profound knowledge of India and Canada gave him a special appreciation of the Society's Indian and Dominions and Colonies Section. He once declared: "Of all the many societies with which I am associated there is none that gives me greater satisfaction than the Royal Society of Arts, with which I have been associated for so many years, and whose work on behalf of India I especially follow with interest. I can never forget India and my connection with that great country."

The portrait of the Duke which hangs in the Council room at the Society's House was the last to be painted of him and was the last work of Philip de László. It was painted in 1938 and was presented by the artist to the Society.

When the Duke of Connaught died in 1942, the nation was in the middle of the Second World War, and for some years the Society naturally turned for its Presidents to three of its most distinguished members, Sir Edward Crowe (1942-3), a former Comptroller-General of the Department of Overseas Trade; Dr. E. F. Armstrong, F.R.S. (1943-5), the eminent chemist and scientist; and Viscount Bennett (1945-7), the former Prime Minister of Canada. But the Society was honoured and gratified when its association with the Royal Family was re-established in August, 1947, by the acceptance of the presidency by Her Royal Highness The Princess Elizabeth.

For the next five years, until she came to the throne in 1952, Princess Elizabeth brought all her particular gifts of youth, sincerity, gaiety and lively intelligence to the service of this ancient Society. It would be difficult to overestimate the importance of her contribution to the Society's fortunes during these difficult post-war years. Her obvious interest in its doings and the very delightful way in which she carried out her official duties on her visits to John Adam Street—both evidenced by the many photographs which appeared in the papers at the time—focused a new attention on the Society's affairs and beyond doubt played their part in the steady increase of the Society's membership. To a learned body, in whose affairs women had had relatively little influence for nearly two centuries, it was a real refreshment and encouragement to have at its head a Princess of such character and charm.

Appropriately, the purpose of her first visit to the Society as President, which occurred on November 5, 1947, was to re-open the Great Room, which had been restored to its former beauty after the severe damage it suffered from a German bomb in 1941. The Society's pictures—having fortunately survived a war-time evacuation—were again on the walls, and Princess Elizabeth sat in the chair used by her great-great-grandfather, Prince Albert.

"The objects to which the Royal Society of Arts addresses itself are worthy of all the support we can give," she said, and she spoke particularly of its work in the field of industrial design: "The spacious days are gone . . . but we should be defeatist and unimaginative indeed if we concluded that because nearly everything we produce to-day must be severely practical, it must also be without taste or beauty." A few days after this visit Princess Elizabeth was married to Lieutenant Philip Mountbatten, soon to become the Duke of Edinburgh. The Society's present to her was a gold box designed by Robert Goodden, R.D.I., with her monogram on the outside and the Society's device on the underside of the lid—a notable piece of British craftsmanship.

Other occasions on which Princess Elizabeth graced the Society's House were the Exhibition of Humorous Art in 1949, of which we have written elsewhere, and the first reception given by the Faculty of Royal Designers for Industry in November, 1950; and her last visit as President was in May, 1951, when she opened the Society's contribution to the Festival of Britain, the "Exhibition of Exhibitions", and, before doing so, announced the award of the Albert Medal for 1951 to her father, King George VI.

This award had been made partly to mark the centenary of 1851, but there were also excellent personal reasons why the Council had decided to offer the Medal to the King "in respectful recognition of His Majesty's life-long concern for the progress of industry and for industrial welfare". King George's interest in the Society dated from 1927, when, as Duke of York, he attended one of the Society's meetings to hear a lecture on "Industrial Welfare in Great Britain and the United States". He was elected a Life Fellow and Vice-Patron of the Society in 1933, and on his accession to the throne became Patron in succession to King Edward VIII. The King's illness and his untimely death in 1952 prevented his receiving the Albert Medal from the Council; but a deputation later waited upon Queen Elizabeth the Queen Mother who received it from them.

With the accession to the throne of Queen Elizabeth II the office of President fell vacant, and the Queen, in her turn, consented to succeed her father as the Society's Patron. On November 5,

1952, five years exactly since the installation of Princess Elizabeth, the Chairman of the Council was able to announce that the Duke of Edinburgh had agreed to follow her as President and had been duly elected. He was installed a year later, on November 18th, 1953. Remembering the Duke's well-known interest in the Arts and Sciences, the Society could well look forward with confidence to his tenure of a presidency to which Prince Albert had brought such lustre a century before.

2

Under the Society's bye-laws, the Council consists of the President; of a number of Vice-Presidents, not exceeding twenty-four; of two Treasurers; and of twelve "Ordinary Members of the Council"—all these to be elected annually. Under Bye-law 8 the Council, at its first meeting after the annual election, elects a Chairman who must be chosen from those members of the Council who are of one year's standing at least. Bye-law 9 lays it down that, after two years' service, the Chairman is not re-eligible to the office for at least one year. This was not always the case, for we find Sir Thomas Phillips (1859-62), Lord Henry Lennox (1868-71) and Sir Richard Webster, Q.C., later Lord Alverstone (1890-3), each serving for four consecutive years. In more recent times three outstanding Chairmen, Mr. J. A. Milne (1932-4), Dr. E. F. Armstrong (1943-5) and Sir Ernest Goodale (1949-51), were asked to continue for a third year of office, the bye-law being temporarily waived, in Mr. Milne's case as a tribute to his strenuous efforts for the Exhibition of British Art in Industry, and in Sir Ernest Goodale's as a recognition of the special duties required of the Chairman in 1951, the Festival year. But these have been the only occasions in this century on which Bye-law 9 has been suspended.

The office of Chairman of the Council demands of its holder —who is, under the President, the practical executive head of the Society—a combination of qualities, of which energy, determination, foresight, tact and the gift of conciliation are perhaps the chief. As a rule these necessary qualities become clear to the future Chairman's colleagues, who elect him, in the ordinary course of their work together on the Council; in fact, the Chairman, in a manner of speaking, usually chooses himself by proving his worth in the actual work of the Council and its committees. There have been exceptions to this rule, where certain distinguished individuals have been appointed Chairman for special reasons that made their chairmanship particularly appropriate at the time, but the normal method of reaching the chair has been by way of long service to the Society, which is as it should be.

Looking back over the list of Chairmen since the eighteen-sixties, we note the energy and capacity of Sir Thomas Phillips, who earned his Knighthood for his action in quelling a Chartist riot in South Wales; the useful chairmanship of Lord Henry Lennox, at one time Under-Secretary of State for War, who accepted office at the desire of his friend the Prince of Wales, thus enabling him to keep in touch with the Society of which he was then President; the tact and common sense of Lord Alfred Churchill, twice Chairman in the 'seventies, who had the warmest interest in the welfare of the Society; and the conscientiousness and thoroughness of Lord Alverstone (formerly Sir Richard Webster), who was successively Attorney-General, Master of the Rolls and Lord Chief Justice.

These are only four of the nineteen Chairmen who held office between 1854 and 1900. Since then their high standard of service has not been lowered. We have only to mention the names of Sir William Abney, F.R.S., the distinguished photographic chemist and education official (1903–4); of Lord Sanderson, an eminent civil servant of the old school (1911–12); of Senatore Guglielmo Marconi, the inventor of wireless-telegraphy (1924); of Sir Thomas Holland (1925–6), remembered equally as scientist and university administrator; of Lord Amulree (1937–8) and Sir Atul Chatterjee (1939–40), to show that the Society has been continuously fortunate in having men of experience and distinction to direct its affairs. During the war years three Presidents of the Society combined with the senior office that of Chairman of the Council—Sir Edward Crowe (1941–2),

Dr. E. F. Armstrong (1943–5) and Viscount Bennett (1945–6)—and since the war the dignity of the Chair has been upheld by Sir Harry Lindsay (Chairman 1947–8), Sir Ernest Goodale (1949–51), Mr. E. Munro Runtz (Chairman 1952) and the Earl of Radnor, Chairman during the bi-centenary year. The names of two of these more recent chairmen, Sir Thomas Holland and Dr. Armstrong, are now commemorated by the periodical delivery of endowed lectures. To go further, and to select for special mention some of the many members of the Council who have given loyal support to their Chairman is an invidious task—except in two cases. Miss Haslett, as she then was, Dame Caroline as she has been since 1947, was elected a member of Council in 1941 and was thus the first woman to hold any such office in the Society, and her election was followed in the next year by that of Miss Anna Zinkeisen, R.D.I.

3

In the first century of its existence, the Society was served by eleven Secretaries; in its second century there have been only five. This is an indication, perhaps, both of the more settled conditions under which the Society has operated and of the confidence which its servants have felt in the usefulness of the work they have been doing.

Peter Le Neve Foster, who succeeded Edward Solly in the secretaryship in 1853 and held it until his death in 1879, was long remembered by those who knew him for his kindly and genial nature, for his patience, tact and common sense. He was a man of simple tastes who was fully contented to serve the Society, as he did with thoroughness and efficiency, with no thought of personal ambition. His association with the Society began in 1837; his father and his grandfather had both been members. When the first Council was formed, he became an *ex officio* member of it, being at the time chairman of the Committee of Accounts. He was then immediately elected Treasurer, and held that office until 1852, when he became an ordinary member of the Council.

Le Neve Foster had therefore taken a full share in the

reorganisation of the Society. By the time that he commenced his secretaryship, it was fairly launched on a new career of prosperity—and much of the credit for the Society's continuing success during one of its busiest and most fruitful periods must properly belong to him. It was largely due to his executive ability that the Society's reputation for practical work stood so high at the time of his death. He had much to do with the organisation of the Exhibitions of 1851 and 1862, though he did not receive the honours or rewards which fell to many of his colleagues.

His sound scientific knowledge, wide reading and general intellectual capacity were always of great benefit to the Society. Born in 1809, he had graduated in the mathematical tripos at Trinity Hall, Cambridge, in 1830, and had been elected a Fellow of his college. Called to the Bar in 1836, he practised for fifteen or sixteen years as a conveyancer. Le Neve Foster was one of the first to experiment, as a scientific amateur, with the new art of photography, and he was one of the founders of the Photographic Society. He was a constant contributor not only to the Society's *Journal* but also to several other scientific and technical periodicals, and for thirteen years he was secretary to the mechanical science section of the British Association.

Le Neve Foster was succeeded as Secretary of the Society in 1879 by Henry Trueman Wood, who was then in his middle-thirties and had already served for several years as Editor of the *Journal* and Assistant Secretary. Born in 1845, he was educated at Harrow and Clare College, Cambridge, of which he was a scholar. At Cambridge he achieved the rare distinction of twice winning the Le Bas Prize for the best English essay on a subject of general literature. On leaving the university, he worked as a clerk in the Patent Office—where he laid the foundations of an extensive knowledge of inventions—until he joined the staff of the Society in 1872. For the whole of his active career thereafter the Society remained his chief interest. Sir Henry Trueman Wood (he was knighted in 1890) held the office of Secretary for thirty-eight years, and had the satisfaction of piloting the Society through the greater part of the First World War before he retired from the secretaryship in 1917. He was then elected Treasurer, and next year Vice-President and member of the Council, serving as its Chairman for 1919–20. A fund was also raised to institute the annual Trueman Wood Lecture, which has since provided the occasion for many outstanding addresses. Sir Henry died in 1929, in his eighty-fourth year.

So indispensable did Sir Henry become to the Society that it seemed almost as if he himself *was* the Society. Certainly the Council left things very much in his hands, and very competent hands they were. Among his other gifts, he shared with his sister Mrs. Annie Besant (who was generally considered the first woman orator of her day) the gift of public speaking, and when he rose to take part in any of the discussions at meetings of the Society, the audience could expect to hear something worth while.

As Secretary, Trueman Wood had been brought into touch with a number of exhibitions with which the Society was more or less directly connected. The Health (1884), Inventions (1885) and Colonial (1886) exhibitions owed much of their success to his energy and enthusiasm, and it was natural that he should be appointed British Commissioner at the Paris Exhibition of 1889 and secretary to the Royal Commission for the Chicago Exhibition 1893. His exhibition work led him to take a deep interest in the history of British industry, and his *Industrial England in the middle of the Eighteenth Century*, in which he described the state of each industry as it existed about 1754, is a valuable handbook of careful research and useful information. This was published in 1910 and was followed in 1913 by his *A History of the Royal Society of Arts*, an admirable achievement to which the present writers have already expressed their indebtedness. Not unnaturally, though one must regret it, he did not fully chronicle the activities of the Society in the years during which he was personally concerned with them.

Sir Henry had various interests outside his official duties. He was a keen photographer, was President of the Royal Photographic Society (1894–6) and later became chairman of the English branch of Kodak. He was one of the best-known figures at the Athenaeum Club, where his popularity led to his election as chairman of the executive committee. In his youth he had, as a runner, won his half-blue at Cambridge for the mile, and till late in life he dodged the traffic in the Strand with an agility that many a younger man might have envied. In maturer years he became a fair golfer and was chairman of the Chorley Wood golf club. All told, Henry Trueman Wood was a man of many parts, beyond doubt a personality, a tower of strength to the Society of Arts, and a very good friend to his friends—though it must be added that his tongue had an uncommonly sharp edge for anyone whom he considered incompetent or undesirable.

Trueman Wood was succeeded in the secretaryship by George Kenneth Menzies, his Assistant Secretary since 1908. Mr. Menzies had come to the Society with a full share of academic and administrative experience, having been on the staff of St. Andrews University, and Secretary in the Academic Department of the University of London, and within a year of his taking over Sir Henry's responsibilities he made what must surely be the greatest personal contribution to the service of the Society of any of its officials—the negotiations leading to the anonymous gift of £30,000 (to be described later) which enabled it to purchase its House. Had it not been for this gift the Society would almost certainly have had to quit its home in 1922 and it is more than doubtful whether it would have survived such a misfortune. Another outstanding contribution of Mr. Menzies, his administration of the Fund for the Preservation of Ancient Cottages, was deservedly recognised by the award of the C.B.E. in 1932, but there is no doubt that the Society also owes a great deal to him for his kindly spirit and sense of humour with which he maintained throughout his secretaryship a harmoniousness at headquarters which had its effect throughout the Society. He will be remembered as a writer of light verse, most of which appeared in *Punch*, and his shorter History of the Society, already referred to, was published in 1934. On his retirement in the following year he was elected a Vice-President and member of Council, in which capacities he has actively served up to an advanced age.

Mr. Menzies' successor was William Perry, who had served the

Society for the previous ten years as Assistant Secretary and secretary of the Indian and Dominions and Colonies Sections. After a brilliant scholastic career, Perry was elected to a Fellowship at St. John's College, Oxford, and then, in 1909, entered the Indian Civil Service. Ill-health soon compelled him to return to England; and after holding a series of administrative posts, interrupted by three years of war service, he joined the Society's staff in 1925. It was tragic that his tenure of the secretaryship should have been cut short after less than three years by his death in 1937 at the age of fifty-five. Happily, these were prosperous years for the Society and saw, among other notable events, the institution of the new distinction of "R.D.I.", but by his untimely passing the Society lost a wise administrator and his colleagues a charming and unselfish friend.

On the death of William Perry, Kenneth William Luckhurst, his Assistant Secretary, was appointed to succeed him. During the latter's temporary absence on war service, Vernon W. Davies, the founder of "Davies's", the famous coaches, served as Acting Secretary from 1942 to 1943 and Miss Jean Scott Rogers in the same capacity from 1943 to 1946. Mr. Davies and Miss Rogers—the Society's first woman Secretary—did splendid work under very difficult circumstances, for which the Society must always be grateful.

As we have seen, all the last four Secretaries of the Society have served an apprenticeship as Assistant Secretary. Among the other Assistant Secretaries of the past hundred years one name is outstanding, that of Henry Benjamin Wheatley, who succeeded Henry Trueman Wood in 1876 and served as Assistant Secretary for nearly thirty years. Wheatley was certainly one of the most distinguished men who have ever served the Society. He was born in 1838, the posthumous son of a well-known Piccadilly auctioneer, and was educated almost entirely by his sister and his brother, B. R. Wheatley, who was esteemed as a bibliographer. At an early age he collaborated with the latter in cataloguing the library of the Athenaeum Club, and he also prepared the catalogue to the library of the Oxford and Cambridge Club. From 1861 to 1879 he was Clerk to the Royal Society, his principal work there being connected with the library, of which indeed he was practically the librarian.

Despite all the hard work that Wheatley's official duties at the Royal Society and the Society of Arts required of him, he was able to live a busy and useful life of authorship. He was possessed of a wide and curious knowledge, and was full of energy and application, his interests lying mainly in archaeology and bibliography. The history of London occupied him particularly. His first important publication was *Round about Piccadilly and Pall Mall* (1876), and in 1891 he produced his *London Past and Present*, which, though nominally a new edition of Cunningham's handbook of London, was really a new book. It remains indispensable to any student of London history. But the work which finally established his reputation was his admirable edition of *Pepys's Diary* (1894–9) which has long been recognised as the standard edition, and for which he was rewarded by the University of Durham with the honorary degree of D.C.L. which he always valued very highly.

It was a varied and most industrious career of scholarship, and as a background to it for thirty years went an earnest and patient devotion to the interests of the Society. On his retirement from the assistant-secretaryship in 1908, Wheatley was granted a moderate pension, and the members of the Council subscribed to present him with a personal testimonial besides electing him a life member of the Society. He lived until 1917, a simple, kindly man, who had won the affection and admiration of a very large circle of friends.

Of others who have held the assistant-secretaryship during the past century space permits the mention only of the most recent. Dr. F. R. Lewis (1937–9), whose historical researches have proved their value to the present writers, was succeeded by Dr. D. C. Martin, who was "lent" by the Society early in 1940 to the Ministry of Supply and did not return to the Society's service. He went instead to the Chemical Society as General Secretary and thence to the Royal Society as Assistant Secretary. Mr. Charles Burns and Mr. C. J. Buchanan-Dunlop then held the post for about a year each, and Mr. G. P. Griggs, novelist and man of letters, for slightly longer (1949–50). He left to become Secretary of the Museums Association and was succeeded by Mr. R. V. C. Cleveland-Stevens, Barrister-at-Law, of Lincoln's Inn.

One might well dilate also, if space permitted, on the services rendered to the Society in latter years by such indispensable officers as the Chief Clerks, G. T. Davenport, H. J. Dack and J. Samson; or by the Accountants, J. H. Buchanan, A. G. Toye and I. Purdam; or by the Examinations Officers (about whom something is said in Chapter 15); or by the Librarians, K. D. C. Vernon and Miss M. L. Clark.

It has always been characteristic of the officials of the Society that they have been anxious not merely to carry out their specified duties efficiently but also, as opportunity offers, to use their position as servants of the Society to be helpful to its members and to the general public. In particular, they are constantly expected, in view of the universality of the Society's interests, to be mines of information on every conceivable subject, and, to be fair to them, they seldom disappoint inquirers. The most common type of question received is one relating to nice points of English grammar (upon which the Society seems to be accepted as a higher authority than Fowler!). But among the odder inquiries have been one from India asking where a special brand of parrot seed could be obtained for a fussy bird which refused to eat any other, and an appeal for instructions for the maintenance of an Egyptian mummy, recently acquired by a Fellow.

4

But we must now turn to consider a few facts regarding the general membership of the Society. The Society's membership figures have always been a fairly reliable guide to its prosperity at any given time. It will be of interest, therefore, briefly to chronicle their rise and fall during the past two hundred years.

The earliest list of members, printed in 1755, contained only 110 names. Thereafter the numbers increased rapidly, and the fourth extant list, issued in 1760, recorded about 1,350 names. After 1770 there was a serious decline to a few hundreds in 1780, but

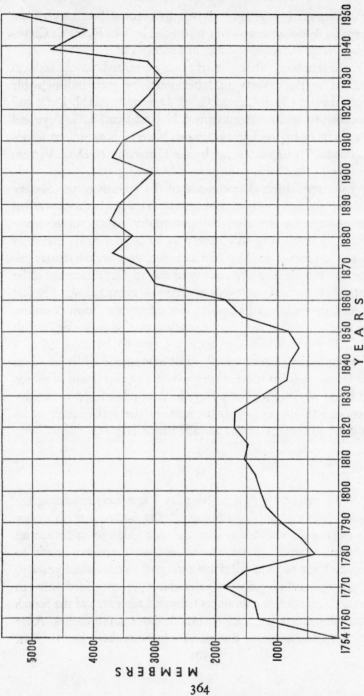

FIG. 7. THE SOCIETY'S MEMBERSHIP THROUGH TWO CENTURIES
(The graph is based on five-yearly calculations)

a steady increase again carried the numbers up to about 1700 in 1820. Then followed the most critical ebb in the Society's fortunes when its membership again fell to a few hundreds in the years before its incorporation.

Soon after the election of the Prince Consort to the presidency the figure only was 685; in 1850 it was just below 1,000; in 1856 it was 1,700. After this there followed a period of regular increase until by 1861 there were 2,263 members and by 1866 the numbers had reached 3,031, owing largely to the publicity resulting from the 1862 Exhibition. For the next seventy years the number of the Society's members did not greatly vary. There were 3,200 in 1870 and 3,128 in 1914. Between those years the figures rose to 3,656 in 1885, fell to 3,078 in 1899, and rose again to 3,490 in 1909. In 1917 there were just under 3,550 members.

After the First World War the membership somewhat declined, particularly in the period of depression from 1927 onwards. But by 1937, when the numbers totalled 4,247—an increase partly due to the success of the British Art in Industry Exhibition in 1935—recovery was in full swing. At the outbreak of war in 1939 the membership stood at the then record figure of 4,650. The war had its inevitable effect, but recovery began before hostilities were over. After the war the figures again rose steadily to 5,362 in 1950 and to 5,835 at the end of 1952. This last increase, won in the teeth of economic adversity, may presumably be partly attributed to the special attention paid to the Society during the 1951 Festival year, for an historian cannot fail to notice that the membership has been sharply affected by the degree to which the Society has, or has not, been in the public eye.

During a period of solid prosperity at the close of the nineteenth century, a reserve fund of investments was built up; in 1905 the value of invested property was estimated at £21,000, and in addition there were Trust Funds valued at £14,700. These funds, especially those held in trust, have since been increased. But it must be remembered that the costs which the Society has to meet —not least in the price of paper and printing, which is such an important factor in connection with the publication of the *Journal* and the organisation of examinations—have risen enormously since 1914. Indeed, the accumulated funds are only significant as a reserve, to meet a deficit in difficult days or some very special item of expenditure. For its revenue the Society has always had to depend almost entirely on the subscriptions of its members, and it is not surprising that the Society had to raise its minimum subscription, which had stood at 2 guineas ever since 1754, to 3 guineas in 1920 and to 4 guineas in 1952. The fact that in nearly two hundred years the rate has only been doubled, whereas the general administrative costs have gone up in a far greater proportion, testifies to the wise husbanding of the Society's limited resources.

5

When we look back over the external dangers that have threatened this philanthropic body during recent years we feel that the Society may well congratulate itself on having maintained and even improved its position. The First World War inevitably meant for it a period of financial stringency, reflected in the lean size and poor appearance of the *Journal* for those years. It was, incidentally, in 1914 that a bye-law was passed allowing subscribers to use the designation Fellow as well as, or instead of, that of Member (a change that seemed to be desired by many). The Society soon discovered that not all Fellows were necessarily going to be Jolly Good Fellows. A paragraph in the following year's annual report, headed "Alien Enemy Fellows", records the Council's decision "to expunge from the List of Honorary Fellows the names of all persons of German and Austro-Hungarian nationality".

In the midst of the depression following the First World War the Society was faced with a grave problem concerning its House. The original lease granted to it by the brothers Adam expired in 1867, and was succeeded by various short-term leases, the last of which came to an end in 1904. For a good many years the Society held its house on a precarious tenure—an agreement terminable on either side at two years' notice. Then, in 1920, it was learned that the landlord, Mr. G. H. Drummond, was unable to continue the lease after March, 1922, but that he was willing to

38. EXHIBITION OF BRITISH ART IN INDUSTRY, 1935

39. EXHIBITION OF EXHIBITIONS, 1951

Her Majesty the Queen (then H.R.H. Princess Elizabeth) with Sir Harry Lindsay, Chairman of the Council, and Mr. H. M. Bateman

H.R.H. the Duke of Edinburgh with Mr. Kenneth Bird (Editor of *Punch*)

40. SUCCESSIVE ROYAL PRESIDENTS OF THE SOCIETY VISITING THE EXHIBITION OF HUMOROU
ART, 1949

sell the freehold for £50,000, this figure being subsequently reduced to £42,000. It therefore became a question whether the Society could raise sufficient funds to purchase the freehold, or whether it would be obliged to leave the historic house in which it had worked for a century and a half. Confronted by this "unthinkable" possibility, the Society decided to make the effort to buy. Prominent members of the Council subscribed about £10,000; a generous donor who desired to remain anonymous contributed £30,000; and, after an appeal had been made to Fellows, enough money was collected to secure the freehold and to carry out a number of repairs and alterations. The gain was not the Society's alone, for the purchase meant that one of the finest masterpieces of the brothers Adam would be preserved for the nation.

Since the Society acquired the house for its own, it has been considerably improved internally to suit modern requirements, but in a manner which has fully maintained its original character, and in 1926 Sir George Sutton, a Vice-President of the Society, generously paid for the cost of decorating the rear wall of the house, which had been brought into unexpected prominence by the widening of the Strand.

Whatever disturbances were caused to the Society by the First World War were negligible compared with the difficulties under which it laboured during the Second World War. First of all, the Society's headquarters were moved. The early months of 1939 found many London firms and institutions planning evacuation in the event of war, and in March the Council decided on a similar policy, in which they were greatly assisted by a generous offer by Mr. Basil Ionides, one of their members, and the Hon. Mrs. Ionides, of accommodation at their house at Buxted Park, Sussex. As the summer wore on as much preparation was made for the expected removal as could be carried out without affecting the normal work of the Society. Temporary offices were made ready in the Buxted Park outbuildings; all the older records were packed and despatched to the National Library of Wales, Aberystwyth, and a roller and crate were prepared for the removal and safe storage of the huge Barry canvases and other paintings.

Thanks to these preparations an orderly evacuation was completed just before the actual declaration of war, and from the beginning of September the official address of the Society became "Buxted Park, Sussex". A skeleton staff remained at John Adam Street, however, for liaison purposes, and to keep the Society's House in readiness for committee and other meetings.

Then came the question of what function, if any, such a body as the Royal Society of Arts could, and should, perform in the grave circumstances in which the nation found itself, but as soon as the Government had made clear its view that the continuation of cultural activities was desirable, the Council at once proceeded with plans for a normal programme of meetings. Thus the Society (alone, it believes, among similar institutions in London) opened its session on the normal date, November 1, and after this good beginning carried out a full programme uninterruptedly throughout the whole of the war. The only change was in the hour of the meetings which, in view of the black-out, was altered from the evening to the early afternoon, and, after the start of the bombing, to the lunch-hour. Although a good many meetings later on were disturbed by the sound of the "Alert", the audiences soon learned to ignore the signals, and the attendances were, on the whole, good and sometimes embarrassingly large.

In April, 1941, a further blow befell the Society through the explosion of a parachute mine on the adjoining Little Theatre. The blast destroyed most of the glass in the Society's House, and severely damaged much of the roof and the general woodwork, and for a few weeks it became necessary to seek the hospitality of the Institution of Electrical Engineers for the Society's meetings. In due course, however, the library was patched up and turned into a temporary lecture hall, and several office rooms were rendered usable. Thanks largely to the faithful services on the roof of Mr. James, the Housekeeper, assisted by a rota of other members of the staff as fire-watchers, no further serious injury was sustained, and as there had fortunately been no serious structural damage, the building was successfully restored after the war to its former beauty, under the skilful supervision of Mr. Oswald Milne. Indeed, when the work was completed and the lecture hall was reopened by Princess Elizabeth on November 5, 1947, many declared that the building looked more charming than ever.

The story of the movements of the staff must now be completed. On a snowy night of December, 1939, the mansion house at Buxted Park, but not, as it happened, the outbuildings used by the Society, was burnt down, and in May, 1940, when there were reliable reports that coastal areas might be compulsorily evacuated at any time, the Council decided to bring the staff back to London. At the same time they sent all the more important books in the library, and the pictures, which had been at Buxted, to join the records at Aberystwyth. When the serious bombing began, in the autumn of 1940, a second evacuation was decided upon, this time, however, only of the examinations department and the small printing press which had been established in the Adelphi building in the 'twenties. As a great deal of the work of these two staffs does not depend on speedy communications, it was felt that it would be advantageous for them to be somewhere out of London where they could work a full day and enjoy undisturbed nights. They were accordingly removed to the village of Upper Quinton in Warwickshire, and then in 1942, as these hurriedly occupied quarters were scattered and primitive as well as remote, the examinations department suffered its fourth move, to more civilised conditions in a country house near Pangbourne, Berkshire, leaving the printing press still at Upper Quinton.

This emergency splitting up of the Society's staff proved in the end to be permanent. The old building in John Adam Street had for some time been overcrowded with the increased staff necessitated by the expansion of the Society's examinations, and on their return to London after the war the examinations department settled at new offices at Victoria Street and the printing press moved to the suburb of Clapham.

The war naturally brought changes of personnel as well as of location to the staff, and by the middle of 1942 the only remaining members of the permanent secretarial staff were the Accountant and the Housekeeper, while several members of the Examinations staff, deferred initially, had been called up for service. Until this time, and even during the First World War, the Society had always employed an all-male staff, but it now found the assistance of women indispensable even in some of its senior posts. Thus occurred another change which has also in considerable measure proved to be permanent, for although since the war a return has been made at the Society's headquarters to an all-male administrative and clerical staff, the other departments now employ a considerable proportion of the other sex.

Another change in the composition of the staff traces its origin to the wartime period: this is the creation of a whole-time librarianship. Hitherto the care of the Society's collection of books (it could for long scarcely be called a library) had been combined with their other duties by busy members of the staff, but in 1943 the Council decided that, as soon as circumstances permitted and the books had returned to their shelves, the library should be reorganised and a full-time staff appointed. In the meantime the services of a temporary librarian were secured, who, by preparing a catalogue of the Society's books, present and absent, prepared the way for Mr. K. D. C. Vernon, who was given the first permanent appointment in 1947. Thus even the wartime period made its contribution of progress in the internal affairs of the Society.

6

The time has come to bring this history to a close. No one could be more fully alive to its imperfections than the historians themselves, for this versatile and ancient society has not been an easy subject for biography. As they have contemplated the innumerable achievements of two centuries, the Society has sometimes reminded them of Dryden's famous verdict on Buckingham:

> A man so various that he seem'd to be
> Not one, but all mankind's epitome.

Dryden's lines cannot be further adapted to the Society. Though it has made its mistakes, the Society has not been "stiff in opinions, always in the wrong". Though it has often chosen to initiate improvements and then retire into the background, it would be misleading to suggest that it has been "everything by starts, and nothing long". The Society has been "chemist" and "fiddler", agreed; it has even played the "statesman" on occasion. "Buffoon?"—certainly not! (one must cautiously admit that it has sponsored an exhibition of humorous art).

The Society has remained steadfast in its purpose—to do all the good that it can consistent with its declared aim of encouraging "Arts, Manufactures and Commerce". Probably no Society has ever had objects more nearly universal. There is very little, as this record of two hundred years has shown, that cannot be brought within the scope of that phrase. And, contrary to a widespread belief, the Society has never received any assistance from the State, but has paid its way entirely by its voluntary efforts. It has kept its own sturdy independence. Never was the independent, public-spirited philanthropist more necessary to our salvation than in these days of the all-mothering, all-smothering State. As Mr. Munro Runtz, Chairman of the Council, said in 1952: "I believe the Society will prosper, provided that it maintains its complete independence of thought and action, and avoids any flirtation with Government control or assistance, whatever party may be in power. . . . This should not deter the Society," he added, "from co-operating for specific objects."

It is, one hopes, not too presumptuous to see something peculiarly English in such an institution as this. The Society has been English in the pride of standing on its own feet, English in its sense of compromise and adaptability. Like England, it has had its ups and downs, its anomalies and non-sequiturs. Like England, it has somehow survived, and in the process has contributed to the progress of mankind. Certainly, the life of every Englishman now living has in some degree been affected by the operations of the Society. If England is to flourish, then there is no reason why the Society should not flourish with it. There is plenty of work to be done yet. May it be so.

At genus immortale manet, multosque per annos
Stat fortuna domus, et avi numerantur avorum.

The Society's Officials : 1754–1953

PRESIDENTS

Viscount Folkestone	1755–1761
Lord Romney	1761–1793
The Duke of Norfolk	1794–1815
H.R.H. the Duke of Sussex, K.G. . .	1816–1843
H.R.H. Albert, Prince Consort, K.G. . .	1843–1861
William Tooke, F.R.S.	1862
H.R.H. the Prince of Wales, K.G. (King Edward VII)	1863–1901
Sir Frederick Bramwell, Bart., F.R.S. . . .	1901
H.R.H. the Prince of Wales, K.G. (King George V) .	1901–1910
Lord Alverstone, G.C.M.G., F.R.S. . . .	1910
H.R.H. the Duke of Connaught, K.G. . .	1911–1942
Sir Edward Crowe, K.C.M.G. . . .	1942–1943
E. F. Armstrong, Ph.D., D.Sc., LL.D., F.R.S. .	1943–1945
Viscount Bennett, P.C., K.C., LL.D. . . .	1945–1947
H.R.H. the Princess Elizabeth . . .	1947–1952
H.R.H. the Duke of Edinburgh, K.G. . .	1952–

CHAIRMEN OF COUNCIL

Edward Speer ⎫ Joint Chairmen	1846–1848
George Bailey ⎭	
Edward Speer	1848–1849
Francis Fuller	1850
Henry Cole	1850
W. W. Saunders, F.R.S.	1851
Henry Cole, C.B.	1852
Captain Owen, R.E.	1853
Harry Chester	1853
Viscount Ebrington, M.P.	1854
Rev. James Booth, LL.D., F.R.S. . . .	1855

Colonel W. H. Sykes, M.P., F.R.S.	1856
C. Wentworth Dilke	1857–1858
Sir Thomas Phillips	1859–1862
William Hawes, F.G.S.	1863–1865
Sir Thomas Phillips	1866
William Hawes, F.G.S.	1867
Lord Henry G. Lennox, M.P.	1868–1871
Major-General F. Eardley-Wilmot, R.A., F.R.S.	1872–1874
Lord Alfred Spencer Churchill	1875–1876
Major-General F. C. Cotton, C.S.I.	1877
Lord Alfred Spencer Churchill	1878–1879
Sir Frederick Bramwell, Bart., F.R.S.	1880–1881
Sir William Siemens, D.C.L., LL.D., F.R.S.	1882–1883
Sir Frederick Abel, G.C.V.O., K.C.B., D.C.L., D.Sc., F.R.S.	1883–1885
Sir Douglas Galton, K.C.B., F.R.S.	1886–1887
The Duke of Abercorn, C.B.	1888–1889
Sir Richard Webster, Q.C., M.P.	1890–1893
Major-General Sir John Donnelly, K.C.B.	1894–1895
Major-General Sir Owen Tudor Burne, G.C.I.E., K.C.S.I.	1896–1897
Sir John Wolfe-Barry, K.C.B., F.R.S.	1898–1899
Sir John Evans, K.C.B., F.R.S.	1900
Sir William Preece, K.C.B., F.R.S.	1901–1902
Sir William Abney, K.C.B., D.C.L., F.R.S.	1903–1904
Sir Owen Roberts, D.C.L., F.S.A.	1905
Sir Steuart Colvin Bayley, K.C.S.I., C.I.E.	1906–1907
Sir William White, K.C.B., F.R.S.	1908–1909
Sir John Cameron Lamb, C.B., C.M.G.	1910
Lord Sanderson, G.C.B., K.C.M.G., I.S.O.	1911–1912
Colonel Sir Thomas Holdich, K.C.M.G., K.C.I.E.	1913–1914
Dugald Clerk, D.Sc., F.R.S.	1915–1916
A. A. Campbell Swinton, F.R.S.	1917–1918
Sir Henry Trueman Wood	1919
A. A. Campbell Swinton, F.R.S.	1920–1921
Lord Askwith, K.C.B., D.C.L.	1922–1923
Senatore Guglielmo Marconi, G.C.V.O., LL.D., D.Sc.	1924
Sir Thomas Holland, K.C.S.I., K.C.I.E., D.C.L., LL.D., F.R.S.	1925–1926
Sir Philip Magnus, Bart.	1927

Sir George Sutton, Bart., M.I.E.E. 1928
Llewelyn B. Atkinson, M.I.E.E. 1929
Sir Edward Gait, K.C.S.I., C.I.E. . . . 1930-1931
John A. Milne, C.B.E. 1932-1934
Colonel Sir Henry McMahon, G.C.M.G., G.C.V.O.,
   K.C.I.E., C.S.I. 1935-1936
Lord Amulree, P.C., G.B.E., K.C., LL.D. . . 1937-1938
Sir Reginald Glancy, K.C.S.I., K.C.I.E. . . 1939
Sir Atul Chatterjee, G.C.I.E., K.C.S.I. . . 1939-1940
Sir Edward Crowe, K.C.M.G. . . . 1941-1942
E. F. Armstrong, Ph.D., D.Sc., LL.D., F.R.S. . 1943-1945
Viscount Bennett, P.C., K.C., LL.D. . . 1945-1946
Sir Harry Lindsay, K.C.I.E., C.B.E. . . 1947-1948
Sir Ernest Goodale, C.B.E., M.C. . . 1949-1951
E. Munro Runtz, F.R.I.C.S. . . . 1952
The Earl of Radnor, K.C.V.O. . . . 1953

SECRETARIES

William Shipley 1754-1757
George Box 1757-1760
Peter Templeman, M.D. 1760-1769
Samuel More 1769-1799
Charles Taylor, M.D. 1800-1816
Arthur Aikin 1817-1839
W. A. Graham 1839-1842
Francis Whishaw 1843-1845
J. Scott Russell, F.R.S. 1845-1850
George Grove 1850-1852
Edward Solly, F.R.S. 1852-1853
Peter Le Neve Foster, M.A. . . . 1853-1879
Sir Henry Trueman Wood, M.A. . . 1879-1917
G. K. Menzies, C.B.E., M.A. . . . 1917-1935
William Perry, M.A. 1935-1937
Kenneth W. Luckhurst, M.A. . . . 1937-

APPENDIX B

The Albert Medal

LIST OF RECIPIENTS, 1864–1953

1864 Sir Rowland Hill
1865 His Imperial Majesty Napoleon III
1866 Michael Faraday
1867 Sir W. Fothergill Cooke and Sir Charles Wheatstone
1868 Sir Joseph Whitworth
1869 Baron Justus von Liebig
1870 Vicomte F. de Lesseps
1871 Sir Henry Cole
1872 Sir Henry Bessemer
1873 Michel Eugène Chevreul
1874 Sir William Siemens
1875 Michel Chevalier
1876 Sir George Airy
1877 Jean Baptiste Dumas
1878 Sir William (afterwards Lord) Armstrong
1879 Sir William Thomson (afterwards Lord Kelvin)
1880 James Prescott Joule
1881 Professor A. W. Hofmann
1882 Louis Pasteur
1883 Sir Joseph Hooker
1884 Captain J. B. Eads
1885 Sir Henry Doulton
1886 Samuel Cunliffe Lister (afterwards Lord Masham)
1887 *Her Majesty Queen Victoria*
1888 Professor H. L. Helmholtz
1889 John Percy
1890 Sir William Perkin
1891 Sir Frederick Abel, Bart.
1892 Thomas Alva Edison
1893 Sir John Bennet Lawes, Bart., and Sir Henry Gilbert
1894 Sir Joseph (afterwards Lord) Lister
1895 Sir Isaac Lowthian Bell, Bart.
1896 Professor D. E. Hughes
1897 George James Simons
1898 Professor R. W. Bunsen
1899 Sir William Crookes
1900 Henry Wilde
1901 *His Majesty King Edward VII*
1902 Professor A. Graham Bell
1903 Sir Charles Hartley
1904 Walter Crane
1905 Lord Rayleigh
1906 Sir Joseph Swan
1907 The Earl of Cromer
1908 Sir James Dewar
1909 Sir Andrew Noble
1910 Madame Curie
1911 Hon. Sir Charles Parsons
1912 Lord Strathcona and Mount Royal

1913 *His Majesty King George V*
1914 Chevalier (afterwards Marchese) Guglielmo Marconi
1915 Sir Joseph Thomson
1916 Professor Elias Metchnikoff
1917 Orville Wright
1918 Sir Richard Glazebrook
1919 Sir Oliver Lodge
1920 Professor A. A. Michelson
1921 Sir Ambrose Fleming
1922 Sir Dugald Clark
1923 Major-General Sir David Bruce and Colonel Sir Ronald Ross
1924 *H.R.H. The Prince of Wales*
1925 Lieut.-Colonel Sir David Prain
1926 Professor Paul Sabatier
1927 Sir Aston Webb
1928 Sir Ernest (afterwards Lord) Rutherford
1929 Sir Alfred Ewing
1930 Professor H. E. Armstrong
1931 *H.R.H. The Duke of Connaught and Strathearn*
1932 Frank (now Sir Frank) Brangwyn

1933 Sir William Llewellyn
1934 Sir Frederick Gowland Hopkins
1935 Sir Robert Hadfield, Bart.
1936 The Earl of Derby
1937 Lord (now Viscount) Nuffield
1938 *Her Majesty Queen Mary*
1939 Sir Thomas Holland
1940 John A. Milne
1941 President Franklin D. Roosevelt
1942 Field-Marshal J. C. Smuts
1943 Sir John Russell
1944 Sir Henry Tizard
1945 Winston Spencer Churchill (now Sir Winston Churchill)
1946 Sir Alexander Fleming and Sir Howard Florey
1947 Sir Robert Robinson
1948 Sir William Reid Dick
1949 Sir Giles Gilbert Scott
1950 Sir Edward Appleton
1951 *His Majesty King George VI*
1952 Sir Frank Whittle
1953 Edgar Douglas Adrian

Publications of the Society

SERIAL PUBLICATIONS

Transactions of the Society, instituted at London, for the encouragement of Arts, Manufactures and Commerce . . . [annual], vol. I, 1783 —vol. LVII, 1850–1.

Abstract of Proceedings and Transactions, etc., during the session 1844–1845, and Premiums for the sessions 1845–6, 1846–7.

[Weekly notices], session XCII [1845–6]—session XCV [1848–9].

Notes of Proceedings of the Society of Arts, session XCV [1848–9]—session XCVI [1849–50].

Proceedings of the Society of Arts . . . the ninety-seventh session, 1850–1.

Journal of the Society of Arts and of the Institutions in Union, vol. I, no. 1, November 26, 1852—[weekly to March 22, 1940; fortnightly April 5, 1940 +].

BOOKS AND REPORTS

[Items marked with an asterisk were published with the cooperation or approval of the Society]

Premiums offered by the Society . . . 1754–1850.

A List of the Society . . . 1755 + .

Rules and Orders of the Society . . . 1758–1846.

*Catalogue of the Pictures, Sculptures, Models, Drawings, Prints, &c., of the Present Artists. Exhibited at the Great Room of the Society . . . [Society of Artists.] 1760.

*Catalogue of the Paintings, Sculptures, Models, Drawings, Engravings, etc., now exhibiting in the Great Room belonging to the Society . . . [Free Society of Artists.] 1761–4.

*Museum Rusticum et Commerciale: or, select papers on agriculture. commerce, arts and manufactures. Revised . . . by members of the Society of Arts, vol. 1–6. 1764–6.

The Complete Farmer: or, a general dictionary of husbandry, in all its branches; ... To which is added The Gardener's kalender, calculated for the use of farmers and country gentlemen ... By a Society of Gentlemen, members of the Society for the encouragement of arts, manufactures, and commerce. 1765.

Practical Observations on the Culture of Lucerne, Turnips, Burnet, Timothy Grass, and Fowl Meadow Grass, communicated by letters to Dr. Templeman, Secretary of the Society ... an appendix containing comparative estimates of the expense and profit in drill and broadcast husbandry, in different parts of England, and in Ireland, and an account of some new and improved instruments in husbandry, with the prices annexed to most of them. 1766.

Memoirs of Agriculture and other Œconomical Arts. By Robert Dossie. vols. I-III. 1767-82.

Experiments and Observations on American Potashes. With an easy method of determining their respective qualities. By W. Lewis. Made at the request of the Society ... in consequence of an application from the House of Representatives of Massachusetts Bay. 1767.

Observations on the Pot-ash brought from America. With respect to its goodness, sophistication, &c., verified by experimental examination: together with instructions for determining the comparative value of any parcel, by expedient methods: to which, is subjoined, processes for making pot-ash and Barilla, in North-America. The whole communicated to the Society ... by R. Dossie: and printed, at their request, in consequence of an application made to them on these points, by the Hon. House of Representatives of the Province of Massachusetts-Bay. 1767.

A Catalogue of the Machines and Models in the Repositories of the Society ... 1771, 1775 and at intervals. (This was also published in *Memoirs of Agriculture*, vol. II, in William Bailey's *Advancement of Arts*, and in A. M. Bailey's *One Hundred and Six Copper Plates* ...)

The Advancement of Arts, Manufactures, and Commerce; or, descriptions of the useful machines and models contained in the repository of the Society for the encouragement of arts, manufactures, and commerce: illustrated by designs on fifty-five copper-plates. Together with an account of the several discoveries and improvements promoted by the Society ... By William Bailey. 1772, 1776. (Revised and added to by A. M. Bailey, 1782. *See below.*)

A Register of the Premiums and Bounties given by the Society . . . from the original institution in the year 1754, to the year 1776 inclusive. 1778.

*An Account of a Substitute for Verdegris in Dyeing Black, by Mr. [James] Clegg. 1782.

One Hundred and Six Copper Plates of Mechanical Machines, and Implements of Husbandry approved and adopted by the Society for the encouragement of arts, manufactures, and commerce, and contained in their repository, . . . carefully corrected and revised . . . By Alexander Mabyn Bailey. 1782.

Catalogue of the Books, Pamphlets, and Maps, belonging to the Society . . . and reserved in their office, for the use of members. 1790, 1828, 1953.

A Description of the Series of Pictures painted by James Barry and preserved in the Great Room of the Society . . . To this is added a short account of some other works of art with which the room is ornamented. 1792, 1800.

Report of the Committee of the Society of Arts &c., together with the Approved Communications and Evidence upon the same, relative to the Mode of Preventing the Forgery of Bank Notes. 1819.

A Catalogue of the Select Specimens of British Manufacture and Decorative Art, exhibited at the House of the Society . . . 1847–[1849].

Charter and Bye-laws. 1847+.

A Catalogue of the Models in the Museum of the Society . . . 1850.

Catalogue of Specimens of Recent British Manufactures received in competition for the Society's special prizes. 1850.

Catalogue of Works of Ancient and Mediaeval Art, exhibited at the house of the Society of Arts, 1850.

Catalogue of a Collection of Articles Invented, Patented, or Registered, since 1849—[1851], exhibited at the house of the Society of Arts . . . in November 1850—[1852.]

First, [second, and third] Report from the Committee of Legislative Recognition of the Rights of Inventors, ordered by the Council to be printed. 1850, 1851, 1852.

Catalogue of an Exhibition of Recent Specimens of Photography, exhibited at the house of the Society of Arts . . . in December 1852.

The Prize Essay on the Application of Recent Inventions collected at the Great Exhibition of 1851, to the Purposes of Practical Banking. By Granville Sharp. 1852.

Reports of the Committee appointed by the Council of the Society of Arts to inquire into the Subject of Industrial Instruction; with the Evidence on which the Report is founded. 1853.

Catalogue of a Collection of Photographs from the Society of Arts, London; first set [and second set]. 1854.

Lectures on the Results of the Great Exhibition of 1851. Delivered before the Society of arts, manufactures, and commerce, at the suggestion of H.R.H. Prince Albert, president of the Society. [First and second series.] 1854.

Catalogue of the Pictures, Drawings, Sketches, etc., of the late John James Chalon Esq., R.A., with a selection from those of Alfred Edward Chalon Esq., R.A., . . . exhibited at the house of the Society . . . 1855.

Catalogue of the Seventh [–thirteenth] Exhibition of Inventions . . . 1855–61.

*Prize Essay on the Prevention of the Smoke Nuisance. By Charles Wye Williams. John Weale, 1856.

Addresses delivered on Different Public Occasions by His Royal Highness the Prince Albert, President of the Society . . . (also, People's edition.) 1857.

Middle Class Education and Class Instruction in Mechanics' Institutions, considered in two reports of the Society of Arts, with extracts from the evidence received by a Committee appointed by the Council of the Society. 1857.

Report of the Artistic Copyright Committee to the Council. [1858.]

Uniform Musical Pitch. Report of the Committee appointed by the Council of the Society of Arts, June 3rd, 1859.

Catalogue of the Miniatures, Drawings, and Pictures of the late Sir William C. Ross, R.A., collected for exhibition at the Society of Arts . . . 1860.

Uniform Musical Pitch. Minutes of a meeting of musicians, amateurs, and others interested in music . . . when the report of the Committee was received and adopted. 1860.

Union of Institutions. Subjects for discussion classes. 1862.

International Exhibition 1862. Reports by the Juries on the subjects in the 36 classes into which the exhibition was divided. 1863.

*Hand-book of Mechanics' Institutions, with priced catalogue of books suitable for Libraries and periodicals for reading rooms. Prepared . . . by W. H. J. Traice, and published with the sanction of the Council of the Society . . . Second edition. Longman, Green, 1863.

Report . . . by the Special Committee on the Statistics of Dwellings Improvement in the Metropolis. 1864.

Report of the Committee on Dwellings for the Labouring Classes. [1865.]

Report on the Acts providing for the Removal of Nuisances, prepared by the Committee on Dwellings for the Labouring Classes. 1866.

First Report of the Committee appointed to inquire into and report on the State of Musical Education at Home and Abroad, together with the evidence taken before, and information collected by the Committee. 1866.

Reports of Artisans selected by a Committee appointed by the Council of the Society of Arts to visit the Paris Universal Exhibition, 1867.

★*On Harvesting Corn in Wet Weather.* Prize essay by W. A. Gibbs. Bell and Daldy, 1868.

Technical Education. Report of the Committee appointed at a Conference held . . . January 1868.

A Standing or a Popular Army; three speeches delivered at a Conference at the Society of Arts on the efficiency and economy of a national army, in connection with the industry and education of the people. 1869.

Information collected by the Society of Arts in Relation to Musical Pitch in Continental Cities. [1869.]

Proceedings of a Committee appointed by the Council of the Society of Arts to report upon the best way of dealing with the Thames Embankment. [1869.]

Proceedings of Conferences held by the India Committee of the Society, on Subjects connected with the Arts, Manufactures, and Commerce of India. 1869.

Programme of instructions for delegates to the meetings to be held for the consideration of an improved national system of education. [1869.]

Report of meetings . . . when a paper on the economy and efficiency of a national army, in connection with the industry and education of the people, was read by Henry Cole . . . 1869.

Educational Condition and Requirements of One Square Mile in the Eastend of London. Prepared at the request of the Council by George C. T. Bartley. 1870.

Inquiry into the Existing State of Education in Richmond, Twickenham, Mortlake, and neighbourhood. 1870.

Report of the Council of the Society of Arts on the Existing State of Education in Ealing and Brentford. 1870.

Inquiry into the Existing State of Education in Battersea. 1870.

Reports on the Exhibition of 1873; prepared by the direction of the Council of the Society of Arts. Pts. 1, 2 and 3. 1873.

Labour Banks. An essay on the advantages that would be likely to arise if railway companies and limited companies generally were each to establish a savings' bank for the working classes in their employ. By J. Mason. 1874.

Report of the Committee on the Means of Protecting the Metropolis against Conflagration. 1874.

Stove Competition. [Report.] 1874.

Report on the Application of Science and Art to the Street-paving and Street-cleansing of the Metropolis. [1875.]

Conference [and *second conference*] *on the Health and Sewage of Towns,* . . . 1876—[1878].

Administrative Organisation. Functions of a general Police Force for the extinction of fires . . . A special report . . . by Edwin Chadwick, Esq. . . . Second edition with additions. 1877.

Insecurity from Fires, and from Panics at Theatres and Place of Public Resort. [1877.]

Report of the Congress on Domestic Economy to be taught as a Branch of General Education . . . held in Birmingham . . . 1877.

Suggestions for the Competition in the Sanitation of the Dwellings of the Wage Classes, for the prize of a gold cup, of the value of five thousand francs, to that municipal or local authority or private association which shall, by the improvement of the dwellings of the wage classes, effect the greatest reduction of their death rates at the lowest cost, to be awarded by the King of the Belgians, at the next International Sanitary Congress. By Edwin Chadwick. 1877.

National Water Supply. Notes on previous inquiries, prepared in connection with the Congress . . . 1878.

National Water Supply. Congress . . . May 1878.

Report of Second Yearly Congress on Domestic Economy and Elementary Education . . . at the Town Hall, Manchester . . . 1878.

Artisan Reporters. Report of the Joint Committee of the Royal Commission for the Paris Exhibition and the Society of Arts. 1879.

Annual Conference on National Water Supply, Sewage and Health, held . . . May 1879.

Report of the Committee on Saving Life at Sea . . . 1879.

A Note on the Pictures by James Barry in the Great Room of the Society of Arts. By H. Trueman Wood. 1880.

Annual Conference on the Progress of Public Health . . . to which is added a report of the meeting of the Sanitary Section of the Society of Arts . . . 1880.

Exhibition of Photographic Appliances (in connection with Capt. Abney's Lectures), February, 1882. Descriptive catalogue. 1882.

Report of a Committee appointed to consider the Prevention of Fires in Theatres. [1883.]

Report of the Conference on Water Supply, held at the International Health Exhibition, Thursday and Friday, July 24 and 25, 1884.

Catalogue of Art-Workmanship Competition. 1887.

Colonial and Indian Exhibition, 1886. Reports on the Colonial sections of the exhibition. Edited by H. Trueman Wood, M.A. Issued under the supervision of the Council of the Society of Arts. 1887.

Report of the Conference on Canals and Inland Navigation, held on Thursday and Friday, May 10 and 11, 1888. With a map of English canals. 1888.

Report of the Committee on the Deterioration of Paper . . . 1898.

Report of the Committee on Leather for Bookbinding, edited for the Society of Arts and the worshipful Company of Leathersellers by the Rt. Hon. Viscount Cobham and Sir Henry Trueman Wood. 1901.

★A history of the Royal Society of Arts, by Sir Henry Trueman Wood. John Murray, 1913.

Report on the Competition of Industrial Designs, 1924–1933, 1938–1939.

★The Stability of Ships, by George Johnson. Liverpool, Journal of Commerce, 1932.

British Art in Industry 1935. Illustrated souvenir [of the exhibition] (published in conjunction with the Royal Academy). 1935.

Exhibition of British Art in Industry, January–March 1935 [catalogue].

★The Story of the Royal Society of Arts, abridged from Sir Henry Trueman Wood's official history, and brought up to date by G. K. Menzies, C.B.E. John Murray, 1935.

Report on the Industrial Art Bursaries Competition, 1941, 1947+.

★Agriculture : To-day and To-morrow ; edited by Sir John Russell. Michael Joseph, 1945.

★Education : To-day and To-morrow ; edited by R. W. Moore. Michael Joseph, 1945.

★British Commonwealth objectives ; edited by Sir Harry Lindsay. Michael Joseph, 1946.

Design at Work . . . Exhibition handbook. 1948.

A Descriptive Note on the Barry Paintings in the Lecture Hall of the Royal Society of Arts [by K. W. Luckhurst]. 1951.

Exhibition of Exhibitions. Illustrating the origin and development of exhibitions in Great Britain and commemorating the centenary of the Great Exhibition of eighteen-fifty-one . . . [A catalogue]. 1951.

SOME OTHER PUBLICATIONS RELATING TO THE SOCIETY

A Letter to the Members of the Society . . . containing some remarks on the pictures to which the premiums were adjudged; with some cursory observations on history painting . . . 1761.

A Concise Account of the Rise, Progress, and Present State of the Society . . . By a Member of the said Society. [Thomas Mortimer.] 1763.

A Short Account of the Great Benefits which have already arisen to the Public, by means of the Society instituted in London, in the year 1753, for the Encouragement of Arts, Manufactures and Commerce. By a member of the same. [Edward Bridgen.] 1765.

Arts, Manufactures, and Commerce: a poem. By George Cockings. [1766.]

A Messieurs de la Société d'Emulation de Londres. [Dupont on some regulations proposed to the Society of Arts, etc.] Versailles, 1767.

An Account of a Series of Pictures, in the Great Room of the Society . . . By James Barry. 1783.

Auszug aus den Transaktionen der Societät zu London zu Aufmunterung der Künste, der Manufakturen und der Handlung. Aus dem Englischen, nebst Anmerkungen, übersetzt von J. G. Geissler, Mitglied der Naturforschenden Gesellschaft in Halle. Erster Band. Dresden, 1795.

A Memorial, read to the Society . . . December 18, 1799; and a speech, delivered before the same Society, January 29, 1800; by Edmund Cartwright . . . with an appendix, containing letters from the late Sir William Jones, Dr. Thurlow, late Bishop of Durham, and other distinguished characters. To which are added, certificates of the power of his improved steam engine, and the useful application of his other mechanical inventions. 1800.

Prize Model Cottages. Detailed working drawings, plans, . . . of a design for labourer's cottages . . . being the same for which the Society of Arts awarded the first and second prizes to T. C. Hine and S. J. Nicholl in the competition of May, 1848. Thomas Dean, [1848].

Index

The letter *l.* after a page number indicates that the reference is to a list only; *Pl.* indicates Plate.

INDEX

INDEX

Thomas Gray Memorial Trust, *see* Gray, Thomas, Memorial Trust
Thompson, Silvanus, lectures, 293, 318
Thomson, J. M., 340
Thomson, Sir Joseph, Albert Medal, 376 *l.*
Thrale, Henry, early member, 28 *l.*
Thurloe, John, memorial tablet, 231 *l.*
Tide mills, 112
Timber production, 86–9 *pass.*
Tizard, Sir Henry, Albert Medal, 376 *l.*
Tobago, award for indigo growing in, 160; award for bread-fruit growing in, 166
Tonson, Jacob, early member, 28 *l.*
Tooke, William, Solicitor to Society, assists with Royal Charter, 179; Dr. Swiney's will, 180; President, 350, 372 *l.*
Town and Country Planning Act, 306
Towne, Francis, award for design, 44
Townshend, Charles, 2nd Viscount, 62
Toye, A. G., Accountant to Society, 363
Trade, Board of, lists of imports, 155; and Great Exhibition, 194, 200; scheme for Institute of Industrial Art, 282; receives Society's report on merchant navy, 329
Trade, Committee of Colonies and, *see* Colonies and Trade, Committee of
Traffic, lectures on, 327–8
Tramways Act, 325
Transactions, originated, 17, 32; references to, 55, 64, 71, 73 *n.*, 74 *n.*, 75 *n.*, 78, 79, 88, 89, 92, 103 *n.*, 104 and *n.*, 107, 113, 115, 116 *n.*, 117, 123, 124 *n.*, 127, 131 *n.*, 135 *n.*, 136, 138 *n.*, 140 *n.*, 141 *n.*, 147, 148, 151, 156 *n.*, 158 *n.*, 165 *n.*, 166 *n.*, 180; publication ends, 234
Tree-planting, 86–9 *pass.*
Trengrouse, H., award for rocket apparatus, 147
Trevelyan, Sir William, gives prize for meat preservation, 299, 301–2
Trinidad, award for clove plantation in, 165
Trueman Wood Lectures, instituted, 359; on radio, 334; on sound track, 339
Tuckwell, E. G., Registrar, 174
Tufnell, B. C., on Food Committee, 300
Tull, Jethro, inventor of drill husbandry, 62, 71–2, 73, 74, 75, 80
Tulley & Sons, achromatic telescope, 117
Turkey, dyeing secrets obtained from, 121
Turk's Head, Gerrard Street, 35, 36
Turner, J. M. W., declines offer of exhibition in Society's House, 52; new building for Turner collection, 219, 220
Twickenham, report on education in, 240
Twining, Thomas, instigates committee on model dwellings, 305
Tyler, Sir Henry, lecture on railway brakes, 322

Union of Institutions, formed, 237–8; examinations of, 238, 245–6, 248; activities discontinued, 238; colonial members, 344
Union of Lancashire and Cheshire Institutes, examinations of, 244
United States of America, reaping machine, 82; meat preservation, 301; Chicago Exhibition, 215; essays submitted from, 306; *see also* Colonies
University College, London, Society's models presented to, 294
Unwin, George, award for exporting tin, 125
Unwin, Sir Raymond, paper on housing, 306
Unwin, Samuel, award for stocking-frame, 130
Ustinov, Peter, paper, "The Modern Theatre", 276

Valtravers, Rodolph, letters on winter feeding-stuffs, 69
Van Diemen's Land, *see* Tasmania
Vane, Sir Harry, memorial tablet, 231 *l.*
Vanilla production, 165
Varley, Cornelius, award for achromatic telescope, 117; invents dynamo, 316; at "glow lamp" lecture, 317
Varley, S. A., paper on submarine telegraphy, 333
Velarde, F. X., award for Colombo Cathedral design, 289
Ventilation, papers on, 310
Verdigris, production of, 219, 220
Vernon, Edward, award for silk production, 92
Vernon, K. D. C., Librarian, 363
Victoria, Queen, portrait of, in Society's House, 49; loans gilt centre-piece to 1849 exhibition, 195, *Pl.* 23; maintains examinations prize, 257; contributes to India Exhibition, 344–5; Albert Medal, 350, 375 *l.*
Victoria and Albert Museum; Henry Cole's tea-set in, 192; educational collection in, 237–8; Modern Illustration Exhibition at, 273; arranges industrial design competitions with Society, 278
Vine products, 163–4
Virginia, corresponding member in, 154, 160
Voycey, C. F. A., appointed R.D.I., 287

W.A.A.F., literary competition, 288
Wade, Edward, pamphlet on tree-planting, 87
Walker, Dr. Ernest, music examiner, 272
Wallich, Dr. N., director of botanical gardens, Calcutta, 154